The Bengal Diaspora

India's partition in 1947 and the creation of Bangladesh in 1971 saw the displacement and resettling of millions of Muslims and Hindus, resulting in profound transformations across the region. A third of the region's population sought shelter across new borders, almost all of them resettling in the Bengal delta itself. A similar number were internally displaced, while others moved to the Middle East, North America, and Europe.

Using a creative interdisciplinary approach combining historical, sociological, and anthropological approaches to migration and diaspora, this book explores the experiences of Bengali Muslim migrants through this period of upheaval and transformation. It draws on over 200 interviews conducted in Britain, India, and Bangladesh, tracing migration and settlement within, and from, the Bengal delta region in the period after 1947. Focusing on migration and diaspora 'from below', it teases out fascinating 'hidden' migrant stories, including those of women, refugees, and displaced people. It reveals surprising similarities, and important differences, in the experience of Muslim migrants in widely different contexts and places, whether in the towns and hamlets of the Bengal delta or in the cities of Britain. Counterposing accounts of the structures that frame migration with the textures of how migrants shape their own movement, it examines what it means to make new homes in a context of diaspora. The book is also unique in its focus on the experiences of those who stayed behind and in its analysis of ruptures in the migration process. Importantly, the book seeks to challenge crude attitudes to 'Muslim' migrants which assume their cultural and religious homogeneity and to humanize contemporary discourses around global migration.

This ground-breaking new research offers an essential contribution to the field of South Asian Studies, Diaspora Studies, and Society and Culture Studies.

Claire Alexander is Professor of Sociology at the University of Manchester, UK. Her publications include *The Art of Being Black* (1996) and *The Asian Gang* (2000).

Joya Chatterji is Professor of South Asian History at the University of Cambridge, UK. Her publications include *Bengal Divided* (1995) and *The Spoils of Partition* (2007), and she is the co-editor of the *Routledge Handbook of the South Asian Diaspora* (2014).

Annu Jalais is Assistant Professor of South Asian Studies, National University of Singapore, Singapore. Her publications include *Forest of Tigers* (2010).

Routledge Contemporary South Asia Series

For a complete list of titles in this series, please visit www.routledge.com.

78 **The Political Economy of Ethnic Conflict in Sri Lanka**
Nikolaos Biziouras

79 **Indian Arranged Marriages**
A social psychological perspective
Tulika Jaiswal

80 **Writing the City in British Asian Diasporas**
Edited by Seán McLoughlin, William Gould, Ananya Jahanara Kabir and Emma Tomalin

81 **Post-9/11 Espionage Fiction in the US and Pakistan**
Spies and 'terrorists'
Cara Cilano

82 **Left Radicalism in India**
Bidyut Chakrabarty

83 **"Nation-State" and Minority Rights in India**
Comparative perspectives on Muslim and Sikh identities
Tanweer Fazal

84 **Pakistan's Nuclear Policy**
A minimum credible deterrence
Zafar Khan

85 **Imagining Muslims in South Asia and the Diaspora**
Secularism, religion, representations
Claire Chambers and Caroline Herbert

86 **Indian Foreign Policy in Transition**
Relations with South Asia
Arijit Mazumdar

87 **Corporate Social Responsibility and Development in Pakistan**
Nadeem Malik

88 **Indian Capitalism in Development**
Barbara Harriss-White and Judith Heyer

89 **Bangladesh Cinema and National Identity**
In search of the modern?
Zakir Hossain Raju

90 **Suicide in Sri Lanka**
The anthropology of an epidemic
Tom Widger

91 **Epigraphy and Islamic Culture**
Inscriptions of the Early Muslim Rulers of Bengal (1205–1494)
Mohammad Yusuf Siddiq

92 **Reshaping City Governance**
London, Mumbai, Calcutta, Hyderabad
Nirmala Rao

93 **The Indian Partition in Literature and Films**
History, politics, and aesthetics
Rini Bhattacharya Mehta and Debali Mookerjea-Leonard

94 **Development, Poverty and Power in Pakistan**
The impact of state and donor interventions on farmers
Syed Mohammad Ali

95 **Ethnic Subnationalist Insurgencies in South Asia**
Identities, Interests and Challenges to State Authority
Edited by Jugdep S. Chima

96 **International Migration and Development in South Asia**
Edited by Md Mizanur Rahman and Tan Tai Yong

97 **Twenty-First Century Bollywood**
Ajay Gehlawat

98 **Political Economy of Development in India**
Indigeneity in Transition in the State of Kerala
Darley Kjosavik and Nadarajah Shanmugaratnam

99 **State and Nation-Building in Pakistan**
Beyond Islam and Security
Edited by Roger D. Long, Gurharpal Singh, Yunas Samad, and Ian Talbot

100 **Subaltern Movements in India**
Gendered Geographies of Struggle against Neoliberal Development
Manisha Desai

101 **Islamic Banking in Pakistan**
Shariah-Compliant Finance and the Quest to make Pakistan more Islamic
Feisal Khan

102 **The Bengal Diaspora**
Rethinking Muslim migration
Claire Alexander, Joya Chatterji and Annu Jalais

Forthcoming

Mobilizing Religion and Gender in India
The Role of Activism
Nandini Deo

Social Movements and the Indian Diaspora
Movindri Reddy

Identity Politics and Elections in Malaysia and Indonesia
Ethnic Engineering in Borneo
Karolina Prasad

Religion and Modernity in the Himalaya
Edited by Megan Adamson Sijapati and Jessica Vantine Birkenholtz

The Bengal Diaspora
Rethinking Muslim migration

**Claire Alexander, Joya Chatterji
and Annu Jalais**

LONDON AND NEW YORK

First published 2016
by Routledge
2 Park Square, Milton Park, Abingdon, Oxon OX14 4RN

and by Routledge
711 Third Avenue, New York, NY 10017

Routledge is an imprint of the Taylor & Francis Group, an informa business

© 2016 Claire Alexander, Joya Chatterji and Annu Jalais

The right of Claire Alexander, Joya Chatterji and Annu Jalais to be identified as authors of this work has been asserted by them in accordance with sections 77 and 78 of the Copyright, Designs and Patents Act 1988.

All rights reserved. No part of this book may be reprinted or reproduced or utilised in any form or by any electronic, mechanical, or other means, now known or hereafter invented, including photocopying and recording, or in any information storage or retrieval system, without permission in writing from the publishers.

Trademark notice: Product or corporate names may be trademarks or registered trademarks, and are used only for identification and explanation without intent to infringe.

British Library Cataloguing-in-Publication Data
A catalogue record for this book is available from the British Library

Library of Congress Cataloging-in-Publication Data
Names: Alexander, Claire E. | Chatterji, Joya. | Jalais, Annu.
Title: The Bengal diaspora : rethinking Muslim migration /
   Claire Alexander, Joya Chatterji, and Annu Jalais.
Description: Milton Park, Abingdon, Oxon : Routledge, 2016. | Series: Routledge contemporary South Asia series; 102 | Includes bibliographical references and index.
Subjects: LCSH: Bengali (South Asian people)—Migrations. | Muslims—Migrations. | Bengali (South Asian people)—Social conditions. | Immigrants—Social conditions. | Bengali (South Asian people)—Ethnic identity. | Bengali (South Asian people)—Interviews. | Bengal (India)—Emigration and immigration—Social aspects. | Ganges River Delta (Bangladesh and India)—Emigration and immigration—Social aspects. | Great Britain—Emigration and immigration—Social aspects.
Classification: LCC DS432.B4 A43 2016 | DDC 306.0954/14—dc23
   LC record available at http://lccn.loc.gov/2015022409

ISBN: 978-0-415-53073-6 (hbk)
ISBN: 978-1-315-66006-6 (ebk)

Typeset in Times New Roman
by Apex CoVantage, LLC

This book is dedicated, with much love,
To
Ann Rosemary Alexander
Sarah Jane Alexander
To
Valerie Ann, or 'Psyche', a gypsy to the last
And to
Shyamali Khastgir and Shanu Lahiri,
who both crossed borders and pushed boundaries
. . . .

Contents

List of figures	xi
List of tables	xii
Acknowledgements	xiii
Introduction	1
1 Pre-histories of mobility and immobility: The Bengal delta and the 'eastern zone', 1857–1947	18
2 Dispositions and destinations in the Bengal Muslim diaspora, 1947–2007	52
3 Belonging, status, and religion: Migrants on the 'peripheries'	80
4 Making home: Claiming and contesting diasporic space in Britain	102
5 'Always/already migrants': Brides, marriage, and migration	131
6 Building a *tazia*, becoming a *paik*: 'Bihari' identity amid a hostile Bengali universe	161
7 Rituals of diaspora: The Shahid Minar and the struggle for diasporic space	191
8 Narrating diaspora: Community histories and the politics of assimilation	219
Conclusion	245

Glossary 255
Appendix 1: Shamsul Huq's family tree 258
Bibliography 259
Index 281

Figures

1.1	Interprovincial migration during the census decade, 1911–1921	19
1.2	Bengal's railway network by 1914	25
2.1	Migration of Muslims from West Bengal, Bihar, and Assam to East Pakistan, 1946–1970	53
2.2	Internal displacement of Muslims in West Bengal, India	55
2.3	Brothers Shahid and Jalal Gazi, separated by the border	70
6.1	Smiling *paiks* in Town Hall camp	162
6.2	Character certificate issued by the Dhaka City Corporation	170
6.3	Route taken by *paiks* through Dhaka	173

Tables

I.1	Field sites and respondents	9
1.1	Persons employed in the railway, irrigation, post, and telegraph departments in Bengal 'proper', 1931	31
5.1	Mean age at marriage, by sex and economic class, Char Gopalpur, 1976	139
5.2	Mean age at first marriage by year of marriage, for females	141
5.3	Immigrants and emigrants by sex and major categories of reasons for migration, Matlab, 1978	142
6.1	Migrants from eastern United Provinces and Bihar in Bengal, 1903	165

Acknowledgements

This book has taken an inordinately long time to finish. In part, this is because it represents the outcome of years of individual and collective research by its authors, in part because much has happened in our lives since its inception. It began as a conversation in 2005 in the Senior Dining Room in the London School of Economics and Political Science (LSE), where we met to discuss the possibility of applying together for a large grant from the Arts and Humanities Research Council (AHRC) to study 'Diaspora, migration, and identities'. By the time we sat down to write up the research, each of us had (perhaps appropriately) migrated to different institutions and, in one case, different continents, and the demands of life and work meant finding time to work together was challenging.

Our first debt is to the AHRC, which, in 2006, sponsored this ambitious, sprawling and idiosyncratic project as part of their 'Diaspora, Migration, Identities' research programme. Willem van Schendel's support was crucial in winning support for the project – we owe him much. Thanks are due to the programme director, Kim Knott, and to David Feldman, our project mentor, who supported us through the life of the project. The AHRC has continued to support our work generously through two follow-on grants focused on public engagement and impact. We thank them, and the Runnymede Trust, especially Vastiana Belfon, Rob Berkeley, and Debbie Weekes-Bernard, who took our work to a broader audience through the Banglastories website and the Making Histories project and website.

Next we thank Shahzad Firoz, research assistant on the project, who carried out interviews among UK Bengali migrants. Without this bedrock of interviews, as well as those conducted by Annu Jalais in her role as research assistant in India and Bangladesh, this would have been a very different, and far poorer, book.

We are grateful to everyone who helped us finally bring this book to completion – to Dorothea Schaeffer, Jillian Morrison, Rebecca Lawrence, Deepti Agarwal, and Sophie Iddamalgoda at Routledge for their patience and support. Michele Greenbank stepped in to help us smooth out an unwieldy manuscript. Tina Bone drew the maps with her characteristic combination of accuracy and art.

Most importantly, we thank the many interviewees in India, Bangladesh, and Britain, who let us into their homes and lives, and shared with us experiences that were deeply intimate, and often traumatic. Each one of them has our heartfelt gratitude. We hope we have done them justice.

xiv *Acknowledgements*

And then there are the individual debts that each of us is delighted, at last, to be able to acknowledge:

Claire:

I send love and thanks to the many people who supported me through the project and the writing. In particular, I thank Joya for never losing faith in the work, for her intellectual inspiration and generosity, and for, finally, putting her foot down about deadlines.

The research project and writing was undertaken while I was based at the Department of Sociology at LSE and the School of Social Sciences at the University of Manchester. I would like to thank my colleagues in both places, especially Suki Ali and Paul Gilroy, who helped shape my thinking around diaspora. Thanks too to Manali Desai, Louise Fisher, Carrie Friese, Suzi Hall, Claire Moon, Pat McGovern, and Fran Tonkiss. At Manchester, I am particularly grateful to Wendy Bottero and Brian Heaphy for their support, for luring me north and for providing me space to think and write. I have benefited greatly from the expertise and generosity of Manchester colleagues, including Laurence Brown, Bridget Byrne, Alice Bloch, Virinder Kalra, James Nazroo, Naaz Rashid, and James Rhodes. I am grateful to Sarah Burton for the insightful discussions around writing. Thanks are due to my PhD students, past and present, but especially Ajmal Hussain, Malcolm James, Helen Kim, Sanjiv Lingayah, Victoria Redclift, and Kjartan Sveinsson, whose work and energies continue to challenge me intellectually, and whose gift of a shiny blue umbrella when I moved north was both delightful and useful.

I would like to thank *Ethnic and Racial Studies*, the *British Journal of Sociology*, and the *Journal of Ethnic and Migration Studies* for permission to reproduce revised versions of articles.

As always, there are innumerable and immeasurable debts owed to friends and colleagues for their support, guidance, and wisdom, usually dispensed over tea and cake. Thanks are due especially to Wendy, who was always on hand with the requisite 'encouragement' or 'hear my pain' talks, and to John Solomos and Caroline Knowles, whose friendship, intellectual inspiration, and astute advice has been unfailing and invaluable. Thanks too to Les Back, Shamus Khan, Michael Keith, who helped guide me through the mysterious byways of East London; Sean Carey, who took me on a memorable tour of Brick Lane; and Ansar Ahmed Ullah for his generosity to Shahzad and myself, and for helping with the Making Histories project. I am grateful to Amanda Eastell-Bleakley for keeping *Identities:Global Studies in Culture and Power* ticking over, and so much else. Love, as ever and always, to my other friends who continue to see me through every day – Mark Arundel, Rob Berkeley, Zalihe Hussain, Brett St Louis, AnnMarie Sylvester-Charles, Kate Reed, Shuel Uddin, Rachel Wicaksono, and the Rahman family. Special thanks are due to Aditya Chakrabortty for his continued interest in the work (and when it would be finished), and for his kindness and support through the past couple of years.

For me, the project is framed by two internal dialogues in particular – with Chhanda, who wanted me to know 'my homeland', and with Stuart Hall, who is always the voice in my head. And, most of all, thanks and love to my family, especially my much loved and much missed mother and little sister, to whose memories this book is dedicated.

Joya:

It is difficult to know how to thank Claire. She brought strengths to this project that I signally lack, such that I simply cannot imagine having done it without her. She was also always sane, practical, robust, and firm; always utterly reliable; always caring. As Jack Gallagher might have said, she is 'a good woman to go tiger shooting with'.

Shahzad and Annu, thank you for making it possible for me to find answers to questions that had long troubled me. Annu deserves special acknowledgment for her courage in the field and her talent as an ethnographer, which have added immeasurably to this work.

Friends, colleagues, and institutions were generous to me. This project began when I was at LSE and continued when I moved to the University of Cambridge, and I accrued many debts at both places. Arne Westad encouraged me to apply for the AHRC grant, without which a book of this kind could not have been written. Trinity College, Cambridge, helped with additional travel grants, and much other practical support. Professor M.K.A Siddiqui was a font of knowledge about Bengal's Muslims, which he shared liberally. Alan Strathern, Justin Jones, Peter Mandler, Prasannan Parthasarathi, Samita Sen, and Tim Hochstrasser read and gave feedback on individual chapters, as did Ali Khan Mahmudabad – thank you all for pointing out errors of argument, transliteration and fact. P.K. Datta's detailed comments on one chapter in an earlier incarnation as an article (as a referee who waived his anonymity) were invaluable. David Washbrook not only read chapters: his conversation, friendship, stimulus, and example were critical throughout. Sunil Amrith generously shared his work before publication. Tim Harper, Tim Hochstrasser, Rosamond McKitterick, Peter Mandler, Ornit Shani, Hans Van de Ven, and Erica Wald suggested additional readings, and Janaki Abraham facilitated my access to the Ratan Tata Library. Jasdeep Brar assisted with research – help most gratefully received. Sara Adhikari and Shaffiq Essajee – my 'intelligent lay readers' – pointed out unintelligible verbiage. Anjali Bhardwaj-Datta was a lifesaver at the concluding stages of this book, checking footnotes, borrowing library books, and much else. Barbara Roe, Kevin Greenbank, and Sue Allerton gave me back up at times when I most needed it. Huge thanks to them all.

It is a pleasure to be able to thank the staff at the Cambridge University Library, the Centre of South Asian Studies Library in Cambridge, the British Library, the British National Archives, the National Archives in Delhi, the Ratan Tata Library and the Nehru Memorial Museum and Library, who were unfailingly helpful. I owe special gratitude to Jaya Ravindran and Kevin Greenbank, who went well out of their way to assist me.

My graduate students have, over the years, helped shaped ideas far more than they perhaps realize: I thank them all. Students who took my MPhil seminar on migration and diaspora will recognize in this book some of the ideas we discussed. I also thank the audiences at the conferences at which I have presented this work.

I would like to thank *Studies in the Humanities and the Social Sciences* and *Comparative Studies in Society and History* for permission to reproduce articles that appear here (in revised form) as Chapters 2 and 8.

Finally, there are the people who have kept me going through difficult times. I thank my doctors, Mel Lobo, Shane Delamont, Nick Gall, and Ajit Banerjee as well as John Brown, Navin Sakhuja, Vandana and Arun Prasad, and Rishad Faruqi. Mark Goldie was deeply compassionate as Faculty Chair at Cambridge, allowing me the respite from faculty duties when I most needed it. Jasdeep Brar was, and is, an inspiration on so many levels. I thank Tanika Sarkar for her enduring support; and Humeira Iqtidar, Kamal Munir, Nikki Wagle, Thomas Hillas, Alicia and Tony Constantinou, Dave Roberts, Alison Talbot, and Ingrid Freese for innumerable acts of kindness. Humeira Iqtidar, Jennifer Davis, Ornit Shani, Prasannan Parthasarathi, Samita Sen, Shalini Sharma, Shaffiq Essajee, Shohini Ghosh, Simon Longstaff, and Tim Hochstrasser endured my mitherings about this subject, and laughed with and at me. Kamal Munir mainly laughed at me. Raj Chandavarkar would have laughed too: every word was written with him in mind as a reader. I miss the many arguments we would surely have had, especially about 'culture', in which he professed not to believe. (Those who knew Raj and his demanding standards will understand why the book has taken so long).

I thank my mother, to whom this work is dedicated, and who, at the end, did not grudge me the time I spent on it. Thanks also to my beloved family for all the good times, and for helping me see my work and life in perspective. Above all, I thank Kartik and Anil, without whose support the tough times would have been so much tougher. Kartik's humane intelligence was a source of clarity in the midst of confusion. Anil encouraged me to keep going when I was plagued by self-doubt (which was often). As he kept saying, this is not 'straight history', and of course he is right. Yet he read every chapter patiently. I cannot thank him enough.

Annu:

My gratitude is first owed to Joya, who placed her trust in me when she asked me to work with her and Claire on this project. It has been a heady experience working with them, and it was a struggle to keep up with the pace they set. Their rigorous approach to words and concepts, methodology and research, down to the tiniest of ethnographic details, helped me become a better researcher. I can never thank Joya and Claire enough for this.

As a PhD student in London, I was inspired by Urmi Rahman, who spoke about childhood holidays in the Sundarbans and growing up in Bangladesh. I learned much from Leesa and Faisal Gazi, Zubaer Mahboob, Sohini Alam, Nobonita Chowdhury, Asif Saleh, Eeshita Azad, Ahsan Akbar, and Imtiaz Haque about human rights in Bangladesh. They also introduced me to their friends and family in Bangladesh, where I was welcomed by Khushi Kabir, Sara Hossein, Rahnuma Ahmed, Indranil Chakraborty, Lupia Khalamma, and Kamal Khalamma. To Hana

Acknowledgements xvii

Shams Ahmed, Shabnam Nadiya, Mahmud Rahman, and Naeem Mohaiemen, I am grateful for conversation, food, and laughter; and to Ishtiaq Ahmed, Mahatab Hasan, Batul Towfique, Bitopi and Abhijit Chowdhury, Mun Parbeen, Afsar Hira, and Robin AR for enlivening my days.

The list of people who helped me in the field is unending, but my greatest debt is to Noor Islam Pappu, who introduced me to Town Hall Camp, to Geneva Camp, and to Saidpur; and to Khalid Hussein, Zayed Hossein, and Md Hasan. I am indebted to Zahed Hasan Saimon, who introduced me to *pirs* and Urs festivals in Chittagong, to Mohon Kumar Mondol of LEDARS in Satkhira, and to the late Chairman Alam of Shyamnagar.

My first interview in Dhaka was with the writer and social worker Ahmed Ilias, who introduced me to Bangladesh's 'Biharis' and their search for dignity and recognition. Conversations in Al-Falah with his companions, and also with Tanvir Mokammel, were a crucial part of my journey. I remain very grateful to them, as well as to Asad Chowdhury and Afsan Chowdhury. Abu Mohammad Jehangir helped me understand the shrines and the genealogies of the saints of Dhaka's Old Town. Abu Jafar, the adept translator of Joya's *Bengal Divided*, kept me going with his encouragement.

In Syedpur, Md Ashraful Haque Babu, or 'Babubhai' as he is popularly known, introduced me to all his political 'friends and foes'. Jinnahbhai, chairman of the Community Development Association in Dinajpur, greatly facilitated my research in the area. In Rajshahi, the writer Hasan Azizul Huq shared stories from his childhood, and Mahbubar Rahman introduced me to what is undoubtedly the largest library of pamphlets and posters in Bangladesh.

The late Shyamoli Khastgir introduced me to many friends in Bangladesh and West Bengal who had roots on both sides of the border, as did the late Dolly Mukherjee. Their passing, along with that of wonderful Shanu Lahiri who livened my days in Singapore, strengthened my resolve to write about this little known subject. In Birbhum, Manisha Banerjee inspired me. I am proud to call Ayesha Khatun, the fiery writer, my friend. In Tilutia, Sri Biswajit and his father's visionary writings gave me hope for the future of our region.

In Calcutta, I thank Ananya Jahanara Kabir who introduced me to her family; Pradyut Kumar Sarkar, my constant guide; Atiya Sen and her gifted daughter, Ashna Sen; P. K. Sarkar, who introduced me to Zakir Hussein, Ibrahim Kutti, and Syed Mustak Murshed. Shahenshah Jahangir was very generous with his contacts and sent me off to Dhulian to meet the people of his constituency. I am immensely grateful to them all.

It is a pleasure to acknowledge the support of Professors Sivaramakrishnan and James Scott, and Yale University's Agrarian Studies community. I was fortunate to have Professor Willem Van Schendel's guidance at the International Institute of Social History in Amsterdam and that of Philippe Peycam at the International Institute for Asian Studies in Leiden. At the Jawaharlal Nehru Institute of Advanced Studies, I benefited from the guidance of Shubhra and Kunal Chakrabarti and Gyanesh Kudaisya. I owe them a great deal.

Introduction

Since India's partition in 1947, there have been diasporas in the Bengal delta on a scale unparalleled in modern times. When the British quit their Indian empire, it was divided into two nation states, India and Pakistan. The latter was a fractured entity, with its eastern wing, carved out of Bengal and Assam,[1] separated from the dominant western wing by over 1,000 miles of Indian territory. In 1971, after a brief but savage war,[2] East Pakistan wrested itself out of West Pakistan's control and became the sovereign nation of Bangladesh.

Two partitions within twenty-five years in this densely populated region sparked off colossal displacements and migrations. Roughly 20 million Muslims and Hindus – about a third of the region's population in 1947 – have since sought shelter across new borders in the 'right' country, almost all of them resettling in the Bengal delta itself. A similar number were internally displaced within the new national borders, with profound consequences for the region.[3] Comparatively few – about 2 per cent – moved overseas, some to the Middle East, and most others to Europe. In 2011, the Census recorded nearly 450,000 people from the region in the UK, mainly Bangladeshi Muslims who had settled or been born in Britain, where they have been the focus of concerns about segregation, social exclusion, and radicalization.

Yet despite the scale of these migrations, scholars of global migration have largely ignored them. In the past fifty years, their leading journal, *The International Migration Review*, has published not a single article on them – an omission that speaks volumes. Scholars of refugees in South Asia, concentrating chiefly on the Punjab with its stark exchanges of population and its spectacular violence, have, for their part, failed to engage comparatively with the wider field of migration studies. As for studies of 'partition in the east',[4] their focus has been on Hindus – mainly from the upper and middle classes – who moved to the towns and cities of West Bengal.[5] In the teeming field of partition studies, poorer migrants and refugees, particularly the Muslims among them, remain opaque, while internal displacees – all but invisible – have no memorial.

These diasporas, while exceptional in scale, have much in common with other migrations in the developing world. Forged on the anvils of nation-making, they were, for the most part, self-driven: states had little or no role in helping to settle the new arrivals, and their efforts to control movement across borders had little effect. Left to their own devices, migrants settled where and how they could, in patterns that mirror those of refugees throughout the non-Western world.[6] Vast numbers of displaced Bengalis, Hindus and Muslims alike, moved within their region of origin, clustering densely on both sides of the new borders between India and East Pakistan (later Bangladesh) and in enclaves inside Calcutta, Dhaka, and other lesser towns in both countries. As this book will show, their position on both sides of the border remains ambiguous and uncertain several decades after they first moved. This is also the case among Bengali Muslim migrants in Britain, whose patterns of clustering and dispersal have many similarities with those in the delta.[7] In both South Asia and Britain, Bengali Muslim migrants are a growing object of political intent and popular anxiety, yet they remain shadowy figures, often of uncertain citizenship,[8] who live precariously on the margins of society.

In many respects, the Bengal diaspora is a typical case of the postcolonial upheavals and the mass migrations of the late 20th century, in what Castles and Miller call 'the age of migration'.[9] By 2013, 213 million people, more than three out of every 100,[10] were 'international' migrants, a number itself dwarfed by 'internal' migrants. In China alone, between 1979 and 2009, some 340 million people moved from villages to towns.[11] In India, perhaps one in five of the country's 1.2 billion people is an internal migrant.[12] In Bangladesh, a constant migration from the countryside to towns (at over 3 per cent a year between 1975 and 2009) has led to one of the highest rates of urbanization in the world.[13] And, as we show in this book, this picture of people on the move does not include the innumerable shorter journeys of people in the Bengal delta itself across and within its porous borders.[14]

In the past three decades, there has been an explosion of interest, both scholarly and political, in migration and diaspora, largely generated by 'new' migration from the global south to America and Western Europe. Two concerns have dominated the field: first, to identify and understand the causes driving this migration, and second, to assess its implications – cultural, social, economic, and political – for the 'multicultural' societies of the West.[15] Not surprisingly, existing theories of migration and diaspora are largely shaped by Western preoccupations.

Yet the majority of the world's migrants – and over 95 per cent of its refugees – have not settled in the West. They have remained in the global south, within or close to their countries or regions of origin.[16] *The South is not just a 'source' of migration, but its preeminent destination.* South-south diasporas are the largest in the world,[17] yet this simple fact has not been taken into account by most scholars of diaspora, whose concepts remain dominated by models of rational, male, and individual labour movement over long distances, across borders, and between continents.[18] Similarly, theories of diaspora, circulation,[19] and transnationalism,[20] which challenge reductive, unidirectional, and crudely economic accounts of global mobility, remain concerned chiefly with diasporas in the west and north, and on processes of place-making and claims-staking in Western countries of arrival.[21]

This book challenges this Eurocentric bias by looking at the Bengal diaspora from a very different perspective. It starts by acknowledging the fact that *there is a Bengal diaspora within Bengal as well as outside it*. It investigates both 'ends' of that diaspora, seeking to compare them and understand their similarities and differences. Exploring the histories of Muslim migrants within the Bengal delta and also in Britain, we ask not only *how many* but who, when, and how, and why they moved in one direction rather than another. Why did almost all remain within the region and only a few travel to distant lands overseas? Crucially, we enquire why so many stayed behind. The very scale of Bengal's diaspora raises profound questions about these stayers-on. Why, despite being subjected to the same 'push factors' – communal violence and intimidation, social discrimination, and political and economic marginalization – did so many not move at all, until some were forcibly displaced? Unusually for a work on migration, this book pays careful attention to immobility, to the 'sticky' connections between people and place, and to the factors that militate against movement.

This work thus asks large and ambitious questions about global migration from a comparative viewpoint, but it seeks the answers in the life histories of very ordinary people. Our methodology has been unusual, but has its roots in a multi-sited, multidisciplinary, and multilayered study of the Bengali diaspora in South Asia and Britain. Our aim was to develop a historically sophisticated and empirically rich ethnography of processes and relationships,[22] of movement and immobility, in very different contexts of nation creation. Our project traces intersections between 'small' family histories and personal lives and 'large' transnational, national, and local contexts. By bringing the stories of migrants themselves together with the grand sweep of history, the book is a portrait of a South Asian diaspora 'from below' in rich and textured detail. So often theorized in the abstract, diasporas are studied here in their real-life embodiments. In so doing, the book captures the resilience and inventiveness of individuals, families, and 'communities' caught up in (but also helping to shape) the dramatic transformations of postwar decolonization and nation building.

In both the Bengal delta and in Britain, we argue, contemporary patterns of migration and settlement, citizenship and exclusion, status and discrimination can best be understood by grasping the historical connections between places of origin and places of arrival and the influence of political and social structures at both 'ends' of the migration process, as well as the complex mix of resources, cultures, and identities of the migrants themselves.

The book insists that diasporas must be situated within particular historical conjunctures, but it also addresses a broader set of issues. The history of the Bengal diaspora, we contend, provides insights into wider global patterns of migration (and immobilization) and suggests ways of understanding them. Our study also throws new light on decolonization, state-building, and partitions and on emergent and resurgent forms of border creation and border crossing.

Our focus on Muslim migration is deliberate. It addresses a glaring lacuna in partition studies, of course. But it also challenges essentialized accounts of 'Muslim identity' in a global climate of Islamophobia. We question representations of Muslims either as an ahistorical and a priori 'community' transcending time and place[23] or as a pathologized,[24] anachronistic, and 'suspect' group who threaten a 'clash of civilisations',[25] whether from without and or within national borders. Instead, we look at how (South Asian) Muslim identities were created in specific historical contexts, keeping in sight the shifting, 'blurred' – but occasionally 'bright' – boundaries[26] between individuals and groups categorized by their religion, ethnicity, region, and nation. If one thing emerges from these stories, it is just how inadequate these categories are in capturing lived history and yet how easily they lend themselves to violence, exclusion, and control.

Starting points: The Bengal Diaspora Project

Ambitious though the book's goals have become, its beginnings were mundane. The research project on which it is based was born of a serendipitous diasporic encounter, one lunchtime in 2005, in the senior dining room at the London School of Economics and Political Science (LSE). Both lead researchers – Joya Chatterji and Claire Alexander – were then teaching at LSE, though both have since moved on. The initial contact was personal rather than academic, brokered by a mutual acquaintance who thought we might find each other interesting, despite (or perhaps because of) our differences. Chatterji, a Bengali with connections with Britain on her mother's side, is a historian of modern South Asia who has published widely on Bengal's partition and its consequences;[27] Alexander, a British sociologist and ethnographer, has explored issues of race, ethnicity, and identity with a focus on youth – most recently Bangladeshi Muslims in London[28] – but has her own diasporic roots in Bengal. Over an otherwise undistinguished lunch, Chatterji mentioned the Arts and Humanities Council's research programme 'Diaspora, Migration, Identities', and suggested a project that deployed our complementary interests and skills.

In previous work, Chatterji had identified highly distinct patterns of clustering and settlement in the Bengal diaspora after partition, but their explanation remained elusive.[29] She had read Zolberg and Schmeidl's recent work, which suggested that such patterns were not unique to Bengal but occurred worldwide.[30] Our plan was to combine different disciplinary approaches to diaspora and migration to research this phenomenon in Bengal, hoping that this would not only explain it but also throw light on wider global patterns. We were of course aware that history and sociology conceptualized diaspora in quite different ways, and this influenced our project's design, key questions, and methods. One early decision was to work with Annu Jalais, then a postdoctoral researcher at LSE, whose anthropological work on the delta region of the Sundarbans[31] promised textured insights into how diaspora and migration was 'lived' by migrants in Bengal. Another, later, decision was to enlist as another member of the team, Shahzad Firoz, a Bangladeshi, Sylheti-speaking researcher in development studies, to help with fieldwork in Britain.

We began with four main aims. The first was to test key concepts in the study of migration, in particular by interrogating the distinction between 'forced migration', which downplays the agency of migrants, and 'economic migration', which diminishes the structuring role of history and culture and attachments to place, people, and 'community'. Second, we wanted to examine the historical circumstances that shaped patterns of migration and settlement of Bengali Muslims in South Asia and Britain. Third, we aspired to learn more about the role of place – national and local – in shaping the experience of settlement and identity. Finally, we hoped to understand better how the experience of migration and settlement affected, and sometimes transformed, social, cultural, and religious relationships and identities among migrants themselves. We thought of these 'layers' – historical, structural/social, and cultural – as integrally linked to one another and mutually constitutive. Recognizing that each was necessary but not sufficient for a multidimensional account of diaspora and migration, we studied these 'layers' with particular attention to their relation to one another. We examined processes of continuity and change set against a large historical canvas and explored tensions between 'being' and 'becoming' in individual lives. We looked at how 'sameness' and 'difference' were produced and sustained over time. We analysed how structures and circuits of power both enabled and constrained movement. This approach, we hoped, would yield insights that would redefine, or at least refine, existing concepts of diaspora, migration, and identity.

Placing the Bengal diaspora: National and local contexts

Our project was based in three countries. India (chiefly in the state of West Bengal, but also in Bihar and eastern Uttar Pradesh), Bangladesh, and Britain. Our period covered the six decades after partition, from 1947 to 2007, with 1971 and the birth of Bangladesh as a significant caesura half way through that period. We did the fieldwork between 2008 and 2014. At each geographical 'end' of the project, we selected four sites typical of 'primary' settlement. In South Asia, these were: (i) urban centres with concentrated settlements of Muslim migrants; (ii) rural areas where internally displaced people had settled; (iii) borderlands with clusters of migrants; and (iv) areas (both urban and rural) with populations of stateless peoples, sometimes still living in camps. Of course, these were not wholly replicated in the UK, where we selected four sites of Bengali Muslim settlement, which were (i) urban settlements; (ii) suburban areas attracting recent internal migration; (iii) deindustrialized, small-town communities; and (iv) dispersed networks across the country.

A key premise of the project and the book is that the experience of diaspora is located in space and time. So a sketch of the national contexts and the local sites where we conducted our research is given to provide a sense of 'place' for the Bengal diasporas in India, Bangladesh, and Britain at the time of our research.

The Bengal diaspora in South Asia

The first two chapters give a detailed account of the contours of the diaspora in Bengal, so here we give only the headlines. Muslims began to flee their homes in Bengal and the neighbouring province of Bihar in 1946. After major riots in 1946, 1950, and 1964, they moved in large waves; at other times they left in steady trickles. By 1964, their number had risen to about 3 million.

In the main, Muslim migrants moved eastwards towards East Bengal (or East Pakistan, as it was known after 1956) and, to a lesser extent, to Assam in eastern

India. Some gravitated to particular cities – Dhaka (the capital of East Pakistan), Chittagong (a large port town), Syedpur (a major railhead in the north), and smaller administrative headquarters such as Bogra and Dinajpur, closer to the border with India. Others – mainly refugees from the countryside – moved to rural areas on both sides of the border along its entire length, where they clustered in dense settlements.

In rural areas of West Bengal, Hindus and Muslims who had previously lived cheek by jowl now separated, like curds from whey or oil from water. Muslims fled to areas where their coreligionists already lived in concentrated settlements. Hence some parts of Birbhum, Murshidabad, Malda, West Dinajpur, and 24 Parganas, all in West Bengal, became even more densely and exclusively inhabited by Muslims, with stayers-on now living alongside rural Muslim displacees. The same pattern of 'unmixing' was evident in towns, notably Calcutta, where small Muslim groups took flight from their old neighbourhoods and sought security in numbers in 'Muslim areas' of the city, which increasingly now took on the characteristics of ghettos.[32]

In 1971, another seismic wave of migration carried almost 10 million people from their homes in East Pakistan in an effort to find shelter in India. Most Bengal speakers in this human tsunami are thought to have returned home soon after the war ended.[33] But those 'Bihari'[34] survivors who stayed on in Bangladesh (many of them partition refugees) were seen as collaborators of the hated Pakistani regime and were now driven underground or into camps. In 2008, there were nearly 300,000 'Biharis' in Bangladesh, over half of whom still lived in camps all over the country.

These patterns of migration, settlement, and ghettoization influenced our choice of the sites in Bengal. Our fieldwork was in the two biggest cities on each side of the new borders – Dhaka and Calcutta – at sites where large camps and ghettos are situated. In Dhaka, our main site was Town Hall Camp; in Calcutta we worked at a number of sites with dense concentrations of Muslims. Our two main rural sites were along the border, one in the north, the other in the south. In the northern borderlands, our fieldwork was conducted in villages on both sides of the border, in Malda in India and Dinajpur and Rangpur in Bangladesh. Further south, we worked in South 24 Parganas and the Sundarbans in West Bengal and Khulna in Bangladesh. In addition, displacees and stayers-on were interviewed in rural Birbhum (West Bengal, India) and Syedpur (Bangladesh). Descriptions of these various sites are given in the chapters that follow, but each site was selected because it was representative of wider patterns.

The Bengal diaspora in Britain

In Britain, most Bengali Muslims are from Bangladesh, particularly the northeastern region of Sylhet.[35] The 451,529 Bangladeshis (or British Bangladeshis) in Britain recorded in the 2011 Census comprised less than 1 per cent (0.8 per cent) of the UK's total population.[36] The overwhelming majority[37] lived in England, and about half in London. Other smaller clusters were to be found in the West Midlands, notably Birmingham, and in the northwest, chiefly in the Greater Manchester area, including Oldham. Over 90 per cent identified themselves as Muslims, and they made up around 15 per cent of the total British Muslim population.[38]

Mobility between Bengal and Britain has a long history. From as early as the 17th century, Sylheti lascars were employed by the East India Company,[39] and regular travel between Sylhet and Britain can be traced back to the 19th century. From the 1850s onwards, Bengali lascars were crucial in the workforce of the imperial merchant marine, and many manned the engine rooms of British merchant ships during the two world wars. From the 1920s onwards, a few ex-lascars began to settle in East London, their numbers slowly rising until 1945.[40]

After partition, many former lascars sought work in Britain, where cheap, unskilled labour was in demand. By 1962, about 6,000 Bengalis had settled in the UK. Many worked in East London's garment industry,[41] while others moved to the textile mills and heavy industries in Birmingham, Oldham, and Bradford.[42] After the 1962 Commonwealth Immigrants Act, however, migration patterns changed. The act restricted primary migration from the Commonwealth to three categories: those with a specific job to go to in Britain; those with a recognized skill or qualification in short supply; and 'others' (unskilled labourers).[43] This encouraged Bengalis already in Britain to seek 'voucher visas' for friends and relatives, marking the start of a period of sustained 'chain' migration.[44]

In the early 1970s and 1980s, further restrictions on immigration encouraged family reunification. By 1987, the Labour Force Survey counted around 116,000 Bangladeshis living in the UK, including a growing British-born population[45] and larger numbers of women.[46] The family reunification of this period coincided with economic recession characterized by a marked decline in those manufacturing industries in which Bengalis were chiefly employed, and this led to further changes in their patterns of settlement and employment. Chapters 4 and 7 show how these decades saw the 'coming of age' of Britain's Bangladeshi communities, whose cultural and religious institutions and events now claimed their place in an increasingly multicultural Britain.

In the next 25 years, changes to Britain's immigration laws curbed primary migration from Bangladesh. From 1991 to 2006, only 40,000 grants of settlement were given to Bangladeshis.[47] In the main, these went to students or other high-skilled migrants, often from regions other than Sylhet, or to migrants joining their spouses.

Bangladeshis are often portrayed as classic example of the failures of migration and multiculturalism in Britain, but the reality is more complex. While Bangladeshis remain among the most densely clustered ethnic minority groups in Britain, they are also to be found in small but increasing numbers across the UK, usually because of the expanding restaurant trade and shifting marriage patterns. Education outcomes have improved and employment opportunities grown for younger generations, and many have moved out of zones of dense settlement to neighbouring, more affluent areas.

Our field sites in Britain were chosen to capture these nuances while mirroring, as far as such different contexts permitted, our selection of sites in South Asia. We settled upon two 'dense' clusters – one in inner city Tower Hamlets, London, and the other in the former mill town of Oldham in Greater Manchester. Both have long, but very different, histories of Bengali Muslim settlement, which Chapters 4 and 7 explore. We also chose two sites of dispersal designed to reflect Bengali mobility within Britain itself. The first was in Newham in East London, close to Tower Hamlets and one of the most ethnically diverse boroughs in Britain.[48] The second was a *set of networks* dispersed across the country, straddling smaller, settled communities in Bradford, Birmingham, and Blackburn, and also the less ethnically diverse towns of Colchester and Stoke-on-Trent.

Research methods

This brief description of our sites is admittedly crude and broad brush. Categorizing groups under convenient ethnic labels with easily digestible captions tied to particular places has obvious dangers for the researcher. It runs the risk of producing the very object under investigation. These categories erase internal heterogeneity, and they ignore the inherent instability of categories, the changing nature of conveniently labelled 'communities', the shifting parameters of the social history of space, and the porosity of borders.[49] Since these instabilities and changes are a central preoccupation of our work, we offer these 'facts and figures' here only as the roughest of introductions.

Our project did not take 'the Bengal diaspora' as a given 'fact' but as lens through which to examine complex processes and ambiguous experiences. While seeking to historicize the diaspora, in all its specificity, we were also alert to its symbolic, emotional, and imaginative resonances. We have taken history seriously but were always aware of the complex choices, negotiations, and constraints that shaped the lives of our respondents, who made history in their turn.

The fieldwork tried to capture these different dimensions through a multiscalar approach.[50] Published and archival sources, as well as oral history, helped us to track a century of growing mobility in and from the greater Bengal region and the more sudden processes of uprooting, flight, and settlement in the turbulent period after 1946. Chatterji analysed national archives, gazetteers, censuses, 'grey' literature, legal cases, newspapers, community histories, genealogies, family photographs, and ephemera to consider the ways in which large external events and national borders shaped and constrained individual and family migrations and the formation of migrant 'communities', and how these changed (or were challenged, evaded, or resisted) in different local contexts and political climates. We set these alongside the accounts of migrants themselves, using a combination of interviews, participant observation, and ethnography. Our aim was to engage 'big' and 'little' histories in dialogue, to simultaneously take both a 'bird's eye' and 'worm's eye' view, and to explore points of convergence and dissonance between them.

At the heart of the study stand the 227 people we interviewed (see Table I.1). Some of their extraordinary stories appear in the pages that follow; others do not, but every single interview has informed our analysis and contributed to our conclusions.

Table I.1 Field sites and respondents.

Field Site	Number of respondents
Dhaka, Bangladesh	32
Malda/Dinajpur/Rangpur border villages, India and Bangladesh	28
Syedpur, Bangladesh	20
South 24 Parganas/Khulna/Sudarbans border villages, India, and Bangladesh	25 Bangladesh + 16 West Bengal
Calcutta, India	18
Birbhum, India	1
Tower Hamlets, London	30
Newham, London	20
Oldham, Greater Manchester	20
Dispersed restaurant workers/brides, UK	17
Total	227

These migrants, displacees, and stayers-on were men and women from different places and different backgrounds. Their migration and settlement took place at different times, under different conditions, and at different stages in their personal life cycle. In selecting interviewees, we had two broad criteria: they had to have migrated to, within or from Bengal after 1946/47, and they had to be Muslims. In practice, however, even these apparently unambiguous boundaries were often unclear – as Chapters 1 and 2 show, individuals had long and complex family histories of mobility that crossed and recrossed borders, and, as Chapters 3, 6, and 7 suggest, the category of 'Muslim' was itself malleable and contested. We also made a particular effort to interview women, and married women especially, although this proved challenging in South Asia and Britain alike.

In India and Bangladesh, interviews were mainly taken by Annu Jalais, and in Britain by Shahzad Firoz. At each site, about twenty shorter interviews were conducted focusing on personal history and the experience of migration (or staying on). In addition, we recorded up to seven longer 'life history' interviews which examined respondents' stories in greater depth, and, where possible, we collected photographs, documents, and genealogies. Some participant observation of family and community events and festivals at each site supplemented interviews, as did occasional, informal conversations with other family members and neighbours. Access varied according to researcher, the site, and the interviewee but can be broadly characterized as a combination of 'snowballing' through community 'gatekeepers', personal networks, and, frankly, the serendipity of opportune meetings. Jalais' access to 'Bihari' migrants in Bangladesh was greatly helped by working with Noor Islam, a local researcher, who acted as guide, gatekeeper, occasional interpreter and authorizing presence amongst this highly vulnerable, and often suspicious, group. In Calcutta, Professor M.S.A. Siddiqui, an anthropologist and social activist, played a similar role. To supplement Firoz's interviews on Britain, Alexander also conducted eighteen interviews in East London with key community leaders, activists, and representatives of political, religious, and cultural organizations to map some of the transitions in Bangladeshi settlement in this iconic site. In India, Chatterji interviewed six informants, including members of the police force and Muslim community organizers.

One primary objective was to uncover the hidden stories of diaspora – the unofficial, undocumented, and unauthorized accounts of the unheard majority, including women, refugees, illicit migrants, and stateless people, the unnumbered and faceless poor who live below the radar of policy and politics as well as of academic scrutiny. A life history approach has long been recognized as a valuable tool for accessing these narratives, bringing what Ken Plummer has termed a 'critical humanism' to the research process.[51] These personal stories stand here alongside, and in critical dialogue with, official accounts from the archive as well as the chronicles that community representatives and 'organic intellectuals' create, elaborate on, and repeat. They enable us to place individual and group biographies within a broad historical context, recognizing where they challenge and reinscribe national histories and myths.

However, the huge scale of the project (both geographical and temporal), its multiple sites and heterogeneous subjects, meant that the research process has been far from seamless. Perhaps inevitably, the fieldwork reflected our own particular interests and disciplinary biases. Moreover, the 'South Asia end' and the 'UK end' had to negotiate very different terrains. Yet despite their differences, we were struck by the precariousness of our informants' lives at both 'ends': whether the uncertain status of 'Biharis' in Bangladesh, the vulnerabilities of the borderland Bengalis, the insecurities of urban 'ghetto' dwellers of Calcutta, or the marginalized citizenship of British Bangladeshis.

The different interests of our small research team also had an impact on the interviews. For Alexander and Firoz, working in Britain, the emphasis was primarily on issues of social structure – notably racial and ethnic discrimination, minority formation, and the role of Muslim migrants in contesting these processes – and was focused more on arrival and settlement than on journeys and departures. In contrast, Chatterji and Jalais, working in South Asia, were drawn to questions of cultural change – to rituals, customs, and practices – and of status and hierarchy. Consequently, in Britain, the emphasis is more on 'community' and its various incarnations in a broad, multicultural context; whereas in South Asia, it is on individuals and families in the context of emergent and fragile nation-building. In Britain, we deployed a more sociological approach which places individuals in their social setting – looking 'up and out' to explore the relationship between 'personal troubles' and 'public issues'.[52] In South Asia, by contrast, our modus operandi was akin to that of historical anthropologists, looking 'in' at practices of everyday life and their changing textures over time.

There were other differences too. Firoz conducted his interviews with a clear, semi-structured questionnaire and a digital recorder, later translating and transcribing a vast volume of spoken material. Jalais' approach was more intuitive and idiosyncratic, snatching conversations on trains and in marketplaces and writing up her field notes afterwards. Both approaches had merits and drawbacks. The UK fieldwork, with clear common themes and quotable text, helped Alexander's analysis but lacked a sense of the embodied 'voice' and 'face' of the interviewees and their everyday lives – a distancing further exacerbated by the dependence on a researcher, interpreters, and translators.[53] By contrast, Jalais' ethnographic eye and ear enabled her to gather stories that were richer and more human, sometimes stunningly so, but proved more elusive to pin down for analysis.

These differences in approach and technique are reflected in the different 'feel' of our material and the way we present it here. There is more 'thick description' in the South Asian fieldwork and more interview data in the UK material; more texture and depth in the former (accentuated by Chatterji's historical analysis) and more text and context in the latter.

As lead authors, Chatterji and Alexander decided not to 'flatten out' these differences. Rather, we deliberately kept the unevenness to allow light from different disciplines to be thrown on different facets of the subject. The book, which reflects these disjunctures and tensions, represents the outcome of a genuinely multidisciplinary effort to write about migration and diaspora. It is, of course, up to the reader to judge how far our experiment has succeeded.

Chatterji was the primary author of Chapters 1, 2, and 8, and Alexander of Chapters 4 and 7. Chapter 5, as well as the Introduction and Conclusion, were coauthored by Alexander and Chatterji. Chatterji and Jalais coauthored Chapters 3 and 6. Every chapter has benefited, of course, from careful reading by all three authors. It is likely – indeed, desirable – that primary authorship will be discernible, not only in the subject matter itself but in the 'feel' of the data presented, the questions asked, and the imagined readerships engaged with, as well as the distinctive styles of the individual authors. For the sake of these different readerships, we have tried to limit the use of the jargon of our respective disciplines.

On account of this unevenness, we present material from the two 'ends' of the project in separate chapters, the exceptions being Chapter 5 on brides, which is coauthored, and Chapter 8 on migration myths, which is not. However, we have placed chapters with common themes alongside each other to encourage comparisons to be drawn between migrant experiences in very different locations. The ordering of chapters reflects the intellectual conversation that underpins the project as a whole. Tensions of structure that remain are revealing about the difference that place makes. They also hint at what multidisciplinary approaches can add to the distinctive contributions of disciplines.

The structure of the book

Throughout our research and writing, we have been attentive to the differences of place, time, social location, and individual biography. Nevertheless, there is an overarching framework and narrative logic to what follows which provides a powerful thematic structure to the book and its arguments. The book's structure itself resembles a journey. We begin with starting points, analysing the long pre-history of mobility in the Bengal delta and the defining moments of fracture and violent dislocation, notably in 1947 and 1971; next, we focus on arrival and the process of place-making and claims-staking in the new 'homeland'; and finally, we explore the role of imagination and 'myths of return' which invoke emotional ties to the original 'homeland' and negotiate forms of belonging in the places of arrival.

The first two chapters provide the historical and theoretical starting points for the book. Chapter 1 examines the longer history of migration in the Bengal delta and beyond in the century before our study. It identifies and underlines the expanding networks of *internal* mobility in the first half of the 20th century, suggesting that late 19th and early 20th century colonial India witnessed a dual process: the stabilization of populations as well as large flows of migration. Mobility and immobility, we argue, were two sides of the same process: both were consequences of the penetration (albeit unequal) of capitalism and state power deep into the heart of Indian society. The migratory grooves they cut were not rubbed away in the inter- and postwar era of the 20th century. They changed, of course, and these changes – sometimes subtle and sometimes sharp – are addressed in the first two chapters. This period was remarkable, we suggest, for opening up stark cleavages between those who *could* use these existing pathways to move and improve their lot and others who could not.

We argue that postpartition patterns of migration in the region must be placed within the context of this pre-history of mobility (and immobility). Chapter 2 picks up the story of migration in the delta in the wake of partition and independence, the Liberation War, and the creation of Bangladesh. Drawing on the life histories of migrants, it explains why so many – both internal 'displacees' and refugees across borders – settled in the border regions after partition, why a significant number clustered in urban ghettos, and why some – a tiny number in comparison with the vast flows of people within the Bengal delta – migrated abroad. As significantly, we consider why some people *did not* move – whether through choice or inability – and the consequences of 'staying on'. We develop three important arguments: first, that the theoretical division between 'forced' and 'economic' migration is fallacious in this context and obscures the complex and ambiguous intersections between 'choice' and 'constraint'. Second, that mobility and immobility are interlinked concepts and phenomena and that 'staying on' provides invaluable insights into the process of movement. Third, we develop a theory of '*mobility capital*' as a bundle of capacities, predispositions, and connections, often rooted in the family and group histories of mobility, which shape patterns of migration and settlement in Bengal. We propose that the 'Bengal model' presented here might help to explain similar patterns seen in other parts of the world.

Chapters 3, 4, and 5 investigate the contemporary experience of Bengali Muslim migration and settlement in India, Bangladesh, and Britain. We build on earlier chapters to explore the motives and means for migration, but our emphasis here is on the experience of arrival and the processes by which marginal men and women created new lives in very different places and under very different circumstances. In Chapter 3, we consider strategies of 'home-making' by poorer Muslim migrants in the Bengal borderlands and in the urban centres of Calcutta and Dhaka. We bring together stories that reveal the myriad ways in which they confronted the harsh, often violent, consequences of both mobility and of immobility. But we also explore the ways in which they negotiated new forms of status and belonging by making innovative claims based on religion and culture, by redefining boundaries, and by creating novel modes of exclusion.

Chapter 4 takes up these themes in a very different context: the migration of Bengali Muslims to Britain. It explores the settlement of pioneer migrants in two iconic sites – Tower Hamlets in East London and Oldham in Greater Manchester. Although the migrants and the place of arrival are in stark contrast to those of our interviewees in Chapter 3, shared themes and experiences emerge nonetheless. In particular, we note similar patterns of exclusion and similar constraints on movement and settlement. Here too, we find that place itself has both shaped and been shaped by these Muslim migrants. Identities have also changed over time, often in relation to very local conditions, struggles, and transformations. In the context of ongoing debates in Britain about the perceived failures of multiculturalism, we challenge simplistic ideas of ethnic, religious, and cultural difference and insist on the complex and shifting nature of 'community'. 'Community' is seen by us as a site of engagement, of struggle, of exclusion, and of change – of 'being', 'becoming', and 'making home'.

In Chapter 5, we examine the neglected experience of women's migration. Bringing together the stories of women from both 'ends' of our research, we consider the significant role marriage has played in shaping migration historically and also the place of brides in the present day. For the majority of women in our study, irrespective of age, status, or place of departure or arrival, migration was closely bound up with marriage. However, in migration studies, women are marginal and subordinate figures – whether as dependents or as the victims or carriers of anachronistic 'cultures' and 'traditions'. In this chapter, we challenge these conventional wisdoms by placing women's stories at centre stage. Situating marriage migration historically, we suggest that marriage constitutes a complex and multilayered 'social field', and we draw attention to the unexpected and revealing changes it facilitated and underwent.

In the final stages of our journey through the Bengal diaspora, Chapters 6 to 8 return to ideas of 'homeland' and 'origin', examining how 'home' is reimagined and reclaimed in diaspora. Ideas of 'home' and 'homeland' stand at the heart of the definition of diaspora. Migration theorists have long reflected upon the 'myth of return' and its role in establishing and maintaining links to the place of origin – either real or imagined. In these last three chapters, our concern is with myth-making, imagination, memory, and performance – shifting from social and historical accounts of diaspora to its cultural and political dimensions.

In Chapter 6, we explore the role of the festival of Muharram in shaping community and identity among Urdu speakers in Bangladesh. Commemorating the martyrdom of Husain at the Battle of Karbala, Muharram is observed in Dhaka both by Shias and, atypically, by Sunni, Urdu-speaking 'Bihari' migrants. We argue that 'Bihari' Muharram should be understood as a prism for understanding complex, often incoherent and incomplete, processes of community formation among disparate migrant groups. We show that migrants draw upon elements of their history as a symbolic resource, simultaneously reinventing tradition and deploying it to stake 'community' claims in a context of national hostility and precarious citizenship.

Chapter 7 picks up similar themes among the British Bangladeshi community. By looking at the Shahid Minar memorial in East London and the associated annual *Ekushe* commemorations, we trace the ways in which collective memory and identity are evoked, layering upon each other the multiple meanings of transnational, national, and local belonging. We argue that the process of memorialization encapsulates both 'roots' and 'routes' – simultaneously conjuring 'myths' about the creation of the Bangladeshi nation as well as very local histories of migration, antiracist struggle, and place-making in East London. The memorials and the commemorations can be seen, then, much as Muharram, as a form of claims-staking, often in the context of violent social exclusion. As with 'Bihari' Muharram, the very act of memorialization reveals and sharpens divisions and disputes, in turn accentuated by wider religious and generational transformations.

In Chapter 8, we pick up the themes of history and myth to compare two community histories written by migrant 'organic intellectuals' in Bangladesh and Britain. As with the performances associated with Muharram and *Ekushe*, we argue that these texts produce 'origin myths' as well as 'migration myths'. We suggest that these advance the cause of assimilation in the place of settlement even as they vigorously assert their unity, integrity, and separate identity. We argue that people must first be 'assimilated' into a 'community' with a single story or construct about itself before it can begin to negotiate its acceptance as a part of a host nation. Maintaining 'ethnicity' does not prevent assimilation, as some critics have argued. Instead it is often a necessary prolegomenon to it.

Rather than pre-empt the broader theoretical conclusions of our journey through the Bengal diaspora, we have deliberately left them to the end of the book. However, in what follows, we explore four key themes. First, we examine the role of history in shaping patterns of migration and diaspora. Second, we focus on the role and circulation of power in multiple levels and arenas: the nation state, community, and family. Third, we explore the significance of place as actively created through the interaction of histories, structures (social and spatial) and people, and as a site of constraint and agency, of claims-making and contestation. Fourth, and underpinning all our other questions, we focus on the subjectivity and agency of migrants themselves. However, we see subjectivity as socially and historically located and agency as constrained and contingent. Our particular interest is in resilience and resistance and the negotiation of the possibilities (and impossibility) of migration by the very ordinary, but nonetheless remarkable, people of the Bengal diaspora.

Notes

1 Bengal and Assam were provinces in British India.
2 Srinath Raghavan, *1971. A Global History of the Creation of Bangladesh*, Cambridge MA: Harvard, 2013.
3 Joya Chatterji, *The Spoils of Partition: Bengal and India, 1947–1967*, Cambridge: Cambridge University Press, 2011.
4 Ranabir Samaddar (ed.) *Reflections on Partition in the East*, New Delhi: Sangam Books Ltd, 1999.

5 For example, Prafulla Chakrabarti, *The Marginal Men. Refugees and the Left Political Syndrome in West Bengal*, Calcutta: Lumière Books, 1990.
6 Aristide Zolberg, 'Introduction', in A.R. Zolberg and P.M. Benda (eds) *Global Migrants, Global Refugees: Problems and Solutions*, New York and Oxford: Berghahn Books, 2001.
7 John Eade and David Garbin, *The Bangladeshi Diaspora: Community Dynamics, Transnational Politics and Islamist Activities*, London: Foreign and Commonwealth Office, 2005; Claire Alexander, Shahzad Firoz and Naaz Rashid, *The Bengali Diaspora in Britain: A Review of the Literature*, 2010: http://www.banglastories.org/uploads/Literature_review.pdf
8 Willem van Schendel, 'Easy Come, Easy Go: Smugglers on the Ganges', *Journal of Contemporary Asia*, 23, 2, 1993; W. van Schendel, 'Working through Partition. Making a Living in the Bengal Borderlands', *International Review of Social History*, 46, 2001; Joya Chatterji, 'The Fashioning of a Frontier: The Radcliffe Line and Bengal's Border Landscape, 1947–52', *Modern Asian Studies*, 33, 1, 1999.
9 See Stephen Castles and Mark Miller, *The Age of Migration: International Population Movements in the Modern World*, 4th edition, Basingstoke: Palgrave Macmillan, 2009.
10 Organisation for Economic Co-operation and Development, 'World Migration in Figures', OECD-UNDESA, October 2013: www.oecd.org/els/mig/World-Migration-in-Figures.pdf
11 Kam Wing Chan, 'China, Internal Migration' in Immanuel Ness and Peter Bellwood (eds) *The Encyclopedia of Global Migration*, Oxford: Blackwell, 2013.
12 Rameez Abbas and Divya Varma, 'Internal Labour Migration in India Raises Integration Challenges for Migrants', *Migration Policy Institute Newsletter*, 2013: www.migrationpolicy.org/article/internal-labor-migration-india-raises-integration-challenges-migrants
13 Richard Marshall and Shibaab Rahman, *Internal Migration in Bangladesh: Character, Drivers and Policy Issues*, Bangladesh: United Nations Development Programme, 2013: www.undp.org/content/dam/bangladesh/docs/Publications/Pub-2013/Internal%20Migration%20in%20Bangladesh%20UNDP%20Final.pdf
14 Willem van Schendel, *The Bengal Borderland: Beyond State and Nation in South Asia*, London: Anthem Press, 2005; M. Sur, 'Through Metal Fences: Material Mobility and the Politics of Transnationality at Borders', *Mobilities*, 8, 1, 2013, pp. 70–89; Annu Jalais, *Forest of Tigers: People, Politics and Environment in the Sundarbans*, New Delhi: Routledge, 2009.
15 Castles and Miller, *Age of Migration*.
16 Zolberg and Benda, *Global Migrants*; S. Schmeidl, 'Conflict and Forced Migration: A Quantitative Review' in Zolberg and Benda, *Global Migrants*.
17 For example, Philip A. Kuhn, *Chinese Among Others: Emigration in Modern Times*, Plymouth: Rowman and Littlefield, 2008; Lisa H. Malkki, *Purity and Exile. Violence, Memory and National Cosmology among Hutu Refugees in Tanzania*, Chicago: University of Chicago Press, 1995; Abner Cohen, *Arab Border Villages in Israel*, Manchester: University Press, 1965; Rosemary Sayigh, *The Palestinians: From Peasants to Revolutionaries*, London: Zed, 1979.
18 Castles and Miller, *Age of Migration*. Note the emergence of critiques of this economistic approach from other social science disciplines, which focus on 'systems', 'networks', and 'fields'.
19 Claude Markovits, Jacques Pouchepadass and Sanjay Subrahmanyam (eds) *Society and Circulation. Mobile People and Itinerant Cultures in South Asia, 1750–1950*, London: Anthem, 2006.
20 Alejandro Portes, Luis E. Guarnizo and Patricia Landolt, 'The Study of Transnationalism: Pitfalls and Promise of an Emergent Research Field', *Ethnic and Racial Studies*, 22, 2, 1999, pp. 217–37.
21 Claire Alexander, 'Diaspora and Hybridity' in P. Hill Collins and J. Solomos (eds) *The Sage Handbook of Race and Ethnic Studies*, London: Sage, 2010; Rogers Brubaker, 'The "Diaspora" Diaspora', *Ethnic and Racial Studies*, 28, 1, 2005, pp. 1–19.

22 Malkki, *Purity*, p. 1.
23 See Chetan Bhatt, *Liberation and Purity: Race, New Religious Ethics of Postmodernity*, London: UCL Press, 1997; and Salman Sayyid, *A Fundamental Fear: Eurocentrism and the Emergence of Islamism*, London: Zed Press, 1997, for two approaches to 'locating' the rise of global Islamic ideologies.
24 Claire Alexander, 'Re-Imagining the Muslim Community', *Innovation*, 11, 4, 1998, pp. 439–50.
25 Samuel Huntington, *The Clash of Civilisations and the Remaking of World Order*, New York: Simon and Schuster, 1996.
26 Richard Alba, 'Bright vs Blurred Boundaries: Second Generation Assimilation and Exclusion in France, Germany and the United States', *Ethnic and Racial Studies*, 28, 1, 2005, pp. 20–49.
27 Chatterji, *Spoils*; Joya Chatterji, *Bengal Divided. Hindu Communalism and Partition, 1932–1947*, Cambridge: Cambridge University Press, 1994.
28 Claire Alexander, *The Asian Gang: Ethnicity, Identity, Masculinity*, Oxford: Berg, 2000.
29 Chatterji, *Spoils*, Chapters 3 and 4.
30 Zolberg and Benda, *Global Migrants*; Schmeidl, 'Conflict'.
31 Jalais, *Forest*.
32 Chatterji, *Spoils*, Chapter 5.
33 Antara Datta, *Refugees and Borders in South Asia: the Great Exodus of 1971*, London: Routledge, 2012.
34 The term 'Bihari' is used colloquially, pejoratively, and often inaccurately, for migrants from north India settled in West Bengal and Bangladesh.
35 Benjamin Zeitlyn, 'Challenging Language in the Diaspora', *Bangla Journal*, 6, 14, September 2008, pp. 126–40.
36 *2011 Census: Ethnic Group, Local Authorities in the United Kingdom*, London: Office for National Statistics, 2012–2014.
37 436,514 in all.
38 Muslim Council of Britain, *British Muslims in Numbers*, London: MCB, 2015: www.mcb.org.uk/wp-content/uploads/2015/02/MCBCensusReport_2015.pdf
39 Caroline Adams, *Across Seven Seas and Thirteen Rivers. Life Stories of Sylheti Settlers in Britain*, London: THAP, 1987.
40 Adams, *Across Seven Seas*; Y. Choudhury, *Sons of the Soil*, Birmingham: Sylheti Social History Group, 1995; A.A. Ullah and J. Eversley, *Bengalis in London's East End*, London: Swadhinata Trust, 2010.
41 Naila Kabeer, *The Power to Choose: Bangladeshi Women and Labour Market Decisions in London and Dhaka*, London: Verso, 2000.
42 Yusuf Choudhury, *The Roots and Tales of Bangladeshi Settlers*, Birmingham: Sylheti Social History Group, 1993; Choudhury, *Sons*.
43 John Solomos, *Race and Racism in Britain*, Basingstoke: Palgrave Macmillan, 2003.
44 Katy Gardner and Abdus Shakur 'I'm Bengali, I'm Asian and I'm Living Here: The Changing Identities of British Bengalis', in Roger Ballard (ed.) *Desh Pardesh, The South Asian Presence in Britain*, London: Hurst, 1994; Kabeer, *Power to Choose*.
45 Ceri Peach, 'The Muslim Population of Great Britain', *Ethnic and Racial Studies*, 13, 3, 1990, pp. 414–19.
46 Kabeer notes a shift from a ratio of men:women from 40:1 to 2:1 between 1960 and 1981. Kabeer, *Power to Choose*.
47 Department for Communities and Local Government, *The Bangladeshi Muslim Community in England: Understanding Muslim Ethnic Communities*, London: DCLG, 2009: www.swadhinata.org.uk/document/Bangladeshi_Muslim.pdf
48 Stephen Jivraj, 'Geographies of Diversity in Newham', Manchester: Centre on Dynamics of Ethnicity, 2013: www.ethnicity.ac.uk/medialibrary/briefings/localdynamicsofdiversity/geographies-of-diversity-in-newham.pdf

49 Claire Alexander and Caroline Knowles (eds) *Making Race Matter: Bodies, Space and Identities*, Basingstoke: Palgrave Macmillan, 2005; Suzi Hall, 'Super-diverse Street: A "Trans-ethnography" Across Migrant Localities', *Ethnic and Racial Studies*, 38, 1, 2015, pp 22–37.
50 Hall, 'Super-diverse Street'.
51 Ken Plummer, *Documents of Life 2*, London: Sage, 2001.
52 Charles Wright-Mills, *The Sociological Imagination*, Oxford: Oxford University Press, 1959; Paul Willis and Mats Trondman, 'Manifesto for Ethnography', *Ethnography*, 1, 1, 2000, pp. 5–16.
53 Bogusia Temple and Rosalind Edwards, 'Interpreters/Translators and Cross-Language Research: Reflexivity and Border Crossings', *International Journal of Qualitative Methods*, 1, 2, 2002, pp. 1–12.

1 Pre-histories of mobility and immobility
The Bengal delta and the 'eastern zone', 1857–1947

When we met Mohammed Shamsul Huq in 2008, this spry, cheerfully toothless gentleman claimed to be 108[1] years old. The son of a railwayman, he was born, he said, in 1901, near the Kidderpore[2] docks in Calcutta. Fascinated by the great steamships that were repaired '[at] the *ghat* (jetty) just in front of our house', as a young man he joined the British merchant marine and travelled the world, from Calcutta to London, taking in Rangoon, Colombo, Singapore, Jeddah, and 'Africa' along the way.

Shamsul's *gusti* (or clan) was 'Khan', a patronymic that he dropped at some point in his life. In all likelihood they were Pathans from Afghanistan, who, in the winter months, plied their wares in upper India.[3] Shamsul's grandfather peddled warm clothing, travelling slowly from Punjab to Noakhali on Bengal's southeastern seaboard. There, romance blossomed and brought his sojourning to a halt. He fell in love, married, and settled down with his Bengali bride in this humid, riverine tract – very distant, and very different, from the arid uplands of Afghanistan.

Not all his male children followed in his footsteps. Of six sons, three moved, albeit along different routes and with different purposes. One settled in the neighbouring town of Barisal to the west, and one (Shamsul's father) moved north to Assam (see Figure 1.1). A third travelled further afield, and ended up 'over there', in London, where he married an English woman and set up a wine shop.[4] The remaining three sons stayed on in Noakhali. Shamsul did not speak of his aunts, but, presumably, like his sisters and daughters, once married, they moved to their husbands' homes, within the region itself.

For decades, Shamsul toiled in the sweltering heat of the ship's boiler room, stoking the glowing furnace deep below deck, where he learned to speak a little English and 'Laskari', the pidgin dialect used by Indian crews. But he abruptly gave up his seafaring life during the Second World War, when his ship was bombed by the Japanese. After a spell on a hospital ship recovering from grave injuries, he swore he would never go to sea again. He returned to Kidderpore and set up a small tea stall.

Shamsul settled contentedly into this new life, chattering with his lascar customers by day and going home to his family at night. But the Calcutta riots of 1946 and the partition of India in 1947 tore his comfortable world apart. The aftershocks of these events forced him to move again and again in search of a

Pre-histories of mobility and immobility 19

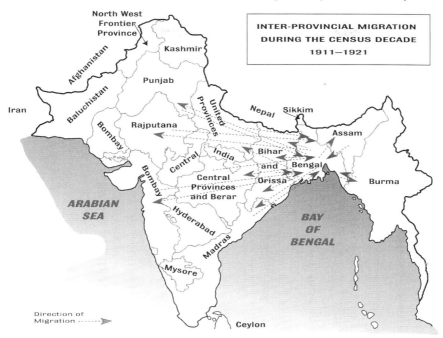

Figure 1.1 Interprovincial migration during the census decade, 1911–1921.

safe haven. At first he and his family fled to Assam, where they had relatives, and where Shamsul's father had worked as a railwayman. But they faced troubles there as well because they were Muslims, and Assam – now part of India – was not welcoming to Muslim migrants. In the 1960s the family was 'pushed out', Shamsul told us, and 'told to go to Arabia'. Finally Shamsul found shelter of sorts in a small village in the district of Dinajpur in present-day Bangladesh, where the government of East Pakistan gave him a tiny plot of land as part of its measures to rehabilitate refugees. All five of his sons live in Bangladesh. His three daughters live nearby with their husbands, or with him, at the modest home where we met him.

What are we to make of Shamsul's complex and peripatetic history? We will return to him again later in this book to tease out the many intricate processes that his life story illuminates. But here we must discuss the one bold theme at its centre, which must be the starting point of this chapter and, indeed, of this book: the widespread mobility in eastern India *before* the partition of 1947. To understand the scale and contours of the Bengal diaspora in the later 20th century, we must give up our nostalgic belief that partition ripped through a comfortably settled society.

Our arguments depart from existing scholarship on South Asian mobility in other significant ways. That scholarship is preoccupied, ever more overwhelmingly, with diasporas overseas. When scholars in the 1970s, many of them influenced by Marxism, began to write the history of the 'taming' of the 'coolie beast',[5] a particular focus was indentured labour, famously described as 'a new system of slavery'.[6] Dominated, on the one hand, by labour historians[7] and, on the other, by sociologists of labour diasporas,[8] this has remained a powerful focus of study. In the 1990s, coinciding with the coming of age of the second and third generations in Asian diasporas in the West, anthropologists generated a lively body of work on 'the cultural dimensions of globalisation'.[9] Yet another, more recent, tradition has grown out of the fin-de-siècle historical fascination with 'the Indian ocean world', which has produced rich studies of merchant diasporas[10] and the cosmopolitan port cities of the European empires. While each of these approaches has yielded important (and different) insights, they are united by their focus on diasporas overseas.

Where scholars have considered mobility within the subcontinent, a second characteristic reveals itself: the influence of compelling accounts of the progressive 'sedentarization' and 'territorialization' of South Asia in the colonial period.[11] Keen to challenge the colonial shibboleth that Indians were a 'stay-at-home race', influential historians have shown that, on the contrary, before 1800, perhaps half the total population of the subcontinent was habitually itinerant for much of their adult lives.[12] These patterns of mobility changed dramatically in the colonial era, and it is now widely accepted that British colonial policy settled Indians in place so that they could be more easily taxed, governed, and observed. While the 'sedenterization' thesis describes processes in the 18th and early 19th centuries, its influence is perceptible in studies of the century that followed. Even when historians recognize that between 1840 and 1940, the imperial state and economy created both pressures and opportunities for movement,[13] they tend to emphasize emigration overseas,[14] underlining the imperial state's capacity to encourage, 'or even forc[e], millions of Asians to move over long distances', while ensuring 'that others stayed firmly in place'.[15] We are given a picture of a society in which internal migration had become rare and agrarian colonization an exceptional activity.

This emphasis on emigration overseas is problematic, both empirically and conceptually. Between 1859 and 1945, overseas migrants accounted for only a small proportion of the millions of South Asians on the move. The *Imperial Gazetteer* suggests that in 1901, at the height of the era of indenture, 1.37 million Indians had gone overseas to Ceylon, Malaya, and Burma, where they were most numerous, and also to the West Indies, Mauritius, Natal (in South Africa), and Fiji.[16] Kingsley Davis, the pioneering demographer of the subcontinent, estimates that from 1926 to 1930, when overseas emigration peaked, some 3.2 million Indians travelled abroad, while 2.8 million returned.[17] By contrast, the Census of 1921 recorded more than 15 million internal migrants,[18] and this figure underestimated the true extent of internal movement for reasons that will be discussed later in this chapter. Moreover, after 1921, as it will show, internal migration grew by leaps and bounds. So the presumption that overseas emigrants are in some way *representative* of the modern migration process is misleading. To be sure, overseas emigration was a striking feature in some parts of the subcontinent,[19] notably peninsular southern India, where internal migrations were indeed relatively rare and overseas migrations, at least before the Depression, were significant.[20] Unquestionably, the history of these emigrants is complex and fascinating, richly deserving of the scholarly attention it has attracted. But emigration abroad was always only the most visible tip of the iceberg of human movement in the subcontinent.

This is no arcane statistical point. We raise it not to deny the significance of these journeys to faraway places, but to draw attention to the sheer volume of movement over shorter distances. Scholars have not paid sufficient heed to the scale, complexity, and impact of more local and intraregional migration in late colonial India, and this oversight has distorted our understanding of South Asia's history of mobility in the late 20th century. This chapter tells the story of a dramatic rise in new forms of internal migration tied to the emergence of a novel economic and political order. It also uncovers the persistence of older patterns of mobility, albeit adapted to the new order.

It faces up, moreover, to the conceptual fallacy that true migration constitutes *only* movement across the borders of states, preferably across oceans. This fallacy unwittingly reproduces two misconceptions: first, that British India was a single, unified cultural and economic zone, and hence migration within it was not migration in a real sense, its social, economic, and cultural effects being minimal. Second, the emphasis on the crossing of formal political borders is a state- or nation-centred approach that most historians today rightly eschew.[21] It implies that migration within a state and migration beyond it are inherently different activities, a proposition which this book will challenge.

Inevitably, then, a central focus of this work is the small journeys, often only from one locality to another within the region, which made up the vast majority of human movement in South Asia. These journeys were profoundly significant. Not only did they add up slowly, sometimes imperceptibly, to large changes in the character of regions, they also left legacies in their wake: connections, memories, and the knowledge, even hope, of potential for future journeys. They are important too for another reason: their links, still imperfectly understood, with cross-border 'refugee' movement after independence. This chapter identifies significant streams of movement that cut their criss-crossing channels through the deltaic region before the huge international upheavals of the mid- and late 20th century; and subsequent chapters will aim to illustrate the connections among these apparently distinct migrations.

There is a further point to be made here. Influential historians argue that 'in the 1930s and 40s, patterns of inter-Asian migration broke down and went into reverse',[22] and they stress that, for migrants, 'the middle decades of the 20th century were a period of disconnection', 'shattering', and 'returning home'.[23] Amrith claims that 'the Second World War broke the links of labour migration altogether, while stimulating the mass movement of refugees', and that a 'further wave' of *forced* migration followed with the creation of new nation states after 1947.[24]

This picture is, of course, true, but only in part. As this chapter will show, internal migrations were not as dramatically affected by the Depression and world wars or were affected in quite different ways. Between 1880 and 1939, new technologies of movement had facilitated massive migrations, while the emergence of modern sectors of the economy had generated an enormous 'zonal' labour market in eastern India. The onset of war did not simply obliterate these pathways, although their uses often changed. Indeed, war accelerated employment in several sectors, intensifying the pace and scale of movement while leaving others intact. The transformations of the late 19th and early 20th centuries had altered family structures in ways that had a particular impact on women.[25] These changes were not reversed by warfare, nor were they easily reversible. As global demand fell, agrarian colonization did not cease; on the contrary, it was driven forward by new forces, not least local hunger. Nor did depression, war, or famine shrink the state. If anything, it expanded, and it continued to drive migration.

The conventional account of Asian mobility has another flaw: it distinguishes too sharply between the circulating labour diasporas of the late colonial era and the 'forced' cross-border migration of the 1950s and 1960s. Challenging this conceptual distinction between 'economic' and 'forced' migration is another key purpose of this work. It will question another persistent assumption in refugee studies: namely, that the migrations and displacements that accompanied partition and independence were catastrophic *precisely because* the creation of new borders ruptured a profoundly settled, even static, agrarian society. We argue, on the contrary, that these postcolonial migrations were so large and took the directions that they did because they flowed along dynamic *existing* channels of regional and local mobility, which survived the Depression, the world wars, partition, and independence.

How, then, can these starkly divergent accounts of South Asian mobility in the late-colonial era be explained? They key is this – late 19th- and early 20th-century colonial India witnessed a dual process: *both* the stabilization of populations *and* large flows of migration. Mobility and immobility were two parts of the same process: both were consequences of the penetration (albeit unequal) of capitalism and state power deep into the heart of Indian society. The migratory grooves they cut were not rubbed away in the inter- and postwar era. They changed, and these changes – sometimes subtle and sometimes sharp – are a focus of this book. This period witnessed, we suggest, the opening up of cleavages between those who *could* use these existing pathways to move and improve their lot and others who could not. A more nuanced picture will emerge which contrasts regional pockets of high emigration with localities untouched by the late 19th-century revolution in mobility and reveals the widening gulfs between social groups *within* the same locality – and, indeed, within the same families – as the emigration of some members created pressures for others to stay behind.

Our concern to track these complex effects shapes the structure of this chapter. The first section analyses changes stimulated by the creation of new sectors of the economy and describes the zonal labour market that emerged to serve them. The second discusses mobility generated and sustained by the expansion of the state. Section three looks at processes of agrarian colonization which continued well into the period when agrarian frontiers are assumed to have closed. The final section draws attention to the one form of female migration that persisted even as others declined – the migration of wives to their husbands' homes. Each of these migratory trends is examined not only for its continued significance in the age of independence, partitions, and mass migration but also to reconcile apparently irreconcilable trends in our understanding of the wider subject.

The mobility revolution in upper India, 1857–1945

In the late 19th and early 20th centuries, upper and eastern India were transformed, suddenly and swiftly, into a densely interconnected region with highly mobile populations. The change was staggering in scale and pace. In early modern times, mobility in the eastern region had been surprisingly limited given its advanced and productive economy. Historians speak of a boom in Bengal between the 16th and 18th centuries under the aegis of the Mughal state, which flowed from the 'expansion in the agrarian frontier, a flourishing textile industry, urbanization, trade with the Western Gangetic plains, and the Indo-European maritime trade'.[26] But that boom, Tirthankar Roy points out, had a limited impact and reach. The central alluvial plains along the river Bhagirathi flourished because they lay astride the only reliable route in the vast deltaic region connecting the Bay of Bengal to the Mughal heartlands. It was here the British established Calcutta and laid the foundations for their Indian empire.

But elsewhere, to the west and the east of this narrow zone of prosperity, the picture was very different. To the west, the forested uplands of Chota Nagpur had never been integrated into the Mughal empire, and the 'penetration of trade and authority dropped away sharply' the further west one went.[27] To the east, high-yielding rice cultivation did expand,[28] but interregional trade was constrained by geography.[29] The myriad smaller rivers that broke up the delta made travel by road difficult and in the rainy season, impossible. As for the great rivers of the eastern delta – the Brahmaputra and the Meghna – their dangerous currents and whirlpools rendered them treacherous for boat travel for much of the year. In consequence, different parts of Mughal Bengal were unable to trade with each other for much of the year. Some commerce existed between the eastern parts of the delta and points further east – chiefly, the Arakan coast, Malacca, and Java – but this too was interrupted by struggles between rival Portuguese, Arakanese, Bengali, and Mughal powers in the region. Piracy was an ever-present threat, and the dangers of shipwreck in the crocodile-infested mangrove swamps of the Sundarbans put a dampener on the expansion of trade.

Roy persuasively describes the Bengal conquered by the British as a region of profound internal fragmentation. Its three distinct ecological zones – the western uplands, the central alluvial plains, and the eastern seaboard – were only loosely connected to each other by commerce and government. Only the central zone had strong links with the burgeoning overseas trade between India and Britain. Long after the British conquest, internal travel in Bengal for most of the year was dangerous and prohibitively expensive. As late as the 1830s, travel between Dacca and Calcutta, the two principal cities of the province, was feasible for only half the year and then involved twenty-two 'stages' and twenty changes of ferry.[30] In 1854, the road between Nowgong and Tejpur in Assam (where Shamsul Huq and his family fled in 1947) carried only ten to fifteen horses, fifteen to twenty elephants, eight to ten palanquins, and 5,000–6,000 travellers on foot during the whole year, while the roads between Sylhet and Cachar and Dacca and Sylhet (all places that will play a large part in our story) saw barely any traffic.[31] Travel upcountry from Bengal to the eastern United Provinces (UP) was arduous in the extreme. In 1831, the journey upstream from Calcutta to Allahabad 'for officers proceeding by water' could take 130 days.[32] Even when steamers began to ply the Ganges after 1834, they 'were few and ran at long intervals . . . rates were high and booking uncertain' – and it still took almost a month to travel to Allahabad by river.[33] Writing of his journey from Calcutta to the North Western Provinces to his first 'station', John Strachey describes how he was 'carried about a thousand miles in a box – for a palanquin is nothing better – on men's shoulders, and it took some three weeks to toil through a journey which is now [in 1884] accomplished in two days'.[34]

The Strachey brothers, like many colonial administrators, described 'giving' India the railways in profoundly whiggish terms, as among the Raj's greatest contributions to India's material progress. This condescending self-congratulation may explain why historians in more recent times, with a few notable exceptions,[35] have been so reluctant to analyse the impact of the transport revolution on the subcontinent's social history. This is not the place to write that history, but the student of migration can ill afford to ignore it.

By the early 20th century, rail, road, and steamer had linked eastern India together, transforming the conditions of travel. The zone was now crowded (if unevenly) with railways, which also connected it to upper, central, and western India. The 1,468-mile long Bengal and North Western railway linked Bengal to the populous, labour-exporting districts of Oudh, Rohilkhand, Benaras, Jaunpur, and Shahbad and carried 13 million passengers in 1904 alone.[36] The Bengal-Nagpur Railway linked Calcutta and Bombay, transporting almost 8 million passengers each year. More than 25 million passengers jostled for space on the East Indian Railway from Howrah to Kalka and Simla, the distant summer capital of India. The Assam-Bengal railway, 740 miles long, ran from Chittagong[37] on the south-eastern seaboard of Bengal through the Surma river valley and Sylhet and across Cachar into North Assam and transported over 2 million passengers a year by the turn of the century,[38] not to mention the numerous smaller gauge railways which criss-crossed Bengal itself, carrying local traffic (see Figure 1.2).

By the 1910s, another element in the transport revolution had come into play: a 'very complete steamer system' now plied the region's waterways. While always subordinate, in the official mind, to the railways, canals had a profound impact on internal travel. To the west, the development of canal systems connected Orissa and Midnapore to Calcutta, allowing small craft to avoid the treacherous waters of the Bay of Bengal.[39] The significance of these small sailboats plying inland waters in the age of steam should not be ignored. On the night of the 1881 Census in Bengal, Bihar, and Orissa, over 300,000 people were counted sleeping in boats,[40] and in 1910, small boats still carried a million tons of cargo a year.[41] But the heaviest investment in the steamer system was in eastern Bengal and Assam,

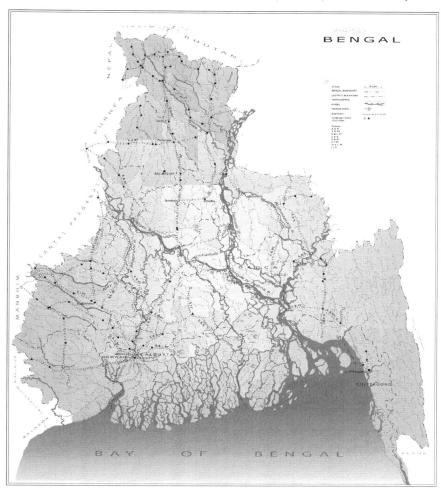

Figure 1.2 Bengal's railway network by 1914.

where topography rendered railways expensive to build and where connections by water were vital for the development of the (chiefly British-owned) jute and tea industries. By 1909, no less than thirteen stations in the eastern region had a minimum of thirty-four steamer services a month.[42] In addition, rivers previously too treacherous to navigate during the monsoons, such as the mighty Brahmaputra, were now regularly served by 'small feeder-steamers' throughout the year.[43]

Nor should the improving road network be overlooked, although it was undoubtedly the Cinderella of Bengal's transport system and chronically starved of funds. Here again, priority was given to the 'trunk' roads, which connected key centres of British power: over a thousand miles of trunk roads were built (or repaired) in Bengal by 1930. But some 'feeder roads' were also constructed, usually with the aim of supplementing and supporting the railways, and they were a significant innovation. As Ahuja notes, in just three months between December 1882 and February 1883, over 5,000 carts carrying oilseeds and salt crossed the Baramul hills, previously impassable by vehicular traffic.[44] Significantly, given our focus on migration, by the 1930s the railways were beginning to see roads as a threat, particularly as far as passenger traffic was concerned.[45]

What drove the construction of these networks of transportation and the particular paths they forged was the special place of eastern India in the British Raj. Here, the interplay of private capital and the imperatives of empire – for security, profit, and cheap but safe governance – played out in specific ways. Some of the earliest railway projects connecting Calcutta to Delhi were driven by strategic considerations brought into sharp focus by the rebellion of 1857. But after the eastern front had been 'pacified' with the annexation of Lower Burma in 1885 and the Lushai Hills in 1891, such imperatives became secondary to the promotion of industry and trade.

By happenstance, three commodities that would become crucial for the imperial commerce of India – tea, jute, and coal – were all discovered in this region at about this time. Native varieties of tea had been 'discovered' in Assam and Sylhet as early as 1824, but its commercial production only began in earnest in the 1850s. By 1859, there were already fifty-nine gardens in the region, chiefly state-run enterprises. These were transferred to private (mainly European) ownership on very liberal terms and the industry began to expand rapidly thereafter. By 1903, 820 square miles had been converted into tea plantations, producing over 200 million pounds of tea annually,[46] enabling Indian tea to 'oust the produce of China' from British markets.[47]

Local people had long cultivated jute, a natural fibre, for its robustness. But after the Crimean War interrupted the supply of hessian in world markets, jute began to be manufactured commercially as a strong and breathable packaging fabric. As global trade boomed in the late 19th century, demand for jute spiralled. To exploit the region's competitive advantage, enterprising British businessmen set up mills around Calcutta to vie with Dundee in the processing of this prized commodity. By 1903–1904, India's annual jute export was valued at about twelve crore (a hundred million) rupees. Bengal emerged as the world's sole supplier of raw jute and one of two centres where it was processed.

Neither the jute or tea industries, nor indeed the railways, could have survived long without supplies of coal. As steamships began to replace sailing vessels in the 1870s and 1880s, they too demanded huge quantities of coal. As luck would have it, a long strip of 'black country' was discovered in southwest Bengal and eastern Bihar. Raniganj, a coalfield in southwest Bengal, was the first to be developed in India because of its proximity to Calcutta, and for the rest of the 19th century and the early part of the 20th, it remained India's largest supplier of coal. One of the first stretches of railway line in India was built to connect the big city to the coalfields of Raniganj. Soon afterwards, in 1894, lines in neighbouring Jharia began to be opened up intensively after 'its connection to a branch line of the East

Pre-histories of mobility and immobility 27

India Railway', followed in quick succession by new fields at Giridih and Bokaro, west of Raniganj.

This concatenation of developments sparked off a voracious appetite for labour. Upper India and Bengal's interconnected transport system was developed chiefly to transport labour, coal, and other vital commodities swiftly and cheaply to the points where they were in demand.

Largely as a consequence of the growth of these industries and the transport networks built to support them, by the early 20th century a vast swathe of territory stretching beyond the Chota Nagpur plateau into parts of northern Madras, the Central Provinces, Orissa, eastern United Provinces, and Bihar had come to be linked closely with central, eastern, and North Bengal, with Assam and Burma to the east and Nepal to the north. The whole region had developed into a vast, interconnected, zonal labour market serving these different, often competing, sectors (see Figure 1.1).

By the early decades of the 20th century, the Bengal region had become part of an exceptionally intense zone of mobility. To grasp the pace and magnitude of change, it is instructive to compare the early modern Bengal that Roy describes with the region in the early decades of the 20th century. By 1907,

> Assam contains *three-quarters of a million* immigrants, or one-eighth of its total population. These belong for the most part to the hardy aboriginal tribes of the Chota Nagpur plateau in Bengal and the adjacent parts of the Central Provinces and Madras; and upon the expiry of the labour contracts which they execute on coming to the Province, large numbers settle down as cultivators, or as carters, herdsmen, and petty traders. The drain from Bengal to Assam is almost *counterbalanced by an influx of nearly half a million natives of the United Provinces*, who come to seek employment in the mills of Calcutta and Howrah and the coalmines of Burdwan, and as earth workers, palanquin-bearers, and field labourers all over Bengal proper . . . . In Burma, as in Bengal, the profits of cultivation are so great, and the amount of wasteland so enormous, that very few labourers are available locally and the Province is dependent on outsiders for its harvesters and workmen in the rice-mills. These aggregated nearly *half a million* at the time of the last Census [1901], *about three quarters of whom were natives of Madras and Chittagong*. . . . The aboriginal tribes of the Chota Nagpur Plateau are spreading to the north-east [of Bengal], and are bringing under cultivation the desolate uplands of the Barind, while large numbers of them have gone to the tea gardens of Jalpaiguri, whither they find their way without the elaborate recruiting agency on which the Assam tea gardens depend. Again, *three or four hundred thousand* persons born in Upper Burma were found in Lower Burma at the Census.[48]

In addition, a quarter of a million people had migrated from Nepal into this region, more than half settling in contiguous British districts.[49] Between 1911 and 1931, the eastern zone consistently recorded the highest numbers of internal immigrants and emigrants in British India. This was true both for males and females.[50] By 1931, 6 million persons had moved within and from the greater Bengal region,[51] a number *already* twice as large as *the entire Indian diaspora worldwide* in 1947,[52] and almost twice the size of the Chinese diaspora in the USA in 2010.

But migration in this zone was profoundly uneven, whether in terms of where migrants came from or who had access to these opportunities to work. The government assumed that local people would provide most of the labour these industries needed, and in railway construction, to begin with, this largely proved correct. In excavating earth and breaking rock or carrying materials to build an embankment, most of the heavy labour was done by people from neighbouring localities when work in the fields was slack. But in time, railway companies took against local labour, as it tended to dry up in the sowing and harvesting seasons, and looked for more 'reliable' workers 'who had taken up more completely the life of circulating wage labour and who usually came to work-sites from a distance'.[53] Skilled earth workers, masons, and carpenters,[54] as Kerr notes, became the 'shock troops of construction', providing 'mobile labour who tramped from one [railway] project to another'.[55] Even if these itinerant labour gangs supplemented locally recruited labour, rather than wholly supplanting it (as Kerr suggests), a pattern emerged where some regions and some people were deemed more desirable for recruitment than others. Migrants who had travelled too far from their villages and fields to be drawn back into the cycle of sowing and harvesting or were not trapped into forms of servitude by local agrarian elites were emerging as the 'modern' employees of choice.

So it was no coincidence that the bulk of the labour force in the tea, jute, and coal industries and in the railways came to be made up of migrants, colloquially known as '*pardesis*' (foreigners). Employers had concluded that *pardesis* were more 'reliable' and 'amenable to discipline'. Unaware, perhaps, of the harsh logic that gave migrant workers these attributes, nonetheless – in tune with the times – they turned to unthinking racial stereotypes in their understanding of the matter: local people were deemed to be 'lazy', and some immigrant 'races' and 'peoples' made good workers by contrast.

Soon, each of these industries relied heavily on immigrants. The tea gardens in Darjeeling recruited 'Gurkha' workers from the hill populations of Nepal and drew off Santal labour from Champaran to the west. The Assam tea gardens found it much more difficult to enlist labour and soon achieved notoriety for the unscrupulous ways in which they recruited workers from Chotanagpur, Bihar, and the United Provinces and then forced them to stay on, despite the brutal conditions of work and life in the plantations.[56] The majority of mill hands in the jute industry were also migrants from upper India, particularly from Bihar and the United Provinces, and also from famine-prone parts of northern Orissa and the Madras Presidency.[57]

In time the stereotyping became more elaborate, so that particular kinds of labour within each industry came to be deemed appropriate for people from a certain place and of a specific 'type'. Santals were favoured by tea planters for their 'hardiness' in withstanding the humid climate and harsh conditions of the Assam gardens; by 1884, only 5 per cent of all workers in Assam's plantations were local people. Santal women and children were believed to have the nimble fingers and build best suited to the plucking of tea. Charles Forsyth of the Tea Districts Labour Association was typical of the planters in declaring these 'hardy aboriginals' to be the best workers because they were allegedly immune to malaria, willing to work long hours, and, above all, docile.[58] '*Poorbeas*' (men from eastern United Provinces/Uttar Pradesh and Bihar) were preferred in the jute mills. In the coalfields, the bulk of the colliers belonged to the Kamia class of landless labourer, although some were agriculturists holding land at a distance from the coalfields. (Both groups, for reasons that had nothing to do with 'race', were unlikely to 'abscond' to the fields in the harvesting season.) *Poorbeas* soon came to dominate the regular staff on the railways. Men from Noakhali and Sandwip in East Bengal were ubiquitous on Calcutta's docks. Sylhetis soon came to monopolize the boiler rooms of steamships. And so on.

In most industries, single, able-bodied men dominated the migrant working population. As Samita Sen has shown, women found it increasingly difficult to find employment in the jute industry.[59] The coal industry routinely hired both women and children, but paid them lower wages for carrying coal to the tubs and the mineshafts.[60] On tea plantations, women and children were employed chiefly in plucking and hand-weeding – again, tasks that were deemed 'unskilled' and were poorly paid. All of this is well known to labour historians, but just how powerful gender and age were in shaping access to mobility is less well appreciated. We will return to this point, and its far-reaching implications, later in the book.

That recruitment relied increasingly on *sardars* (foreman) or jobbers of various kinds is also well known, particularly in the jute industry but also in the recruitment of lascars for steamships. *Sardars* enlisted men from their own caste, community, and village. This reinforced the links between particular areas of recruitment and specific sectors of the economy. Even within these recruitment 'hotspots', however, opportunities for movement came to be restricted to particular networks, access to which *sardars* tightly controlled. In time, the 'segmentary'[61] labour market in these 'modern' sectors of the economy became less open to the population at large, even when recruitment figures swelled to record levels. Working in these sectors was not an option open to all comers.

Admittedly, labour conditions in these sectors were exploitative in the extreme. As historians know well, employers paid as little as they could and workers endured appalling hardship. Yet scholars of migration cannot ignore that the mobility afforded by these new industries – mobility that in times of famine, epidemic or riot, could make the difference between life and death – was asymmetrically distributed.

The Depression and the Second World War affected regional labour migration patterns, of course, but the 'shattering and disconnection' suggested by Baker and Amrith are better described as rearrangements. Rural credit dried up in the 1930s and 1940s, food prices were highly volatile, and landlessness increased. But as the insightful author of the 1951 Census noted, the consequences of these developments were paradoxical: they generated 'a much greater mobility of labour' rather than its converse, since 'the landless labourer, formerly the most destitute of all, [now] has staying power'.[62] More ready to travel, having lost his stake in the countryside, he commanded the seasonal labour market while adapting himself more easily to various kinds of more long-term employment in the 'modern' sectors. In the census commissioner's view, for this class, the Japanese invasion of Burma created a huge boom in employment. Between January 1941 and October 1944, 1.3 million men joined the army, and most were stationed on the eastern front. To move troops to the front, infrastructure needed urgently to be improved. Japanese airstrikes in the Bay of Bengal not only sank ships (almost drowning Shamsul Huq), they forced the closure of all ports on the eastern seaboard; and railways were hamstrung by acute shortages of rolling stock. So, at long last, roadworks came of age. Assam finally had to be connected to Bengal and Burma, and a great new arc of metalled road, thousands of miles long, was the result.[63] The scale of mobilization of resources was such that the budget of the Engineering Department increased twenty-five-fold, from Rs 40 million in 1939–1940 to Rs 1,000 million in 1944.[64] Bayly and Harper suggest that the Indian Tea Association, stepping up to the plate, supplied 100,000 porters to work on roadworks between 1942 and 1945.[65]

But roads, though necessary, were not sufficient: airpower was essential to fight Japan. Before the war, only Calcutta had one adequate airstrip. By the end of the war, the region had 145 aerodromes and runways.[66] In the same period, labourers had built 'a fine network of . . . feeder roads' to the aerodromes. Protecting the health of the American air forces and British and Indian troops required massive scrub clearance and anti-malarial programmes, and all of this demanded labour.[67]

Of course, historians are correct to argue that, broadly speaking, war forced some sectors of the economy to retrench. Jute mills, for instance, dealt with the fluctuations of demand and commodity prices by downsizing the labour force while placing ever greater demands upon those workers who were kept in employment.[68] But other sectors expanded, notably coal and iron, both of which 'substantially increased' their output. New downstream or derivative industries provided unprecedented opportunities for both skilled and unskilled work,[69] and construction boomed as never before.

But perhaps because historians have taken a granular approach to the study of industrial labour (typically studying one industry only and rarely crossing industrial boundaries), they have failed to appreciate the extent to which workers moved flexibly *between* sectors. They had, after all, precious little choice given the worsening conditions in the countryside and the varied and changeable quality of urban demand. Laid-off jute workers took up jobs in the booming coal industry or found work as drivers, mechanics, firemen, cartmen, 'and hundreds of unspecific jobs'.[70] Tea garden labourers moved to build roads. Workers migrated between different types of labour within the city, from industrial to 'casual', formal to informal, and back again. Sardari systems of recruitment could not survive intact in such an economic environment. The long 'decline of the jobber'[71] had begun, and this allowed labour great freedom of manoeuvre.

During the Second World War, then, labour mobility did not decline in the eastern zone. On the contrary, it increased, becoming more agile, better connected, and – above all – more desperate.

State expansion and migration, 1857–1945

The economic transformations of the industrial age are well recognized as drivers of migration, in India as elsewhere. Less well understood is the migration driven by the late-colonial state. In early modern times, the rise, decline, and competition between states triggered the migration of soldiers, skilled artisans, and service elites;[72] so too as the British colonial state expanded, it afforded opportunities for employment for Indians with the right skills who were able and willing to move. There was more continuity than has hitherto been recognized: the 'new' service groups were drawn largely from much the same social groups who had worked for precolonial states.

But these groups swelled in size. The eastern region witnessed an enormous expansion in state employment as, after the rebellion, the Raj took on the classic features of a bureaucratic and military empire. The elite corps of 900 Indian civil servants who manned the top posts were supplemented – in clearly subordinate roles – by a much larger body of lesser civil servants, most of whom were Indians. Below them, hundreds of thousands of lesser public functionaries worked at the district and village level.[73] By 1921, in Bengal 'proper'[74] alone, over 47,000 people worked in public administration, and 67,000 in the army and police ('the public force').[75] By 1931, almost 200,000 Indians were employed in the allied services such as the railways, irrigation, post, and telegraph departments in the province (see Table 1.1).

Each of these arms of the state tended to be dominated by men from particular castes with particular skills. After the 1857 rebellion, *poorbea* men were no longer favoured in the Indian army (although they continued to provide more than one in six of all regular troops until the First World War),[76] but they took over the constabulary in Calcutta and the suburbs.[77] Together with 'Anglo-Indians', they also dominated the railways. By 1914, Gurkhas made up almost a fifth of all regiments

Table 1.1 Persons employed in the railway, irrigation, post, and telegraph departments in Bengal 'proper', 1931.

	Europeans/Anglo-Indians	Indians
Railway	4,050	153,000*
Irrigation (directly employed)	45	4,074
Post offices	42	20,087
Telegraph	37	3,397

* This figure does not include the vast numbers of people employed in building and earthworks.

Source: *1931 Census Bengal*, Subsidiary Table VI, p. 301.

in an army now composed of supposedly 'martial' races.[78] In a replication of patterns of old, high-caste Hindu literate castes (Brahmins and Kayasthas) and elite Urdu-speaking groups dominated the clerical services.

In time, as educated Bengali Brahmans and Kayasthas set off to serve the Raj 'upcountry' and beyond, 'white collar', outward-bound migration became as marked a feature of this region as labour immigration. This trend was so marked that, by 1931, the majority of *all* Bengali-speaking immigrants in Orissa, Bihar, the United Provinces, Punjab, Rajputana, and Bombay belonged to the 'white collar category'; indeed, there were almost *2 million* Bengal speakers in Bihar and Orissa alone.[79] By the beginning of the 20th century, there were so many Bengalis in administrative positions in Assam that Bengali was made the medium of instruction in local schools.[80] Burma, too, became a destination for educated Bengalis, among whom 'could be counted municipality officials, advocates, attorneys, judges, jail officials, surgeons, physicians, Postmasters, businessmen [and] contractors'.[81]

Most of these men – including those in clerical and administrative jobs – led highly mobile lives. Once employed, they were liable to be 'posted' again and again before they were promoted to the next grade. As Abedin notes,

> Mr B. [an] officer who held the rank of SDO/SDM[82] might . . . be required to move from one post to another post [of the same rank]. . . . In the course of his movements, he might . . . be required to hold the same post twice or thrice or even more [at a different station]. Later on, when he held higher posts . . . the nature of his mobility was [the] same.[83]

It was not unusual for such an officer to move five or more times at the same grade and fifteen times over the course of a career. Whether or not these men took their families with them often depended upon the educational facilities available at their new post, since most were determined to educate their sons to at least the same level as themselves. Landed families would send sons to nearby towns and cities to attend Higher English schools and colleges. This pattern of movement by the educated between the ancestral village and the urban centres was so common that it became ingrained in the Bengali language: as Nirad Chaudhuri's autobiography recalls, the term '*basha*' was given to the digs in the town, with the more emotive term '*bari*' reserved for the ancestral village home.[84] Among Muslims from less affluent backgrounds, the practice of sending young boys to stay in families where they paid their way as tutors while pursuing higher studies also acquired its own special Bengali word: *jagirthaka*. Thus Tamizuddin Khan, who would go on to become a leading figure in the politics of Bengal and East Pakistan, was only able to study at Cooch Behar's Free College because one of his teachers found him a place as 'a resident student-cum-tutor' at the house of a Muslim subinspector of police.[85]

Even Indians on the lowest rung of government employ had to move 'in service'. Once the railways had been built, they required a considerable workforce to run them, and by 1904, in Bengal alone, the railways employed over 150,000

Indians at the lower levels,[86] whether as railway attendants, linesmen, or maintenance and repairs staff at railway workshops. By definition, these men were constantly on the move. For the staff of the ever-expanding post and telegraph system, mobility was part of the job description. In 1884, the government introduced the telegraphic money order system, which used fingerprints to identify illiterate migrants remitting their savings to payees back at home. In 1904, over 77,590 postmen across India delivered almost 16.5 million money orders.[87] This way of life in service of the state was essentially migratory, and it created its own history of connections, friendships, dreams.[88]

Critically, state employment and the mobility it generated did not fall off in the 1930s after the Depression. Jobs in 'public administration' declined by 4 per cent between 1921 and 1931, but those in the 'public force' rose by 20 per cent in the same decade.[89] And this was *before* the introduction of provincial autonomy in 1935. After popularly elected governments took charge in 1937, politicians in official employ influenced recruitment. Pressures for more evenly distributed communal ratios and heightened political competition trumped any pressures for 'downsizing' the state.

Within months of the fall of Rangoon in 1942, the state had ballooned to a size hitherto unimaginable. The army called over a million more men to arms, and they were largely concentrated in Bengal (and, to a lesser degree, Ceylon).[90] Building roads, constructing airfields, and scrub clearance required the creation of specialized 'labour battalions' composed largely of the 'aboriginal tribes' of Bengal, Bihar, and Orissa.[91] But this was not all: the fall of Burma also pushed the government to intervene in the economy as never before. Spectacular investment in strategic road building was one aspect; another was state intervention in the market in foodstuffs. The 'Limited Denial' policy, intended to starve the advancing Japanese army of essential resources, led the government to remove or destroy boats and vehicles and to move foodgrains en masse from the coast to the interior. The Foodgrains Control Order of 1942 and the Bengal Rationing Order of 1943 are now widely deemed to have had a disastrous effect, making the catastrophic famine of 1942–1943 worse and driving starving people off the land in their thousands in search of food. Not only did these interventions (and the Grow More Food campaign of 1943) 'end free trade for the rest of the decade',[92] they required thousands of men to implement them and forged new migratory pathways through the disaster.

Economic slump and war did disrupt, massively, the economy of eastern India, but they did not have quite the effects that Baker and Amrith suggest. On the contrary, the crisis of the imperial state drove internal migration as never before.

Local 'micro-mobility'

By the early 20th century, local movement between neighbouring districts had increased to levels unimaginable a century before. In 1904, nearly 200 million third-class passengers, paying an average fare of 2.34 *pice*,[93] travelled by rail.[94] That year, over 2 million third-class passengers used the Assam-Bengal railway. More than 12 million passengers bought third-class tickets on the Bengal and North Western railway, and 7.25 million passengers in this class used the Bengal-Nagpur railway. On the smaller-gauge East Bengal railway, whose largely local traffic travelled to and from places that could only be reached by a combination of river and rail, 14.5 million passengers took the train in 1904.[95] In the five years from 1900 to 1904, over 12 million persons moved relatively short distances by steamer along the main routes connecting different parts of Assam and Bengal.[96]

However, access to these new modes of mass travel was profoundly uneven. Conditions in the so-called 'coolie class' of wagons were shocking. Dangerously overcrowded and unsanitary, overflowing with men jostling for every square inch of space,[97] they were not suited to the old, the disabled, or the frail and posed particular risks for women and girls.

What is more, the transport infrastructure was built only in areas of political or commercial consequence or of particular religious significance. Young, able-bodied men who lived in the vicinity of these transport networks were able to travel far more readily, cheaply, and quickly than ever before, but those who dwelt far away from them could not.

Three clusters of infrastructure were exceptionally well connected. One was southwestern Bengal, centred around Calcutta; the jute mills townships of Hooghly and Howrah; the coalmine districts of western Bengal and Bihar; and the railway hub at Asansol. The second was in eastern Bengal, with Narayanganj and Dacca, which had excellent steamer facilities, as its hub. The third was the ribbon of territory extending south to north from the port at Chittagong, through the Surma Valley in present-day Sylhet, and into the tea garden districts of Assam, linked from end to end by the Assam-Bengal railway.

However, these three 'infrastructure clusters' were not adequately linked to each other. Beyond them, modern transport facilities penetrated unevenly or not at all. In theory, roads were intended to connect the 'interior' to the 'railheads', but well into the 1930s, little money was spent on them, and such that was went to towns that served as district or subdivisional headquarters (and later, airports). Every effort was made to provide infrastructure to the areas that had commercial prospects. The logic of capital and imperatives of government plainly drove infrastructure provision.

Elsewhere, away from these focal points, the picture was very different. Providing cheap transport to every Indian was no part of the British agenda in India. A study in the 1970s compared three villages in present-day Bangladesh, largely unchanged since colonial times. The first was on a metalled road, and the second and third were one-and-a-half and six miles away, respectively, from an all-weather road. In the first village, half the respondents had seen a government official in the preceding three months; in the third village, only 14 per cent had had that dubious privilege.[98] Government officers still struggled to get to parts of their jurisdictions off the beaten track, so one can imagine how hard it was for ordinary people to move from isolated villages to market towns, courts, temples, and shrines, and how daunting was the task of migrating from a rural area even further from a road to places where public works or the seasonal patterns of agriculture afforded opportunities for work.

In consequence, most people off the grid had little or no experience of the dramatic effects of 'space-time compression' of modern modes of travel. As Ahuja has shown, late-colonial 'development' in Orissa opened up new lines of inequality *within* regions.[99] They did not merely compound and reshape old differences of wealth and status, they created a new type of inequality altogether – *that of access to mobility*. Since this book is as concerned with stasis as it is with mobility, this point calls to be kept constantly in mind.

Even so – and stasis notwithstanding – local micro-mobility over relatively short distances accounted for a far greater element in internal migration than we have been led to believe. The scale of such migration is notoriously difficult to assess, since censuses tended to list a person's birthplace and to count the numbers of people born either outside their district or outside their province – and even this practice was abandoned in 1931 to cut costs. A person's place of birth or enumeration often was different from where he or she was ordinarily resident, as first-born children often were delivered in their maternal grandparents' village, and this could distort the figures. Alternatively, since the censuses only recorded those who crossed administrative boundaries, they overlooked many who moved *within* the same district. This led to underrecording of local migration on a huge scale, particularly of women who migrated as brides to neighbouring villages, who, all demographers agree, constituted a significant proportion of all local migrants, a point to which we will return.

Yet with all these caveats, the census figures suggest that by 1921, almost one in ten of India's population, or some 30 million people, were internal migrants.[100] In other words, in 1921, the number of *people* who were enumerated as internal migrants totalled more than the total number of *journeys* overseas migrants made *over the course of an entire century*. Have we then been concentrating on the plumage and forgetting the living bird?

Who were these people, so numerous and yet so invisible to historians of South Asia? In northern and northeastern India, substantial numbers, of course, were persons moving relatively long distances to work in the so-called 'modern' sectors of the economy – the tea plantations, jute mills, railway townships, coalfields, and offices in Calcutta and other towns. Yet why did these folk continue to be drawn to the towns and cities after their capacity to absorb and employ became saturated and urban labour markets experienced the glut in supply characteristic of the era? Why did women from neighbouring areas also begin to flock to the city, driving the number of female domestic workers in Bengal's towns and cities up fourfold in a single decade?[101]

The answer to these questions lies in the countryside, where conditions – already desperate by the end of the First World War – were made immeasurably worse by demographic pressure. All over India, as Kingsley Davis puts it,

> Something appears to have happened after 1920 . . . [when] the alternating process [of decades of growth followed by decades of decline] stopped. From

1921 to 1931 the increase, almost 11 per cent, was the highest on record for India, and during the following decade, 1931–1941, the record was broken again by a 15 per cent growth. . . . It was the first time in India's known history that she experienced rapid growth in two successive decades. At a time when Western nations were approaching demographic stability, India with its much larger population was just starting what appears to be a period of rapid and gigantic expansion.[102]

In the greater Bengal region, this unprecedented expansion was particularly marked, and the thirty years after 1921 witnessed 'steady and rapid growth'.[103]

This demographic shift accounts for a new and significant phase in the expansion of eastern India's agrarian frontier. Urban Bengal simply could not absorb the growing numbers of impoverished people on the move after 1920, and as a consequence, land reclamation projects – large and small – unfolded across the region, from western Bengal to Assam and Burma. But unlike the first wave of agrarian expansion in the age of Akbar, so admirably described by Richard Eaton,[104] this second wave frequently involved the extension of cultivation into marginal lands, whether tracts with low yields or areas at high risk of flooding.

Some of these migrants came to till the soil as tenants on government-owned land in newly 'opened up' interiors. This was particularly striking in North Bengal, 'where the need to people government *khas mahal* lands'[105] offered the migrants opportunities.[106] Another factor, as Iqbal has shown, was that the government grew more energetic in its efforts to bring new areas under cultivation so that it could be taxed more efficiently. In their turn, *zamindars*, hereditary landlords who collected taxes for the British government, tried to grab for cultivation any and every piece of new land they could – whether forest, riverbank, or newly formed river sandbank – to keep it out of the grasp of the taxman.[107]

This cat-and-mouse game between the Raj and landowners created opportunities for would-be rural migrants. In the 1920s and 1930s, a novel phenomenon began to be observed in many Bengal districts: the settlement 'of immigrants in regular tenancies'.[108] Before this period, 'nowhere in Bengal was the Bihari or Oriya permitted to acquire rights in the land, neither is he employed as an agricultural labourer'. Rights to land were guarded jealously by those who held them. Now that picture changed. Increasingly, 'the Santal, the Oroan and Munda [were] found in appreciable numbers in old alluvium zones of Birbhum, Bankura, Murshidabad, Western Midnapore, Malda and West Dinajpur'.[109] They joined the smaller numbers who had come into this area before them over the previous half century, 'a constant stream of Santals, Mundas, Malpaharis and others crossing the Ganges at Raj Mahal and moving into northern Bengal'. While some had made this crossing at the instigation of landlords, many others moved on their own initiative in order to capture for themselves the region of North Bengal known as 'the Barind'. This outcrop of old alluvium, geologically an extension of the Chota Nagpur plateau, was hitherto largely unoccupied because the soil was rocky. Now people migrated there from Chota Nagpur in large numbers as they found that 'the soil [here] is the soil of their own country' where 'their methods of agriculture [could] be used with advantage'.[110] They also moved further east to the more fertile, but largely unoccupied, forested tracts of Dinajpur, where the local population (despite rapid growth) was still too small to clear the forest, settle the land, and build roads. So migrants began to reap rewards as this district was 'opened up' for agriculture. The 'Grow More Food' of the 1940s campaign thus merely accelerated a trend that was already well underway.

A marked feature of this period was, thus, rural North Bengal's emergence as a 'hotspot' for immigration. While a handful of settlers were traders or businessmen,[111] the great majority laboured in the fields. Immigrants from Nepal – for long a marked presence on the indigo plantations of Champaran and the Darjeeling tea estates – began to take up cultivation in these new tracts, and also in Assam. Conspicuously, these migrants were accompanied by their wives and children. They settled as peasant families with some form of title – however nugatory[112] – to the produce of the land.

Few of these people were Bengali speakers. Thousands came from neighbouring Bihar, but they were not 'Urdu speakers', a category that plays a large part in our story. They were, for the most part, neither 'Hindus' nor 'Muslims'. In the following decades, a fierce competition would ensue between Hindu and Muslim communal leaders to convert or 'purify' these people and enlist them as members of their religious community to boost claims to demographic majority. But even if the migrants signed up in later censuses as 'Hindus', 'Muslims', or as 'Christians', they often continued to practise forms of worship and life-cycle rituals of the 'tribal' Chota Nagpur and the Santal Parganas from where they had come. This would prove significant in the upheavals of 1947 and again in 1971, when religious affiliation and spoken language would become sharp markers of national belonging.

A second trend, particularly marked in North Bengal but widespread throughout this riverine region, was the increasing rush of migrants in search of new land created by the changing course of rivers. Just as population growth created powerful pressures for movement in the 1920s and 1930s, so too did the ecology of the region. The borderlands between western Bengal and eastern Bihar are made up of higher rocky ridges and plateaus, with relatively poor topsoil. Moving from west to east, this terrain falls away gradually into flatter alluvial plains, many parts of which are (or once were) fertile and ideally suited to the cultivation of rice. These plains are cut through by two enormous rivers systems – the Ganges and the Brahmaputra – and both wind their way through them to the sea, carrying with them many thousand tons of alluvium. They discharge this alluvium into the Bay of Bengal, where it meets the countervailing force of tidal currents, which shape the dumped alluvium into a series of islands. Collectively, these islands are known as the Sundarbans.

But this is a restless, shifting landscape. Over time, riverbeds become choked with alluvial deposits. Often, during the monsoons, rivers burst their banks, flooding the surrounding fields. Periodically the course of the great rivers shifts as a new course cut during a flood eventually takes over as the main channel to the sea. In general, the rivers have shifted gradually eastwards, away from the rocky uplands of the west to the softer, more yielding alluvial plains of the eastern delta. Every year, footloose rivers submerge some fields, laying bare new river banks and throwing up *chars* (alluvial islands).

In times of ever more intense demographic pressure, it is easy to see how the smallest shifts in this fluid ecological zone could prompt migrations, even of formerly settled peasants. Many of these movements have been so small and so localized that they have gone entirely unnoticed by historians of migration. Yet in the most volatile areas of the delta, there has been a series of modest but nevertheless significant migrations by people known collectively as '*bhatias*' or '*diarias*' (after *diar*, meaning river). Often they were erstwhile smallholders or tenant victims of flooding who left in search of fresh fields and found them on river banks and *chars*. Made up of new alluvium, these were of course highly fertile, but given their location, they constantly faced the risk of being washed away in the next monsoon. Over time, these *diarias* formed communities of migrating peasants who moved from *char* to *char* every year when the rivers reclaimed fields yielded up by the previous monsoon.

Theirs was a precarious existence. Nonetheless, during the 1920s a significant number of people began to take up this perilous mode of shifting cultivation. Every census reported their movement. In Bogra, for instance, 'a number of districts in Shariakandi were washed away between 1921 and 1931, with the result that some of the inhabitants of the affected villages moved into Mymensingh',[113] while others moved to more proximate, but unaffected, parts of Bogra itself. The locality of Bera in Pabna district, which lies between the Jamuna and Padma rivers, attracted a host of migrants from as far afield as Dacca, Faridpur, and Mymensingh to settle on its new *chars*. Migrants also flocked to the Sujanagar *chars* in Pabna.[114] In Malda, *chars* were captured by migrants from Shershahbad in Bihar, forming a community whose distinctiveness in manners and faith was obvious to Asok Mitra when he arrived there as a district officer in 1948.[115]

As a consequence of these many streams of movement, large tracts of North and Gangetic Bengal – from Nepal, the Himalayan foothills of Darjeeling, where the tea plantations had attracted Gurkhali and Santali workers; moving south to Malda, where tribal peoples from Chotanagpur had reclaimed the Barind; from Murshidabad to Dinajpur, Bogra, and Pabna, where *bhatias* and *diarias* moved fast from flooded fields to new *chars* – became a region whose population grew ever more dense and cosmopolitan, speaking different tongues, following different faiths, or practising different, recently adopted versions of Hinduism and Islam.

A second thrust in this wider process of land reclamation occurred further south in the Sundarban islands, where the rivers met the sea. Here, man's struggle to tame the environment was even more epic. Many of the islands were covered in mangrove forests through which the Bengal tiger prowled and swamps that were the habitat of snakes and crocodiles. Their dangers were the stuff of legend and fable.[116]

But the rewards for the brave who dared could be great. The islands were, after all, pure alluvium – so fertile that each year the forest had to be fought back anew.

Hence there was no shortage of people willing to take on leases to clear them for cultivation, and they were willing to pay good wages to labourers ready to face the hazards the islands posed. Gangs of labourers from Jessore, Khulna, and Pabna would arrive in the Sundarbans as soon as the rains of April had loosened the soil so they could plant *aman* (winter) rice. They would remain there in temporary huts until the sowing season ended in July, and then return again in the harvesting season a few months later. Also visible in the Sundarbans, particularly after the monsoons, were parties of woodcutters. In the 1930s and 1940s, seasonal migrants made their way in ever-larger numbers to the wooded islands.[117]

Indeed, migrant labour gangs were ever more prominent in the countryside of greater Bengal from 1921, as population growth began to make its impact felt, through the Depression, right up until the 1940s (and indeed beyond). These were decades of insistent, deepening hardship for the poor, as credit dried up and food prices rose. They marched by foot or travelled by train or steamer in search of wages just a rupee or two higher than that which they could scrape together locally. They would do any work they could find: sowing and harvesting crops in season and, at other times, repairing embankments or constructing roads. A growing proportion of these 'short-distance' travellers were impoverished field workers (of whom more below), moving mainly in all-male gangs during the harvesting season.[118] East Bengal, which had previously been a region of relative agrarian prosperity and of relatively settled peasants, was hit hard by the hammer blows of population growth, inflation, and credit scarcity; it turned the region into a significant zone of rural emigration. The horrifying famine of 1943 exacerbated trends in rural migration that had been evident – albeit on a lesser scale – long before that tragedy.

A third trend, albeit more controversial and politically charged, was the eastward march of peasants from overpopulated parts of East Bengal into the forested river valleys of Assam and Burma. In the first decades of the 20th century, peasants – predominantly from Mymensingh – began to move upstream along the Brahmaputra into the uncleared river valleys of Assam, attracted by the incentives local landlords offered them to clear land for cultivation. Once the Assam-Bengal railway was built, their numbers grew and they travelled further afield.[119] The government took a benign view of these migrants who brought new land under the plough and generated fresh streams of revenue. By 1911, there were already almost 200,000 immigrant Bengalis in Assam. By 1921 that number had doubled to roughly 400,000. Within the next ten years it had climbed to about 600,000.[120] In the same period, Bengali Muslim immigrants also flooded into the Surma valley in Sylhet, where they introduced the cultivation of jute. By 1931, the Bengali-speaking population in Assam outnumbered the 'locals' two to one,[121] and the government introduced the so-called 'line system' to try to stem a tide it had once encouraged.[122] Even so, between 1930 and 1950, over 83,000 hectares of land were brought under the plough for the first time, mainly through the endeavours of migrants.[123]

Burma, likewise, became a magnet for peasants spilling out of Chittagong district. Since the 1870s, the government had encouraged migration into Burma to clear land and grow rice, which was promoted as a cash crop for export, but these schemes had little success.[124] Now, as pressure on the land grew intense in neighbouring Chittagong, its people began, of their own accord, to move into the Arakan. Some arrived by sea and steamer; many more arrived by land on foot. Many stayed on in Burma with their families, working on the land in the sowing and harvesting season and migrating to Rangoon in the off-seasons to work as labourers in rice mills.[125] They were joined by Tamil mill workers, Bengali clerical staff, Sikh policemen, and Chettiar merchants, who dominated the trade in Burma rice.

Once rice cultivation had become widespread across Burma, seasonal migrants from Chittagong joined the pioneers in the sowing and harvesting seasons. By 1931, there were almost 400,000 Bengali speakers in Burma,[126] and the numbers continued to grow until 1941, when the government of Burma introduced migration controls to prevent the influx from India.

Agrarian colonization in eastern India and Burma thus continued well into the 20th century, long after other parts of the subcontinent had reached the limits of their land frontiers. Rather than 'going into reverse', migration accelerated faster than ever after the Depression and during the war. It was a process that was in some places barely discernible except to the careful observer, and in other places, it was dramatic. Either way, as we will see, it had a considerable impact upon patterns of mass migration after 1947.

The changes of this era had particular implications for women, which demand analysis in their own right.

Broadly speaking, the economic changes of the late 19th century had two interlinked effects upon rural women. The first was the decline of handicrafts, chiefly weaving, and the concomitant falling off of work such as spinning, which in the past had given work to many rural women. The second was the increasing dependence of peasant households – hit hard by revenue and rent demands, high interest rates, and corvées extracted by landed elites – on the unpaid labour of women and children. As Sen has shown, families resisted women's emigration and incorporation into the waged proletariat, preferring to deploy their labour more intensively in the countryside.

The new sectors of the economy gave some opportunities to women seeking work: by 1920, for instance, almost four out of ten coal workers were women.[127] In the early 20th century, however, these opportunities gradually shrank. Bosses in jute mills and coalmines preferred to lay off women rather than pay the surcharge that emerging labour laws demanded. (After women were prohibited from working underground, by 1937, almost two-thirds of all women in the coal sector had lost their jobs.)[128] In the tea plantations of Assam, where females continued to be in high demand for the intensive work of plucking, other factors conspired against the free emigration of women to plantations. In 1901, the furore over the 'enticement' of women and young girls to plantations led to legislation which prevented women from emigrating to Assam without the consent of their families, and such consent was rarely given. Women were deemed to lack the capacity to enter into a free contract in their own right[129] – a move that had considerable implications for their mobility.

After this, some women continued to migrate to the 'modern' sectors. But most were those whose families were unwilling to support them and happy to see them go – widows, the barren, and the deserted. Overall, however, the capacity of women to move declined steadily as a result of these intertwined pressures. So the Depression and war had a more muted impact upon women – representing the further contraction of an already shrunken labour market.

But women's migration *within the context of marriage* itself was not as vulnerable to such pressures. Most colonizing peasants – whether Santals in the Barind or Bengalis in the Brahmaputra Valley – migrated as 'nuclear' families, with young wives and children accompanying the men. Elderly relatives or frail brothers were left behind, and the women who stayed back to take care of them were trapped ever more tightly by their domestic obligations. (We will return to the themes of disability, caring, and immobility in Chapter 2.) But the wives and daughters of able-bodied men who moved to grab marginal lands did join the menfolk. The closer and more accessible the destination, the greater was the presence of women and girls among the migrants. Officials interpreted their presence as a sign that these migrants wished to settle permanently in their new locations, harbingers of long-term social and demographic change, and, unusually, they were correct in their predictions.

The nature and scale of female migration can only be fully understood, however, if we extend our focus beyond dependent women accompanying men. *Marriage itself was a form of migration that was almost universally experienced by women.*

Demographers agree that 'in marriage migration, females generally predominated in the past as they do in the present',[130] and that in rural-to-rural migration, 'a large proportion of such moves [were] made in contracting marriages'.[131] This pattern arose because throughout North India (with few exceptions) women and girls moved to their husband's homes upon marriage. Remaining a spinster was almost entirely unknown. Village exogamy prevailed, as Karve showed, throughout North India, where 'the woman ... spends her life, except for her few childhood years, with her affinal family with whom she is not acquainted up to the moment of her marriage'.[132]

Yet despite the ubiquity, and hence vast scale, of marriage migration, it has rarely been studied with the degree of attention it warrants. Perhaps because they regarded wives and their work as 'uneconomic', census officers categorized such migrations as 'casual'. In truth, they were anything but. Migration to a husband's household was a profound and permanent transition, for which girls, not only in Bengal but all over North India, were assiduously prepared from childhood. A young girl would be typically regarded as a temporary visitor in her father's home. Since her birth, then, she was an 'always-already' migrant. Both Hindu and Muslim brides, on arrival in their *shashur-bari* (in-laws' home), were expected to learn their duties and responsibilities as wives, mothers, daughters-in-law, and household workers. They had to adopt the ways and conduct (*niyom koron*) of their husbands' 'lineages'.[133] A young bride would be instructed in these duties by her *shashuri* (mother-in-law) in an initiation no less intimidating than modern citizenship tests and in an acculturation process no less demanding. She could return to her father's house, but only at times preordained, such as the birth of her first child. If widowed, she would stay on in her late husband's home, but she would be treated as an 'inauspicious' person, with little authority or autonomy. She could perhaps migrate again, as a pilgrim in a holy place, and many Bengali Hindu widows did end up in Benares – where, with their shaven heads, white saris, and emaciated bodies, they stood out among the pious masses. Others might be driven to seek work in the mills or as domestic workers in urban homes. The Royal Commission of Labour found many women like Narsama Kumari, who came to work in the mills 'after the death of her husband' since 'her brothers were not willing to receive her back into the family on account of the extra work it would give them to keep her'. Mangari at Titagarh mill was also a widow, and her widowed mother and barren sister worked at the same mill.[134] These women could not return 'home', since they owned no share of their fathers' property and their brothers had no responsibility to support them.

Marriage, then, was indeed a migration far more final than most, but because of its submersion into the realm of 'culture', it has rarely been seen as such. It is remarkably difficult to find the migrant-wife in the historical record. Censuses mention these women, but only *en passant*. Gazetteers refer to them only to show how communities punished 'disorderly' or 'deviant' wives; the great majority who did as they were told have no memorial.

Some wealthy women travelled to *shashur-bari* hundreds of miles away, but they were exceptions. Given the dangers and rigours of travel for poorer women, the vast majority migrated relatively short distances, although the building of roads and steamer services allowed even humble families to negotiate alliances somewhat further afield. A study of a caste Hindu Bengali village in western Bengal suggested that the wives of the village came from some ninety different villages and towns, most within a thirty-five mile radius.[135] Thirty-five miles is not very far as the crow flies, but the significance of these journeys was no less for that. Henri Lefebvre's maxim that 'social space' is produced 'through social practice'[136] encourages us to recognize that the social distance the migrant-bride travelled was vast, and that her experience *as a migrant* is worthy of research.

Any assessment of the scale of local migration in India must surely include women. No one appears to have even tried to number them. The best figure we have is in the 1921 Census, whose commissioner put the number of *interdistrict* migrants down at 6 million people for Bengal proper alone,[137] admitting that the number of short-distance migrants, who did not cross the district boundary (and among whom women predominated), was much larger. To get the roughest order of magnitude of marriage migration, let us simply recall that the Bengal population was about 60 million by 1947, and that 44 per cent of this population, or about 28 million, were women. Each, when she married, was transformed by her journey to a new place.

As Sen has pointed out, what migration meant for women often meant something different than it did for men – whether within or, more rarely, outside the context of marriage. 'Its history merits exploration', she argues.[138] Taking the cue, this book will seek better to understand the movement of brides to their *shashur-bari*. In a later chapter, we analyse the experience of migrant-brides whom we interviewed, who travelled both near and far *as wives*, in all its complex variety.

Conclusion

The eastern zone in 1945 can be imagined as a vast web of connections whose strands linked the region densely and intricately, albeit unevenly. Of course the web was also connected by longer filaments to distant parts of the globe. These extended links multiplied in the late 19th and early 20th centuries. But they were less numerous and more fragile than the networks of internal movement that straddled the region. Over the years, these internal networks developed to such an extent that by the middle of the 20th century, the region was like a richly woven tapestry of interdependent humankind.

This is not to diminish the importance of long-distance migration. As eastern India became more closely connected to global trade, many more Indians from these parts began to travel the world. Even before the construction, in 1885, of the wet docks at Kidderpore where Shamsul Huq grew up, Calcutta had come to rank among the great commercial ports of the world. By 1904–1905, about 84 per cent of India's trade was carried out under the British flag, and almost two-thirds of this involved trade either with Britain itself or other British possessions.[139] A large proportion of the seamen employed in that merchant marine were 'Asiatic' lascars like Shamsul Huq, who were valued by the shipping companies for their apparent 'docility' and their low rates of desertion and pay.[140] Among these lascars, men from the eastern region figured prominently.

It is hard to gain even a rough estimate for the late 19th century of the numbers of lascars from Bengal. It was only in 1931 that the government began to try to obtain figures through the captains of vessels hiring Indian crews. But that count (admittedly anecdotal and impressionistic) suggested that, while a majority of the lascars were indeed from the greater Bengal region, their total numbers were not large. Only 12,540 Indian men were enumerated at all ports where the exercise was carried out (in Aden, Karachi, Bombay, Calcutta, and Rangoon). Of them, 6,806 were born in Bengal proper, 2,927 in Assam, and 258 in Bihar and Orissa[141] – miniscule numbers when set against the vast scale of internal migration in the same period.

The numbers of indentured labourers abroad was, of course, considerably larger: between 1831 and 1920, 1.3 million Indians were indentured abroad, from Trinidad in the west to Fiji in the east. During the decade from 1851–1860, when their numbers peaked, some 275,000 Indians were exported abroad.[142] Calcutta was the port from which the majority set off, accounting for more than 60 per cent of such embarkations.[143] The vast majority were men and women from the eastern zone. Before 1870, ship lists reveal that a substantial number of 'tribal' emigrants were drawn from Chota Nagpur and the Bihar plains, as well as from Bankura and Midnapore in present-day West Bengal. But after that date, the indenture ships struggled to find enough recruits to fill their holds: they had to look further and further afield, to the eastern districts of the United Provinces of Agra and Oudh, which 'remained the principal suppliers of labour for the remaining period of indentured emigration', until its abolition in 1922.[144]

Even at its height, despite the support of imperial governments, it was obvious that indenture was a failing project. This was not merely a matter of Indian nationalist protest against the system's inherent exploitation and abuse. Despite the pressure of population growth, famine, and pestilence, potential recruits from the eastern zone proved increasingly reluctant to embark on the indenture ships. While within the subcontinent itself, as the authorities recognized, 'the native of India' was 'often ready to move within a certain radius from his home or even to travel to considerable distances [for] temporary work on roads or harvest operations, returning home after a few weeks or months', he was 'not a ready emigrant' overseas.[145]

Why was this the case? This is among the key questions this work hopes to address. Why, after 1870, did labour migrants from the eastern zone begin to reject the blandishments of the recruiting agents for '*Mirich*' (Mauritius)? One factor surely was that word had got round about the unspeakable conditions on filthy, overcrowded ships on which so many of their compatriots had already perished. Between 1851 and 1870, Indian migrants en route to the British West Indies 'perished at the rate of 65 per thousand' – a mortality rate which Northrup estimates was higher than that of the slave ships of the Atlantic slave trade at its notorious height.[146] Thanks, not least, to the impressive corpus of evidence gathered by Marina Carter,[147] historians now accept that there was a far greater degree of information-sharing between migrants about the working conditions in the plantations overseas than previously supposed. Many would-be emigrants from the eastern zone can thus be expected to have heard from those who had served out their contracts about the harsh realities of life on the ships and across the black waters.[148]

But there were other factors too, and the surge in opportunities to work closer to home was one of the most significant. As Lal notes, the so called 'Dhangars' from Chota Nagpur stopped going overseas in the late 19th century because they knew there were jobs to be had nearer at hand, whether in the rapidly growing Assam tea gardens (which had yet to acquire their own fearsome reputation) or in Bengal's burgeoning coalmines. As for the former hunting grounds of the recruiting agents in the Bihar plains, would-be migrants in these parts too began to be 'attracted to employment opportunities closer to home'. They favoured 'internal over colonial migration' because it enabled them to circulate more easily, to 'return to their villages in the planting and harvesting seasons'.[149]

A more self-propelled stream of overseas travellers were pilgrims, almost all of them pious Muslims, travelling to the holy places in the Hejaz. This was a marked trend in Bengal with its large Muslim population. By 1911, when the government issued a manual of instructions for religious travellers to the holy places, the so-called 'pilgrim passport' furnished a list of admonishments not only in Arabic, Urdu, and Farsi, but also in Bengali.[150]

But the numbers of travellers overseas remained small, however computed, when compared with the millions on the move within the region. Even among pilgrims to Mecca, who were the most willing sojourners abroad, their numbers remained infinitesimal compared to the teeming crowds who flocked to local shrines and religious festivals. The scale of internal pilgrim traffic stunned the British, and they remarked upon it with bemusement and awe. In the mid-19th century, when the railways first began to be constructed in India, the British had calculated 'that there would be little passenger traffic on account of the poverty of the people, and that the chief business would be derived from goods. They had not recognized how important a part pilgrimages ... would play in the daily life of the population'.[151] In the greater Bengal region, Hindu sacred sites at Puri and Jagannath in Orissa drew unprecedented crowds,[152] and by 1915, railway lines had to be built especially to serve the rush of worshippers flocking to temples at Kalighat and Tarakeshwar in Bengal.[153] So too did the attendance of the faithful at major Sufi shrines. By the early 20th century, the three-day *Isal i Soab* at Furfura, the seat of the famous Pir Abu Bakr, 'was attended by over a [hundred thousand]' people every day.[154]

Indeed, this comparison of scale reveals the same trends across the board. Internal migration vastly outstripped overseas migration, and local mobility far surpassed both – although this has been begging to be discovered.

The social changes generated by high local mobility in the eastern region were not undone by the shocks of the middle decades of the century. They were simply too dense, too deep-seated, too multifaceted. To remind ourselves of the scale of these changes, let us return to Roy's account of 18th-century Bengal with its three distinct zones – the Chota Nagpur plateau to the west, the Bhagirithi basin at its centre, and the alluvial seaboard to the east. By the mid-20th century, their respective populations were profoundly intermingled. The region had also absorbed millions of the inhabitants of eastern United Provinces and Bihar to its west. It had sucked in Nepalese hillmen from the North and exported millions of Bengal speakers to Assam. These changes simply could not be rolled back in 1929, 1939 or, indeed, as this book will show, in 1947. Calcutta to this day is teeming with Bhojpuri, Bihari, and Oriya speakers. Northern Bengal and Assam still have huge Santal populations. Gurkhalis are so numerous in North Bengal that they are demanding a state of their own. Several districts of Assam have Bengali-speaking majorities. In the heart of Dacca a large community of Bhojpuri speakers lives to this day, despite efforts to rid the nation of them in the 1970s.

If we return to the life history with which this chapter began, it is clear that Shamsul Huq's family history can be read in one of two ways. One reading would place Shamsul himself the centre of the story and see his sojourning life as the 'essence' of South Asia's diasporic history. A variation on this theme might be to focus on Shamsul's uncle – the one who married an Englishwoman and settled in London – and see his story as typical of the migration process.

This book suggests that a different reading of the family's history may be more fruitful. Without for a second denying how fascinating were the lives of these travellers on the high seas, it suggests that considering Shamsul's grandfather – the lovesick Afghan peddler – and his uncles and brothers who also migrated, but along more local and, at least superficially, more mundane tracks, is vital.

46 *Pre-histories of mobility and immobility*

It is crucial to think about his aunts, sisters, and daughters, whose stories are even more elusive but which demand to be investigated by scholars of migration. The following chapters pay careful attention to these humble histories and their significant afterlife.

Notes

1 In South Asia, the practice is to round up one's age rather than round down, as in the West. Someone born in 1901 therefore would be in his 108th year in 2008.
2 Today, 'Khiddirpur'.
3 *The Imperial Gazetteer of India. The Indian Empire. Vol. I. Descriptive*, Oxford: Clarendon Press, 1907, p. 469; and Robert Nichols, *A History of Pashtun Migration 1775–2006*, Karachi: Oxford University Press, 2008.
4 See Appendix 1: Family trees.
5 Jan Breman, *Taming the Coolie Beast. Plantation Society and the Colonial Order in Southeast Asia*, Delhi: Oxford University Press, 1989.
6 Hugh Tinker, *A New System of Slavery. The Export of Indian Labour Overseas 1830–1920*, London: Hansib, (1974) 1993. Also see Brij Lal, *Chalo Jahaji: On a Journey of Indenture through Fiji*, Canberra: Australian National University, 2000; and David Northrup, *Indentured Labour in the Age of Imperialism, 1834–1922*, Cambridge: Cambridge University Press, 1995.
7 See, for instance, Prabhu Mohapatra, '"Following Custom"? Representations of Community among Indian Immigrant Labour in the West Indies', in Rana P. Behal and Marcel van der Linden (eds) *Coolies, Capital and Colonialism: Studies in Indian Labour History*, Cambridge: Cambridge University Press, 2006; G. Balachandran, 'Recruitment and Control of Indian Seamen: Calcutta, 1880–1935', *International Journal of Maritime History*, 9, 1, 1997; Ravi Ahuja, 'Mobility and Containment: The Voyages of Indian Seamen, c. 1900–1960', *International Review of Social History*, 51 (Supplement) 2006; and Patrick Peebles, *Plantation Tamils of Ceylon. New Historical Perspectives on Migration*, London and New York: University of Leicester Press, 2001.
8 Influential examples of such work on Britain include Ballard (ed.) *Desh Pardesh*; John Eade, *The Politics of Community, The Bangladeshi Community in East London*, Aldershot: Ashgate, 1989; S. Vertovec, *The Hindu Diaspora: Comparative Patterns*, London: Routledge, 2000; Katy Gardner, *Global Migrants' Local Lives: Travel and Transformation in Rural Bangladesh*, Oxford: Oxford University Press, 1995.
9 Homi Bhabha, *The Location of Culture*, Oxford: Routledge, 1994; Arjun Appadurai, *Modernity at Large: Cultural Dimensions in Globalisation*, Minneapolis: University of Minnesota Press, 1996; Avtar Brah, Mary J. Hickman and Martin Mac an Ghaill, *Thinking Identities: Ethnicity, Race and Culture*, New York: Palgrave, 1999.
10 Claude Markovits, *The Global World of Indian Merchants, 1750–1947: Traders of Sind from Bukhara to Panama*, Cambridge: Cambridge University Press, 2000; Engseng Ho, *The Graves of Tarim: Genealogy and Mobility Across the Indian Ocean*, Berkeley: University of California Press, 2006.
11 See, in particular, David Washbrook, 'Economic Depression and the Making of Traditional Society in Colonial India, 1820–1855', *Transactions of the Royal Historical Society*, Sixth Series, II, 1993; and C.A. Bayly, *Indian Society and the Making of the British Empire*, Cambridge: Cambridge University Press, 1988, pp. 136–68.
12 David Ludden, 'Presidential Address: Maps in the Mind and the Mobility of Asia', *Journal of Asian Studies*, 62, 4, 2003.
13 See, for instance, Jan Breman, *Footloose Labour: Working in India's Informal Economy*, Cambridge: Cambridge University Press, 1996; Jan Lucassen, *Global Labour History: A State of the Art*, Bern: Peter Lang, 2006; Dipesh Chakrabarty, *Rethinking*

Working Class History: Bengal 1890 to 1940, New Jersey: Princeton University Press, 1989; Samita Sen, *Women and Labour in Late Colonial India: The Bengal Jute Industry*, Cambridge: Cambridge University Press, 1999; Chitra Joshi, *Lost Worlds: Indian Labour and its Forgotten Histories*, London: Anthem Press, 2005; Subho Basu, *Does Class Matter? Colonial Capital and Workers' Resistance in Bengal, 1890–1937*, New Delhi: Oxford University Press, 2004; Dilip Simeon, *The Politics of Labour Under Late Colonialism: Workers, Unions and the State in Chota Nagpur, 1928–1939*, New Delhi: Mahohar, 1995; R. Chandavarkar, *The Origins of Industrial Capitalism in India: Business Strategies and the Working Class in Bombay*, Cambridge: Cambridge University Press, 1994; Ian Kerr, *Building the Railways of the Raj, 1850–1900*, Delhi: Oxford University Press, 1995; Janaki Nair, *Miners and Millhands: Work, Culture and Politics in Princely Mysore*, New Delhi: Sage, 1998; Rana Behal, 'Coolie Drivers or Benevolent Paternalists? British Tea Planters in Assam and the Indenture Labour System in Assam', *Modern Asian Studies*, 44, 1, 2010, pp. 29–51; Jayeeta Sharma, *Empire's Garden: Assam and the Making of India*, Durham: Duke University Press, 2011.
14 This is true of all, otherwise excellent, recent overviews of the subject. See Sunil Amrith, *Migration and Diaspora in Modern Asia*, Cambridge: Cambridge University Press, 2011; Judith Brown, *Global South Asians. Introducing the Modern Diaspora*, Cambridge: Cambridge University Press, 2006; and Gijsbert Oonk (ed.) *Exploring Trajectories of Migration and Theory*, Amsterdam: Amsterdam University Press, 2007.
15 Amrith, *Migration and Diaspora*, p. 29. Also see Sunil Amrith, 'South Asian Migration, c. 1800–1950', in Jan Lucassen and Leo Lucassen (eds) *Globalising Migration History: The Eurasian Experience*, Leiden: Brill Publishers, 2014.
16 *Imperial Gazetteer. Vol. I. Descriptive*, pp. 466, 470.
17 Kingsley Davis, *The Population of India and Pakistan*, Princeton, NJ: Princeton University Press, 1951, p. 99.
18 Ibid., Table XI 'Birth-place', p. 497.
19 A more reliable figure (albeit still resting on sources of variable plausibility) is Baker's approximation of 1.5 million Tamils overseas, spread chiefly across Ceylon, Malaya, Burma, and Fiji by the 1920s. Many of these people were 'circular' migrants who returned home quite frequently. See Christopher Baker, *An Indian Rural Economy, 1880–1955*, Oxford: Oxford University Press, 1985.
20 If Baker's approximation of 1.5 million Tamils overseas, referred to above, is correct, this would suggest that more than one in ten of the Tamil population were overseas migrants. Ibid., p. 180.
21 Ludden, 'Maps'.
22 Christopher Baker, 'Economic Reorganisation and the Slump in South and Southeast Asia', *Comparative Studies in Society and History*, 23, 3 (July) 1981, pp. 325–49.
23 Amrith, *Migration and Diaspora*.
24 Ibid., p. 8.
25 Samita Sen, '"Without his Consent?" Marriage and Women's Migration in Colonial India', *International Journal of Labour and Working-Class History*, 65 (Spring) 2004.
26 Tirthankar Roy, '"Where is Bengal?", Situating an Indian Region in the Early Modern World Economy', *Past and Present*, 213 (November) 2011, p. 115.
27 Ibid., p. 125.
28 Richard M. Eaton, *The Rise of Islam and the Bengal Frontier, 1204–1750*, Berkeley: University of California Press, 1993.
29 Roy, '"Where is Bengal?"', p. 128.
30 James Taylor, *A Sketch of the Topography and Statistics of Dacca*, Calcutta, 1840, in Roy, '"Where is Bengal?"', p. 128.
31 'Note from the Military Board to the Hon'ble J.A. Dorin', cited in Sunil Kumar Munsi, *Geography of Transportation in Eastern India under the British Raj*, Calcutta: K.P. Bagchi, 1980, p. 24.

48 *Pre-histories of mobility and immobility*

32 R. H. Phillimore, *Historical Records of the Survey of India, Vol. IV*, p. 170, cited in Munsi, *Geography of Transportation*.
33 Ibid., p. 23.
34 John and Richard Strachey, *The Finances and Public Works of India from 1869 to 1881*, London: Kegan Paul, 1882, p. 2.
35 Honourable exceptions are Ravi Ahuja, *Pathways of Empire. Circulation, 'Public Works' and Social Space in Colonial Orissa, c. 1780–1924*, Hyderabad: Orient BlackSwan, 2009; and Kerr, *Building the Railways*.
36 *The Imperial Gazetteer of India. The Indian Empire. Vol. III. Economic*, Oxford: Clarendon Press, 1907, p. 389.
37 Misbahuddin Khan, *History of the Port of Chittagong*, Dhaka: Dana Publishers, 1990.
38 *Imperial Gazetteer. Vol. III. Economic*, p. 389. Also see *History of Indian Railways Constructed and in Progress, corrected up to 31 March 1923*, Simla: Government of India Press, 1924.
39 *Imperial Gazetteer. Vol. III. Economic*, pp. 332–56.
40 *Report of the Census of Bengal, 1881*, Calcutta: Bengal Secretariat, 1883, p. 34.
41 *Imperial Gazetteer. Vol. III. Economic*, pp. 358–9.
42 Munsi, *Geography of Transportation*, p. 66.
43 *The Imperial Gazetteer of India. Provincial Series. Eastern Bengal and Assam*, Calcutta: Superintendent of Government Printing, 1909, pp. 8–9.
44 Ahuja, *Pathways*, pp. 238–9.
45 Munsi, *Geography of Transportation*, pp. 38–9.
46 *Imperial Gazetteer. Vol. III. Economic*, pp. 56–62. But also see Amalendu Guha, *Planter Raj to Swaraj*, New Delhi: Indian Council of Historical Research, 1977; and Sharma, *Empire's Garden*
47 *Imperial Gazetteer. Vol. III. Economic*, p. 57.
48 *Imperial Gazetteer. Vol. I. Descriptive*, pp. 467–8. Emphasis added.
49 Ibid., p. 469.
50 K. C. Zachariah, *A Historical Study of Internal Migration in the Indian Subcontinent, 1901–1931*, New York: Asia Publishing House, 1964, pp. 62–9.
51 Ibid., pp. 69–70.
52 Memo by B.F.H.B. Tyabji dated 23 August 1952, Ministry of External Affairs, India (MEAI), (AFR II Branch)/AII/53/6491, 31 (Secret), National Archives of India (NAI).
53 Kerr, *Building the Railways*, p. 90.
54 *Report No. 799 R. C., Railway Construction*, Simla: Government of India Public Works Department, 1887.
55 Kerr, *Building the Railways*, p. 91.
56 Rana P. Behal, 'Power Structure, Discipline and Labour in Assam Tea Plantations under Colonial Rule', *International Review of Social History*, 51 (Supplement) 2006, pp. 143–72; Jayeeta Sharma, '"Lazy" Natives, Coolie Labour and the Assam Tea Industry', *Modern Asian Studies*, 46, 6, 2009, pp. 429–55; Samita Sen, 'Questions of Consent: Women's Recruitment for Assam Tea Gardens', *Studies in History*, 2, 2002, pp. 231–60.
57 This point has long been recognized by historians of labour in the jute industry. See, for instance, Sen, *Women and Labour*, pp. 21–54; Basu, *Does Class Matter?*; Chakrabarty, *Rethinking*.
58 Sharma, *Empire's Garden*, p. 83.
59 Sen, *Women and Labour*, passim.
60 *Imperial Gazetteer. Vol. III. Economic*, p. 164. Also see Sen, '"Without his Consent?"'.
61 Ahuja, 'Mobility and Containment', pp. 111–41.
62 *Census of India, 1951, Vol. VI, Part 1-A. Report*, Delhi: Manager of Publications, 1953 (hereafter *Census of India, 1951*), p. 206.
63 Sanjoy Bhattacharya, *Propaganda and Information in Eastern India. A Necessary Weapon of War*, London: Curzon, p. 19.

Pre-histories of mobility and immobility   49

64 Bhattacharya, *Propaganda*, p. 20, Table 1.1.
65 C. A. Bayly and T. Harper, *The Forgotten Armies: The Fall of British Asia, 1941–1945*, Cambridge, MA: Harvard University Press, 2006, p.185.
66 Bhattacharya, *Propaganda*, p. 19.
67 *Census of India, 1951*, pp. 75–8.
68 Chakrabarty, *Rethinking*.
69 *Census of India, 1951*, pp. 75–8.
70 Ibid., p. 320.
71 R. Chandavarkar, 'The Decline and Fall of the Jobber System in the Bombay Cotton Textile Industry, 1870–1955', *Modern Asian Studies*, 42, 1, 2008.
72 Tirthankar Roy and Douglas Haynes, 'Conceiving Mobility: Weavers' Migrations in Pre-colonial and Colonial India', *Indian Economic and Social History Review*, 36, 1, 1999; Rosalind O'Hanlon, 'Scribal Migrations in Early Modern India', in Joya Chatterji and David Washbrook (eds) *Routledge Handbook of South Asian Diaspora*, Oxford: Routledge, 2013.
73 Anil Seal, *The Emergence of Indian Nationalism. Competition and Collaboration in the Later Nineteenth Century*, Cambridge: Cambridge University Press, 1971, p. 118–9.
74 'Bengal proper' comprised the Bengali-speaking districts of the Bengal Presidency and did not include Bihar, Orissa, and Assam.
75 *Census of India, 1931, Vol. V, Part I, Report*, Calcutta: Central Publications Branch, 1933, Statement No. VIII-3, p. 261 (hereafter *1931 Census Bengal*).
76 David Omissi, *The Sepoy and the Raj*, London: Macmillan, 1994, p. 11.
77 W. N. Souttar, *Annual Report on the Police Administration of the Town of Calcutta and its Suburbs For the Year 1879*, Calcutta: Bengal Secretariat Press, 1880, pp. 17–18.
78 Omissi, *Sepoy*, p. 11.
79 Haraprasad Chattopadhyaya, *Internal Migration in India: the Case of Bengal*, Calcutta: K. P. Bagchi and Company, 1987, Chapter 6.
80 Ibid., p. 471.
81 Ibid., p. 477.
82 Subdivisional officer/subdivisional magistrate.
83 Najmul Abedin, *Local Administration and Politics in Modernising Societies, Bangladesh and Pakistan*, Dacca: National Institute of Public Administration, 1973, pp. 182–3.
84 Nirad C. Chaudhuri, *The Autobiography of an Unknown Indian*, London: The Hogarth Press, 1988, p. 48.
85 Tamizuddin Khan, *The Test of Time. My Life and Days*, Dhaka: University Press, 1989, p. 69.
86 *Imperial Gazetteer. Vol. III. Economic*, p. 387.
87 Ibid., p. 421.
88 Rabindranath Tagore, *The Post Office* (translated from Bengali by Devabrata Mukherjee), New York: Macmillan, 1914.
89 *1931 Census Bengal*, Statement No VIII-3, p. 261.
90 Ashley Jackson, 'The Evolution and Use of British Imperial Military Formations', in Alan Jeffreys and Patrick Rose (eds) *The Indian Army, 1939–47, Experience and Development*, Farnham: Ashgate, 1988, p. 28.
91 Bhattacharya, *Propaganda*, p. 20.
92 *Census of India, 1951*, p. 84.
93 The old Indian rupee was divided into 16 *annas*; each *anna* was subdivided into 4 *paise* or 12 *pice*. Thus there were 192 *pice* in a rupee.
94 *Imperial Gazetteer. Vol. III. Economic*, pp. 385–6.
95 Ibid., p. 389.
96 C. A. White, *Waterways in East Bengal and Assam*, Preliminary Report on the Improvement for Navigation of the Most Important Waterways on Eastern Bengal and Assam, 1909, cited in Munsi, *Geography of Transportation*, p. 74.

97 Aparajita Mukhopadhyay, 'Wheels of Change? Impact of Railways on Colonial North Indian Society', PhD thesis, School of Oriental and African Studies, University of London, 2013.
98 Abedin, *Local Administration*.
99 Ahuja, *Pathways*, passim.
100 Davis, *Population*, pp. 107–8.
101 *1931 Census Bengal*, p. 261.
102 Davis, *Population*, p. 28.
103 *Census of India, 1951*, p. 202.
104 Eaton, *Rise of Islam*.
105 *Khas mahal* was a tract of government-owned agrarian land.
106 Ranajit Das Gupta, *Economy, Society and Politics in Bengal: Jalpaiguri 1869–1947*, Delhi: Oxford University Press, 1992, pp. 26–44.
107 Ifthekar Iqbal, *The Bengal Delta: Ecology, State and Social Change, 1840–1943*, Basingstoke: Palgrave Macmillan, 2010.
108 *Census of India, 1951*, p. 315–16.
109 Ibid.
110 Ibid., pp. 315–16.
111 Chattopadhyaya, *Internal Migration*, p. 63.
112 As Das Gupta has shown, this period saw the proliferation of forms of tenure, which gave the cultivator less than half the produce of the land tilled. Das Gupta, *Jalpaiguri*, pp. 48–9.
113 Chattopadhyaya, *Internal Migration*, p. 81.
114 Ibid., pp. 81–2.
115 Asok Mitra, *The New India, 1948–1955*, Delhi: Popular Prakashan, 1991.
116 Jalais, *Forest*.
117 Amitav Ghosh, in his novel *The Hungry Tide*, gives a vivid sense of how dangerous these jungles were for woodcutters and boatmen. Amitav Ghosh, *The Hungry Tide*, London: The Borough Press, 2005.
118 Chattopadhyaya, *Internal Migration*, p. 57.
119 Sharma, *Empire's Garden*, p. 101.
120 Chattopadhyaya, *Internal Migration*, p. 250.
121 Ibid., pp. 250–1.
122 Sharma, *Empire's Garden*; also Guha, *Planter Raj*.
123 Sharma, *Empire's Garden*, p. 101.
124 Chattopadhyaya, *Internal Migration*, pp. 302–3.
125 J.S. Furnivall, *Colonial Policy and Practice: A Comparative Study of Burma and Netherlands India*, Cambridge: Cambridge University Press, 1948; Chattopadhyaya, *Internal Migration*, pp. 297–310.
126 Chattopadhyaya, *Internal Migration*, pp. 315–16.
127 Sen, '"Without his Consent?"', p. 85.
128 Ibid., p. 86.
129 Ibid.
130 Chattopadhyaya, *Internal Migration*, p. 4.
131 *Census of India, 1921, Vol. V, Bengal, Part 1*, Calcutta: Bengal Secretariat Book Depot, 1923.
132 Irawati Karve, 'The Kinship Map of India', in Patricia Uberoi (ed.) *Family, Kinship and Marriage in India*, Delhi: Oxford University Press, 1993, p. 60; Irawati Karve, *Kinship Organisation in India*, Bombay: Asia Publishing House, 1968.
133 Lina Fruzetti, *The Gift of a Virgin: Women, Marriage and Ritual in a Bengali Society*, New Brunswick: Rutgers University Press, 1982, p. 65.
134 *Report of the Royal Commission of Labour in India*, London: 1931, p. 5, cited in Sen, '"Without his Consent?"', p. 84.

Pre-histories of mobility and immobility 51

135 Ronald P. Rohner and Manjusri Chaki-Sircar, *Women and Children in a Bengali Village*, Hanover and London: University Press of New England, 1988, p. 45.
136 Henri Lefebvre, *The Production of Space* (translated by Donald Nicholson-Smith), Oxford; Cambridge, MA: Basil Blackwell, 2004, pp. 73, 77.
137 *Census of India, 1921, Bengal. Part I*, p. 131.
138 Sen, '"Without his Consent?"', p. 78.
139 *Imperial Gazetteer. Vol. III. Economic*, p. 275; and *Report connected with the Construction of Docks at Calcutta*, Part I, *(Selections from the Government of India Public Works Department, No. CCIX, Public Works Department Serial Number 4)*, Calcutta: Superintendent of Government Printing, India, 1885, p.47.
140 Ahuja, 'Mobility and Containment'.
141 'Indians enumerated on the high seas on 26th February 1931', Statement No. 111–6, *1931 Census Bengal*, p. 101.
142 Northrup, *Indentured Labour*, p. 156, Table A.1.
143 Brij V. Lal, 'Indian Indenture: Experiment and Experience', in Chatterji and Washbrook (eds) *Routledge Handbook*.
144 Ibid.
145 *Statistical Atlas of India (Second Edition, 1895)*, Calcutta: Superintendent of Government Publishing, 1895, p. 67.
146 Northrup, *Indentured Labour*, p. 89.
147 See, for instance, Marina Carter, *Voices from Indenture: Experiences of Indian Migrants in the British Empire*, London: Leicester University Press, 1996.
148 For 'coolie' voices on how wretched these conditions could be, see Carter, *Voices*; Y. S. Meer, *Documents of Indentured Labour: Natal 1851–1917*, Durban: Institute of Black Research, 1980; and Marina Carter and Khal Torabully, *Coolitude. An Anthology of the Indian Labour Diaspora*, London: Anthem Press, 2002.
149 Lal, 'Indian Indenture'.
150 *General Instructions for Pilgrims to the Hedjaz*, Calcutta: Superintendent of Government Printing, 1911.
151 *Imperial Gazetteer. Vol. III. Economic*, p. 385.
152 Indeed, the railway line connecting Moghul Sarai with Puri was built chiefly in order to serve pilgrim traffic. *Report No. 799 R. C.*, 1887.
153 *History of Indian Railways up to 31 March 1923*, pp. 238, 261.
154 Abdul Bari, *Isal I Soab Darshan*, P. O., Rajgunj: Noakhali, 1924, p. 5, cited in Pradip Kumar Datta, *Carving Blocs. Communal Ideology in Early Twentieth-century Bengal*, Delhi: Oxford University Press, 1999, pp. 88–9.

2 Dispositions and destinations in the Bengal Muslim diaspora, 1947–2007

In 1947, a new international border cut through the lush deltaic plains of Bengal. A consequence of India's partition along religious lines, the Radcliffe line divided Bengal – by now a profoundly cosmopolitan region, as Chapter 1 has shown – between India and Pakistan. Over the next two decades, between 12 and 13 million Hindus and Muslims crossed that border as refugees, seeking to rebuild their lives in the 'right' nation. Millions stayed on where they were as uneasy minorities, but, among them, countless numbers were internally displaced.

In 1971, civil war broke out in East Pakistan. As Bengali nationalists fought Pakistan's army in one of the most brutal conflicts in recent times, another ten million migrants fled from East Pakistan to India. When the war ended, most were able to return home,[1] but a second wave of violence swept through what was now the independent nation of Bangladesh. This time its target was 'Biharis',[2] many of whom were refugees of the first partition and who were believed to have collaborated with the Pakistani regime which the war had overthrown. Thousands of 'Biharis' died in grisly reprisals against their community. A few were able to escape abroad. Most of those who remained inside Bangladesh were internally displaced: many live – to this day – in the makeshift camps set up by international agencies after the 1971 war.[3]

Two surges of nation-making thus tore through the fabric of Bengal in the latter half of the 20th century, producing some of the largest migrations and displacements in recorded history. Patterns of migration among these displaced millions display striking and counterintuitive features. These have occasionally been noted[4] but have never been adequately explained. If we look at Muslim migrants, the focus of our study, it is plain that only a tiny number of the displaced – between 1 and 2 per cent – migrated to the West (in the main to Britain) in this period. The overwhelming majority stayed on in the region itself.

Perhaps 3 to 4 million Muslims crossed the Radcliffe line as refugees seeking shelter in East Bengal (or East Pakistan, latterly Bangladesh).[5] But, again, their migration followed distinct and unexpected patterns. About half the refugees moved to urban centres, but they moved only to specific towns, resolutely shunning others.[6] Further, in a trend that confounded all observers, the remainder resettled in clusters on the Pakistan side of the mainly rural border (see Figure 2.1).

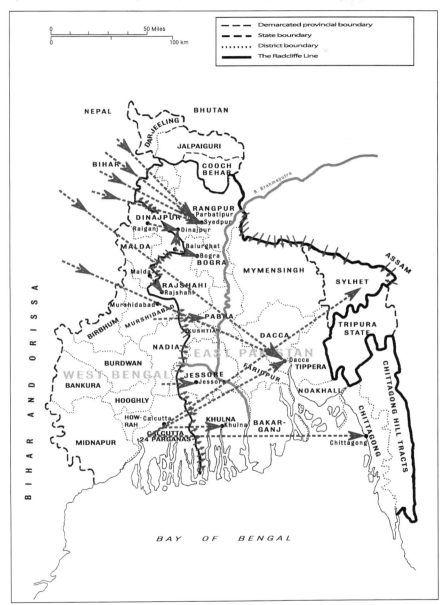

Figure 2.1 Migration of Muslims from West Bengal, Bihar, and Assam to East Pakistan, 1946–1970.

The largest numbers of postpartition Muslim migrants crossed no international border, however. They remained inside the Indian province of West Bengal, where they clung on, despite harassment, displacement, and ghettoization.[7] In another remarkable trend, thousands of these displacees gravitated close to the new border that divides India from Pakistan/Bangladesh[8] (see Figure 2.2). Hindu refugees fleeing in the opposite direction also followed the same patterns.[9] As a result, the Bengal borderlands – on both sides of the Radcliffe line – are now populated by large communities of displacees and refugees.

Prima facie, then, the Bengal diaspora appears to lend powerful support to Aristide Zolberg's two most significant claims: first, that 'nation-making is a refugee generating process'[10] and, second, that the vast majority of the world's refugees since the Second World War have stayed within their regions of origin in the developing world, with only a tiny minority migrating to the countries of the industrialized West.[11] Zolberg also observed that where refugees did cross national borders, most have stayed close to the borders of their countries of origin.[12] In this respect too, Bengali migrations exemplify these larger global patterns.

The aim of this chapter is to explain these patterns in all their specificity. While it has long been a truism in migration studies that particular areas, even a handful of villages, can account for the origins of a significant global diaspora, few scholars have paid detailed attention to migrants' destinations, particularly when these are located not in the Western world but in their regions of origin. One exception is Nicholas van Hear, who, in a comparative study of Sri Lankan and Somali refugees, argues that the wealthiest refugees, propelled by a mixture of money and social capital, reached the most distant and 'desirable' destinations, usually in the West.[13] But our own research did not bear this out, and this chapter seeks to understand why. Drawing on our interviews, we excavate the complex calculations migrants make about whether and when to leave and where to go. The chapter teases out the subtle interplay between migrants' agency and structures of coercion as well as between histories of mobility and of attachment in the shaping of their choices. It hopes thereby to illuminate how the recurrent patterns identified by Zolberg were produced in a regional context of critical but unexplored significance.

Another goal is to look at the reasons why, in a period of great flux and violence, so many people did not move at all. The very fact that so many people stayed on in a zone of violent nation-making (while millions migrated) poses questions of great significance. Scholars of migration have tended to neglect the questions raised by its obverse – immobility. This chapter hopes to tease out its dynamics and is as concerned with inertia as it is with movement.

It follows that one imperative is to better understand the nature of the brakes upon 'cumulative causation' in the migration process. In a brilliant and influential essay published in 1990, Douglas Massey argues that a dynamic interplay between processes gives migration – particularly across borders – 'a strong internal momentum'.[14] Massey places migrant networks at the heart of the process of cumulative causation, since these networks minimized the risks and maximized the advantages associated with migration. Yet by uncovering the factors that

Internal displacement of Muslims in West Bengal, India

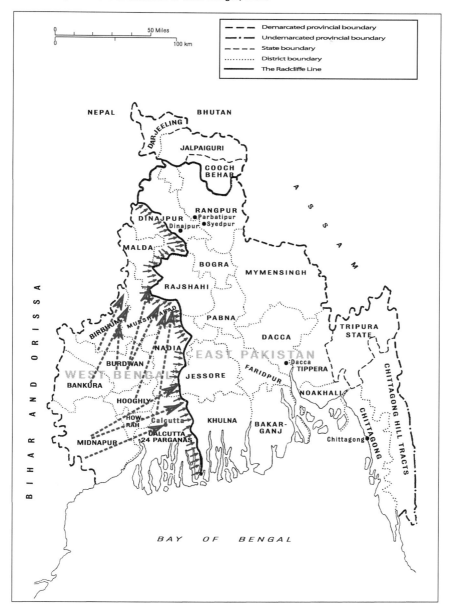

Figure 2.2 Internal displacement of Muslims in West Bengal, India.

persuade many people to stay on even when they are in danger and by highlighting the fragility of some networks, we suggest that this persuasive model needs to be qualified.

Another key question addressed in this chapter is the impact of new national borders on older forms of mobility in the region. Building on the picture presented in Chapter 1, it uncovers the continuing interconnections between historic patterns of mobility (and immobility) and the international and transoceanic migrations that took place after decolonization and two partitions.[15] In doing so, it challenges the assumption that 'forced migrations' caused by political upheavals such as partition are fundamentally different phenomena from the 'economic migrations' driven by the demands of labour markets.

The chapter suggests that, disproportionately when compared to the general population, the delta's migrants tended to have very particular bundles of assets, competences, or dispositions. These are described (after Bourdieu[16]) as 'mobility capital' and include relatively high levels of literacy or other portable skills (in many cases, artisanship and hereditary craftsmanship) and some transferable assets. Migrants tended to be youthful. They were able-bodied, fit, and well. Their numbers included more men than women. All our migrants proved to have dense networks of contacts garnered through and obligations earned by personal histories of mobility. By contrast, as will be seen, those who stayed behind tended to lack some or all of these attributes or were held back by complex ties or obligations.

Furthermore, the make-up of a migrant's particular bundle of mobility capital influenced the trajectory of his (or her) movement – or lack of it. People with similar assets and competences tended to head towards similar destinations, and the lack of one asset could be enough to persuade a person to stay on, even in the face of grave danger. Choices which confounded observers at the time are intelligible, as we will see, when viewed from this analytical perspective.

'National' mobility: Migration to urban centres in the new nation state

Commenting on the first (1951) Census of independent Pakistan, the census commissioner of East Bengal was baffled by the sheer numbers of refugees who flocked to a few particular towns – as was his counterpart in West Bengal.[17] These included Dhaka, the new capital of East Pakistan, as well as Dinajpur, Bogra, and Rajshahi, all administrative hubs close to the new border with India.[18] The railway townships of Syedpur and Parbatipur to the north were also favourite destinations, as, to a lesser extent, was Chittagong, a large and growing port city in eastern Bengal (see Figure 2.2).

The commissioner might have been less mystified had he considered the fact that, long before partition, these particular towns had been magnets for migrants. As shown in Chapter 1, for many decades, East Bengal's subdivisional headquarters, (towns which included Dhaka, Dinajpur, Bogra, and Rajshahi) had attracted white-collar migrants.[19] In the early 20th century, the railways were extended into eastern Bengal and Assam, and thousands of men were recruited from North

India (particularly from Bihar) to build them.[20] Large railway townships had also sprung up around the locomotive workshops at Syedpur and Parbatipur.[21] So these were not just any towns: they were towns that, before partition, had drawn large numbers of migrants from the very regions that produced refugees after it.

The migrants who flocked to these towns had rather distinctive profiles. Before partition, they had been overwhelmingly city dwellers or townsfolk. Of those who headed to Dhaka, most were well educated, some were exceptionally well qualified, and a significant number had worked for the government as part of the North Indian Urdu-speaking service elite.[22] After partition, every government employee was offered the choice of serving either in India or in Pakistan, and most Muslims opted for Pakistan.[23]

The notion that this was a wholly 'free' choice is, however, unhelpful. The Calcutta killings[24] in August 1946 and, particularly, the communal violence in Bihar[25] in October and November that year had already driven thousands of Muslims from their homes, and many who had survived these horrors had lost faith in the capacity of Hindu-dominated governments to protect them. Those who were reluctant to move – riots notwithstanding – were 'encouraged' to do so by threats, often quite naked, from Hindu vigilantes,[26] and also more insidious persuasions from the Indian government.[27] So there were subtle, or not so subtle, pressures upon these Muslim 'optees' (as they were known in the bureaucratic jargon of the time)[28] to migrate to Pakistan. It also quickly became apparent that there were openings for them in East Bengal. In the first year after partition, over a million upper and middle class (bhadralok or 'genteel') Hindus had quit East Bengal for India,[29] and the government of East Pakistan faced a formidable challenge in trying to fill key posts in the administration vacated by Hindu officials. This gave educated Muslims many employment opportunities in the new state. And since Dhaka – the new capital of the state – was where most of these jobs were, Dhaka was where most of these highly educated migrants headed. These were people who had traditionally worked for the state, and the nation state now became the chief facilitator of their mobility, just as the colonial state had been in the past. As with the millions of ashraf (elite) refugees who went to West Pakistan at this time, many of the migrants we interviewed were keen to put their skills at the nation's service.[30]

The migrants who moved to nearby district towns across the border also tended to have middle-class backgrounds. Their assets before partition typically included medium-sized landholdings, some modest educational qualifications, and a little gold and cash. Several had previously held posts in these parts of eastern Bengal during their service careers and had friends, relatives, or contacts there who could help them to migrate.

When we interviewed her, Anisa Banu was a schoolteacher at Syedpur in her early thirties. Her family's story reflects the complex mix of imperatives that informed its emigration to this particular town:

> Our family is originally from Mungher [Monghyr] in Bihar. My grandfather was a railway employee and we had relatives here in Syedpur. My father's

58 *Dispositions and destinations*

> family came here in 1946 just after there were riots in Bihar. We came to the largest rail factory in Eastern India. My grandfather said, 'We're Pakistani and we're going to go to Pakistan'.

Anisa's grandfather had connections at many points along the eastern Indian railways and had family in Syedpur – 'the largest rail factory' – and so there were persuasive personal and pragmatic reasons why he decided to go to there (and nowhere else) when riots broke out in Bihar. But also palpable in Anisa's testimony was her grandfather's strong identification with the idea of Pakistan, and it would be a mistake to overlook this. It remains difficult for 'Biharis' in today's Bangladesh to speak of their family histories as 'loyal Pakistanis', so the fact that Anisa volunteered this information is poignant and revealing.

In the early 1950s, Pakistan – just as India – embarked on development designed to build a 'modern' nation,[31] and families like Anisa's tied their own futures to that project. Anisa's father went on to work as a senior technician at the Power Development Board.

In a suburb of Dinajpur town not far from Syedpur, which is populated mainly by refugees, Jinnahbhai[32] was the middle-aged and educated head of a local non-governmental organization (NGO). He explained:

> The place we're in is a satellite town – an *uposhahr* – it has quite a few engineering and administrative offices. Every immigrant was given a small flat with an attached bathroom and kitchen. The sewage system, electrification, water supply was all very modern.

The refugee rehabilitation regime, as Uditi Sen has noted, was an arena in which the Indian state forged many crucial aspects of its practices of governance,[33] and Jinnahbhai's account suggests that something of that drive – to turn refugees into model citizens of a modern state – was at work in East Pakistan. For their part, many educated *mohajirs* (as refugees in Pakistan were known) appear to have embraced the development project with enthusiasm: the very fact that Jinnahbhai's family named him after the founder of Pakistan says much about the depth of its attachment to the idea of Pakistan.

But state patronage, while important, was not the only force driving this wave of migration into specific towns in East Pakistan. Twenty-six-year-old Mushirul Huq's story shows how a complex mix of connections forged in 'British times', kinship networks, and access to capital enabled the family to make their move. In 1947, Mushir's family moved from the Benares region of eastern United Provinces to Parbatipur, a small railway town close to Syedpur:

> My maternal grandfather was an army officer . . . [who came over] from Benares. . . . [His family] set up a confectionary shop in Parbatipur [sometime after 1947]. . . . My [maternal aunt's son] was Parbatipur's Chairman. . . . My paternal grandfather used to work in a train-making workshop or a 'loco-set', and came from India to Parbatipur around 1947. . . . Before 1971 [when the civil war forced this 'Bihari' family to flee Parbatipur] my father used to work

Dispositions and destinations 59

at the Municipality or City Corporation of Parbatipur . . . he used to read and write well.

This family, which went on to become a leading family in the 'Bihari' community in Parbatipur before 1971, had strong pre-existing links with both the army and the railways – two well-established vectors of mobility in the region – as well as relatives well connected in the municipal administration. These overlapping networks enabled them to move across the border, quickly establish themselves, and do well in their new setting. They also had enough capital to start a small business, which was typical of many other refugees who flocked to these border towns. Describing the suburb of Dinajpur where he lived, Jinnahbhai explained that,

> [This] is a place of migrants – especially of rich people, many from West Bengal: first and mainly from [West] Dinajpur [which remained in India], then Malda, then Birbhum and Calcutta; quite a few came from UP[34] and Bihar too. . . . These people who came were rich, they did not necessarily 'come with land' but they bought cash and gold and started businesses here. Many got Government assistance like loans and land to start factories because those who came from India had the know-how – as mainly the educated and the landed came.

Particularly revealing is Jinnahbhai's reference to 'know-how'. He appears to be speaking not just of formal knowledge – mere degrees and qualifications – but of something more subtle and complex: worldly knowledge about how to work the state, how to push for 'loans and assistance', how to get the licences and permissions needed to set up small businesses, and a pragmatic understanding of how to deploy networks of kin, class, and caste to survive in a new place. Again, this echoes the adeptness of middle-class Hindu refugees in deploying all their connections – calling in familial and caste-based obligations as well as solidarities of class and region – to gain a foothold in their new setting.[35]

When pressed to explain what he meant about refugees 'who came with land', Jinnahbhai identified another trend, built around another kind of competence. This was particularly marked among refugees who settled in small border towns. Many heads of migrating families were local magnates who had made deals to swap land with Hindus migrating in the other direction. Musa Ali, a young man of 23 who now works for a local association in Rampur, explains that his father, together with six of his brothers, migrated to East Pakistan in 1971. Scion of a wealthy family in Malda in northwest Bengal, which had owned 400 *bighas* (or over 100 acres), a sizeable amount in land-hungry Bengal, Musa's father had exchanged property with a local Hindu whom he knew who owned an estate of a similar size and who was anxious to move from East Pakistan to India during the civil war:

> They came and lived with Ossini babu – he was a [Hindu] *joddar* [a '*jotedar*', or petty landlord] who had 400 *bighas* of land . . . we also owned 400 *bighas*

60 *Dispositions and destinations*

of land in India (in Kaliaganj) so we got his land . . . and he got ours . . . we also exchanged our leases (*dalils*).

Faruq Hussain, aged 67, now the modestly prosperous owner of a rice-husking mill, also came over in the same way:

[I]n our village [in South Dinajpur] we exchanged land with [a Hindu landholder] who used to live in Parameshpur. They had about the same amount of land as us – 45 *bighas*. . . . We came over because . . . we were being continually harassed. They [the Hindus] never let us celebrate *qurbani* (animal sacrifice) . . . they used to play the drums loudly during *namaaz* (daily prayer) time and if we ever complained they'd beat us up.[36]

The success of such deals depended critically on trust between the two parties to the exchange – trust which, in times of such extreme hostility between Hindus and Muslims, was itself a remarkable phenomenon. Suraiyya Begum's father, who had been president of the Union Board[37] in Itahar in West Dinajpur and who came over in 1956 after exchanging 450 *bighas* of land with Hindu landowners, 'decided to settle in Borobondor because he had many Hindu friends and acquaintances here. It was one of my father's Hindu friends – a High Court Judge – who requested him to settle here. It was he who brought [my father] to his house and oversaw everything'. Migrants who were able to make such land exchanges either – as was the case with Suraiyya Begum's father and his friend – knew each other well or were known for their probity. Their wealth was afforced by robust local networks and reputations as 'men of honour'. Such attributes were as crucial as their riches and formal qualifications in enabling their migratory ventures, particularly when this involved exchanges of property where claims to title could not be enforced legally if trust was breached.

So most Muslims who migrated to urban centres and small towns in East Pakistan had rich and complex bundles of assets and competences. They possessed the goods of education, land, cash, and gold in varying amounts, as well as local standing, networks of contacts, and 'know-how' about how to deploy these assets to make their migrations viable. Indeed, they seemed ideal candidates for a move to Britain, where post-war shortages created a labour market for skilled manpower from the empire and where pay and benefits were much higher than in the delta. But well-to-do Bengalis and 'Biharis' did not seem even to have considered this option. They chose instead to go to East Pakistan, defying Van Hear's prediction.

Pressed to explain why his family decided to move to Pakistan (instead of Britain), 'Anonymous' – a landholder in his late fifties who had left kinsfolk in India and was reluctant to reveal his name – was expansive about his own family's expectations in migrating to the new nation. Also from a modestly landed and literate family background, he explains that:

My forefathers decided to come here because this was Pakistan. The main fact was that Hindustan [India] was for Hindus and Pakistan was for Muslims.

> Around 1965 some Muslims from our village exchanged land and hearth [with Hindus crossing in the opposite direction] to come over to this part . . . I was a student then, in class eight. . . . After putting into context the bleak future that we, as young men, would face in India, we came over. We'll be able to claim our rights in Pakistan, we thought. . . . I am at peace here. I can travel all over Bangladesh and I don't feel scared. I can also progress. . . . I can talk to our politicians, to the military – I feel I can actually go up to them and talk to them and that they will protect me if I ask them.

His words reflect one of our most unexpected findings: namely, the strength of the sense of entitlement among these migrants to citizenship in Pakistan, and the extent to which this influenced their decision to migrate. A surprisingly large number of our interviewees told us that they migrated not only because they wanted to place their skills at the service of 'their' new nation, but because they believed they had a better chance of regaining their standing in a country that was 'for Muslims'. Suraiyya's story put this into sharp focus:

> My parents came in 1956. . . . My father was a landowner in Itahar; he was the Union President of Itahar. . . . We came over because after the country's division my father thought we would be better off in a Muslim country. . . . After coming here he was selected Ward Chairman because he was so influential. The Government gave him that position. Later my elder brother was the Chairman of the Municipality for two years.

Nafissa Begum's father, a highly educated schoolmaster (with a master's degree in history and an excellent command of English) migrated after he had been repeatedly passed over for promotion in favour of less qualified Hindus:

> He repeatedly asked his colleagues why he had not been promoted and he slowly understood that this was because he was Muslim. He then realized the future would be bleak for us [his children], that we wouldn't stand a chance as equals even if we were meritorious and did well at school, and so he decided to migrate to Pakistan. . . . This event happened in the 1950s after which he resigned. We knew that in high posts in India the percentage of Muslims is practically zero.

In Nafissa's testimony we see just how much it rankled among middle-class Muslims in West Bengal when they saw local Hindus who were 'beneath' them being unjustly promoted over them. For many, this bitterness, more than any simple cost-benefit calculation, drove them to migrate to Pakistan with their families. These accounts lend support to the observation of other scholars that a sense of *relative* deprivation plays a powerful role in encouraging individuals and families to migrate.[38]

The other recurring theme in these migrants' stories is their obsession with their dwindling status at 'home'. Thus Abdul Rahim, whose landed family moved in 1950, said that his 'grandfather's elder brother . . . was the village headman (*prodhan*) but [after partition] nobody cared whether he was headman or not'. This theme also comes through in the determination these families demonstrated to exchange like for like when they migrated, whether in terms of their jobs, landholdings, or even the specificities of bricks and mortar. Suraiyya Begum's father did not leave India immediately in 1947. He waited until he had finished the complex business of exchanging all his land 'so that he could initially have a foot in both sides whilst he moved his assets across', and moved only after he had built a house in Dinajpur of the same style and quality as the house he was leaving behind. Nafissa's father, the schoolteacher, waited patiently 'for a good opportunity to present itself in relation to the selling of his land', which he exchanged 'with that of a Hindu gentleman'. Because the 'Hindu gentleman's' house was of an inferior quality ('made of mud', while his own house was a *pucca* or brick structure), he made sure he was compensated by an extra ten *bighas* of land in the transaction.

Given this context of middle-class anxieties about the loss of status and the drive to regain it, it is entirely explicable that so many Muslims from Bengal and Bihar chose to migrate to East Pakistan rather than to Britain, where few believed that they would be adequately 'respected' or 'recognized'. Only in Pakistan could they hope to achieve the dignity of full citizenship and assuage their deep and painful sense of personal and communal dishonour. Of course it helped that there were vacancies they could fill in Pakistan, but the fact that so many left several years after partition indicate that it was not merely the immediate opportunities for advancement that drove them. Todaro's famous insight – that in less developed countries, labour migration is driven not as much by wage differentials as by the probability of finding employment – is borne out by these life stories from the delta.[39] But they also suggest a rider – that migrants are influenced by expectations of finding employment commensurate with their standing and by aspirations of upward mobility for their children. These less tangible benefits must be taken into account to get a full understanding of the reasons why migrants leave home and where they go.

The refugees in these select towns of East Pakistan were not all people from elite or clerical families. Blue-collar workers also made up a large segment of the migrant population. Often drawn from artisan communities, many of them had skills that were in demand in the new 'national' industries of Pakistan. They also had contacts – friends, relatives, former colleagues – who helped them to relocate. Several had worked in the railways before partition, and the railways were the critical pathways along which they now moved.

Mohammad Shaffiquddin's story captures the particular mix of skills and connections that made this kind of mobility possible. He is a 'Bihari' who lives in Syedpur. Known locally as 'Shaffiq *Chacha*' (Uncle Shaffiq), he is now in his seventies:

> I was born in 1935 and came here on the 17th of August 1947 with my maternal uncle. He used to work at the rail workshop of Jamalpur. . . . [After he

came over] he worked in a foundry workshop of the railways. . . . I used to be a rail power operator – my first port of call was Khulna which I joined in 1963, after that I was transferred to Santahar – it used to be a big junction – again as a rail power [electricity] operator. From there I was posted to Pakshi Rail Office and then to Amnura, then TNG Ghat in Gaibandha district and from there in 1971 back to Santahar.

Indeed, it was the extensive and effective network of friendships and allegiances he had formed during the course of a peripatetic life of 'postings' on the railways that enabled Shaffiq *Chacha* – unlike so many fellow-'Biharis' who were killed at Santahar – to survive the horrors of 1971. A former colleague gave him shelter during the riots and later helped him to get another job when things had quietened down, once again on the railways.

Another prominent group among the urban refugee population were mill hands, including many skilled weavers who had migrated to Calcutta from 'up country' long before partition,[40] and who migrated once again in the late 1940s and early 1950s to East Pakistan after anti-Muslim riots broke out in the mill districts of Calcutta and Howrah. In 1950, the Pakistan government established the East Pakistan Industrial Development Corporation, and during the 1950s and 1960s, seventy-four jute mills, thirty-six cotton mills, and several sugar and paper mills were established under its aegis.[41] In consequence, there were jobs for skilled weavers and mill hands in Pakistan's rapidly growing industries. Under General Ayub Khan's regime (1958–1969), the Pakistani state began to invest in infrastructure and housing,[42] and skilled masons, plumbers, and carpenters were much in demand. Among the refugees we interviewed was Abdul Rasul, now of Chamra Godown Camp in Niyammatpur. Abdul, who migrated from Bhagalpur in India to Parbatipur after partition, was 'a carpenter, our whole *gusti* [clan] is of carpenters'. Owais, originally of Shibpur in India, was a plumber with a sideline as a marriage-broker, a business through which he had forged contacts who helped to facilitate his migration. In this period, Pakistan's army grew by leaps and bounds, and many of our respondents had relatives who were employed by the armed forces in various (though usually quite humble) capacities.

Most of these working-class migrants were employed by the Pakistani state in the railways or the army or worked in state-backed private enterprises such as the jute and construction industries. Former railway workers are prominent among the group of 'Bihari' people in Bangladesh who, since 1971, have described themselves as 'Stranded Pakistanis' and have waged a campaign demanding 'repatriation' to (west) Pakistan. They insist that they are Pakistan's 'true' citizens, having migrated to East Bengal after 1947 in order to contribute to the building of the Muslim nation state.[43] However, the blue-collar migrants we interviewed made no such claims, giving much more mundane accounts of their migration to the eastern wing of Pakistan. Their testimony suggests that they left India because partition and communal violence had rendered them physically insecure and economically vulnerable. They moved to Pakistan as refugees because they had contacts and connections forged 'in British times' through older forms of mobility and because

64 *Dispositions and destinations*

Pakistan appeared to offer them physical safety and some prospects of employment. Shaffiq *Chacha* thus came over with his uncle because he had good connections in the railways, but his 'father refused to come because he had a job in Bihar and didn't want to forgo it'. Abdul Jalil of Chamra Godown Camp told us, 'I'll be honest with you. [I came over] because I had fought with my father, I was a hothead'. Mohammad Salauddin, also from the same camp, said he was the only one in his family 'to risk it in Pakistan' because he was offered a good job: 'I worked at the Bhawani Textiles dyeing clothes – the money was much better over there . . . I used to get 1,600 *takas* a month and when I worked overtime, I got more'. Sitara Jubin of Syedpur explained why so many 'Biharis' like him came to Pakistan: 'They did not go there for Pakistan. . . . They went there because they could improve their economic situation, just as now they are going to Saudi or Korea'. These men are candid, admitting that they simply deployed old skills and old networks of mobility and adapted them to new circumstances. State formation and nation-building provided the context for their migration, but a pragmatic search for security and survival appears to have been its primary driver.

Migration and displacement in the rural borderlands

The Radcliffe line of 1947 cut through an overwhelmingly rural landscape. It passed through emerald paddy fields, dense thickets of bamboo, and forests of sal,[44] through shallow fish ponds and mangrove swamps, and along sluggish, muddy rivers. And yet, astonishingly, this bucolic setting was transformed beyond recognition by dense settlements of migrants within a few decades of partition.[45] On both sides of the Radcliffe line today, refugees and displacees cluster along its length; crowded villages of refugees jostle against the settlements of stayers-on and communities of the internally displaced.[46]

There have been few official enquiries or scholarly studies into this remarkable phenomenon. We therefore conducted over sixty interviews in villages in these borderland zones, in West Bengal in India as well as in Bangladesh. Over a period of fifteen months in 2007–2008, we crisscrossed the villages of the region, roaring along dirt tracks on the pillion of a motorcycle since this was often the only mode of transport available in these parts.

One trend quickly became apparent from this extraordinary set of interviews. While almost all the migrants who cluster along Bangladesh's border with India are peasants, they tend to fall into two very distinct groups. The first is a large and very visible segment, particularly along the riverine border tracts in rural North Bengal – the region identified in Chapter 1 as a hotspot of local micro-mobility since the 1920s and 1930s. They are *diarias* or *bhatias*: mobile agriculturists known locally as 'Maldoiyas' ('people from Malda') or 'Chapaiyyas' ('people from Chapai'), who are practitioners of the form of agrarian migration described in Chapter 1. They have all colonized riverbanks, new sandbanks, alluvial islands (chars) or uncleared jungle, which they now cultivate.

This process of agrarian colonization accelerated after partition. A surprisingly large number of the borderland refugees turned out to be *diaria* peasants. They were particularly prominent in the refugee villages in northern Bengal where the river Ganges (known locally as the Padma) forms the border between the Indian district of Murshidabad and the Bangladeshi district of Rajshahi, a region identified as a hotspot of agrarian colonization in Chapter 1. One of these refugees is Ghazi, about 45 years old, originally from Malda in India. He told his family's story:

> As you must have realised, we're all [indicating the inhabitants of the villages in the area] from either of the two sides of the [river] Padma. The others have come from Murshidabad or Rajshahi. We've always been losing our land to the river; when that happens we move elsewhere. We were settled somewhere along the Padma; when we lost our lands [to the river] we settled in Murshidabad; from there we moved to Gangarampur, then Kaliaganj, and from there finally here in Ishwargram when we got *khas* land from the Pakistan government. We are all people from Chapai-Nawabgaj here. . . . We got this land only after we cleared this land and settled here.

In the course of the interview, it transpired that the fertile land on which Ghazi and his fellow Chapaiyyas are now settled had previously belonged to Hindus who had left for India. It is also evident that they have done rather well:

> This place is good. You know the proverb about Dinajpur? It has 'paddy piled up high, sheds full of cows, ponds brimming with fish' ('*gola bhora dhan; goyal bhora goru; pukur bhora machh*'). People in this district are much happier than those in other districts, everything grows easily.

His mother, Bibi Ruha, added, 'After 1947, we Indians came over. We were living in Chapai and losing our land to the river; then one of us got word that this place was a forest and that if we reclaimed it, it would belong to us'.

Here, then, is a group with a rather distinctive form of 'mobility capital'. They belonged to a very particular and localized network – through which information about available land travelled fast. They had no formal literacy but were clearly part of a very particular kind of information community; they also had much experience of moving quickly, grabbing and clearing new tracts of land for agriculture. Traditionally, they lived in light bamboo huts that could easily be taken apart and reassembled when they moved on (as Ghazi puts it: 'Our houses are usually temporary ones; look at the walls here, they're just woven bamboo bark. We can pack up and leave at the drop of a hat, whereas locals have heavy-set mud houses'.). Unlike most of the delta's Sunni Muslims, moreover, they did not revere the graves of their ancestors and had few religious attachments to place.

In consequence, after partition they could cross the border with relative ease and were quick to capture much of the best land vacated by Hindus moving in the opposite direction. They were able to respond swiftly to the opportunities created by partition and have done well. Bibi Ruha's two brothers have both been on the hajj pilgrimage to Mecca, a sign of the family's newfound (albeit modest) affluence.

Two further points are worth noting about the Chapaiyya 'refugees'. They appear to be remarkably free of any ideological baggage committing them particularly to a nation, whether Pakistan, India, or Bangladesh. It is revealing that Bibi Ruha described her community – settled in East Pakistan/Bangladesh since 1947 – as 'we Indians'. Ghazi's daughter is married to Niaz, whom he describes as 'an Indian'. Niaz's brother came over to East Bengal after partition, but then returned to India after his land was 'lost to the river'. They appear to be remarkably pragmatic about taking whatever land they were given by the Pakistan government, but showed themselves to be no less ready to leave it behind if better land turned up elsewhere in India. Secondly, it is plain that they have a lively sense of entitlement to any land that they had reclaimed from nature and cleared by their own labours – harking back to customary practice in the region and legitimized by its moral economy.[47] For its part, the Pakistan government appears to have yielded to their claims, giving sanction after the fact to actions which violate the laws of property as well as crucial agreements with India.[48]

The second group of rural migrants, erstwhile smallholders clustering in the border zones, has been much less fortunate. Before partition, they tended to have been settled agriculturists who cultivated their own tiny plots or smallholdings leased from others. They did not migrate to Pakistan immediately after partition mainly because they had few elements of mobility capital – no contacts across the border, few portable skills, and few possessions they could sell. Such meagre assets as they possessed were rooted in the locality: their diminutive landholdings, seldom owned outright, to which their titles to cultivate were often insecure, and very local networks of creditors who loaned them funds to invest in seeds or to tide them over in lean times. Most of them were tied to 'home' by a complex combination of bonds: the insecurity of their tenure, local obligations, networks of debt, and deference to local creditors and landlords. These peasants tended to leave their homes only in conditions of extreme violence and intimidation, often when they literally had to flee for their lives. Nearly all our interviewees in the South 24 Parganas/Khulna border areas shared this profile. They had fled across the border during the riots of 1950 and 1964. In Tengrakhali, Jaafar Ali Faqir said that his family – together with fifty or sixty neighbouring households – had left together in 1964 when incoming Hindu refugees 'started burning down our houses and fields'. His neighbour, Billal Ali Chowdhury, said that his own family, together with 'seven or eight other houses . . . came here when our houses started being attacked by brick-throwing and our paddy fields were burned down'. Gulam Mohammad Saif Ali of Koikhali gave a more detailed account of the circumstances in which his family fled across the border:

> We were about 500 households to flee over to Bangladesh during the 1964 riots. We used to live in Kalitala in Shamsernagar, and my father was the *Anchal Pradhan* [headman] there. Eight of my family members were killed that night. Had the rest of us not left we would have all been killed. . . . It was a Saturday and we had gone to the weekly market (*haat*) . . . [where] someone

told us there was a plan to kill my father that very night. . . . As soon as we arrived, we pitched tents and waited for the night to end.

The land on which they happened to camp that night turned out to have been a barren plot that belonged to a Hindu landlord who had fled in the opposite direction to India. In due course, the government allotted each household three *bighas* (about a third of an acre) of the same land on which to settle. However, life proved hard for them:

> Nothing would grow on this land. We had been cultivators in India, but here we couldn't cultivate anything [because] the soil was so saline, so we used to fish and work as labourers in other people's fields.

In the context of late-20th century Bengal, it was typical that any 'spare' land was 'spare' precisely because it was uncultivable,[49] since any productive land vacated by emigrant Hindus had been quickly snapped up by the likes of the Chapaiyyas or even more powerful 'locals'. Asked why they chose to run to Koikhali, and not somewhere else, on the night of the killings, Saif Ali explained that 'We had a relative there – and we used to visit him as we just had to cross the river'.

In Saif Ali's story we can see clearly the factors that predisposed people like him not to move at all or to hold on where they were for as long as possible. They lived off the grid of the infrastructure put into place by the colonial state. The world they had inhabited as agriculturists before they moved was extremely circumscribed: their relatives lived close at hand, their daughters and sisters married into homes in neighbouring villages, and their longest journeys had been to markets only a few miles away. The nearby weekly market was their connection to the outside world, and also their main source of information: it was at the Saturday market that Saif Alis's family got wind of the plans to attack his family – too late to save eight of his relatives. Such assets as they possessed – cultivation rights, potential creditors – were rooted in these localities and could not be transferred to new places. Even if they were in reasonable health, they had no skills other than those of cultivators, and they could not easily turn to other work, except manual labour. Their bundles of 'mobility capital', then, were almost nonexistent. So it is hardly surprising to find that the indebted rural poor were deeply reluctant migrants and that, as will be seen below, many did not move at all.

Staying on: Ghettoization among 'national minorities'

Some refugees who have moved into Bangladesh's agrarian borderlands have done well; others are worse off. Yet even so, the comparison with the conditions of their co-religionists on the Indian side of the border is stark. These are mainly rural Muslims who – for a variety of reasons – could not or would not move to Pakistan after 1947. They make up about 85 per cent of West Bengal's Muslim population, which numbers 16 million.[50] Most of them have either clung on precariously where they were, albeit in ever-shrinking spaces, or have been displaced to areas within West Bengal where more of their fellow Muslims live in densely concentrated and economically depressed clusters.[51]

For these Bengali Muslims, 'staying on' in India has meant a rapid downward spiral in prosperity, status, and security. Decades of communist government notwithstanding, they are among the most impoverished communities in the region. Statistics show them to be disproportionately likely – compared to the rest of the population – to be uneducated, unemployed, or underemployed. Despite constituting about 28 per cent of West Bengal's total population, Muslims hold less than 2 per cent of government jobs and less than 1 per cent of all 'service-level' jobs in the private sector.[52] They tend to live in desperately overcrowded spaces with little or no institutional support. Their children are more likely than those of other communities to remain illiterate and have shorter lives. Their daughters are more likely to marry young and to die in childbirth. Their sons, in disproportionately large numbers, fall foul of the law and spend years in prison.[53]

We found it much more difficult to gain access to these settlements and to conduct interviews there. Suspicion of our intentions, and even plain fear, were palpable. However, we were able to conduct an extraordinary set of interviews with two branches of the same family whose members have lost all contact with each other: one branch had migrated to East Pakistan after 1947 and the other had not. These interviews suggest tentative conclusions about patterns of staying on.

Shahid and Jalal Gazi are brothers, originally from the village of Kalitola in the southeast corner of present-day West Bengal. The village was not well connected to the transport network – it was served neither by rail or steamer. After partition, Shahid, together with many other members of the family, migrated across the border to Kalinchi in East Pakistan, but his brother Jalal did not. Today Jalal (aged about 95) is too ill to be able to say much. His son, Fakhruddin Gazi, filled in the gaps in his story:

> We are originally from Kalitola. The Hindus kicked us away from there so we came here [Dokkhin Parghumte] where we had family. Our whole place in Kalitola used to be Muslim. Then one day [around 1950] some refugees who had come from the other side announced that Muslims wouldn't be allowed to live there, that they would have to leave. . . . They went from house to house, sometimes raped and looted, at other times burned down our homes and our granaries. . . . My elder brother . . . felt he wouldn't be able to keep his honour and left for Khupdipur [across the border]. . . . At that time all the Muslims of Jogeshganj, Parghumte, Kalitola, Samshernagar, Gobindokati left this place . . . Our family's land used to stretch all the way to the river; now it ends with the field which surrounds our homestead . . . . One by one, all of my uncles left. But my father, Jalal Gazi, being the eldest, stayed back to look after the mosque and the graves of our ancestors.

Today the community is reduced to about fifty people, cramped into only four homesteads. This Muslim family had clearly once been modestly prosperous.

After riots broke out in 1950, many members of the clan went to Pakistan. Those who were left behind did not lack contacts there – indeed, they had many close relatives and contacts who had made good on 'the other side'. But they stayed on in India because they were bound to 'home', either, as in the case of Jalal, by responsibilities to the graves of his ancestors, by infirmity, or by the need to care for the elderly and infirm. Fakhruddin and Hamidullah Gazi, respectively the son and nephew of Jalal Gazi, have stayed even though there are very few opportunities for them in the locality and despite the fact that the former was 'kicked out' of his job at the local school after being passed over for promotion by a less qualified Hindu. They felt obliged to look after the old man, who is sick and frail. 'Previously', Fakhruddin continued, 'we all wanted to leave as our leaders all left, but it is not so now. We can't go and neither do we want to go'.

As we can see, their decision to stay has resulted in a catastrophic downward spiral in wealth and status. The landholdings of this clan have shrunk to one small field; the younger men in the family are either unemployed or inappropriately employed, and they are deeply pessimistic about their prospects. Interestingly, they have lost contact with their kinsfolk across the border. National borders – even ones as relatively porous as those between India and Bangladesh – and attempts to control movement across them have undoubtedly played a part in this. Since the Enemy Property Act came on the statute book in 1967, maintaining contact with 'enemy' aliens across the border has been an enterprise fraught with danger,[54] and this may explain why two brothers, separated by partition, had neither seen nor heard from each other for several decades. It was only when we took news and photographs of Jalal over to Shahid in Bangladesh that contact between them was re-established (see Figure 2.3).

Their story reveals a critically important point overlooked by much of the literature on networks: namely, that networks atrophy and rupture in adverse circumstances. After the blood brothers lost touch with each other at a moment of upheaval and chaos, the ties between them withered. For the family members who had stayed behind, this meant a big loss in their mobility capital, with assets stripped and familial networks that might have facilitated their movement no longer existing: 'We can't go and neither do we want to go'. Among the less mobile, then, it seems that an initial reluctance to move could have foreclosed their opportunities for migration at a later date, keeping people like Fakhruddin and Hamidullah Gazi stuck in their unenviable locations.

Our research suggests that 'stayers-on' in the cities are no better off, whether in West Bengal in India or in Bangladesh, their different trajectories since partition notwithstanding. These communities have been squeezed into ever more densely packed ghettos where they enjoy few facilities and have few opportunities. A recent study of Muslims 'stayers-on' in contemporary Calcutta showed that four out of every five now live in overcrowded slums, where entire households (with an average of 6.65 people)[55] sleep, eat, and work in tiny one-room shacks, the average size of which is less than 120 square feet.[56] Their levels of literacy are exceptionally low. More than nine out of ten have no 'chance of getting admitted to any kind of educational institution [whether] recognized or unrecognized,

70 *Dispositions and destinations*

Figure 2.3 Brothers Shahid and Jalal Gazi, separated by the border.
Courtesy: Annu Jalais, Bengal Diaspora Project.

or unaffiliated or public'. Drop-out rates among the few lucky children who are admitted to schools are estimated to be as high as 80 per cent. These urban communities survive mainly by self-employment in family-run sweatshops where they work for pitifully low returns embroidering gold thread onto cloth, making paper goods like kites, binding books, and making cheap leather goods.[57] The communities to which the internally displaced interviewees belong have been impoverished not just by the discrimination they continue to face in the labour market or by the loss of their properties, but by the emigration of those family members who had the wherewithal to leave.

In Bangladesh, urban 'stayers-on' among the 'Biharis' gave a vivid sense of the compulsions that persuaded them to cling on, however precariously, where they were. In the troubles of 1971, Salima's husband (who worked in the railways) was tortured by a mob and eventually died from his injuries. She was left with very young children to care for. Using her contacts, she managed to get from Syedpur to Dhaka, to the Town Hall Camp where some members of her family, including her divorced sister, had huddled together for safety. Despite the fact that Salima's father and brother migrated from Bangladesh to Pakistan, the sisters stayed behind. They live together in a tiny shack in the camp where they do piecework as garment embroiderers to earn a few takas or rupees to support their families and jointly care for their children and grandchildren, one of whom suffers from severe disabilities. Why did Salima stay? In the first instance, to care for her wounded husband. After his death soon after the 1971 war ended, as a single woman with very small children, one of whom was disabled, she calculated that she would be better able to survive in Dhaka where she had some networks of familial support. (Indeed, even as the interview was being conducted, one of Salima's female relatives who lives close by dropped in to help Salima complete her quota of piecework on time.)

Mehrunissa Khatun, a 'stayer-on' in Syedpur, also had two very young daughters (aged three years and six months respectively) in 1971. The family was one of hundreds which, during the troubles, fled from Parbatipur – a smaller railway colony – to the much larger neighbouring town of Syedpur, seeking safety in numbers. At this point, one of Mehrunissa's sisters was able to migrate with her husband and children to Pakistan. But Mehrunissa's own husband was 'bedridden' – 'he used to cough up blood' – and she had to take care of him, as well as her children, until he died of tuberculosis in 1978. She has since managed to support her family by working as a maid in the house of a Canadian aid-worker. Like Salima, Mehrunissa had kinsfolk in Pakistan but could not herself migrate because she had to care for her sick husband and her small children. She still lives in Chamra Godown Camp in extremely reduced circumstances. Neither Salima nor Mehrunissa are in touch with their relatives in Pakistan.

What does stand out in these life histories is that the internal displacees and 'stayers-on' who hung on despite threats to life and limb did not always, in the first instance, lack access to networks that might have helped them migrate. But they did lack one or more other vital dimension of 'mobility capital'. Strikingly, most 'stayers-on' we interviewed had physical disabilities or problems with their health, which were more dramatic impediments than any lack of literacy or skills. Or if they were able-bodied themselves, they also had powerful countervailing obligations to care for the vulnerable and infirm, whether infants, the ill, the aged, or the disabled. Many (but not all) in this category were women.

This suggests – somewhat counterintuitively – that while networks, cash, 'know-how', and skills are important elements of mobility capital, good health is vital. So is the 'freedom' to leave others behind, to abandon (socially constructed) duties of care. It points to the role of familial and religious obligations as constraints to people's ability to join the stream of refugees – and hence to the need to consider the impact of patriarchies of various kinds on mobility.[58] These stories suggest, moreover, that the capacity of networks to sustain cumulative patterns of migration in and of themselves might need to be reconsidered.

'Imperial' mobility: Migration to Britain

Set against this backdrop, we can see just how exceptional an enterprise it was for peasants from Sylhet to migrate so far from home and strike out for London. The migration of Bangladeshis to Britain is not a closed book: much is already known about how, when, and why young men from the rural central lowlands of Sylhet began to migrate to Britain.[59] But this chapter suggests that the challenge is not so much to explain why some Bengalis did migrate to Britain but why so few did in a period of mass migration in the delta. This requires some aspects of their history to be revisited.

Before partition, Sylhet was not part of Bengal: it was a district in the province of Assam in British India. Historically, however, the people of this region had close ties both with Bengal to the west and Assam to the east,[60] and these ties had persisted (and, indeed, been strengthened) during British rule. Since the early 20th century, demographic pressure had encouraged some young Sylhetis to emigrate in two separate streams: eastwards to find work on the British-owned tea estates of Assam and westwards, down-river by the Surma and Kashiara to Calcutta and Hooghly, to seek work as boatmen and other employment in the big city.[61] Some, like Shamsul Huq in Chapter 1, found work as lascars (or seafarers) in the British Indian merchant marine, and they soon came to occupy a lowly niche as fire stokers in the boiler-rooms of steamships. A complex recruitment system soon sprang up which gave (typically two-year) contracts to young men from Sylhet (and which, as Ravi Ahuja acutely observes, also contrived to keep people from other parts of Bengal and India out of this monopoly[62]). This system was dominated by a troika of Sylheti hostel owners or *bariwalas* who put the lascars up, several to a room, while they waited in Calcutta for work on the ships; port foremen or ghat serangs; and ship serangs – all from the same region of Sylhet, frequently from a cluster of neighbouring villages – who recruited them for particular shipping lines, in return for a share of their pay when they eventually found employment. As a result, many lascars were embroiled in complex relationships of debt and obligation to particular *bariwalas* and *serangs*, and on these they could not easily renege.

For their part, ship *serangs* had a strong incentive to closely monitor the lascars they had recruited since they owed their own jobs to their white employers' faith in their 'customary' (and supposedly 'Asiatic') command over the workforce. The *serang* had another powerful incentive to prevent lascars from jumping ship, since 'losing' a lascar would mean losing his own cut from the wages of the absconding sailor and would involve squaring with all the other stake-holders – the *ghat serangs* and *bariwalas* – who were also owed a share of the lascar's meagre pay packet.[63] As Ahuja has shown, this complex web of bodily control, debt, and obligation – as much as the highly punitive shipping laws and immigration rules that deterred 'Asiatics' from breaking their contracts or disembarking at European and American ports[64] – explains why so few lascars jumped ship in London. The dubious attractions of the life that awaited them if they did – two years of evading arrest, the challenges of surviving while on the run, the growing racism in white seamen's unions against lascars,[65] not to mention the loneliness, London's long winters, and the ever-present spectre of destitution – were not sufficient incentive to outweigh the great costs of taking such drastic action. Fifty thousand or so Indian seamen each year passed through British ports between 1900 and 1947, and only a few dozen of these transients jumped ship and stayed on in Britain,[66] mainly in London, about which they had none of Dick Whittington's illusions.

After partition and independence, however, workers from Sylhet were abruptly cut off from Assam's tea gardens, since Sylhet became part of East Pakistan and Assam was given to India. From 1948 onwards, the government of Assam began to put pressure on 'outsiders', particularly Muslims, to leave the state, and Sylhetis were among the thousands who were forced to return to East Pakistan.[67] Partition also cut Sylhet off from Calcutta, now the capital of the Indian state of West Bengal. India soon made it clear that Pakistanis (as the Sylhetis were now being classified) were no longer welcome in its merchant marine.[68] As these two traditional streams of labour migration were disrupted by partition, many Sylhetis were forced to return to their district, and some of them began to consider how they might deploy their networks and knowledge of the world to migrate elsewhere in search of work. In consequence, a few ended up in Britain, mainly because they had heard on the grapevine that there was work to be had in the mills and factories up north.

These men tended to be people who had very little money and less education but who had exceptionally rich and far-flung networks established over decades of travel on the high seas and living outside their home district. They were almost all young; all were able-bodied. The great majority of them returned home after doing a stint abroad. Only a tiny handful stayed on, usually for personal and quite idiosyncratic reasons: a love affair with an English woman, for instance, or a falling out with fathers and uncles, or getting into trouble with the authorities back home in Sylhet.

Shamsul Huq's family history, which we encountered in Chapter 1, reflects many threads in this typical pattern. Despite his own remarkable peregrinations as a lascar, and his Afghan ancestry, the great majority of his uncles, brothers, and nephews as well as all the women in his family settled in Bengal itself. Shamsul regarded the fact that his lascar uncle, Hamid Khan, had stayed on in London as an aberration and put it down to his infatuation with a 'crazy' white woman.

Shamsul himself was the only one of several male siblings to have become a lascar, and like most seafarers of his generation, he returned to Bengal after the war ended to set up a small business, as a tea stall owner. Although his brothers also travelled in search of work, they stayed closer to home: one brother worked for the government; a second was in private service as a clerk; a third was a preacher or *maulvi*. His sisters all married men who lived in Assam or Bengal.

Here, then, is a family that had lived for several generations through various forms of circulatory migration. The partition of British India into two hostile countries had ruptured some of the routes along which they had traditionally moved and closed off some of their old options. But they continued to deploy those that were still open (so Assam, albeit in India, remained part of their shrinking canvas of opportunities). They also developed new alternatives and diversified their strategies for survival in the changing context after 1947. Migration to the West was one of them, but clearly not the easiest, nor the only – nor even the favoured – option. Migration to the 'right' nation state afforded more opportunities for work in line with their aspirations and sense of status, enabling many members of the family to rise from their blue-collar backgrounds to join the lower ranks of the 'respectable' service classes.

This suggests that the model of 'mobility capital' can help explain an apparent paradox, namely the fact that, after partition, the boldest migrations to the distant West were undertaken not by those who had the greatest reserves of economic and cultural capital but by people with little money, scant literacy, and little competence in the English language who were part of networks of far-flung connections, who had richly layered histories of mobility, who were young and strong, and who had few onerous obligations back at home. Even among this small, select group, staying on in the West permanently or semi-permanently (since most harboured the dream of an eventual return 'home') was not the norm. Nor was it the case that once one member of the family or network group had established himself in Britain, the rest followed automatically in his wake, as the network theorists of 'cumulative causation' have suggested. For most of those possessing such networks, by far the preferred strategy was to explore other, less risky avenues to achieve security and higher status in their region of origin.

Jubair Ahmed's story reinforces this point. Jubair, who runs a takeaway food business in Newham in London, is the son of a lascar who worked on the supply ships servicing the Royal Navy during the Second World War. His father got this job through one of his own maternal uncles, who was also a lascar 'in an English ship'. After being discharged from the merchant marine in 1945 at the age of sixteen, Jubair's father worked for eighteen years in the steel mills at Scunthorpe and Sheffield, frequently returning to Sylhet to his wife and family. Jubair's grandmother and his younger uncle eventually joined Jubair's father in Britain, to look after him when his health began to fail. His older uncle stayed on in Bangladesh until his death.

Born in Sylhet in 1965, Jubair is one of four siblings. He was educated to college level in Habiganj, where the family was doing well: 'My father was a good earner. Before father came here [to Britain], our financial condition was good. He multiplied it. Everyone was happy'. None of his siblings wanted to move to Britain. Nor did his father intend to bring them to join him there: 'we [were] not interested; my elder brother didn't want to come. My father was also not interested to bring us'.

At college, however, Jubair got mixed up with student movements against the Ershad government, and his mother, concerned for his safety, urged her husband to move him to Britain:

> I was involved in politics in Bangladesh. I was not interested in coming to London. My father kept pushing me; a visa was issued, extended and expired – once, twice, three times, five times, seven times. Last time in 1984, during the movement against Ershad, people were being arrested in Habiganj. Everybody wrote to my father telling him to bring me to London, or else I would be sent to jail. My mother also pressured my father to bring me here. . . . 'You send him ticket, then you see', mother told father like this. Father sent ticket to me. Then I came, otherwise the ticket would be a loss.[69]

So Jubair, along with his mother and younger sister, ended up in Britain, essentially as a political refugee, although he moved there along a network that had been established long before by previous generations of his family who had been sojourners or 'economic' migrants. Not all his siblings followed him there: twenty-five years later, his older brother and sister still live in Bangladesh.

Conclusion

The concept of 'mobility capital' helps unravel the apparently confounding patterns of migration identified at the start of this chapter. It throws light on patterns other scholars have identified, but not explained, elsewhere in the postwar world.[70] It helps us understand not only migration itself, but also internal displacement and staying on. Most postpartition migrants we interviewed had rich and complex bundles of mobility capital; all had local or supralocal contacts or connections that they deployed to facilitate their movement. All had personal prehistories of mobility and ties of affection and obligation accrued on these journeys. Many had the (less easily measurable) goods of 'know-how' – the capacity to work the system and their assets to their best advantage. Most were knitted into knowledge communities through which they learned both of dangers and of possibilities.

The migrants we interviewed all possessed these different elements of mobility capital to varying degrees. Moreover, the constituent elements of each migrant's particular bundle appear crucially to have shaped his or her choice of destination: migrants with similar types of bundles tended to end up in similar places. Particular 'dispositions' among migrants, then, appear to draw them to 'matching' destinations. Migrants who lacked one or another dimension of mobility capital or were tied by obligations to 'home', by contrast, tended to end up in impoverished communities of the internally displaced.

By comparing very different cases in a large and international study, this chapter suggests that mobility capital worked as an interdependent bundle of attributes to enable successful migration. The life stories of our informants demonstrate that the lack of one or more elements of the bundle – particularly something as basic as health – could make all the difference between staying on, being internally displaced or moving abroad. Among the elements that make up this bundle, moreover, actual monetary resources prove not to have been as critical as one might expect (as shown by the effective moves made by the cash-poor Chapaiyya peasant migrants we interviewed). Nor was literacy as important as one might imagine – again, the stories of the Chapaiyyas, but also of many lascars, proves the point.

Scholars of migration will not be surprised to learn that networks played a crucial role in enabling migration within and from Bengal. Indeed, every single one of the migrants we interviewed was tied into complex webs of overlapping networks. But so too were many persons who did not move at all and were unable or reluctant so to do. By themselves, it seems, networks were not sufficient to enable migration in the Bengal upheavals, let alone to produce it. This was particularly significant when these networks were very local, off-the-grid places unconnected

76 *Dispositions and destinations*

by 20th century modes of transport. This is important to recognize, given the powerful influence that 'cumulative causation' and network theory has exercised over a generation of scholars of migration. These posited that once a critical mass of people from a particular source had migrated abroad, migration would continue until every member of their network joined the pioneers in the West. But when the tiny fraction of a huge body of Bengali migrants in Britain (or, indeed, of 'Bihari' migrants in Bangladesh) is studied alongside the vast majority in the diaspora who stayed on in the region of origin, a very different picture emerges. It is plain that very large numbers of people who could (and should, according to this theory) have moved abroad to join their kin have not done so. They have instead made highly complex personal choices to stay on in their region of origin or not to move at all.

Secondly, looking closely at how these networks worked in practice, over time, reveals not only how they could atrophy and rupture, but how important they were in limiting and constraining migrants' choices and their trajectories of movement. Networks were not neutral spaces, easily capable of being penetrated by 'outsiders'. The networks we studied were closed arenas in which hierarchy was perpetuated more frequently than challenged, and status was reconstituted more often than it was subverted. These points are well understood in many classical studies of migration, but they call to be underlined in South Asian and cultural studies, which tend to valorize networks and 'diasporic spaces' as sites of radical possibility.

This also raises doubts about one of the most persistent assumptions of migration studies by undermining the notion of a clear conceptual distinction between 'forced' migrants (or refugees) and economic migrants. All the migrants we interviewed straddled this divide. All moved (or stayed on and were internally displaced) within a context of nation formation, ethnic discrimination, and religious violence, and in this sense were classic 'refugees'. But all moved in 'grooves' (as Adam McKeown has vividly described them)[71] created by older forms of 'economic' mobility. Put differently, the 'refugees' we studied were all people drawn from communities that historically have been itinerant (whether for economic, political, cultural, or environmental reasons). When faced with physical violence, or threats to their livelihood or status during partition riots and civil war, those who migrated possessed the wherewithal (itself partly a product of past movement) to move to safer and more propitious settings.

Notes

1 A.F.M. Kamaluddin, 'Refugee Problems in Bangladesh', in L.A. Kosinski and K.M. Elahi (eds) *Population Redistribution and Development in South Asia*, Dordecht: Springer, 1985.
2 The term 'Bihari' has come to be used to describe non-Bengalis, mainly Urdu- and Bhojpuri speakers, though by no means all of them come from Bihar. It has acquired pejorative connotations: hence our use of inverted commas. See Chapter 6.
3 Papiya Ghosh, *Partition and the South Asian Diaspora. Extending the Subcontinent*, Delhi: Routledge, 2007; Ahmed Ilias, *Biharis. The Indian Emigres in Bangladesh. An*

Objective Analysis, Syedpur: Shamsul Huque Foundation, 2003; Victoria Redclift, *Statelessness and Citizenship: Camps and the Creation of Political Space*, Abingdon: Routledge, 2013, Chapter 6.
4 Chatterji, *Spoils*; Nahid Kamal, 'The Population Trajectories of Bangladesh and West Bengal During the Twentieth Century: A Comparative Study', PhD thesis, London School of Economics and Political Science, 2009.
5 Kamaluddin, 'Refugee Problems'; Mahbubar Rahman and Willem van Schendel, '"I Am *Not* a Refugee": Rethinking Partition Migration', *Modern Asian Studies*, 37, 3, July 2003, pp. 551–84.
6 *Census of Pakistan, 1951, Vol. 3, East Bengal* (hereafter *Census of Pakistan, 1951*), p. 39.
7 Chatterji, *Spoils*, pp. 188–94. Also see N. K. Bose, *Calcutta, 1964: A Social Survey*, New Delhi: Lalvani Publishing House, 1968; and M.K.A. Siddiqui, *The Muslims of Calcutta. A Study in Aspects of their Social Organisation*, Calcutta: Anthropological Survey of India, 1974.
8 Chatterji, *Spoils*, pp. 188–9; *Census of India, 1961, Vol. XVI, Part I-A, Book (1)* (hereafter *Census of India, 1961*), p. 222.
9 Chatterji, *Spoils*, passim; Kamal, 'Population Trajectories', passim.
10 A. R. Zolberg, 'The Formation of New States as a Refugee-generating Process', *Annals of the American Academy of Political and Social Science*, 467, 1, 1983.
11 Zolberg and Benda (eds) *Global Migrants*, p. 9. Also see Schmeidl, 'Conflict', in the same volume, for quantitative evidence supporting this assertion.
12 The mass migration after the partition of India was not taken into account in Zolberg's study, despite its scale, because the millions who crossed the Radcliffe line were not counted as international refugees by the legal conventions of the time. B. S. Chimni (ed.) *International Refugee Law: A Reader*, New Delhi: Sage, 2001. Had they been included, they would have enormously bolstered this conclusion, particularly in regions such as Bengal and Assam, where refugees resettled themselves with minimal interference (or support) from the state.
13 Nicholas van Hear, '"I Went As Far As My Money Would Take Me": Conflict, Forced Migration and Class', COMPAS Working Paper No. 6, University of Oxford, 2001. Van Hear also takes into account cultural, social, and symbolic capital but maintains that wealth per se has become the most significant factor, particularly since the 1990s, when the costs of seeking asylum in the West escalated. Ibid., p. 9.
14 Douglas Massey, 'Social Structure, Household Strategies and the Cumulative Causation of Migration', *Population Index*, 56, 1 (Spring) 1990, p. 3.
15 It thus develops, in a rather different context, the research agenda outlined by Leslie Page Moch, 'Dividing Time: An Analytical Framework for Migration History Periodization', in Lucassen and Lucassen (eds) *Migration History*.
16 Pierre Bourdieu, 'The Forms of Capital', in J. Richardson (ed.) *Handbook of Theory and Research for the Sociology of Education*, New York: Greenwood, 1986.
17 *Census of India, 1951*, p. 305.
18 *Census of Pakistan, 1951*, p. 39.
19 Chattopadhyaya, *Internal Migration*.
20 Ibid., p. 47.
21 I. J. Kerr, *Railways in Modern India*, Delhi: Oxford University Press, 2001.
22 The classic work on the elites remains F.C.R. Robinson, *Separatism Among Indian Muslims. The Politics of the United Provinces' Muslims 1860–1923*, Cambridge: Cambridge University Press, 1974.
23 All but one of undivided Bengal's nineteen Muslim Indian Civil Service officers opted to serve in Pakistan. Saroj Chakrabarty, *With Dr. B.C. Roy and other Chief Ministers. A Record Until 1962*, Calcutta: S. Chakrabarty, 1974, p. 45. Nationally, only twelve out of 100 Muslim officers opted for India, and similar patterns were reflected at lower levels of the services. Government of India (GOI), Ministry of Home Affairs (MHA)/51(346)/48-Public, NAI.

78 *Dispositions and destinations*

24 Suranjan Das, *Communal Riots in Bengal, 1905–1947*, Delhi: Oxford University Press, 1993.
25 Ghosh, *Partition*, pp. 6–10.
26 In the summer of 1947, several Muslim policemen were murdered in broad daylight in Calcutta. No one was ever brought to book. Government of Bengal, Intelligence Branch (GBIB) File No. 614/47 and 1123/47, NAI.
27 GOI/MHA/F. 40/5/48-Appts, NAI.
28 Rahman and Van Schendel, '"I Am *Not* a Refugee"'.
29 Chakrabarti, *Marginal Men*, p. 1.
30 A classic exposition is to be found in Chaudhuri Muhammad Ali, *Emergence of Pakistan*, New York: Columbia University Press, 1967. Also see A.R. Siddiqui, *Partition and the Making of the Mohajir Mindset, A Narrative*, Karachi: Oxford University Press, 2008.
31 The East Pakistan Industrial Development Corporation was set up in 1950. Ilias, *Biharis*, p. 61.
32 The respondent asked specifically to be identified, so this is his actual name.
33 Uditi Sen, 'Refugees and the Politics of Nation-building in India, 1947–1971', PhD thesis, University of Cambridge, 2009.
34 UP stood for 'United Provinces' in British times; the name was changed to 'Uttar Pradesh' in 1950.
35 Ibid., Chapter 3.
36 Nakatani's finding that many of immigrants had exchanged land in this way is confirmed by this data: it was a common feature in the rural borderlands. Tetsuya Nakatani, 'Away from Home. The Movement and Settlement of Refugees from East Pakistan to West Bengal, India', *Journal of the Japanese Association for South Asian Studies*, 12, 2000.
37 A Union was a group of *taluks*, the smallest unit of administration for revenue-gathering purposes in British India.
38 Oded Stark and J. Edward Taylor, 'Relative Deprivation and International Migration', *Demography*, 26, 1 (February) 1989.
39 Michael P. Todaro, 'A Model of Labour Migration and Urban Development in Less Developed Countries', *American Economic Review*, 59, 1, 1969.
40 On artisanal mobility in South Asia, see Roy and Haynes, 'Conceiving Mobility'.
41 Ilias, *Biharis*, p. 61.
42 Marcus Daeschel, 'Sovereignty, Governmentality and Development in Ayub's Pakistan: The Case of Korangi Township', *Modern Asian Studies*, 44, 1, 2011.
43 Ilias, *Biharis*, pp. 150–3; Ghosh, *Partition*, pp. 50–6.
44 *Sal* is the common name for *Shorea robusta*.
45 *Census of India, 1961*, p. 222.
46 Interview with the chief commissioner of police, Calcutta, July 2006.
47 Iqbal, *Ecology*.
48 In the Calcutta and Delhi agreements (of 1948 and 1950 respectively), the governments of India and Pakistan agreed that land abandoned by outgoing refugees in both parts of Bengal would be held and managed for them until they were able to return. GOI, Ministry of External Affairs (MEA) F.8–14/48-Pak1, NAI; GOI/MEA/F.8–7/48/Pak-1, NAI; GOI/MEA/F.3(49)-BL/1950 (Secret), NAI.
49 Joya Chatterji, '"Dispersal" and the Failure of Rehabilitation. Refugee Camp-dwellers and Squatters in West Bengal', *Modern Asian Studies*, 41, 5, 2007.
50 M.K.A. Siddiqui, *Muslim Educational Uplift. How to Achieve this Goal?* Calcutta: Institute of objective Studies, 2008.
51 Chatterji, *Spoils*, pp. 181–94.
52 Siddiqui, *Muslim Educational Uplift*, p. 7; also see Jeremy Seabrook and Imran Ahmed Siddiqui, *People Without History. India's Muslim Ghettos*, London: Pluto Press, 2011.

53 Vol. I of papers submitted by the Chief Secretary of West Bengal to the (Sachar) High Level Committee on Social, Economic and Educational Status of the Muslims of India, 2005–6, Nehru Library, Delhi.
54 Joya Chatterji, 'South Asian Histories of Citizenship, 1946–1970', *The Historical Journal*, 55, 4 (December) 2012, pp. 1049–71.
55 Siddiqui, *Muslim Education Uplift*, p. 26.
56 Ibid.
57 Ibid., pp. 23, 29.
58 These themes are explored further in Chapter 5.
59 Adams, *Across Seven Seas*; Choudhury, *Roots*; G. Balachandran, 'Circulation through Seafaring: Indian Seamen, 1890–1945' in Markovits et al., *Mobile People*.
60 Ibid.; also see S.N.H. Rizvi (ed.) *Bangladesh District Gazetteers: Sylhet*, Dacca: Bangladesh Government Press, 1975.
61 W. W. Hunter, *Statistical Account of Bengal, Vol. 3*, London: Trubner and Co., 1877, p. 284; Chattopadhyaya, *Internal Migration*, p. 57.
62 Ahuja, 'Mobility and Containment'.
63 Indian lascars earned between one-third and one-fifth of the wages that white seamen were paid for doing the same jobs. See Ahuja, 'Mobility and Containment'. On the constraints on the power of foremen or 'jobbers' over Indian workers, see Chandavarkar, 'Decline and Fall'.
64 'Lascar agreements' denied lascars shore leave in North American and African ports; ship masters could discharge lascars only in Indian ports, and England's Merchant Shipping Act of 1894 entitled ship owners to transfer even unwilling lascars to any other vessel as long as it was bound for India. See Ahuja, 'Mobility and Containment'; and Balachandran, 'Recruitment'.
65 Laura Tabili, *'We Ask for British Justice'. Workers and Racial Difference in Late Imperial Britain*, New York: Cornell University Press, 1994.
66 Ahuja, 'Mobility and Containment'.
67 *A Study of the Report of the Commission of Enquiry (Jabbar Commission) on Expulsion of Pakistani Infiltrants from Tripura and Assam*, New Delhi: Government of India, Ministry of Home Affairs, 1964.
68 GOI/MHA, C.S. Section, 36/3-c.s., 1949, NAI; and GOI/MHA, F-I Section, 199-FI, NAI.
69 Interview with Shahzad Firoz, Newham, 2009.
70 Sayigh, *Palestinians*; Malkki, *Purity*.
71 Adam McKeown, 'Global Migration 1846–1950', *Journal of World History*, 15, 2, 2004.

3 Belonging, status, and religion
Migrants on the 'peripheries'

Many of the migrants in the Bengal diaspora, as the last chapter has shown, were people with little mobility capital. They stayed on or were internally displaced within the new borders of partitioned Bengal. Some only barely crossed them, settling only a few miles beyond the Radcliffe line. Others remained within the boundaries of the nation but were pushed out of the villages and neighbourhoods where they used to live, becoming displaced persons.

Significant though they are in number, these groups remain a shadowy presence in the literature on partition's refugees. Perhaps because they do not fit neatly into the conceptual categories into which migrants are divided, scholars have largely ignored them.[1] International law does not give internally displaced people the status of refugees, so they do not figure even as statistics and tend to be discounted in studies of refugee experience.[2] As for the very poor people who did cross an international border – people like Shamsul Huq, Jaafar Ali Faqir, Billal Ali Chowdhury, and Gulam Mohammad Saif Ali, whose accounts we heard in the last chapter – they too for the most part have been ignored. Because they crossed over so late in the day and so long after partition and also because they were so poor, administrators doubted their claim that they were refugees. They dismissed them as 'economic migrants' trying to take advantage of rehabilitation programmes designed to help 'genuine refugees'.[3] As a result, they were often written out of the script and ignored in reports on refugee populations, and they have not received the attention they deserve in scholarly (and indeed popular) discussion of the subject.[4]

More than a decade ago, Van Schendel and Rahman made a plea that partition studies include these groups in its ambit,[5] a call which has remained largely unheeded. And yet the histories of these people throw much fascinating light on the experience of migration. Their very poverty and immobility rendered them particularly vulnerable to violence, so their stories require us to recognize squarely the impact of that violence on the region's history. Whether they crossed borders or were forced to move within them, or somehow stayed on where they were despite intimidation, they suffered the brute processes of nation-making in the delta in ways that elites were largely able to avoid. Yet as this chapter will show, they were not hapless victims of communalism and nationalism (in all their evolving forms). They too deployed a variety of strategies to build a sense of belonging and status – indeed, hierarchy – in the places where they settled. They did not merely transplant preexisting 'communal' identities and match them to the 'right' country. These strategies involved complex processes of refashioning, building new alliances and affiliations, and realigning – often in quite radical ways – their beliefs, practices, and lifestyles. In the process, they changed themselves as well as the places they now called 'home'.

This chapter will focus on this category of poorer migrants who settled on the peripheries – whether geographical or social – of a changing world. Their life histories sit uneasily within the grand narratives of the nation states of South Asia. The identities they have fashioned are at odds with conceptions of 'legitimate majorities' and 'illegitimate minorities', which partition and nation-making supposedly produced.[6] Van Schendel, for instance, has argued that refugees were 'citizens by proxy' and that 'their trek across the boundary line – the spatial delimitation of the nation – was a homecoming: they joined the nation to which they belonged and in which they had full rights'.[7] However, as the accounts below demonstrate, impoverished Muslim refugees – both Bengali and 'Bihari' – were not welcomed in Pakistan nor, later, in the new state of Bangladesh, despite having the 'right' religious affiliation. As with Muslim stayers-on in India, albeit in different ways, their identity as 'true citizens' remained in question, both in the Pakistan era and after Bangladesh was created.

Nonetheless, in the ways they have chosen to live, some of our respondents found unusual and courageous ways to transcend the neat binaries of 'majority' and 'minority' status. Others fashioned for themselves novel identities as Muslims. Their accounts force us to question both the presumed stability of communal identities and the homogeneity of 'majorities' and 'minorities' in postcolonial South Asia. They upset the idea of the subaltern refugee as an unwitting object of national governmentality[8] and destabilize settled chronologies that have clear turning points, foundational dates and milestones. Viewed from their perspective, the history and experience of communalism – as well as of partition, independence, the Liberation War, and the migrations that accompanied these epochal events – is a strange and unfamiliar narrative.

The 'refuz' in the Bangladeshi borderlands

Dinajpur: immigrant *'kafirs'* and *'razakars'*

In previous chapters, we encountered Shamsul Huq, the erstwhile lascar who claimed to be 108 years old when we interviewed him. He was a small-framed, wiry, loquacious man, dressed in the checked lungi and plain shirt typically sported by Muslim men in these parts. His beard and white skullcap marked him out as a believer. He came up to us just as we were packing up to leave the Dinajpur border village in which we had been conducting interviews. He said, with some urgency, 'I'm from Kidderpore, I've been to London, and I speak Laskari'. He rattled off some strange words, making everyone laugh, and then asked, 'Why don't you interview me?' We obliged.

Born in Kidderpore, the docklands area of Calcutta, Shamsul had, 'in British times', travelled the world ('. . . Colombo, London, Africa, Singapore, Jeddah . . .') while working in the merchant marine. But, as the reader will recall, the cataclysms of the mid-20th century – riots, war, partition, and independence – had brought his global circumnavigations to a halt. It is not always certain precisely when the events he describes took place – Shamsul's account of his life story had few dates. The only date he remembered was 1901 – the year, according to his proud assertion, of his birth – and this in itself is significant, given the huge burden historians, nationalists, and many middle-class refugees place on 'key dates' such as 1947. At some point in the mid-1940s, possibly during the Calcutta killings of August 1946, his neighbours ransacked his home and the family moved to Assam where they had relatives. But they found no safety there. Shamsul tells us that in Assam, the Indian army set fire to the family homestead and fields, 'cleansing Hindustan of foreigners' while their neighbours stood by and watched.[9] Eventually, probably around 1964, when 'Pakistani infiltrants' were expelled en masse from Tripura and Assam, Shamsul ended up in a camp with other Bengali Muslim refugees in Dinajpur, in the shadow of the Radcliffe line.

The district of Dinajpur, partitioned in 1947, lies to the northeast of present-day Bangladesh. Its population in 2001 was 2.26 million, of whom the great majority (77 per cent) were Muslims. But it was also home to large numbers of Hindus, who accounted for over 20 per cent of the district's total population. Since the 1920s, as Chapter 1 describes, it had attracted agrarian migrants in large numbers, including Santal 'tribals' from Bihar, who cleared its abundant forests and settled the land, helping to build a prosperous agrarian economy famed for producing the finest rice in Bangladesh. But refugees were given very little of that prime land and had to squeeze themselves into tiny plots where the soil was often of poor quality, frequently (as it would turn out) seized from others weaker than themselves. 'Adivasis' or low-status 'tribal' peoples dwelt in abject poverty in neighbouring villages.

From the start, Shamsul and his fellow refugees were under no illusion that the new nation had embraced them into its fold. They were made to feel only marginally 'above' the despised Adivasi communities. Soon after Shamsul's arrival in Dinajpur, sometime in the mid-1960s, he was insulted by being called a '*kafir*' (unbeliever) when he went to ask for food from 'a rich Pakistani's house'.

'What do you mean – a rich "Pakistani"?', we asked. 'Weren't you also a Pakistani?'

'I mean Punjabi – those big tall guys with names starting in "P". Punjabis, Pathans, Pakistanis – all the same'.

'But didn't you say you're also part Punjabi, at least on your father's side?' we asked.

'Would you believe me? No, right! Well, nobody does. Look at me, I'm so small', he laughed a little nervously. Punjabis are not popular in Bangladesh.

'But why did he call you a *kafir*?' we persisted.

'I had found a brass bowl when bathing in the river and had gone to his house to beg with it'.

The 'Punjabi', an officer, had bellowed at Shamsul: 'Brass belongs to Hindus and not Muslims, you *kafir*'. The use of brass utensils in the region of Dinajpur was widespread; brass utensils were a marker of class rather than of religion, and those who could afford it used brass, while the poor used aluminium. But the 'Punjabi' officer knew little (and perhaps cared less) of local customs. He turned Shamsul away with a rough contempt that still echoes in Shamsul's memory five decades later.

Shamsul's troubles did not end there. When the war broke out in 1971, his neighbours questioned his loyalty to the cause of Bengali liberation. Since Shamsul and his fellow refugees lived on plots that the East Pakistan government had given them, the neighbours denounced them as quislings, people 'from India', 'not real Bengalis', and even as *'razakars'* (as collaborators of the Pakistani regime were known). Some suspected that Shamsul had 'conveniently' become a 'freedom fighter' or *muktijoddha* late in the day, with the cynical motive of grabbing more land.

Until this point, Shamsul told us, religion had never been particularly important to him. He had been persecuted for being a Muslim but had never given much thought to what 'being a Muslim' actually meant. (When asked whether there was a designated room for *namaaz* prayers on the ship where he spent so many years, he said no, although he had not volunteered this fact in his rather nostalgic account of his days on board the *S.S. Arenda*). But in his late sixties, stuck in a barely liveable 'camp' in Dinajpur, taunted for being a 'foreign' traitor, and with food hard to come by, he decided to join the Tablighi Jama'at: he and some others had heard they might be fed if they did so.

Founded in northern India in 1934 by the Deoband-trained Maulana Ilyas Thanavi, the Tablighi Jama'at's purpose was to root out ignorance and superstition among Muslims (in particular, Muslim women). Declaring itself to be 'apolitical', the Tablighi Jama'at in the 1940s had remained aloof from the campaigns for Pakistan, focusing instead on promoting personal piety among illiterate or poorly educated rural Muslims who knew little (or so Thanavi concluded) of the true essentials of their faith.[10] The Jama'at is essentially a peripatetic movement: its modus operandi was (and still is) to use groups of itinerant lay preachers to promote the communal study of a few simple texts.[11] Preachers go on *chillas* (periods of forty days spent travelling with other members) visiting Muslim communities and urging them to go to the mosque to pray. The Tablighi Jama'at thus spreads its message literally by word of mouth, through travel, direct contact, and face-to-face persuasion.

After the upheavals of partition, Tablighi preachers had resumed their work in North India while keeping a low profile. By the later 1960s and early 1970s, however, they had emerged as a significant proselytizing force, promoting a reformed Sunni Islam in new settings in West Pakistan[12] and in Britain,[13] although much less is known about this, in Bangladesh,[14] especially in the districts bordering West Bengal.

It was at this stage that Shamsul appears to have joined the Tablighi Jama'at. Jama'atis from the Kakrail Mosque in Dhaka (now a global hub for Tablighi activities) gave Shamsul and a few others from his camp some 'basic advice and teachings and then sent them off in groups of ten all over Bangladesh'. While on their *chilla* travels, Shamsul and his fellow converts stuck together. They bought food with money the Tablighis had given them and cooked their meals communally. Shamsul told us that it was hard work travelling from mosque to mosque as a preacher but that the sense of brotherhood kept him going. It was as a Tablighi preacher, interestingly, that Shamsul first visited Karachi in West Pakistan and first set eyes on the Red Fort in Indian's capital, Delhi – new destinations for a veteran traveller.

Late in his life, then, Shamsul took up a quite different itinerant career, one that took him to the new refugee townships of West Pakistan, the ghettoes of stayers-on in Old Delhi, and many mosques, both regional and local. Once he had sailed the world as a lascar and had been to Mecca and Medina when his ship dropped anchor at Jeddah. Now he was drawn into an emerging network of Islamic religious circulation more focused on South Asia.

It was within this religious network, he says, that he felt truly welcome. He had been directly caught up in the creation of the new nations of South Asia, but neither 'East Pakistan' nor 'Bangladesh' had much to offer a man of his background. His new neighbours had not been sympathetic when he arrived in Dinajpur as an impoverished refugee, nor had the East Pakistani state treated him with much concern or respect. Bangladesh did not feed him when he was starving. That had been done by the Tablighi Jama'at, and it was within this religious network that he rebuilt his life and sense of worth.

Satkhira: *'Refuz'* and 'others'

In Koikhali village far to the south, poised on Bengal's southern seaboard, Jafar Ali Faqir had his own story to tell. Koikhali is in Satkhira district in southwest Bangladesh, along the border with India. To its north lies the district of Jessore; to its east, Khulna; and to its south, the Sundarbans forest and the Bay of Bengal. The sluggish River Ichhamati separates Satkhira from the West Bengali districts of North and South 24 Parganas. A bit smaller than Dinajpur, the district's population in 2001 was 1.8 million but, as in Dinajpur, that population includes a significant 'minority' presence. Muslims make up just over 78 per cent of the population, with Hindus constituting most of the balance at just over 21 per cent.

Satkhira is one of the poorest regions of Bangladesh. People live by growing rice, foraging in the Sundarbans forests or by fishing, while some work in recently established tiger-prawn farms. Local transport is poor. In 2007, at the time of our research, people still travelled in boats or crossed rivers by bridges made of bamboo. Most roads were no more than mud tracks, and nearly everyone travelled by foot or by boat. A few had cycles and fewer still had motorcycles, which they loaded onto boats when they had to cross the district's many coastal rivers and creeks.

This was the unlikely setting where Jafar Faqir sought refuge. Originally from a village on the other side of the Ichhamati river, his family – together with fifty or sixty neighbouring households – had left en masse in the 1960s when incoming Hindu refugees 'started burning down our houses and fields'. Ayub Khan's government eventually gave them shelter of sorts in a camp in the village of Koikhali, barely ten miles due east from their own abandoned village in India.

Faqir was about seventy years old when we met him. A short, thin, Bengali-speaking man with a bushy beard and two loudly warring wives, he was the self-styled leader of the '24-Parganas Mohajirs Society'.[15]

Despite the fact that their own village was only a few miles away, the people among whom these families settled and with whom they shared customs, occupations, and even kinship relations, were not welcoming. Adopting a 'sons of the soil' attitude, they called the newcomers '*refuz*', a new word that soon acquired pejorative connotations. Even refugees who did relatively well, working hard and setting up small businesses, were shunned for being 'Indians'. According to Faqir, it was this relentless hostility that spurred him to organize his fellow refugees and set up the 24-Parganas Mohajirs Society. Collecting from its members a subscription of 10 *takas* each year, he promised them that one day, when the world learned of their plight, funds would pour in to rescue them from their misery.

But the world took no heed of their predicament. As time went on, things went from bad to worse for them. When the Liberation War broke out in 1971, the neighbours regarded Faqir and his fellow migrants as potential traitors to the Bangladeshi cause.

We checked his bleak account with the local people in whose midst he and his fellows had settled. They confirmed that they do not intermarry with the '*refuz*', even though (as they acknowledged) there was little difference between them and the newcomers in economic, cultural, or religious terms. The local people told us of rumours that most '*refuz*' had been '*razakars*' who had provided secret information to the Pakistani army. In any event, so they said, the '*refuz*' were all '*dhandabaj*' (makers of shady deals) who exploited others. They were not 'real Bengalis': they lacked affection for their fellow countrymen and had no affinity with the lofty ideals of the 'Bengali nation'. Nearly forty years after Bangladesh's creation, despite decades of living cheek by jowl with their neighbours and despite the fact that their own village was a mere ten miles away from their new encampment, nothing had erased the stamp of their 'Indianness', and their '*refuz*' (and supposedly '*razakar*') past. Many still lived in camps, their second-class status plain for all to see.

However, a fascinating trend could be discerned when we observed '*refuz*' interactions with their Adivasi neighbours. This trend was palpable at both sites, despite their many differences. In Dinajpur, Shamsul's camp was set up on land, we were told, that had originally 'belonged' to the local Adivasi community. Of course, it is not clear what the precise nature of that Adivasi entitlement had been, given the hugely complex structure of property ownership in colonial-era Bengal, but it is safe to assume (see Chapter 1) that tribal communities were established migrants who had cleared the forests and earned cultivating rights. In both Dinajpur and Koikhali, however, the refugees treated these Adivasis, as well as Hindus of low caste, as their social inferiors. Having arrived and pitched their tent in new territory, they denied Adivasis access to the land on the grounds that this new place was theirs 'by religion'. As Muslims, they asserted their status as legitimate citizens of the state and hence as more 'entitled' to the land than 'non-Muslims'. While their Bengali Muslim compatriots – the 'sons of the soil' of the area – treated them with suspicion and contempt, they, for their part, refused to accept non-Muslim stayers-on in their new-found 'homeland' as their equals.

So, for instance, in Koikhali, as we accompanied Jafar Faqir round the area, talking to people along the way, we noticed that Faqir walked briskly past one house, refusing to speak to its inhabitants. Pressed to explain why, he said that the house in question belonged to a family belonging to the 'rishi caste – you know, the leather-workers or Valmikis.[16] ... They're dirty'. Brushing aside Faqir's protests, we insisted on visiting this home as we had visited all others. We were surprised to find that its occupants seemed to be no worse off, in material terms, than Faqir himself. Yet the refugees considered this family to be dirty and polluting and refused to share food with them.

We pressed the refugees to explain this social segregation in the neighbourhood. Their justification was that 'in Islam' they were banned from accepting food from women who wore shell bangles (such as those worn by married Hindu women) 'as these are "dirty"'. We pointed out that Muslim women too wore bangles. 'But ours are thin', they replied, 'whereas the Hindus wear thick bangles with designs, so there's more dirt encrusted in them'.

Similarly, Ghazi, the Chapaiyya refugee we met in Chapter 2, commented that the Chapai families do not mix with local Adivasis: 'Adivasis are lazy and don't want to work their land, so people buy it off them for nothing ... So you'll find the Chapai people living next to the Adivasis, but they will never want to mix with them'. Ultimately', he stated, 'at the end of the day, for them, we're from India'. Even as the local Muslims reviled the incomers for their poverty and their association with India and for being refugees, '*razakars*', and potential betrayers of the nation, the refugees themselves showed no love for the Hindus already there, especially those of low status. Perhaps they hoped to improve their own social standing and be accepted by fellow Bengali Muslims if they played out new rituals of hierarchy towards 'lesser' beings than themselves.

A tale of two brothers: Mirror images and reflections across the Radcliffe line

These trends could be seen on the other side of the border as well. The story of two brothers separated by partition is revealing in this regard.

In Chapter 2, we met the brothers Shahid and Jalal Gazi, originally from the village of Kalitola in present-day West Bengal on the western bank of the River Ichhamati. Kalitola lies along the water's margin in the southeast of the district of 24 Parganas South. The district is densely populated, with almost seven million inhabitants in 2001, a third of whom were Muslims. Some years after partition, Shahid, along with many members of the family, migrated across the border to Kalinchi (in Satkhira) in rural East Pakistan. His brother Jalal did not leave Kalitola, staying on to tend the graves of his ancestors.

When we visited Shahid's home across the border in Satkhira, it displayed the accoutrements of rural prosperity in Bangladesh – the granary in the courtyard was piled high with rice, the homestead had a large pond and a bathroom and toilet, and the children were bright-eyed, curious, and well-nourished.

In contrast, back in Kalitola in West Bengal, the home and fields of Shahid's brother, Jalal, now in his nineties, were desolate. Paralysed and barely able to speak, Jalal lay against a half-broken and virtually empty grain store. He and his family were afraid to talk to strangers bearing news of relatives 'on the other side'. 'It was so many years ago', he whispered.

One of Jalal's great-nephews, a teenager, blurted out that the local mosque had been destroyed five years ago. The elders nodded in confirmation but remained silent.

We realized then that a crowd of neighbours had gathered and were watching us intently. Suddenly, one of them, a Hindu man in his mid-twenties, stepped forward. He said curtly, as if to bring the discussion to a close: 'Those events were many years ago. We all get along fine now. There is no use dwelling on old memories. We have nothing to report to journalists'.

Taken aback by his aggressive tone, we did not press the issue. In rural Bengal, the elderly usually are treated with respect, even by those more 'learned'. In this context, the behaviour of this young Hindu man in Jalal's courtyard was a shocking disregard of traditional manners.

As the day progressed, we witnessed similar reactions elsewhere. When we visited the next village to ask about the mosque that had been destroyed, within a trice another group of young men had surrounded us and ordered us to stop asking 'Hindu-Muslim questions'. 'Everyone is fine now, all living happily together', they said, before escorting us out the Muslim neighbourhood where we had been.

Exasperated by their blatant efforts to intimidate us and realizing that the Hindu youths were migrants from East Bengal, we asked, 'You're from the other side, aren't you? When did you come over?'

'So what, we're Hindu, and we're in Hindustan', they shot back, chillingly unfazed.

Asserting an East Bengali refugee identity (which, as Neelanjana Chatterjee has pointed out, claimed 'communal victimhood' and often 'explicitly demonized Muslims'),[17] these young men seemed absolutely convinced of their superior standing to local Muslims who had stayed on. They belonged to the 'majority religion' of India, after all.[18] Even as recent immigrants of dubious legality, they saw themselves as 'legitimate Indians'. Nor did they have any doubts about the low status of local Muslims who had stayed on, let alone outsiders who dared visit them and ask awkward questions.

Later that evening, as dusk fell over deceptively peaceful paddy fields, we spoke to Fakhruddin, Jalal's nephew. He said he had refused to follow his five brothers to East Pakistan despite the killings because he was 'too old to call a new place "home"'. His village was his 'homeland', he told us. But living there had become harder with every new departure of his Muslim kinsfolk:

> When even the Union Board President, Doctor Sofed Ali, went missing, many of us had felt that they had nobody who could protect us anymore. A few more

families then left, and our village, from being a Muslim-majority one, became a Hindu-majority one. Geographies became religious – you were either in 'Hindustan' or 'Pakistan' and, depending on your religion, you were either in the 'right' or the 'wrong' country, whatever the majority of your village.

Becoming a 'minority' is about losing the link to power and status. With our community leaders replaced by leaders of the majority religion, our jobs started to disappear, mosques started to be attacked. More than our lives we feared losing our dignity. I was . . . headstrong so I stayed on despite this, but the others, my uncles, they were respectable and established people, and when they started losing their jobs to young upstarts who had half their degrees, age, and qualifications, they left.

Well educated himself, but unemployed, Fakhruddin took solace in tending the graves of his ancestors. Notably, he also sustained his own sense of dignity by denouncing the migrant newcomers as 'upstarts'.

On the other side of the border, in Bangladesh, Shahid's children were prosperous but poorly educated. There was very little opportunity for social mobility through education in this 'backward' area. Schools were few and far between in Satkhira, and only a handful offered secondary education. Those who had 'respectable jobs', such as teaching, were rarely local people, and they invariably returned to Dhaka or other small towns when they retired. Shahid's children had little opportunity to 'learn' to become 'respectable' Bengalis by mastering the ability to speak or write 'proper' Bangla (there were few libraries in the vicinity and little access to literary Bengali) and sing Tagore's songs or to learn English – all essential to gain the respectable status of *shaheb* or *babu*.

Achieving respectability was even more elusive for the refugees than for the other local village people who shared these hardships (and who, in their turn, were looked down on by the well-to-do urban elites as rustic *gramer lok*). The neighbours mocked the refugees for being outsiders and labelled them 'Indians', '*refuz*'. So Shahid's sons had worked hard to amass rather different kinds of social capital. They earned decent sums of money by careful investment in fisheries and spent it not on education (which was not easily available) but on land and religious philanthropy.

Shahid himself had been on the hajj. He had built a mosque in the village. He sought respectability not so much in a 'Bengali identity' (although he is a Bengali-speaker born and bred) but in a modern Muslim one based on piety, prosperity, and the practice of 'proper' Islam. Not for him the futility of tending graves – a practice many reformists viewed as 'backward', even 'un-Islamic'. Nor did *Ekushe* – the nationalist commemoration of Bengali language martyrs – hold much appeal for him.

In the story of how Shahid refashioned his own identity and that of his family after his escape from violence, we can see subtle but significant realignments in their religious practices and lifestyles. In the old days, Shahid and Jalal both came from a family of school teachers whose status rested on their medium-sized holdings, their modest education, and their influence in local politics. But after their move, only a few miles east across the border, Shahid's family focused not on education (as it had done in the past) but on entrepreneurship and profit. His sons were successful businessmen whose local status was based on clever investments. Whereas the family had previously followed the traditional religious practice of the region in which the graves of ancestors played a big part, Shahid's refugee branch of the family had abandoned these old ways for modern ones – for hajj pilgrimage, mosque-building, and a very public adherence to 'modern' Islam.

Van Schendel has argued that those who migrated into the new country were seen as 'sons and daughters of the nation coming home'.[19] Our study suggests, however, that the poorer refugees in the rural borderlands did not experience this sense of homecoming – far from it. New migrants had to try to prove (not once but again and again) their 'allegiance' to their chosen state, which was never seen as established and always remained suspect.

In the Bengal borderlands, it seemed that for many the best strategy to achieve security and respectability, if not acceptance, was by laying claim to the religious symbols of the majority as they understood them. Many found it easier to adopt 'modern' practices of Islam, which were less rooted in place, custom, and ancestry. They became more overtly pious, more 'reformed', more ostentatiously Sunni in their outlook. But we also noted with these realignments came a harsher delineation of divisions between 'us' and 'them' when it came to their relationship with the minority groups who lived alongside them. So while the Bengal borderlands were extraordinarily diverse, full of village clusters inhabited by migrants and the internally displaced, we found that they were riven with deep tensions radiating along a variety of axes.

Marked out as the 'other': Minorities who stayed on

Even when 'minority' settings were situated a long way from the actual borders of states, they can usefully be regarded as 'borderland' spaces. The Park Circus area in the heart of Calcutta, which is predominantly Muslim, was often referred to as 'mini-Pakistan' by the city's Hindus, while Hindu neighbourhoods in Bangladesh were also frequently described as 'mini-Indias'. Similarly, the 'Bihari' camps of urban Bangladesh were often dismissively referred to as 'Pakistani *elaka*' (areas). Each of these, and many less well-known minority neighbourhoods, we suggest, share many of the characteristics of the geographical borderlands described above. In the following sections, we discuss discrimination in such locations but also explore some innovative strategies of resistance against this discrimination.

Prejudice and battles against it: Birbhum district, western Bengal

Birbhum district in western Bengal, as Chatterji has shown elsewhere, witnessed a significant 'unmixing' of Hindu and Muslim populations after partition. Muslims were pushed towards the east and north of the district, close to the Muslim-majority districts of Murshidabad and Malda, while Hindus became concentrated in the western and southern parts of the district.[20] In 2001, Birbhum's

90 *Belonging, status, and religion*

largely rural population had crossed the three million mark – of whom over a million were Muslims, usually densely clustered together. These significant Muslim clusters – the 'Pakistani' *elaka* of Birbhum – give us a sense not only of how the dynamics of 'othering' worked in such places but also of how people resisted these dynamics.

Born in Birbhum, Fatema Khatun is a writer in her thirties. We met her in Calcutta, where she now lives. With her neatly coiffed hair and expertly tied, starched sari, Fatema could be mistaken for a school teacher. Her generous laugh and happy disposition give no hint of the hardships she has faced as a middle-class Muslim woman seeking to make her way in Hindu-majority West Bengal. It was only when we asked her searching questions about her life history that she said: 'It has been a constant struggle for economic stability and social acceptance. You know, having one without the other is of no use really'. She continued:

> Hindu domination is so rooted in our collective unconscious that speaking out against it seems like an affront to our very identity as Bengalis. I have to keep reminding people that 'most of us West Bengali Muslims are Bengalis too, you know'.

As a young girl, Fatema loved playing with her Hindu friends. Her father warned her not to 'argue back if they say something hurtful. Remember, you, who talk about your friends all the time, that they don't let you eat and drink in the same vessels as them, that they wash their hands after having played with you'.

Fatema did not believe her father. Independent-minded from an early age, she decided 'to test it out on my closest friends. I visited [a Hindu girl] Rita Saha's house and was made to sit on a rough blanket made of animal hair' (instead of an embroidered cloth mat of *kantha*[21]).

On another occasion, her Hindu friend briefed Fatema to say when she visited that her name was 'Poornima' (an obviously Hindu name) instead of Fatema (self-evidently a Muslim one).

When we met her, Fatema had led campaigns for the integration of Muslim women into the socio-political fabric of West Bengal. She spoke eloquently of how middle-class Muslims like her were 'othered'. 'As soon as someone hears I'm Muslim', she explains, she is constantly made to feel like a non-Bengali, even though she was born and raised in West Bengal.

Fatema describes, for instance, an incident that took place when she attended evening classes at university. She told us,

> One day I wore a beautiful sari to university. The teacher remarked in front of the whole class: 'Notice how Fatema has worn her sari so well'. The teachers there kept making comments about how 'for a Muslim' I spoke the language very well, I dressed very well, I wrote very well. [To begin with] I kept wondering if they said that because I have a [provincial] accent from Birbhum [as opposed to an urban middle-class accent] when I speak in Bengali. Like, for example, the time when I was asked to read out a poem and I came to the word

'jyotsna'. The teacher pointed out to the whole class how perfectly I had pronounced the word.[22] The constant condescension about how I speak or wear my sari 'like a Bengali', implying of course a 'Hindu Bengali', reminds me of how I am not seen as a Bengali – because I am Muslim, I am a 'foreigner'.

Fatema coped with these trials by writing: she is a distinguished author and winner of the Begum Rokeya prize. She founded an NGO that provided work to young women from marginalized communities. She established a school in Birbhum where she taught young Muslim and Adivasi girls. She is a vocal presence in the media, writing prolifically in newspapers and appearing regularly on television to discuss her work. But others in her position have adopted rather different creative strategies to resist their marginalization.

The small village of Tilutia is also in Birbhum district. Not very far from where Fatema grew up, it is about thirty kilometres from Shantiniketan, where the poet Rabindranath Tagore established a settlement and university based on his humanist philosophy. Enamul Haq, a young resident of Tilutia, was locally renowned for having set up a local spiritual movement to counter religious hatred. Deeply shaken by the 1946 riots during and after partition, many of Enamul Haq's relatives left for East Pakistan. He went with them, spending a couple of years out of India. However, he soon returned to Birbhum, 'his land . . . and the land of Tagore's tradition'. Together with eleven other families from the village, both Hindus and Muslims, Enamul decided make a stand against religious fanaticism and economic exploitation by establishing an unusual cooperative. All in this group gave up organized religion. They pooled their resources and tilled their 55 *bighas* (roughly 18 acres) together as a cooperative. They abandoned the use of surnames (usually markers of community, caste, and status). 'It is as soon as the surname comes into the picture that people decide whether they want to share food with you or not so out it goes. We're Bengalis, this is our primary identity', he declared.

Enamul named his sons 'Biswajit' and 'Surojit', which are not Muslim forenames. After toying first with mystical Islam and later with atheism, he decided in the end that 'spiritualism' would be his new 'religion', which he described in short works with both English and Bangla titles, for example, 'Dinghy', 'Caravan', '*Alo*' (Light), '*Eka*' (Alone).

In the early 1960s, however, the ashram he founded was attacked and a person was killed. Enamul was jailed for six years, from 1961 to 1967. Yet after his release, Enamul Haq persisted with his movement. He continued to write poems denouncing caste and organized religion. He dressed in a simple loincloth, sometimes wearing a *kurta* (short tunic), often leaving his torso bare. Other than these signifiers of dress, often adopted by ascetics in South Asia, he wore no overt mark of religiosity – whether a (Muslim) skullcap or a (Hindu) sandalwood mark on his forehead. His aim was to be 'human', and he hoped to achieve this by being recognized above all as 'Bengali'.

As he grew older, Enamul announced that when he died, he wanted to be neither buried nor cremated. Faced with the dilemma of what to do with his remains on his death, his family decided to bury him but placed his body so that his head faced southwards (and not westwards towards Mecca as Muslim practice ordained). This may have been influenced by the fact that the lowest Hindu castes bury their dead facing south.

Surojit, his son, by then in his early forties, welcomed us when he heard about our research. Handsome, with an open face and ready smile, he has continued to preach his father's message to the world at large 'with my bike on the one side and my voice on the other', he laughed. 'I refuse to be either this or that', he explained, 'and so do you know what happens? I face trouble from both groups':

> Take my two children's marriages. Trying to find a suitable spouse for them, well, I realized then what hypocrisy really means. No 'open' Hindu nor Muslim wanted to marry my daughter despite my father's philosophy and local renown. She finally found a young Muslim man who did not care about her 'background'. But my son is still unmarried and I wonder who will take him on.

His wife, however, wore the accoutrements of Hindu Bengali wife – red *sindoor* (vermillion powder) in the parting of her hair and white and red bangles around her wrists.

Surojit was the headmaster of a high school in the (Muslim-majority) district of Murshidabad. The school's student population was two-thirds Muslim and a third Hindu. Surojit told us that every year the school celebrates '*Nobi dibosh*', the birthday of the Prophet. One year, when preparing the *Nobi dibosh* celebrations, he invited Sidheswar Mukhopadhyay from Tagore's Viswa Bharati University and Halim Shaheb, a Muslim professor also from Viswa Bharati, to sing on the occasion. This angered reform-minded Muslims in the area, 'especially political people', who began to 'make a fuss'. Surojit was left to explain his controversial belief that the Prophet liked music – if he had not done so, he argued, he would not have put the *azan*, the call to prayer, to melody. As Bengalis, he argued, both Hindu and Muslim children should learn and celebrate their musical heritage.

When officials ask him to asked to declare his caste, Surojit insisted that his caste was 'human', but he constantly had to fight clerks who ignored his protests and wrote 'Das' (or some other caste name) in place of his (nonexistent) surname on official forms. He said:

> As a people, we have had Lalon,[23] Tagore, and yet we persist in staying within the confines of prescribed religious doctrine. Partition and its aftermath transformed my father into becoming more human and less a doctrinaire, yet unfortunately, the state and the ruling classes do not allow us to remain as we are – Bengalis and humans before anything else.

Interestingly, then, Fatema, Enamul, and Surjoit all felt the need to ground their 'humanism' in Bengal and to claim for themselves an alternative but nonetheless local and Bengali identity. It is also significant that Enamul Haq's graveyard has become a site marking this alternative humanist vision of Bengali identity.

Recently, the noted artist and activist Shyamali Khastgir chose it as her last resting place. Born a Hindu and raised in Shantiniketan, she asked that she be buried in Tilutia with nothing but a simple *kul* tree over her remains for 'children to play all around her'. Choosing nonorthodox ways of marking death, then, seems to have become a route by which some try to escape the confines of rigid 'Hindu' and 'Muslim' identities and to cross borders even in death.

Engseng Ho has famously remarked that 'graves, while they are endpoints for migrants, are beginnings for their descendants, marking ... a ready point of return in a world where origins keep moving on'.[24] As these stories show, they can also be creative spaces that represent not so much points of return to the past but points of departure to variously imagined utopian, postnational futures.

Seeking a place within the fabric of the nation: Bangladeshi 'Bihari' Muslims: Dhaka

Modhu's canteen is a well-known landmark in the Dhaka University area. One humid summer's evening, we gathered there for tea after watching Tanvir Mokammel's documentary *Swapnabhumi* or 'The Promised Land'. Released in 2007, the Bengali film portrays the dilemmas of Bangladesh's 'Biharis' in a sympathetic light.

'Biharis', as seen in Chapter 2, was the label given to migrants from up-country who survived the violence of 1971 and became 'stayers-on' in Bangladesh. As Ghosh,[25] Hashmi,[26] and Redclift[27] have noted, they were rendered stateless after 1971, unwanted by all three nations – Pakistan, India, and Bangladesh – alike. Descendants of the *poorbea* labour migrants of the imperial age (discussed in Chapter 1) and of post-partition refugees, there were nearly 300,000 'Biharis' in Bangladesh in 2008, over half of whom still lived in camps all over the country. In their peripheral location, they had much in common with Muslim 'stayers-on' in West Bengal, although their marginalization was more acute. Denied or refusing to claim citizenship rights until 2008, most were unable to get their children into good government schools, to rent housing outside the camps, or to be employed in formal jobs, whether in government or the private sector.

Perhaps it was inevitable that our discussion at Modhu's café was fraught: our group included both a Bengali, Nazibul Islam, and a 'Bihari', Saif. Despite Saif's presence, Nazibul, a man in his mid-thirties who worked as a photographer, made no bones about his feelings, whether about the film or its subjects. The director, he said, had been 'too kind to these bastard "Biharis" '. Tempers predictably rose, and Nazibul walked out.

Saif was silent throughout this discussion. We were, after all, sitting in the notoriously 'Bengali' space of Modhu's canteen, where images of the proprietor Modhu, slain in 1971, hung conspicuously on the walls. Finally he spoke, but softly, almost under his breath. Quoting the Urdu poet Faiz, he murmured: 'How many monsoons will it take to wash away the blood?'

Later, we persuaded Saif to tell us more about his childhood. The picture he painted of camp life complicated the crude distinctions Nazibul had drawn between 'Bengali citizens' and '"Bihari" traitors', between those 'inside' and those 'outside'. 'Between 1994 and 1998, when I was a young teenager', he said, relations between the ('Bihari') leaders of the camp and those of the ('Bengali') outside world were far from hostile: they were pragmatic, even cynical. 'There have always been very close links between the [camp] drug lords and the local leaders', he explained. Despite the entrenched rivalry between the Awami League and the Bangladesh Nationalist Party (BNP), the local leaders of both parties, 'along with the drug dealers, demanded a cut from any major celebration – be it a wedding or a religious festival like the coming of a *pir* ((Muslim) saint or holy man). A notorious 'Bihari' dealer managed to conduct his business 'for many years because he was under the protection of a Member of Parliament' – a Bengali – who '. . . was infamous for having captured the properties of many of the Urdu speakers who lived there before '71. . . . The Urdu speakers cannot vote, but their leaders can be bribed to have the camp dwellers come for rallies to increase the numbers of perceived supporters. . .' of both 'Bengali' national parties.

Nor, in Saif's view, were 'Bihari' leaders any more consistent: 'The leaders of the "Stranded Pakistanis" keep talking about repatriation [to Pakistan] every time a foreign journalist interviews them', he said,

> But their kids are all settled in comfortable flats *outside* the camp precincts. They have Bangladeshi ID papers and they go to university and have jobs. . . . Why, if they keep saying they want to be sent to Pakistan, do they play these double games? Let them go to Pakistan and let those amongst us make a life of our own in the country of our birth.[28]

The Awami Leaguers, according to Saif, 'have to demonstrate that they hate the "Biharis", but in actual fact, they use them for all sorts of reasons. . . . They're all in it together, these bastard leaders'.

Saif also spoke with insight about the ways class complicated the Bengali–'Bihari' divide. The 'Biharis' regarded the Bengalis in the adjoining areas as 'posh'. When Saif was a child, he thought Bengalis wanted to shut him and other camp children out of the park not because they were 'Bihari' but because they were poor. And there may have been some truth in this. But as Saif was quick to admit, it cut both ways:

> We were nasty too. 'Bihari' youngsters would take revenge by attacking the poor Bengali hawkers who walked into the camps. They would be abused verbally or sometimes not paid for their wares and there was nothing they could do as they were alone and without connections and we had the strength of being a group.

It is important, then, not to reify 'Bihari'–Bengali–Bangladeshi divides. While respondents sometimes spoke to us as though these were fixed and distinct 'races' ('Biharis' were frequently described as 'tall' and 'fair'; while Bengalis were 'short', 'dark', and 'soft-natured') locked in eternal strife, at other times they talked as if these categories were shifting and unstable, and capable of being breached. People on both sides, moreover, were quite ready to manipulate these categories when circumstances demanded it, for political or other ends.

Nomenclature, categories, and contestations

Speaking to people across multiple marginal sites, it was also clear that 'being a "Bengali"' meant very different things at different times and different places. The three categories – Bangladeshi, Muslim, and Bengali respectively – did not map onto one other neatly or predictably.

While talking to Bengali and 'Bihari' camp dwellers, we began to realize how labile these categories were and how complex their relationship with each other. As an elderly Bengali who had migrated from Burdwan in India and was living in a camp in Dinajpur commented, 'If these guys ['Biharis'] were so happy being Bengali, why did they want Pakistan?' – this despite the fact that he too had migrated to Pakistan. Another Bengali migrant, however, described shifts in his self-perception over time: 'It was only with the war that I learnt I was a Bengali. Before that, I'd always been referred to as "Mussalman". "Bengalis" was what we called Hindus'.

In West Bengal, on the other side of the border, poor 'Bihari' and Bengali Muslims desired above all else to be recognized as 'legal' inhabitants. Regardless of their 'ethnic' backgrounds, both groups feared being mistaken for illegal immigrants from Bangladesh. As Fatema's testimony showed, for many Hindus, the fact that they were simultaneously 'Bengali' and 'Muslim' was a source of considerable unease, as though it was impossible to be both.[29] So, whereas in Bangladesh, many 'Bihari' Muslims found it hard to be accepted as 'Bangladeshis', in West Bengal their lot as Muslims was always to be *assumed* to be Bangladeshi.

The elites and middle classes of Bangladesh, meanwhile, habitually used 'Bengali' as a synonym for 'Bangladeshi Muslim'. It was as if Indian Muslims lost their 'Bengali' identity in 1947 (if, indeed, they had 'owned' it then) and Bangladeshis had gained it in 1971, except that in two places – West Bengal and Bangladesh – 'Bengali' meant very different things. For instance, when we described our research as 'studying Muslim migrants from India after 1947', educated people said, 'Oh, so you're working on immigrants', "Biharis"', to which we would reply, 'Yes, and Bengalis'. In most cases they responded, 'Oh yes, there were some, but they quickly integrated as they settled in Dhaka, Rajshahi, and Chittagong'.

When we mentioned the camps where migrant Muslims from western Bengal had settled in the Bangladesh-India borderlands, most people we met in Dhaka reacted with incredulity, saying, 'Bengali, you said? You're sure? They can't be, they must have learnt up the language and are now trying to pass off as Bengalis'.

Among most 'Biharis',[30] by contrast, the challenge was to be accepted as Bangladeshi. Their strategies to achieve acceptance ranged from the bold to the subtle.

Most dramatic were the legal cases which 'Biharis' fought to be allowed to vote. In May 2001, ten enterprising young residents of Geneva Camp filed a writ in the High Court seeking the right to vote.[31] They won their case. This landmark ruling effectively gave legal recognition as citizens of Bangladesh to thousands of young 'Biharis'.

However, law is one thing and political practice, another. The citizenship status of 'Biharis' still remained ambiguous, and activists went on to make another push to achieve voting rights in reality. On 26 November 2007, in a new writ, Muhammad Sadaqat Khan (popularly known as Fakku), leader of the Urdu Speaking People Youth Rehabilitation Movement, asked for the recognition of *all* Urdu speakers as Bangladeshi citizens.[32] Once again they succeeded: the judge ruled that Urdu-speaking people who were resident in the territories now comprising Bangladesh at the time of its independence, as well as those born after independence and living in camps, were indeed citizens.

In the months that followed, newspapers and magazines debated the issue of giving 'Biharis' the vote. Detractors insisted that they should never be given a place on the official register of citizens of the nation, while sympathizers called upon the public to accept Urdu speakers into their fold. The debate encouraged activist groups to canvas for equal civil and citizenship rights in Bangladesh. Finally, on 18 May 2008, the High Court declared that the 'Biharis' (those who live outside the camps as well as the 150,000 resident in camps) were eligible to be listed on the electoral roll as Bangladeshi citizens.[33] As a result, the Government of Bangladesh proceeded to register all 'Biharis' as voters for the next parliamentary elections.

The cases and the publicity surrounding them have shifted perceptions. We spoke to Karim, a young lawyer in his early thirties, revered by many younger 'Biharis' as a pioneer who has brought their cause to the fore. Interestingly, Karim spoke of shifts in nomenclature as crucial gains:

> Less than ten years ago the media still referred in the main to us as 'Stranded Pakistanis'. However, both the national and international media have now started referring to us as 'Biharis'. This marks a step forward, as 'Stranded Pakistani' is a highly loaded term, chiefly used by the SPGRC (Stranded Pakistani General Repatriation Committee) – a group which has forcefully but ineffectually asked for the repatriation of the 'Biharis' . . . they do not represent the wishes of the majority of the 'Biharis' of Bangladesh. However, 'Bihari', the term now used, has derogatory implications in the Bengali context, as well as being incorrect. It is wrong to refer to us as 'Bihari' as many originally also came from the Indian states of Uttar Pradesh, West Bengal, Madhya Pradesh, and Andhra Pradesh.

According to Karim, although 'the young generation within this community prefer using the term "Urdu-speaker" ' to describe themselves, 'technically we are all bilingual, [and] many of us speak Bengali as our first language'.

Yet, as Karim recognized only too well, the point of this naming and renaming has little to do with technical accuracy. Rather, it is about changing perceptions of what a 'Bihari' is. To this end, at both the national and local levels, community organizations have fought – and continue to fight – with considerable skill. Leaders of the younger generation played a key role. For instance, in Syedpur, where many 'Biharis' remained, Mohammad Ashraful Haque Babu – or 'Babubhai' – runs the Shamsul Haque Foundation, a community organization at the forefront of numerous campaigns to promote a more sympathetic image of the 'Biharis'. The foundation was part of a delegation (along with the Association of Young Generation of Urdu Speaking Community and Al-Falah Bangladesh) which met the chief election commissioner and submitted to him a memorandum seeking the inclusion of camp dwellers on the electoral roll. They also published books by 'Biharis' – the most famous of them being Ahmed Ilias's history of the community: *'Biharis' – The Indian Émigrés in Bangladesh*. As Saif remarked, 'the publication of this book brought a significant change in the perceptions of the Bengali intellectuals, members of civil society, human rights activists, and international . . . institutions about the "Bihari" ' camp dwellers in Bangladesh. Thus voices of other individuals and organizations in support for the demand of citizenship of the camp dwellers were raised'. On the theme of nomenclature, it is significant that Ilias described 'Biharis' neither as Bengalis nor Muslims but as 'Indians'.

The Bengali-Urdu Sahitya Forum has adopted another approach,[34] which was to build bridges across apparently insurmountable barriers through poetry and literature. Its goal was to establish a dialogue through the medium of art and translation so as to enhance the mutual appreciation of the two cultures. To this end, they wrote and distributed tracts urging 'Bihari' youths to come forward and participate in the socio-cultural scene of the Bengali mainstream. Ahmed Ilias, about whom a great deal more will be said in Chapter 8, was a leading figure in this movement. The translation of Ahmed Ilias's *'Biharis' – The Indian Émigrés in Bangladesh* into Bengali under the title *Bangladeshe Bharotiyo Obhibashi* was another important step by middle-class activists, both Bengali- and Urdu-speaking, in this campaign.

At Modhu's canteen, Saif saw the consequences of such moves as significant and wanted us to write about them. Observing that it was easier 'nowadays' to 'become' more 'Bangladeshi', he said:

> Like the film [*The Promised Land*] . . . has sort of rehabilitated us. With the coming of the new millennium, things have radically changed. The children of the Bengali kids who used to kick us out from the park now come and play with our children. They have also started addressing us as '*tumi*' instead of '*tui*' [derogatory when used for someone not related or close]. Sometimes I dare feel that we are no more the enemy. We still have a long way to go, but we're aware of these things, and we now work towards making Bangladesh a more inclusive space for all.

Yet Saif shifted from at one moment deploying an 'us' and 'them' discourse to including himself and the rest of the 'Biharis' within a more 'open', cosmopolitan Bangladesh at another, a move that was familiar across sites. 'Bihari' respondents often said that they wanted to be recognized as part of Bangladesh while remaining concerned to highlight what made them 'different' from Bengalis.

This ambivalence was nowhere more evident than in the practice of moving out of the camps and seeking to 'pass' as Bengalis. Our research suggested that many people tried to do this, although the scale, for obvious reasons, is hard to judge precisely. Durba Ghosh has discussed the strategy of 'racial passing' among 'Anglo-Indians' or 'Eurasians' in British India,[35] where fairer-skinned persons sought to 'pass off' as Britons. We observed rather similar processes among 'Biharis' as smaller people with darker complexions tried to pass themselves off as Bengalis.

For instance, the first thing Saif did when he had put aside enough money was to move out of the camp. When we asked Saif's sister, Pinky, how it had felt to move to their new place, she said, 'I finally felt like I could breath and stretch my limbs, and I felt people stopped seeing me as a pariah'.

But Saif had to lie about his origins to be able to rent a flat. He joked when he told us this, saying, 'See, I'm dark like most Bengalis and I speak impeccable Bangla; they couldn't see through me'. We observed similar trends in the borderlands when people (like Shamsul Huq, who made the point by saying, 'Look at me, I'm so small' to set himself apart from 'Pakistanis') played down their mixed ancestry to pass themselves off as Bengali.

In 2010, however, after his sister's marriage, Saif moved back to the camp. His decision to return was influenced by several factors. The first was insecurity. After 'Biharis' were awarded citizenship in May 2008, there were rumours that the government might take over camp property, and Saif worried that he might lose his place in Geneva Camp (which is small, but, being in the centre of town, prime property in a 'safe' zone). The ruling of June 2008 deems 'Biharis' born after 1971 to be 'citizens', but, as Saif said, 'It's not as if they've stopped mistreating us'. His three brothers worked as *zari* embroiderers: their business was based in the camp and their outlets were the camp market. His wife, who was also from the camp, missed her mother; his brothers missed their friends.

As Saif's story underlines, 'passing' was not always straightforward – it required cutting (or at least loosening) economic and social ties that were crucial for security and survival. It also points to the ties of affect that made such moves painful, even impossible, to sustain. In any event, the option was not open to the poorest who could not afford to pay rent in Bengali neighbourhoods, even if they could find a landlord willing to take them in.

It would be a mistake to see the camps themselves as unambiguously 'Bihari' domains. Just as 'Biharis' could move out, Bengalis could move in. Poor Bengal hawkers enter the camps regularly to ply their wares. Walking through the camps in the morning, the songs of Arnob and Habib (famous Bengali singers) blared on transistor radios. In many homes, Bangla was the first language. There were many mixed Bengali-'Bihari' couples. Many camp people 'felt' more 'at home' in Bangladesh despite their exclusion from the mainstream. The 'felt' Bangladeshi. Those among them who had been to Bihar or Pakistan describe the people there as 'very rough', not like the 'kind Bengalis'. Outside Bangladesh, where they are not among their 'own people', they feel 'like total aliens'.

Belonging, status, and religion 99

When we asked Vicky, a young man, why he wanted Bangladeshi citizenship, he answered: 'Where else should I go? I have my family and my friends here. One wants to live where one's heart is happy'.

Conclusion

The historical effects of the fracturing of the subcontinent had a huge impact on migrants in and from 'the peripheries', but these have largely escaped scholarly attention. As Rahman and van Schendel have noted,[36] the scholarship on 'partition in the east' has been dominated by two themes: the relationship 'between the refugees and the state' and 'the voices and identities of a particular group of refugees to West Bengal, the Bengali *bhodrolok* (the educated upper and middle class), with their often traumatic and nostalgic memories of a lost homeland in East Bengal'.[37]

If the region's troubled history is examined from other, less privileged, perspectives, we discover just how challenging it was for the poor to move even a few miles. They may have crossed the border, but their inclusion in the new country posed problems despite their 'right' religious and cultural identity. Their struggle for acceptance continues fifty years later, and this struggle has been multifaceted, varying over space and time. Attempting to penetrate the national 'majority' as an outsider pushed many 'migrants from the periphery' to accrue different forms of social capital, to reinvent themselves in a variety of ways. We found that taking up 'modern', reformed, and very public forms of piety was one significant strategy. Another was the invention of novel forms of social hierarchy and structural (or very real) violence between incomers and 'stayers-on'.

As for 'stayers-on', who after partition and Liberation became part of 'national minorities', their predicament has been harsh, but their responses to it have been different. Class location proves to have been a significant factor in this variation. Those with some wealth and education (like Fatema Begun, Ahmed Ilias or Saif) often deployed their education to engage in debates within and about their 'community'. They could 'opt out' of religion altogether, like Enamul Huq, and found new humanistic or secular associations. Or they could 'move out' if they were prepared to try and 'pass' as a member of the majority religion.

Yet one group of people on the periphery – the poorest stayers-on – had only one choice: to tolerate in silence their ever-growing marginalization, immiseration, and vulnerability. The 'rishi' family in Satkhira or Jalal's family in Koikhali were withdrawn, nervous, markedly reluctant to discuss their predicament. Or if they dared speak, they were intimidated into silence by overbearing neighbours, often recent migrants themselves. This throws a different perspective on what 'toleration' means in the national contexts of South Asia. At the borderlands, where the nation marks itself out from its 'other', it is not the 'majority' who 'tolerate' the minority. It is rather the marginal men and women of the *minority* who tolerate the violence meted out to them (in the name of the nation) in fearful silence, a silence so complete that they have been rendered almost wholly invisible.

Notes

1. See also Rahman and Van Schendel, '"I Am *Not* a Refugee"', pp. 551–84.
2. Although see Redclift, *Statelessness*.
3. Joya Chatterji, 'Right or Charity? The Debate over Relief and Rehabilitation in West Bengal, 1947–1950', in Suvir Kaul (ed.) *The Partitions of Memory: The Afterlife of the Division of India*, Indiana: Indiana University Press, 2001, pp. 74–110; Kamaluddin, 'Refugee Problems'.
4. Notable exceptions include Sen, 'Refugees'; and Nilanjana Chatterjee, 'Interrogating Victimhood: East Bengali Refugee Narratives of Communal Violence', Department of Anthropology, University of North Carolina at Chapel Hill, NC: www.swadhinata.org.uk/misc/chatterjeeEastBengal%20Refugee.pdf.
5. Rahman and Van Schendel, '"I Am *Not* a Refugee"'.
6. Van Schendel, *Bengal Borderland*, p. 193. Also see Willem van Schendel, 'Stateless in South Asia: The Making of the India-Bangladesh Enclaves', *The Journal of Asian Studies*, 61, 1 (February) 2002, pp. 115–47.
7. Van Schendel, *Bengal Borderland*, p. 193. Anthem Press.
8. Vazira Fazila-Yacoobali Zamindar, *The Long Partition and the Making of Modern South Asia: Refugees, Boundaries, Histories*, New York: Columbia University Press, 2007.
9. For an account of purges in Assam at the time, see the *Jabbar Commission Report*.
10. Maulana Khalid Masud (ed.) *Travellers in Faith: Studies of the Tablighi Jama'at as a Transnational Islamic Movement for Faith Renewal*, Leiden: Brill, 2000; Barbara Daly Metcalf, *Perfecting Women: Maulana Ashraf Ali Thanawi's Bihishti Zevar*, Berkeley: University of California Press, 1990; Barbara Daly Metcalf, *Islamic Revival in British India: Deoband, 1860–1900*, Princeton: Princeton University Press, 1982; Barbara Daly Metcalf (ed.) *Islam in South Asia in Practice*, Princeton: Princeton University Press, 2009; Barbara Daly Metcalf, 'Living Hadith in the Tablighi Jama'at', *The Journal of Asian Studies* 52, 3, 1993, pp. 584–608; Barbara Daly Metcalf, *Islamic Contestations: Essays on Muslims in India and Pakistan*, Oxford: Oxford University Press, 2006; and Khatija Hafesji, 'Transnationalism, Migration, and Piety in the Growth of the Tablighi Jama'at Between India and Britain from 1926 to 2001', History Tripos dissertation, University of Cambridge, 2011.
11. These include *Bihishti Zewar* (heavenly ornaments), *Fazail-e-Amal*, and *Talimul-Islam* (Lessons in Islam). Hafesji, 'Transnationalism'.
12. Yogender Sikand, *The Origins and Development of the Tablighi Jama'at (1920–2000). A Cross-country Comparative Study*, New Delhi: Orient Longman, 2002; Robert Hefner and Muhammad Qasim Zaman, *Schooling Islam: The Culture and Politics of Modern Muslim Education* (Princeton Studies in Muslim Politics), Princeton: Princeton University Press, 2007; Muhammad Qasim Zaman, *Modern Islamic Thought in a Radical Age: Religious Authority and Internal Criticism*, Cambridge: Cambridge University Press, 2012.
13. Hafesji, 'Transnationalism'.
14. Although see Maimuna Huq, 'Reading the Qur'an in Bangladesh: The Politics of "Belief" Among Islamist Women', *Modern Asian Studies*, 42, 2/3, 2008, pp. 457–88.
15. 'Muhajir', or 'Mohajir', was the term used for refugees in Pakistan. Originally, the term was used to describe those who accompanied the Prophet from Mecca to Medina in 622 CE.
16. A subcaste.
17. Chatterjee, 'Interrogating Victimhood'.
18. Annu Jalais, 'Geographies and Identities: Subaltern Partition Stories along Bengal's Southern Frontier', in David N. Gellner (ed.) *Borderland Lives in Northern South Asia*, Durham, NC: Duke University Press, 2013, p. 254.
19. Van Schendel, *Bengal Borderland*, p. 192.
20. Chatterji, *Spoils*.

21 *Kantha* work is typical of Bengal: several layers of fine cotton are sewn together to form thin but beautifully embroidered blankets or mats.
22 The word '*jyotsna*' has Sanskrit, and hence 'Hindu', roots. In Bengali, the word is pronounced in a Sanskritic, rather than Bengali, manner.
23 Also known as Lalon Sain, Lalon Shah, or Lalon Fakir, Lalon (*c.* 1774–1890) was a renowned Baul saint, mystic, songwriter, social reformer, and thinker. In Bengal he is held up as an icon of religious tolerance.
24 Ho, *Graves of Tarim*, p. 3.
25 Ghosh, *Partition*.
26 Tajul Islam Hashmi, 'The "Bihari" Muslims of Bangladesh: Victims of Nationalisms', in Mushirul Hassan (ed.) *Islam, Communities and the Nation: Muslim Identities in South Asia and Beyond*, New Delhi: Manohar, 1998.
27 Redclift, *Statelessness*. Also see Chapter 6.
28 Emphasis added.
29 Joya Chatterji, 'The Bengali Muslim: A Contradiction in Terms? An Overview of the Debate on Bengali Muslim Identity', *Comparative Studies of South Asia, Africa, and the Middle East*, 16, 2, 1996, pp. 16–24.
30 The obvious exception were the self-styled 'Stranded Pakistanis', who demand 'repatriation' to Pakistan as citizens of that country.
31 Md. Abid Khan and others vs The Govt. of Bangladesh and others, Writ Petition No. 3831 of 2001, Supreme Court of Bangladesh, High Court Division (Special Original Jurisdiction).
32 Md. Sadaqat Khan (Fakku) and 10 others vs The Chief Election Commissioner, Bangladesh Writ Petition No. 10129 of 2007, Supreme Court of Bangladesh, High Court Division (Special Original Jurisdiction).
33 Md. Sadaqat Khan and 10 Others vs The Chief Election Commissioner, Bangladesh Writ Petition No. 10129 of 2007.
34 *Sahitya* means culture. The forum was organized by the Bengali poet and activist Asad Chowdhury and the journalist and freedom fighter Kamal Lohani, among others.
35 Durba Ghosh, *Sex and the Family in Colonial India. The Making of Empire*, Cambridge: Cambridge University Press, 2006. Also see Uther Charlton-Stevens, 'Decolonising Anglo-Indians: Strategies for a Mixed-Race Community in Late Colonial India during the First Half of the Twentieth Century', DPhil thesis, University of Oxford, 2012.
36 Rahman and Van Schendel, '"I Am *Not* a Refugee"', p. 555.
37 Ibid., p. 556. For examples of this kind of writing, see Dipesh Chakrabarty, 'Remembered Villages: Representation of Hindu-Bengali Memories in the Aftermath of the Partition', *South Asia*, 28, 1995; Gautam Ghosh, '"God is a Refugee": Nationalism, Morality and History in the 1947 Partition of India', *Social Analysis*, 42, 1, 1998, pp. 33–62; Manas Ray, 'Growing Up Refugee: On Memory and Locality', *Hindi: Language, Discourse, Writing*, 1, 3–4, 2001, pp. 148–98. For similar research on refugee memories and identities in East Pakistan/Bangladesh, see Niaz Zaman, *A Divided Legacy: The Partition in Selected Novels of India, Pakistan and Bangladesh*, Dhaka: University Press Limited, 1999; Tazeen M. Murshid, 'Nations Imagined and Fragmented: Bengal', in Willem van Schendel and Erik Jan Zürcher (eds), *Identity Politics in Central Asia and the Muslim World*, London: I. B. Tauris, 2001, pp. 85–105; Meghna Guhathakurta, 'Families, Displacement', *Transeuropéennes*, 19/20, 2001, pp. 131–42.

4 Making home

Claiming and contesting diasporic space in Britain

In 2008, when we interviewed him, Jubair Ahmed was in his early forties and living in the East London Borough of Newham, where he owned an 'Indian' takeaway. Jubair came to Britain as a teenager with his mother and younger sister in 1985, as part of a larger wave of family reunification that took place within the British Bengali Muslim community in the wake of the Liberation War, and settled with his father in Manor Park. We met Jubair earlier in Chapter 2, where we discussed how his family's history of mobility in Bengal laid the foundations for Jubair's later migration to the UK. Jubair's father had arrived in London in 1945, aged just sixteen. Discharged from the Merchant Navy supply ships onto the dockside in East London, Jubair's father followed in the footsteps of his maternal uncle, travelling the ship's route along the Kushiara river in Sylhet, through the port at Calcutta, to the docks in the Borough of Tower Hamlets at the heart of the imperial metropole. From there, he journeyed by land northeast to Scunthorpe and then Sheffield to seek work in the burgeoning postwar steel mills.

> Jubair recalled his father's stories of that time:
> Some people from our area [in Sylhet] worked there; when my father came, he worked with them. Earlier, there was no proper recruitment system; everyone was recruited verbally, there was no form. If you had a friend in any company, and you asked him to find a job for you, he just informs the foreman about you . . . then the foreman would say 'Tell him to come tomorrow'.

Like many of the early migrants, Jubair's father shared a flat with his countrymen and struggled with the harshness of the weather and the work:

> Earlier, people would live together. They would rent a three bedroom flat for fifteen, sixteen, twenty people. All fifteen, sixteen, twenty people would share the rent. The rent was ten shilling, fifteen shilling, very cheap. They would work in shifts; say six people went to work in one shift, others slept in their beds. Then they went to work in another shift, others slept in their beds. They had a hard life. At that time, there were no modern features. All was based on coal and gas. The street lights were gas, not electricity.

Five years later, Jubair's father returned to live with family in East London after a spell of ill health and settled in Upton Park. The area had no mosque, and he and his friends would gather to pray in a room in a local shop:

> There was a Pakistani shop. One room of this shop was spared for prayer. . . . The shop owner saw it as work for Allah, 'as you will say prayer, you can pray here. No rent for this'. There was no other place to gather. At first, four, six people gathered here, then eight people and then ten people. . . . They started collecting donations to buy a room for prayer. . . . Gradually they bought the shops, one, two, three, four, and then built a first floor. Day by day it turned into a big mosque – the mosque was named 'Shahzalal Mosque'.[1] It is the biggest mosque in this area.

When Jubair arrived to join his father, who had since moved to nearby Manor Park, Jubair noted that there were comparatively few Bengalis in the area. But 'gradually Bengalis gathered. Now Bengalis are a big community. You can see Bengalis from all sides'. Many had moved from neighbouring Tower Hamlets, attracted by the more spacious terraced houses and gardens, the multiethnic shops and community and religious institutions, good transport links, and the presence of family nearby. As Manor Park too became crowded, Jubair noted, some Bengalis like himself moved further eastwards along the Central line towards Essex – Chadwell Heath and Redbridge. Jubair moved with his wife and two children to Chadwell Heath in 2007 because:

> This place is just outside London . . . the kids can walk to school, they don't depend on transport. . . . All important institutions are very near to our house. Communication is good, I've good connection with East London so I can still keep in touch. . . . There are three or four Bengali shops, there is a Bengali mosque. . . . We can meet our acquaintances, people from our area [in Sylhet].

The story of Jubair Ahmed and his father is typical of migration stories to Britain, and the intertwining of these cross-generational familial histories – of two lives in one (family's) migration (hi)story – provides revealing insights into the process of migration and, particularly, of Bengali Muslim settlement. They point to movement and consolidation; to the constraints and contingencies of mobility; to the creation of, and struggle for, community across time and place; to diasporic and local reformulations of 'home'; and to unfinished journeys as part of the broader landscape of multicultural Britain.[2] It is a story of multiple journeys – not only of Jubair and his father themselves in the initial passage across the 'Seven Seas and Thirteen Rivers'[3] between Bangladesh and Britain, but also of Jubair's great-uncle who travelled on the British ships and inspired Jubair's father, and of the staging posts in their individual journeys – Calcutta, East London, Scunthorpe, Sheffield, back to East London and then eastwards towards Essex and beyond as well as regular movement between the UK and Bangladesh and, in Jubair's father's final years, to Mecca. It is a story too of multiple temporalities, of continuity and change, and the entanglement of histories. It speaks to the longer histories of migration across, within, and from Bengal discussed in Chapter 1; to the histories and legacies of empire; to the ways in which the classic stories of early male migrants – of casual work, communal living, makeshift mosques, and the 'myth of return'[4] – carried within them the seeds of community; to the way those uncertain beginnings took root in particular places and provided the foundations for the greater aspirations of the later generations. And, as with the stories explored in Chapter 3, it is a story of struggle: of borders and barriers; of exclusion and inclusion; of sometimes violent racism and the struggle for recognition, for space, and for acceptance; of resistance and transformation; of community, nation, diaspora in all their complexity.

This chapter traces the formation and transformation of the Bengali Muslim 'community' in Britain through a focus on two key sites and through the narratives of pioneer migrants who helped shape these diasporic spaces. As with the previous chapter, it focuses in particular on the process of settlement, of building new homes away from home, and on the places where migration stops – albeit temporarily – and shapes new communities and new landscapes. The chapter emphasizes the creation of place and the ways in which place-making imbues meaning and emotion to particular locations.[5] Tracing the changing contours of the Bengali 'community' historically and paying attention to its contested contemporary boundaries, the chapter explores the process of 'community' formation in Tower Hamlets in East London and Oldham in Greater Manchester. Through a portrait of these iconic British Bengali diaspora spaces, the chapter explores how historical process and contingency along with intersections of diaspora movement with local people and places have worked to create and transform community identities, challenging simplistic dominant notions of ethnicity and difference and insisting on the complexity and mutual imbrication of what Brah has termed 'diaspora spaces'.[6] Its arguments are fourfold: first, that rather than a natural and pre-given aspect of ethnicity, 'community' takes shape as part of broader political and social processes, exclusions, and solidarities; second, that 'community' and ideas of 'home' are shaped in local settings and with reference to locally rooted histories and struggles; third, that 'community' is contested and changing and constitutes a site of struggle and transformation; and fourth, that in acknowledging the constructed and contested nature of community formation, a historically and spatially sensitive understanding of diasporic 'community' also recognizes the strong emotional and symbolic attachment to place and 'home' and its significance in claiming space to belong.

A tale of two (sub)cities: Tower Hamlets and Oldham

Tower Hamlets

The London Borough of Tower Hamlets sits at the heart of the traditional East End of London. Bordered by the City of London to the west, Newham to the east, and Hackney to the north, the river Thames forms its southern border. The borough contains the West India Docks, which linked London to its empire from the early 1800s onwards,[7] and the Isle of Dogs at its southern reaches, developed from the 1980s onwards as part of the Docklands regeneration, including the new business district of Canary Wharf.[8] The 2011 Census recorded a population of nearly 238,000 people.[9] Of this population, 47 per cent were estimated to be of black or ethnic minority heritage, and 36 per cent of whom identified as Muslims. The Bangladeshis are the largest of these groups. The 2011 Census recorded around 75,300 Bangladeshis in Tower Hamlets, making up about 32 per cent of the local population and 55 per cent of the under twenties group. Bangladeshis are concentrated in particular wards of the borough.[10] Tower Hamlets is home to over two-fifths of the Bangladeshi population of Greater London.[11]

The glittering glass towers of Canary Wharf notwithstanding, Tower Hamlets has entrenched patterns of social marginalization: the borough ranks third (out of 354) of all local authorities in England in terms of social deprivation.[12] The period 2005–2011 showed that Tower Hamlets had the second highest level of unemployment in London, at around 13 per cent,[13] the highest levels of child and pensioner poverty rates nationally,[14] and one of the youngest populations in the country, whose average life expectancy is the sixth worst of any group in London. These indicators are more pronounced among the Bengali community, of whom 35 per cent are in the 0–15 year age group (compared to 14 per cent of white British residents). It also suffers nearly three times the level of unemployment (20 per cent compared to 7 per cent average). According to the analysis of 2011 Census data for London, only 54 per cent of Bangladeshi men and 24 per cent of Bangladeshi women aged over 16 were in employment.[15] Of those in work, nearly half work in hotel and catering or in the wholesale and retail trade sectors.

Poverty and deprivation have been integral to the history of London's East End and are closely intertwined with ideas and experiences of migration and marginality. Historically, for centuries the East End has been home to waves of immigrants including French Huguenot silk weavers, Irish dockworkers, Jewish refugees, Chinese opium dealers, Greek and Turkish Cypriots, and sailors from across the world.[16] Perhaps because of this, it has attracted a rather ambiguous reputation for disorder and dysfunction. The East End has long been popularly associated with crime and vice, from the opium dens of Limehouse – London's original Chinatown – to Jack the Ripper and the notorious Kray gang.[17] The area also has a long tradition of radical politics and social dissent and of both racist and anti-racist mobilization – most famously, the Battle of Cable Street in 1936, when Jewish anti-fascists and communists confronted Oswald Mosley's British Union of Fascists, a precursor to the anti-racist struggles of the Bengalis in the 1970s.[18] It is perhaps surprising, then, that the area has most usually been represented in social and historical accounts – from Young and Wilmott's classic 1957 study to Dench et al. in 2006 – as the last bastion of 'indigenous' Britain, of Blitz spirit, and 'authentic' white working class 'community'.[19]

This longer history is the context within which the Bengali 'community' in Tower Hamlets takes shape. Viewed conventionally as a latecomer to this story, the Bengali 'community' is often reduced to a footnote or a few pages.[20] In contrast, Tower Hamlets Council's 'Cultural Walk 3'[21] reveals that Bengalis have been present in London for nearly 400 years and points to the links between Bengal and East London's Docklands forged by the trade routes of the British East India Company.[22] From the 1920s a small number of ex-lascars living in East London provided shelter and guidance to Bengali sailors passing through London or, occasionally, jumping ship.[23] The numbers of Bengalis in London rose slowly throughout the 1930s and in the period up to the end of the Second World War; the establishment of 'community' institutions, such as the Indian Seamen's Welfare League in Christian Street, Aldgate, in 1943, underlines the continued intricate connections between the docks and migrant settlement in the area.[24] This period also saw the opening of Bengali 'coffee shops' catering for the new arrivals, which later became the first Sylheti owned 'Indian' restaurants, laying the foundations for the recent Banglatown development.

After the Second World War, the numbers of Bengali migrants grew as part of a broader recruitment of workers to fill Britain's postwar labour shortage. However, it was only in the 1960s and 1970s that the number of Bengalis began to increase substantially. The arrival of women and children from the late 1970s into the 1980s – again stimulated by the relaxing of British immigration restrictions and flux and famine in Bangladesh – laid the groundwork for the present concentration of Bengali families in the area.

Arrivals

Because of its distinctive demography and history, Tower Hamlets is generally understood as the symbolic historical, social, and cultural 'heartland' of the Bengali Muslim 'community' in Britain and indeed is often regarded as metonymous with the 'Bangladeshi community' nationally. However, this position was the outcome of more contingent historical processes and struggles than its current status suggests. Bengalis were not present in large numbers in this area until the late 1970s. Many early migrants spoke vividly of the ethnically diverse community that greeted them and, for them, Tower Hamlets is a place of multiple migration histories and settlements.

Ansar Ahmed Ullah was born in Birmingham but lived Bangladesh until the age of sixteen. He then returned to Luton in Bedfordshire and has worked in Tower Hamlets as a youth and community worker since 1982. An active oral and community historian in his own right,[25] Ansar placed the history of the Bengali community as part of a longer and broader picture of migration to the area, with the iconic Brick Lane as its primary symbol. He told us:

> Brick Lane is an historic place because here our society has evolved. When the Bengalis first came here, they landed in the area of Cable Street or Shadwell area. They used to land here because historically the seamen lived here. Before Bengalis, there were Somali, Yemeni seamen, and the Chinese lived here. Then the Bengalis came. . . .

Making home 107

Once Brick Lane area was under the control of the Jewish community. They had businesses, shops, factories . . . the Bengalis used to work at their businesses and factories. Gradually the Jews moved to other areas . . . and the Bengalis started coming in. One day all the area had been emptied by the Jews and replaced by the Bengalis. . . .

For people like Jubair's father, who arrived in the 1950s, Tower Hamlets was a place of arrival but not necessarily of settlement as many moved around the country in search of work.[26] This remained true throughout the 1970s, until recession and growing national unemployment led people back to more densely populated settlements. One of our oldest UK based interviewees, Altaf Ali, aged 80, came to Britain in the 1950s and initially stayed at the flat of a *murabbi* (elder) from his village along with five other Bengalis. He worked for six months in a local wood factory:

The work was very hard. I had not seen the machinery before. I would take the logs on my shoulder and lift them from downstairs to the upstairs, and from upstairs to the downstairs. Logs would hit my face and my nose, and sawdust would come out when I coughed. At the end of the week I would get 40 pence.

In 1959 Altaf moved to Lancashire to work in Preston's Thread Factory, but a year later he returned to Bangladesh. He only came back to Preston, where he owned a small house, in 1962; then in 1968 he again returned to Bangladesh for six years. He returned reluctantly to Britain in 1974 because of conditions in Bangladesh, where political instability and economic uncertainty had fuelled a famine of horrifying proportions. He worked in a restaurant in Manchester before ending up in London in 1978, where he opened a restaurant.

Similarly Boshir Ahmed, following several cousins and uncles, arrived in London in 1963 but worked in cotton mills in Darlington, sugar mills in Preston, textile mills in Burnley, and then for British Steel and the Ford Motor Company in Birmingham before opening his own business in East London in 1979. He was pragmatic about this experience: 'My movement basically depended on the opportunities available. Say, if I thought I could earn more in Birmingham, I went there'.

East London, for this generation, was a point of entry into life in Britain. Rushanara Ali, MP for Bethnal Green and Bow, is the first member of parliament of Bangladeshi descent.[27] She told us that when her father arrived in the 1960s, he stayed first with his uncle, who had come to London in the 1930s:

That's where a lot of Bengali men started. You arrived in London and landed there because Brick Lane had a long history of association with what is now Bangladesh, with the history of the merchant navy and that connection. . . . You'll find when you talk to people that many men of my father's generation

108 *Making home*

came through those connections – had an uncle or a cousin . . . people who came in the interwar or postwar era.

The comparatively small number of Bengalis who settled locally provided accommodation and contacts for new arrivals. Mojibur Rahman, who was 74 when we interviewed him and sadly died shortly afterwards, arrived in Britain in 1959, joining relatives in Birmingham. There he worked in a factory before moving to East London in 1968, where he trained and worked as a tailor. He told us of his uncle, who had helped Mojibur and many other Bengalis when they first arrived:

In the old days, people helped each other. There was a house in Arthur Street [near to the docks in East London] which was partially damaged by bombing during the Second World War. People used to live in one part of that house. There was no-one in the Bengali community who did not know about the house. It was a kind of shelter that was open to everyone. Whenever new people came from Bangladesh, they would go to the house and could stay there. No one would ask who they were or whether they have anyone here. . . . He [his uncle] passed his life by helping people like that.

The area, still scarred by its history of social marginalization, wartime destruction, and postwar neglect, was not a welcoming one, however. Mahmoud Rauf, a local community activist and accountant who arrived in Tower Hamlets in 1968, described it:

The area was a very run-down area. Very, very run-down, Brick Lane was. All the houses were falling apart, the landlords were not repairing anything. I saw a few houses in the area in Brick Lane where you would go upstairs and find pigeons' nests, so you can imagine how dilapidated, how run-down the buildings were.

Husna Ara Begum[28] arrived in London at the end of 1972 with her husband, who was posted to the new Bangladeshi embassy in London. After renting for a year in Surrey, the family moved to cheaper housing in East London. Husna recalled the living conditions at that time:

After moving into the house, we suffered quite a lot. At that time, the area was full of old houses which did not have shower and toilet facilities inside the house. For fourteen years we had to go to the public baths. It was like a village in Bangladesh.

She recalled too that the local white community was extremely hostile to the new arrivals:

We faced other problems also. We had to face skinheads. They created lots of problems for us. They used to call us Paki. . . . They used to beat us wherever

Making home 109

they could get us. . . . There was no telephone in anyone's house at that time. I had to go outside to make a call from the public phone at the corner of the road, . . . but it was risky because there was a possibility of being hit by someone.

Helal Abbas, who came to Tower Hamlets as a child in 1971, told us what his daily life was like:

> People were living with real fear, fear of being murdered, fear of being beaten up, fear of walking the streets safely. I used to live on the Chicksand Estate, which is about 400 yards away from my school, and the number of times I used to duck and dive to get to the school and come home safely – that was the major issue.

Shiraj Haque, now a prominent local restaurant owner, arrived in Tower Hamlets in 1976 as a 20-year-old and also had a violent introduction to the area:

> I'll tell you what happened on the day of my arrival . . . we came with a black taxi from the airport, and when I came, one or two of my uncles were there waiting for us . . . they were attacked as they were coming to the flat and were bleeding when they arrived. . . . And I was told that this was something which happened quite frequently, . . . [but] people never used to mention it. They were a more closed community at that time.

Nevertheless, the number of Bengalis in the area was growing. A strong sense of solidarity had begun to emerge among them, shaped partly by local conditions in London and partly by the struggle for independence from the late 1960s onwards. The Swadhinata Trust's oral history of the area[29] reveals the active involvement of London Bengalis in raising money for the struggle as well as awareness among the international community. As the authors argue, 'the liberation war was not just fought in the Bengal delta'.[30] These contexts generated an increasing political engagement in the area, both formal and informal. Shiraj recalled that the day after his arrival his uncle took him to a cafe in Brick Lane, which was a meeting place for the local Bangladeshi men. He explained:

> In those days running a cafe in the area was more a meeting point for the Asian community. . . . And in those cafes, people who used to work in and around Brick Lane used to come as well for tea and coffee and socializing in the evening and politics, discussing what's going on back home.

These informal networks consolidated into more formal meetings and campaigns as the settlers grew in strength and confidence. In 1976, the synagogue on the corner of Brick Lane and Fournier Street was purchased as the site for a mosque – the Jamme Masjid – and the same period saw the purchase of a site for the East London Mosque, which was to open its doors a decade later.[31] There were older links too: the Pakistan (and later Bangladesh) Welfare Association (BWA) had been established on Fournier Street off Brick Lane and, from the 1950s on, provided an initial point of contact for the new migrants.[32] Shiraj Haque told us that when he first arrived the BWA was closed due to infighting, but it had provided a forum for 'community' activism:

> I was fortunate because my uncle used to be president of that [BWA] before – my dad was president of the Pakistan Welfare Association before the liberation struggle – so because of that connection managed to find some other activist people who were willing to support my effort to reopen the centre and utilize it for the community benefit. . . . I thought we must organize, we must do something about what's happening, why people are being attacked and so on.

'Here to stay, here to fight': Building community

Although this generation was active in the politics of Bangladesh, from these more global beginnings, Bengali migrants in Tower Hamlets began increasingly to engage in the local situation in East London.[33] What is apparent, however, are the multiple dimensions integral to the building of 'community' in this local space. As Shiraj Haque made clear, on the one hand, there are the transnational links to regions and villages in Sylhet arising from chain migration, which formed a basis for mobilization; on the other, there are local links to the historic processes of settlement of Bengalis in East London across generations and the institutions that facilitated and supported settlement. Shanu Miah, who arrived in Britain in 1967 and worked as a tailor in Hanbury Street, off Brick Lane, made this connection clear:

> In this country, we struggled a lot. After coming here, my grandfather also struggled. They fought one kind of war. Step by step we progressed. We all struggled, generation after generation. Today's face of Brick Lane has not come suddenly.

There are, however, two additional and significant dimensions to community building in Tower Hamlets in this period. The first is the changing picture nationally and the impact of this on Bengalis in Tower Hamlets. This includes the economic crisis of the 1970s, which led to deindustrialization and high levels of unemployment; the growth of virulent, populist racist movements such as the National Front; the increasingly explicit hostility of the state towards immigration in the period from 1968 onwards; and the emergence of a younger generation who were becoming increasingly vocal and active in their resistance to discrimination and victimization.[34] The late 1970s and early 1980s witnessed a series of confrontations between black and Asian young men and the police as well as the National Front. These sparked off widespread demonstrations, culminating in urban disorder, most famously in London, Liverpool, Birmingham, and Manchester in 1981 and 1985.[35]

Second, East London and other sites of Bengali settlements grew increasingly dense at this time. Rising unemployment and insecurity nationally played a part in this, as did the migration of wives and children from Bangladesh in increasing numbers. In particular, this period saw the arrival in Britain of a number of young men in their teens or early twenties trained in political activism in the charged decade of the Liberation War and its unstable aftermath. These young people were largely left-leaning, and they brought their primarily leftist, secular political activism and organizational experience to the streets of Tower Hamlets.[36] They established links with other Asian youth movements across London and in Birmingham, Manchester, Bradford, and Leicester,[37] but they also established links with local leftist and antiracist groups to take on the National Front on the streets of Tower Hamlets.

Such mobilization and community formation then must be seen as multiscalar – spanning familial and local, pan- and cross-ethnic, national and global contexts and networks.

Rajonuddin Jalal, who came to Tower Hamlets in 1972, as a 13-year-old, described the emergence of the youth movements in Tower Hamlets:

> As the community grew in Tower Hamlets, Bengalis became noticed and the murders of Altab Ali, Ishaq Ali, and Michael Ferreira in Hackney[38] took place against a background of persistent racial attacks in the East End, on the housing estates, in the streets. Every day [there was] harassment. I was beaten up a few times and most other people who lived here. And so I think the younger generation realized that they had to stay in this country and decided to fight back. . . . And I think there was a phase in the mid-'70s, the Bengali community came of age. These murders . . . created the impetus for going public with the resistance, and eventually the racist thugs were polarized and were driven out of the area.

Through the mid-1970s and into the 1980s these self-defence groups transformed into organized antiracist resistance.[39] Helal Abbas told us that there were two local Bangladeshi youth organizations: the Bangladeshi Youth Front and the Bangladeshi Youth Movement (which still exists). Helal was secretary to the latter and explained:

> We used to fight for Bangladeshi equal rights – it was very clear, the organization was founded to establish equal rights for young people in our community. . . . Unfortunately, it wasn't just about campaigning, it was about safety. . . . There were some physical confrontations but, . . . many of us never believed this was the solution. But we did stand up for our rights, and we defended ourselves physically.

Shiraj Haque was also actively involved in organizing local youths to challenge racist threats during the 1970s. He described the group's strategy:

> We used to take control of some of the youth clubs in the area where our boys were not allowed to go. We directly forced ourselves into it, fighting our way. . . . Also street battles we used to fight. We had a lot of bad experiences.

At the end of Brick Lane there used to be a large group of racists selling their literature, newspapers and so on – every Sunday in their hundreds, and our people used to be scared about it. So we would occupy that particular spot early on so they don't have this position.

Sajjid Miah, who arrived in Britain in 1974 and is now chair of Brick Lane Mosque, recalled:

Almost every Sunday we had to face attacks by the skinheads and the racist National Front. In Bethnal Green, they used to sell their leaflets and . . . we have to fight for it, a long, long fight, and then they moved away. . . . I was young, and along with a lot of my friends we had a meeting and said, 'This Sunday from 10 o'clock to this time some people will stand outside, some people stay here, protecting ourselves and our elders and shops'.

As the campaign progressed, its base within the community grew:

We got politically started, say, fifty, sixty young people who had a network of 500, 600 friends. But about two years into the movement, the antiracist struggle, even older people would have come out, occupying streets, police stations and so on, demanding action. And by that time you had a thousand coming out, 'Here to stay, here to fight', 'Not going back'. These slogans were important.

The racist murder of Altab Ali, a young garment worker, in May 1978 is seen by many as a definitive turning point in Bengali community self-organization in Brick Lane.[40] Ten days after the murder, a large group marched from Brick Lane to Westminster, with a rally in Hyde Park.[41] Rajonuddin Jalal, who was one of the organizers of the march, described the events:

For the first time, Bengalis marched from Whitechapel to Parliament House, on the way round Hyde Park corner and back to Whitechapel. It took about eight hours. About 10,000 people. That was the first time Bengalis came out.

Shiraj Haque similarly recalled:

We mobilized a big demonstration demanding justice for Altab Ali . . . in six days we managed to mobilize a very big crowd that no ethnic minority community had ever been able to do. It was a rainy day, people started marching with a symbol of the coffin of Altab Ali to Hyde Park[42] . . . It was a bit of a wake-up call, you know, that we shouldn't take that easily, we should fight back.

These struggles, along with the growth of the Bengali population in the area from the late 1970s onwards, placed Brick Lane as the heartland of Britain's Bengali community. Ansar Ahmed Ullah reflected:

In the '70s and '80s, you could say this place did offer a sense of safety, because of the sheer numbers of people here. . . . I think a racist would think

Making home 113

twice before launching an attack or attacking a member of the community here. . . . So in the '70s and '80s it did provide a safe haven, I guess, for our people.

Dilowar Hussain Khan, now chair of East London Mosque Committee, who had also been part of the antiracist battles of the 1970s, also told us:

> I used to live in Wapping, and our windows used to be broken almost every other week . . . and I was even attacked physically many times out on the streets. So that was there everywhere apart from this area, Brick Lane, and this little island we had, this was like a safe haven.

(Re)generating community: The rise of Banglatown

The changes to the area at that time were not always viewed unequivocally, even by those at the heart of 'community' building and shaping. Ansar Ahmed Ullah, for example, told us that while the levels of violence decreased through the 1980s, levels of segregation increased, particularly with the increasing numbers of Bengali women and children arriving in the area:[43]

> I think by the 1990s the number of racist attacks decreased, where I guess our numbers increased *(laughs)*. And in some areas there was white flight, so as more of our people moved into housing estates, and as our kids moved into schools, the white people moved out. So it became more Bengali and less white.

This spatial and social marginalization was exacerbated by the migration outwards not only of local whites, but also other minority groups, including the Jewish factory owners in the area. The local cinema, the snooker hall, and the shops selling Indian music all closed, as did the local leatherwork factories where many Bengalis were employed. Amjad Ali came to London in 1973 to join his father, who had previously been employed in a local leather factory. Amjad, who himself worked as a tailor until the factories closed, recalled:

> Up to '90, tailoring factories existed. After then, these decreased. . . . Most of the factories were declared closed. . . . Clothes and leather factories closed down. Carpet factories were shifted to Stratford, Hackney. Tailoring factories, clothes-making – this business was captured by Pakistan, India, Turkey, Morocco. When the factories were declared closed, the Bengalis were unemployed. Then they entered into the restaurant business.

Amjad noted the shift in the restaurant trade from the Bengali-oriented coffee houses of the 1970s towards more outward-facing businesses:

> The restaurant business started with 'Sonar Bangla', a restaurant-styled shop: tea, chicken curry, and one, two items were available. Another cafe, called

'Nirula', was there. Bengalis owned these two restaurants. . . . In the '80s the number of restaurants increased. . . . The Bengalis would go there and eat rice. . . . When regeneration started, this area came to the forefront. People started coming to this area. Then the restaurant business also flourished. . . . Then, when the whites started coming, the restaurant owners presented themselves in different ways.

This period was also one of intense political change as activists from the youth movements moved into mainstream British party politics. Nine Bengali candidates stood for the 1982 borough council elections and the first Bengali councillor, Nurul Huque, was elected that year.[44] The most successful candidates had previously been community activists involved in the Altab Ali campaign. As Eade notes, this reflected a shift from a 'Bangladeshi' politics to a more a Britain-centred series of political interests and alliances.[45] Rajonuddin Jalal, who himself became a councillor in 1990, commented:

There were three or four Bengalis who stood as independents supported by us because the political parties, namely the Labour party, was not allowing us to join the party. So by filtering independent candidates we were able to take one seat. . . . And that's when they realized that the Bengali community has to be listened to. And then the gates opened. And then we joined in large numbers.

Helal Abbas, who was the first Bengali leader of Tower Hamlets Council from 2002–2006, was elected as a Labour councillor in 1985, and saw the move into mainstream party politics as a necessary progression from his activist days:

Gradually I realized instead of someone shouting from the steps of the Town Hall, you join the party, it's better . . . . your chances of being heard are better if you are inside the tent rather than outside the tent. . . .

These three factors – the numeric expansion and spatial concentration of the Bengali population, the decline of industrial employment in the area, and the entry into mainstream British politics at the Council level – laid the groundwork for the partial transformation of the area in the mid-1990s, which saw the regeneration of Brick Lane in Spitalfields into its current iconic incarnation as 'Banglatown'. Part of a broader programme of gentrification of Spitalfields's picturesque Georgian streets around Brick Lane, the trend (which began in the 1970s) was bolstered by regeneration funds aimed at Britain's inner cities in the late 1980s.[46] Mahmoud Rauf, who was chair of the Banglatown Consultative Forum, told us that the 'Banglatown' idea was originally developed by a white British planning officer in the council in the 1970s:

The concept came from Chinatown. . . . Why not create a Banglatown and make it a developed area? When he put these words into the air, we Bangladeshis caught it. . . . So there the movement, or the talking or the discussions started. . . . [But] there was resistance, inside and outside the council as well. So our muscle wasn't strong at that time. . . . But we wanted to keep it alive. Anywhere in meetings, anywhere we get the chance, we raise the question of Banglatown.

It was only with the election of a Labour majority to the Council in the mid-1990s that the situation changed:

> We had about fourteen Bengali councillors at that time in the council. So the Labour party were indebted to the Bengali people. . . . Bengali people were going to the polling station like anything, like ants . . . so we started our demands again: 'We want our Banglatown'.

The redevelopment started on the site of the old Truman Brewery and grew to include a neighbouring site owned by British Rail – 27 acres in total. The development initially focused on the 'Indian' restaurant trade along Brick Lane to the south of the Brewery site. Carey notes that in 1997 the area had six Indian restaurants and four cafes, but by 2003 this had grown to 46 outlets (and counting),[47] making it the largest cluster of Indian/Bangladeshi restaurants anywhere in the UK and a focal point for supply businesses across Tower Hamlets, London, and the South-East. In 1999 the Council officially labelled the area around Brick Lane 'Banglatown', and in 2001 the electoral ward of Spitalfields changed its name to Spitalfields and Banglatown.

Ansar Ahmed Ullah was critical of the way in which the concept was first adopted and then adapted by the regeneration committees:

> The idea came from the community . . . as an acknowledgement of the strong Bengali community here. . . . [But] for them it was the branding of this area in order to attract tourists and businesses to this area. . . . We wanted to give it a more physical look of Banglatown . . . we wanted all the signs in Bengali, we wanted a gate, a lamppost, we wanted colourful drawings on the road, we wanted some balconies on the buildings, to give it more of a feel of the streets from Bengal. But that hasn't happened, they are still fantasies in our minds.

Mahmoud Rauf, who was chair of the Banglatown Consultative Forum, similarly commented:

> At this moment in time, Banglatown is in name [only]. We wanted some sort of library with the history of the local immigrants over the years, including the Bengali people. . . . But that never materialized . . . Banglatown was mostly to be involved with culture rather than the economy, that was our idea.

Jalal reflected:

> The only thing you can see that are tangible achievements would be a few community centres, a few shop fronts on the restaurants, the Banglatown

arch, the Shahid Minar. . . . The Banglatown concept, though it officially exists . . . hasn't really taken off.

Nevertheless, as Helal Abbas reflected, the creation of Banglatown was significant as a recognition of the presence and contribution of Bengalis to the local area:

> I think the symbol of Banglatown and Bangladeshis was an issue and the declaration of Banglatown . . . was 'this is our community, we are part of this borough'. Psychologically, it was an important factor.

Moreover, Banglatown was viewed by many as the culmination of this longer Bengali presence, history, and struggle. Ansar Ahmed Ullah evoked this history as underpinning a strong, affective attachment to place and to 'community', both ethnic and local:

> I have called Brick Lane the blood-centre of the Bengalis because centring on Brick Lane, they have been organized. Here, they built a mosque, they brought out papers, they developed a political base, and the leaders of the Bengali community live here. . . . On every occasion, every Bengali rushes to this area. . . . This area can be called 'Bengali *para* (neighbourhood)'. You can get everything from Bangladesh you need – food, magazines, CD, DVD, everything.

Similarly, when we asked Shamim Azad, a local poet and cultural activist who has lived in the area for twenty years, whether she 'liked' the Banglatown image, she responded 'it's more than a like, it's more than a look – it's a metaphor'. She continued, 'Bangladeshi sailors came here to this area . . . our forefathers came here . . . this is our forefathers' area, where people smelt the curry first'.

Oldham

The small town of Oldham forms part of the Greater Manchester metropolitan county.[48] In the northwest of England, six miles to the northeast of the City of Manchester, the town forms the administrative centre of the Metropolitan Borough of Oldham. The borough was home to nearly 225,000 people in 2011.[49] Of this population, 18 per cent were from a South Asian background and nearly 18 per cent were Muslim, predominantly of Mirpuri (Pakistani) and Sylheti (Bangladeshi) descent, in total about 65,000 people.[50] The Bangladeshi population in 2011 comprised 7.3 per cent (or approximately 16,310 people) of the larger metropolitan district of Oldham, the second largest population outside London.[51]

Historically linked to the textile trade from the 19th century until the mid-1970s, Oldham was a centre of cotton and textile manufacture for the global market. A hub for the imperial trade of the British East India Company, it imported raw materials from the plantations of the United States and India via the nearby port of Liverpool and exported cloth across the British empire. Virinder Kalra notes that by the mid-19th century, Oldham had come to rely almost exclusively on imported Indian raw cotton, and India, in turn, became one of the area's largest markets for exported finished cloth. At its peak in the 1920s, there were 320 mills in the town; however, the industry began a steady decline after the Second World War, and by the 1970s, technological advances, industrial restructuring at home, and the increase in cheaper foreign imports from abroad shut down the vast majority of mills. By the 1980s, only 12 mills were left. The last textile mill closed in 1998.[52]

Industrial growth and rapid deindustrialization had a profound impact on the demography and labour market of the town. At its peak in the 1920s, the mills employed 60 per cent of the town's workforce – about 600,000 people,[53] a large percentage of whom were women. There was also a long history of migrant labour recruited to unskilled work in the industry: Irish immigrants in the 19th century, Eastern Europeans after the Second World War, and South Asian migrants from the 1950s onwards. Kalra notes that there were small numbers of Pakistanis in Oldham from the mid-1960s (around 700 people in 1966)[54] but that this number rose to 11,500 people by the 1990s. In 2001 there were nearly 23,000 Pakistanis and Bangladeshis across the borough,[55] and this number rose by 2011 to nearly 39,000, a rate of increase well above the national average.[56] Both South Asian men and women were employed in the mills from the 1960s onwards, with men concentrated in the night shifts to minimize contact with the local white women who dominated the day shifts.

The closure of the mills by the mid-1980s hit the local Asian population hard, therefore, with many ageing migrants facing a future of long-term unemployment. Many were in poor health, and the only employment available to them was badly paid work in the clothing warehouses of Manchester or self-employment in the taxi ranks or restaurant trade.[57] This has had longer term ramifications for ethnic minority communities: Bangladeshis in Oldham are over four times as likely to be unemployed as local whites (23 per cent compared to 5 per cent). They own fewer homes (28 per cent compared to 60 per cent for whites and Pakistanis), and these homes are often severely overcrowded.[58] Oldham, along with Tower Hamlets, has been identified as one of the most unequal districts of England and Wales for ethnic minorities, according to a recent Index of Multiple Inequality.[59]

The Bangladeshi community in Oldham originates chiefly from two regions of Sylhet: Biswanath and Habiganj.[60] Bangladeshis live in all areas of the town, but are particularly concentrated in the Coldhurst electoral ward (over 60 per cent).[61] This contains the neighbourhoods of Glodwick, which was, infamously, the site of 'riots' in 2001 (discussed below) and Westwood, known locally as 'Bangla Para' because of the concentration of Bangladeshi families and community institutions and also for the replica of the Shahid Minar memorial[62] and Shapla roundabout. The formation of the Oldham Bangladeshi community is inseparable from, and intertwined with, the longer history of this postindustrial town – its history of migration, of industrial decline, of Far Right political mobilization, and of often unwelcome ethnic diversification. But it speaks too to the creation of new communities, new spaces, and new forms of belonging.

Arrivals

Despite its status as the British Bengal diaspora's second most significant settlement, the establishment of Oldham's Bengali community was serendipitous and, as with Tower Hamlets, achieved through a circuitous route, reflecting the mobility of the early Bengali migrants within the UK itself. Abdul Jabbar, for example, arrived in England in 1962. He travelled to Oldham the following year via Northampton, Halifax, and the neighbouring mill town of Burnley, using networks of relatives and fellow villagers from Bishwanath *thana*, and settled even though, at that point, 'there was not much employment opportunity here'. Mizanur Rahman, likewise, arrived in Oldham via London and Manchester in 1965, first joining his father who (like Jubair's father) had worked on the British merchant ships in the Second World War and had disembarked in London in 1945. Mizanur's father had lived first in London, then in Birmingham, and then moved north to Manchester, where he tried unsuccessfully to open a restaurant. When his father returned to Bangladesh in 1966, Mizanur moved to Oldham to be with his elder brother but struggled to find work or housing. He commented, 'There was no family environment. We developed it later on. . . . When I came, my brother told me to stay in a separate house [because] there was no environment to stay together'. He lived in Oldham to be near fellow Bengalis but worked in a nearby town. 'I lived in Oldham. My factory was in a different town. It would take half an hour for the bus. . . . It was the place for the factory, not for living. Very few people lived there. I was also afraid . . . of racists. We would be attacked at any time'.

However, the fledgling Bengali community in Oldham was already beginning to expand and establish itself; Mizanur noted 'for shopping, for *halal* items, we would have to come to Oldham. After we came here, these [things] became available'. He noted too the significance of a close support network among the mainly young Bengali migrants:

> We all worked in the factory. For work, we would go together. The day we had no work, we would go to town walking or on the bus. . . . But if you were alone and there were some rough boys, you might be beaten up or abused, or they would shout at you.

As opportunities for work in the town expanded through the late 1960s, more Bengalis arrived. Tasarul Ali, who arrived as a teenager in 1967 and came to Oldham the following year to work in the mills, where he worked for nearly twenty years, estimated that there were around 500 Bengalis in Oldham at that time but that most were single men. He told us: 'At that time, the situation was good. People would get a job and work the whole day. There was no intention from people that they'll settle here. . . . They never thought of bringing their families here'. Hasib, a school teacher who arrived in a later wave of family settlement, describes this time in terms familiar in many tales of early South Asian migration:

> In the 1970s, when our people came to this country, they landed in Oldham. Oldham at that time was a mill area – cotton mills. Everyone would work

there – 15 people living in one house.... A batch of one shift would sleep; when another batch would come, this shift-batch would go to work and others would sleep in the same bed. It was their life.... They had a system for cooking – they would take it in turn to cook. One day was the day-off. All would go out. There was a cinema hall – they would go to the cinema. Indian films were shown...

Their focus was on Bangladesh. Whenever they got money, they would send it to Bangladesh.... They came here just to earn some money. Their intention was, after getting a reasonable amount of money, they would go back to Bangladesh and settle over there.

Kamal Hossain came as a child with his mother to Oldham in 1970, ahead of the wave of family reunification that followed. He recalled what life was like for him, aged just four, and his mother in the fledging Bengali 'community':

In Oldham, there were only two Bengali families.... The English did not see other Asian boys, so they responded warmly to me.... In the afternoon, the English kids would come to play with me. They would come because I was only one little Asian. All the people in the neighbourhood liked me and gave me sweets, but I did not eat sweets much, so I kept the sweets and gave them to the English kids when they would come to play with me.

His mother and Kamal lived with his father, an uncle, and three 'cousin-brothers' in a three-bedroom house on a street where they were the only Asian family; later another Bengali woman relative came from Bradford to keep his mother company. Kamal reflected:

That time, people would work at the factory, and they would live in chaos. There was no family environment. The women faced many problems to live. Bath, toilet were outside, not integrated into the house. My mother cried to go home. She didn't see anyone. She wouldn't stay any longer.

His mother returned back to Bangladesh with Kamal the following year and only returned in 1986 once the community had established itself.

Things were already changing by the time Kamal's mother returned home to Bangladesh, however. By the time Mohammed Aziz moved to Oldham in 1973, he recalled, with some nostalgia:

At that time, Oldham was a business centre. There were many textile mills. Many Bangladeshis worked there.... At that time, Bengalis would only work and eat. The Bengalis were mostly single men, not family centred. That time was very good. We had friendship with each other. Now it's not like that. Now everybody is very busy.

Mohammed saw the growing numbers of Bengalis as a business opportunity, and he opened a *halal* food store with a relative and, later, two restaurants catering to white Oldham residents, which are still running over 30 years later. Most Bengalis, though, worked in the mills, and, to begin with, work was easy to come by. Its casual nature facilitated easy movement between England and Bangladesh. Abdul Jabbar recalled:

> I can remember, I came to Oldham on 27th May 1963. On that day, I was going with one of my village friends to look for a job. We went to a possible employer. Her daughter opened the door. Then a man came. He asked me 'What do you want?' I told him 'Can you give me any job?' I replied in English. I learned English in Bangladesh. Then he told me to enter the house – 'Only you come' he said, and I went inside. He showed me a machine in the house, a circular knitting machine. Clothes are knitted with this machine. 'Can you work with this?' he asked me. I replied 'I can'. Then he said, 'You can come from today if you like'. . . . I went back to my house and bought some work trousers and in the afternoon, I went for work.

Building community

From its early and temporary beginnings, the Bengali presence in Oldham began to grow throughout the 1970s and establish itself within the town. The late 1970s to the 1980s saw the arrival of families – wives and children – which swelled the numbers and shifted the priorities of the migrants towards their life and future in Britain. According to the census data, the number of Bangladeshis in Oldham grew from 2,000 in 1981 to 5,200 in 1991 – a settlement pattern replicated in the neighbouring larger Pakistani communities.[63] The arrival of women and children precipitated the establishment of more settled, and more visible, communities, with families moving out from temporary, multiple occupancy houses in the town centre to the surrounding areas, sometimes sparking tension with local white Oldham dwellers. Tasarul Ali, who lived in Westwood ward, told us 'When the density of Bengalis increased in any area, we started calling it Bangla Para'. He recalled:

> After the Liberation War, gradually people started bringing their families and moved to these areas. No black [people] lived in these areas at that time. All were whites. Now the whites have gone. Once I asked them, 'Why are you leaving this place?' They replied that the scent of our curry spread to their houses, crossing [through] the walls.

Mohammed Aziz described the spread of the Bengali community across the town:

> Chadderton, Coldhurst, Westwood, Werneth Coppice – Bengalis lived in these areas. Some Bengalis are still there. Now Bengalis have increased in Coldhurst, Westwood areas. When Bengalis became concentrated in one area, some started calling it *Bangla Para*. . . . Now, we are all over the town. Bengalis are living everywhere.

Making home 121

As the communities became more established, visible institutions emerged – community centres, welfare associations, shops, and mosques. Abdul Jabbar, who worked in an advice centre as an interpreter from 1978 to 2000, described these developments and transitions:

> I settled myself in Oldham in 1963. When I first came to Oldham, there was a society – its name was 'Pakistan Association'. It was organized by people from East Pakistan and West Pakistan. . . . The society was run by a Bengali. . . . The Liberation War started . . . [and] we thought of starting a separate society. First we formed an Action Committee to help the freedom fighters. Then we organized the Bangladesh Welfare Association. This association still exists. In 1980, with Oldham Council for Race Equality, . . . we developed a community centre.

Mohammed Aziz helped form the Bangladesh Welfare Association in Oldham, which grew from the 1970s onwards. By the 1980s, it had established an institutional structure for the local Bengali community:

> I tried my best for the Oldham dwellers. For the Bangladeshi community, we built up a central Jamme Masjid, we've done a lot of community projects, we've built up Bangla schools, we built up a community centre. . . . At that time there was no community centre for Bangladeshis anywhere in England. . . . Oldham Welfare Association is one of the biggest welfare associations in England.

Slowly, as Abdul Jabbar noted with pride, the community established itself socially and culturally within the town:

> The Bengalis' achievements are: we built the first Shahid Minar outside Bangladesh[64] – this was in '80 – we built the Shapla Chhattar on the basis of our national flower. The council has borne all the expenses. We've developed an advice centre, an association was organized for the youth – Oldham Bangladesh Youth Association [established in 1978] – we've also built an organization for women. It is called the Bangladesh Women's Association.

Such changes are marked too in the religious institutions of the town, which were closely associated with the community organizations and activists. Mohammed Aziz told us:

> We came forward to solve the space problem in the Jamme Masjid. Earlier in Oldham, there was only one Jamme Masjid. It was difficult to provide a space for the people for prayer. Society is expanding very fast. Earlier, Oldham was a place for 700 Bengalis – now 15,000 Bengalis are living here. So we thought of building a mosque in every area. *Inshallah*, we now have 10 mosques in Oldham . . . We are trying to build a beautiful central mosque in Oldham.

The 'success' of the Oldham Bengali community derived in part from its partnership with the local town and metropolitan councils in the construction of these community institutions – something that is reflected too in Tower Hamlets – particularly in the heyday of British multicultural policy in the 1980s and 1990s. These institutional sources and supports are highly significant in thinking about how ethnic 'communities' take shape in particular locales and in conjunction with the activism of local people themselves.

It is also worth noting the role of Tower Hamlets as a source of both identification and distinction in the creation of a specifically northern/Oldham Bengali community identity; the community centre, the Shahid Minar, the Shapla Chhattar all stand as symbols of a nationally competitive and locally feted Bengali identity in opposition to other, particularly East London-based, communities and histories. Ethnicity and location thus stand in a creative tension with each other, and both underscore and undermine the role of simplistic appeals to ethnicity in the creation of 'community'.

While the Bengali community in Oldham has worked to consolidate and mark its presence in the town, it is also true that it has come under increasing pressures for change both internally – through expansion, regionalism, and the growth of a British-born second generation – and externally – in terms of broader structural changes around employment, intercommunity tensions, and increased segregation, particularly in the spheres of housing and education.[65] 'Community' here is not always understood by migrants themselves as an unmitigated 'good'. Nor do they necessarily see it as a clearly defined and bounded sense of belonging. Their accounts reflect, rather, processes of transformation, contestation, and often profound ambivalence, even (or perhaps especially) from those who were active in its formation. Thus, some of the 'pioneer migrants' recalled nostalgically the earlier sense of brotherhood and support which was lost as the community expanded. Tasarul Ali commented:

> We were united. . . . After families [came], people became busy with their families. They would also envy each other. But at that time, there was no enmity. We would go to each other's houses, eat over there, stay over there. Nobody would talk about money. There was no problem of 'is he from this *thana* or is he from that *thana*'.

Kamal noted that regional tensions had come to dominate and fracture local community political organizations and mark their engagement with local branches of mainstream political parties:

> Like with the Bangladesh Association, the council elections are dominated by regionalism. People from Nabiganj will give their votes to their candidate; Bishwanath people will give votes to their candidates. The candidate who has many people from his region will win the election. Candidates from another region will not win.

Intraregional identities worked to divide the community even in terms of religion. What can be read as a sign of strength can, then, also be seen as a sign and source of division and fragmentation. Hasib noted:

> Mostly [the people] are from Nabiganj and Bishwanath. There are many people from these districts. One mosque is enough . . . but they say 'in this mosque, Bishwanath people are coming, there is no one from my area. Let's build a mosque for Nabiganj'. It is like this.

The arrival of families coincided too with the closure of mills and increasing unemployment in all the northern mill towns and the search for alternative forms of employment.[66] Hasib described the challenges faced by the migrants:

> The mills were closing down and no alternative was emerging. It was because in every profession the one thing that was needed was education. But our people were not educated. . . . When the Bengalis saw all the employment was closing down, they were thinking what other things they could do. Bengalis are experts in new ideas. They found that there is one business that can be profitable and run forever – that is rice business. . . . Bengalis saw it as an easy business. It only needs labour, nothing else. If some profit remains after all the expenses, that is enough. That time, there were only two, three types of curry, not much. Now it is one of the biggest industries.

Rapid deindustrialization has left its mark on the Bengali community in Oldham and across the north,[67] entrenching the disadvantages faced by the pioneer migrants across the generations and largely unameliorated by the regeneration funding that took place in the major urban centres such as London (and Tower Hamlets). Set against a climate, both national and local, of increased racial tension, the backlash against multiculturalism and the rise of Far Right anti-immigrant and anti-Muslim groups in the North,[68] these social exclusions and inequalities became visible and tangible in the spring and summer of 2001 with the outbreak of violent unrest among the South Asian communities in Oldham. As with the antiracist and community activism of the late 1970s and 1980s in the wake of the murder of Altab Ali in East London, the events of 2001 were to mark a turning point in national discourses around the place of Muslims, migrants, and minorities in Britain, putting the mill towns' hitherto invisible Asian communities on the imaginative map of Britain and indelibly marking the Bengali community in South Asian Oldham and elsewhere.

From cohesive community to parallel lives: The 2001 'riots'

One weekend in late May 2001, 'riots' broke out in the Glodwick area of Oldham. In what *The Guardian* newspaper described as 'a weekend of race riots . . . which were the worst Britain has seen for 15 years',[69] an estimated 500 Asian Muslim young men took to the streets in angry protests, causing damage estimated at £1.4 million.[70] The unrest formed part of a chain of clashes that year across the northern mill towns of England, preceded by Bradford in April and followed by neighbouring Burnley and Leeds in June, returning again to Bradford for a spectacular finale in early July.[71]

At the national level, the repercussions of the violence were profound, shifting the tenor of discussions from the optimistic commitment to racial equality which had heralded New Labour's arrival to power in 1997[72] to an insistence on the need for a reinvigorated ideal of Britishness focused on 'shared norms and values'.[73] Pronouncements about the 'death of multiculturalism'[74] lay the blame for the disturbances on two decades of multicultural policies which had encouraged separation rather than integration. The events in Oldham are central to this new paradigm, as are the policies that have followed thick and fast in its wake.[75] Ted Cantle's report on the disturbances in Oldham, Burnley, and Bradford identified 'parallel lives' as their defining cause:[76]

> Separate educational arrangements, community and voluntary bodies, employment, places of worship, language, social and cultural networks means that many communities operate on the basis of parallel lives. These lives do not seem to touch at any point, let alone overlap and promote meaningful exchanges.[77]

The claims around segregation that underpin this analysis have been strongly criticized[78] for erasing the messier contours of separation and mutuality and the often-fraught textures of the events themselves.[79] These are often rooted in very local situations, histories, events, and micro-encounters, which can be lost from a broader focus on ethnicity, religion, and 'community'. In Oldham, for example, the context for the unrest can be traced both to longer histories of social marginalization linked particularly to employment and housing and to more recent tensions linked particularly to youth unemployment, crime, and policing and 'triggered' by the arrival of the National Front in the town in the month before the 'riots'.[80] While the events have resonance and consequences at a national level, then, they must also be placed within the context of a strong and emotional sense of local identity which imparted a powerful sense of ownership and belonging, of collective agency, and of community defence and which cut across gender and generation. Kamal Hossain, a restaurant worker in his thirties, traced the origins of the violence to the earlier mugging of pensioner Walter Chamberlain by a group of Asian young men in the town in April:[81]

> It began in 2000, but the real cause of the riot was an old white man . . . he was going along the road. Then some Asian boys beat him. They were Bengalis. The police rescued him and he was seriously injured. When he was hospitalized, the media photographed him and published it as a news story. . . . The BNP, British Nationalist Party, took it as an opportunity. They came to protest and demonstrate against it.

Tensions escalated. On the last weekend in May, after a football match in the town, violence broke out as crowds passed through the streets of Glodwick. Monsur Hossain commented:

> This is a main road to go to the stadium from the city. . . . Police could have put barricades on the side roads, which is the residential area. People live there. But they were allowed to go through the side roads, where Bengalis are living, and they [the racists] got their chance.

The football crowds contained many National Front members, who attacked the predominantly Asian homes. Mohammed Aziz described the initial events and the community response:

> Several times there were riots. With the help of the Pakistanis, we tried to resist the National Front. . . . They wanted to march in our areas, we prevented them . . . when they marched, they damaged houses on both sides of the streets and threw stones and broke window panes.

Similarly Kamal Hossain told us:

> There was a football game. They (the BNP) came with the team. While passing through the street, they kicked the doors, broke down some windows, they were shouting and making noise. All our boys and girls came out of the houses on all sides with the things they had . . . and chased the BNP people.

As the violence grew, however, clashes were not between Bangladeshis and the BNP or NF, but between Pakistani and Bangladeshi young men and the police. Mohammed Aziz noted:

> The clash did not happen with the National Front people; unfortunately it happened with the police. When our people gathered, the police told them not to gather. . . . They wanted our boys to leave the place. At one stage of the argument, clashes erupted. Our boys set fire to the police vehicle. But the way the media spread the news – it did not happen on that scale. The media exaggerated it.

Similarly Kamal Hossain, who had been out on the streets during the violence, perceived police–community tensions as at the heart of the way the events unfolded and escalated:

> Then a big number of police came. . . . The police escorted the BNP along the barricades to the railway station. Then the Bengalis started fighting with the police. . . . There were two to three thousand Bengalis, they came with banners to protest. . . . The police released dogs to chase the youth, and they arrested many people.

From this trigger event, the violence grew. Hasib told us:

> In Glodwick, they [Asian youth] set fire to tyres on the roads and blocked the area. News of the riot spread. . . . Some English people came out of a pub and entered into the Asian area – they broke into some houses, doors and windows, and also hurt a pregnant woman. Our boys did not take it lightly. It is impossible for anyone to take it lightly. That night they started rioting.

Kamal described what happened next:

> The next day, the riots started seriously. This was in Glodwick area. On one side, many whites came, and the Pakistani and Bengalis stood on the other side. The riot started with petrol bombs. The whites threw, and we also threw. . . . Fighting was intense. . . . After about three hours, police gathered. . . . Fighting continued for many hours.

Hasib noted, 'After two days, it calmed down. But there was huge damage. Vehicles were set on fire, houses were broken'. Kamal reflected, 'Bengalis gained nothing politically. The National Front gained something. In the election, National Front candidates got the white votes. They tried to win the Council election – they did not win, but only by a few votes'.[82]

Unlike the 1980s 'riots', which prompted large-scale regeneration of Britain's inner cities and which was to lead to the development of Banglatown in Tower Hamlets, the 2001 unrest has not generated investment. Partly as a consequence of the securitization and integration agendas that have dominated the UK's approach to immigration and 'community cohesion' in the subsequent decade, they marginalized still further Asian Muslim communities in the deindustrialized mill towns. Hasib noted that the events of 2001 had left a legacy of mistrust in the town:

> After the riot, for a year, we were in a panic situation. We were very cautious about other people . . . even if we went into town, we would feel insecure. Everyone was in a panic "anything might happen"! . . . Still this insecurity exists. Anytime, anything can happen.

Conclusion

Stories of arrival and of settlement, of building homes and community are necessarily unfinished, partisan, and partial. They are part of a longer process of claims-staking and of what Jane Jacobs has described as 'how people . . . come to dwell in diasporic identities and heterogeneous histories'.[83] As we will argue in Chapter 8, migration stories involve myths of origin that are oriented to the present as much as they account for the past and, as we will explore further in Chapters 6 and 7, reveal the ways in which ideas of 'community' and belonging are shaped, performed, and contested at the level of the everyday and the demotic.

Making home 127

This chapter has explored the formation of two iconic British Bengali 'communities' through the stories of Bengali pioneer migrants whose lives, histories, and experiences have shaped and been shaped by the process of arrival and of settlement, in spaces formed and transformed at the intersection of transnational, national, local encounters, and personal structures. This examination of these local histories shows that it is possible – and necessary – to trace the broad historical sweep of postwar British migration as it takes shape in particular places and at particular moments.

A comparison between Tower Hamlets and Oldham reveals, on the one hand, shared experiences of labour migration and deindustrialization, struggles against racism, and the routes and roots of community formation. But, on the other, it also suggests significant differences in the patterns and histories of settlement, encounters with majority and other minority groups, engagement with the state and the (changing) British political system. Community mobilization has followed different paths, and these have not always led to local regeneration. Whereas in Tower Hamlets it has created a platform to express visibility and confidence – however ambiguous and contested in reality – in Oldham, the Bengali presence remains perhaps less confident and less visible. However, both 'communities' have shaped both local places and national discourses in profound ways, politically, ideologically, and materially.

Placing 'community' – both spatially and temporally – challenges dominant inscriptions of ethnic minority communities as anachronistic and autonomous alien entities within the broader imagined nation. It recognizes the mutually constitutive formation of diaspora spaces and their integral location in a broader (and changing) social, historical, and political context. 'Community' is a site of engagement, of struggle, of exclusion, and of change. This is not simply to insist on the complexity of 'community' identity, but also to argue that it is *from* this process of struggle, engagement, and change that community identity emerges and is invested with emotional and symbolic significance. 'Community' is thus a place of 'being' and 'becoming', of space won and defended, of arrival and belonging, but also of embarkation and future journeys.

Notes

1 Shah Jalal is the saint who is believed to have brought Islam to Sylhet. We will hear more of him in Chapter 8.
2 This chapter is partly based on an article previously published in the *British Journal of Sociology*: see Claire Alexander, 'Making Bengali Brick Lane: Claiming and Contesting Space in East London', *British Journal of Sociology*, 62, 2, 2011, pp. 201–20.
3 Adams, *Across Seven Seas*.
4 Muhammed Anwar, *The Myth of Return: Pakistanis in Britain*, London: Heinemann, 1979.
5 Alexander, 'Making Bengali Brick Lane'.
6 Avtar Brah, 'The Scent of Memory: Strangers, Our Own and Others', *Feminist Review*, 61 (Spring) 1999, pp. 4–26.
7 Georgie Wemyss, *The Invisible Empire: White Discourse, Tolerance and Belonging*, Aldershot: Ashgate, 2009.

128 *Making home*

8 Janet Foster, *Docklands: Cultures in Conflict, Worlds in Collision*, London: UCL Press, 1999.
9 Tower Hamlets Council, 'Population: Key Facts, Research Briefing 2011–06', 2011: www.towerhamlets.gov.uk/idoc.ashx?docid=a2cee9aa-89ad-48d9-8cd2-00deef8128a4&version=1
10 Shadwell (52 per cent), Stepney Green (47 per cent), Bromley South (44 per cent), Mile End (42 per cent), Bromley North (42 per cent), Spitalfields and Banglatown (41 per cent), Poplar (41 per cent), Whitechapel (38 per cent), Bethnal Green (32 per cent), and Weavers (29 per cent): www.towerhamlets.gov.uk/lgsl/901–950/916_borough_profile/area_profiles.aspx
11 Tower Hamlets Council, 'Population'.
12 Tower Hamlets Council, 'Indices of Deprivation 2010, Research Briefing 2011–03', June 2011: www.towerhamlets.gov.uk/idoc.ashx?docid=7d09b443-cc9a-4913-bb2b-b0a88c654f49&version=-1
13 T. MacInnes, A. Parekh and P. Kenway *London's Poverty Profile, 2011*, London: Trust for London/New Policy Institute www.londonspovertyprofile.org.uk
14 See: www.towerhamlets.gov.uk
15 Tower Hamlets Council, Labour Market, Research Briefing 2013–09 (2013): www.towerhamlets.gov.uk/idoc.ashx?docid=bc69178d-55e2-45d9-alf0-860ba9bec713&version=1
16 John Eade, *Placing London: From Imperial Capital to Global City*, Oxford: Berghahn, 2000.
17 Eade, *Placing London*; Ed Glinert, *East End Chronicles: 300 Years of Mystery and Mayhem*, London: Penguin, 2005.
18 Eade, *Placing London*; K. Leech, *Brick Lane 1978: The Events and Their Significance*, Birmingham: AFFOR, 1980.
19 Michael Young and Paul Wilmott, *Family and Kinship in East London*, London: Routledge and Kegan Paul, 1957; Geoff Dench, Kate Gavron and Michael Young, *The New East End: Kinship, Race and Conflict*, London: Profile Books, 2006. See also Phil Cohen, *The Last Island*, London: Centre for New Ethnicities Research, 1998; Foster, *Docklands*; Les Back, '"Home from Home": Youth, Belonging and Place', in Alexander and Knowles (eds) Making Race Matter: Bodies, Space and Identity, Basingstoke: Palgrave, 2005.
The East End has also been the site of community studies of 'immigrant' communities, beginning with Banton's 1955 study through to Eade's analysis in 1989 in Tower Hamlet's Bangladeshi community. See Michael Banton, *The Coloured Quarter*, London: Jonathan Cape, 1955; and Eade, *Politics of Community*.
20 See Glinert, *East End Chronicles*, in which he devotes less than seven pages to the Bengali presence, which he dates from the 1960s – part of a chapter tellingly entitled 'Dark Ages'.
21 'Exploring Banglatown and the Bengali East End': www.towerhamlets.gov.uk/idoc.ashx?docid=780619a3-6997-43cf-8e6f-5b1d52fb4b20&version=-1
22 Adams, *Across Seven Seas*; Humayan Ansari, *The Infidel Within*, London: Hurst and Company, 2004; R. Visram, *Ayahs, Lascars, and Princes: Indians in Britain 1700–1947*, London: Pluto Press, 1986; Ullah and Eversley, *Bengalis*; Wemyss, *Invisible Empire*.
23 Adams, *Across Seven Seas*; Choudhury, *Roots*; Choudhury, *Sons*.
24 Adams, *Across Seven Seas*; Ullah and Eversley, *Bengalis*.
25 J. Eade, A. Ullah, J. Iqbal and M. Hey, *Tales of Three Generations of Bengalis in Britain*, London: Swadhinata Trust and CRONEM (Surrey and Roehampton Universities), 2006: www.swadhinata.org.uk/index.php?option=com_content&view=article&id=49&Itemid=53; Ullah and Eversley, *Bengalis*.
26 Adams, *Across Seven Seas*.
27 Rushanara Ali was elected as Labour MP for Bethnal Green and Bow in May 2010.
28 Husna Ara Begum's story is explored in more detail in Chapter 5.
29 Eade et al., *Tales*.

30 Ibid., p. 8.
31 See Chapter 7 for a more detailed discussion of these two significant institutions.
32 Eade, *Politics of Community*.
33 Ibid.
34 Ambalavaner Sivanandan, 'From Resistance to Rebellion: Asian and Afro-Caribbean Struggles in Britain', *Race and Class*, 23, 2/3, 1981/1982; Claire Alexander, 'Imagining the Politics of BrAsian Youth', in N. Ali, V. Kalra and S. Sayyid (eds) *A Postcolonial People: South Asians in Britain*, London: Christopher Hurst, 2006, pp. 258–71; Anandi Ramamurthy, *Black Star: Britain's Asian Youth Movements*, London: Pluto Press, 2013.
35 Michael Keith, *Race, Riots and Policing: Lore and Disorder in a Multiracist Society*, London: UCL Press, 1993; Solomos, *Race*.
36 Eade, *Politics of Community*.
37 Brah, 'Scent'; Alexander, 'Imagining'; Ramamurthy, *Black Star*.
38 Altab Ali and Ishaq Ali, both Bengali young men, were murdered by racists in Tower Hamlets in 1978. Michael Ferreira, an 18-year-old Guyanese mechanic, was murdered in a racist attack in Hackney the same year.
39 Leech, *Brick Lane*; Sivanandan, 'From Resistance'.
40 This is discussed further in Chapter 7
41 Leech, *Brick Lane*.
42 For further discussion of symbolic coffins taken out in procession in Bangladesh, see Chapter 6.
43 The 1991 Census recorded 85,738 Bangladeshis in London, with the largest percentage concentrated in Spitalfields (comprising 60.7 per cent of the ward). The next decade to 2001 saw a 79 per cent increase in the Bangladeshi population of London. Data Management and Analysis Group, *2001 Census Profiles: Bangladeshis in London*, London: GLA, 2004: http://legacy.london.gov.uk/gla/publications/factsandfigures/DMAG-Briefing2004-16-2001CensusProfilesBangladeshisinLondon.pdf
44 Eade, *Politics of Community*.
45 Eade et al., *Tales*.
46 Halima Begum, 'Commodifying Multicultures: Urban Regeneration and the Politics of Space in Spitalfields', PhD thesis, Department of Geography, Queen Mary and Westfield, 2004.
47 S. Carey, 'Curry Capital: The Restaurant Sector in London's Brick Lane', Working Paper No. 6, Institute of Community Studies, London, 2004.
48 The Metropolitan Borough was formed in 1974 and comprises the cities of Manchester and Salford and eight surrounding metropolitan boroughs. The total population of Greater Manchester is estimated at 2.6 million people (see Simon Jones, 'UK population estimates: how many people live in each local authority?', *Guardian*, 21 September 2010: www.theguardian.com/news/datablog/2010/sep/21/uk-population-local-authority). Of these, 8.5 per cent are from an ethnic minority.
49 Oldham Council, *2011 Census: Key Statistics for Oldham, Corporate Research and Intelligence Team*, 2012: www.vaoldham.org.uk/sites/vaoldham.org.uk/files/Census%202011%20key%20stats%20briefing%2014%20Dec%2012.pdf
50 L. Simpson and V. S. Gavalas, *Population Dynamics within Rochdale and Oldham: Population, Household and Social Change*, Manchester: Centre for Census and Survey Research, Manchester University, 2007.
51 Eade and Garbin, *Bangladeshi Diaspora*.
52 Virinder S. Kalra, *From Textile Mills to Taxi Ranks: Experiences of Migration, Labour and Social Change*, Aldershot: Ashgate, 2000.
53 Ibid.
54 This would include both West and East Pakistanis, so the numbers of Bengalis are not clear. Ibid.
55 Simpson and Gavalas, *Population Dynamics*.
56 Oldham Council, *2011 Census*.

130 *Making home*

57 Kalra, *From Textile Mills*; A. Kundnani, 'From Oldham to Bradford: The Violence of the Violated', London: Institute of Race Relations, 2001: www.irr.org.uk/news/from-oldham-to-bradford-the-violence-of-the-violated/
58 Simpson and Gavalas, *Population Dynamics*.
59 Nissa Finney and Kitty Lymperopoulou, *Local Ethnic Inequalities: Ethnic Differences in Education, Employment, Health and Housing in Districts of England and Wales, 2001–2011*, London: Runnymede Trust, 2014: www.runnymedetrust.org/uploads/Inequalities%20report-final%20v2.pdf
60 Eade and Garbin, *Bangladeshi Diaspora*.
61 Oldham Council, *Ward Profile 2014: Coldhurst*: www.oldham.gov.uk/download/downloads/id/2043/coldhurst_ward_profile
62 For other replica memorials, see Chapters 6 and 7.
63 Kalra, *From Textile Mills*.
64 See Chapter 7 for a further discussion of the Shahid Minar and *Ekushe* memorializations in Oldham and Tower Hamlets.
65 Simpson and Gavalas, *Population Dynamics*.
66 Kalra, *From Textile Mills*.
67 Ibid.; Kundnani, 'From Oldham'.
68 C. Alexander 'Re-Imagining the Asian Gang: Ethnicity, Masculinity and Youth after "The Riots"', *Critical Social Policy*, 24, 4, 2004, pp. 526–49.
69 Staff and agencies, 'Councillor's Home Suffers Petrol Bomb Attack', *Guardian*, 1 June 2001.
70 Home Office, *Community Cohesion* (The Cantle Report), London: HMSO, 2001a; Home Office, *Building Cohesive Communities*, London: HMSO, 2001b.
71 Chris Allen, *Fair Justice: The Bradford Disturbances, The Sentencing and The Impact*, London: Forum Against Islamophobia and Racism, 2003; Alexander 'Re-Imagining'.
72 Derek McGhee *Intolerant Britain? Hate, Citizenship and Difference*, Maidenhead: Open University Press, 2005.
73 Alexander, 'Re-Imagining'; Alexander 'Imagining'; A. Amin, *Ethnicity and the Multicultural City*, Report for Department of Transport, Local Government and the Regions, London: DTLG, 2002.
74 Arun Kundnani, A. *The Death of Multiculturalism*, London: Institute of Race Relations, 2002: www.irr.org.uk/news/the-death-of-multiculturalism/
75 Alexander, 'Re-Imagining'; C. Alexander, 'Re-Imagining the Muslim Community', *Innovation*, 11, 4, 1998; McGhee, *Intolerant Britain?*
76 Home Office, *Community Cohesion*.
77 Ibid., p. 9.
78 Nissa Finney and Ludi Simpson *Sleepwalking to Segregation?: Challenging Myths about Race and Migration*, Bristol: Policy Press, 2009.
79 Kundnani, 'From Oldham'; Amin, *Ethnicity*.
80 Kundnani, 'From Oldham'; Kalra, *From Textile Mills*; Alexander, 'Re-Imagining'.
81 Jeevan Vasagar and David Ward, 'The Five Words that Baffle Oldham's Asians', *Guardian*, 28 April 2001.
82 In the wake of the 'riots' that June, Nick Griffin, then leader of the British National Party, came third in the general election as candidate for Oldham West, gaining 16.4 per cent of the vote.
83 Jane Jacobs, *Edge of Empire: Postcolonialism and the City*, London: Routledge, 1996, p. 73.

5 'Always/already migrants'
Brides, marriage, and migration

Husna Ara Begum arrived in Britain with her children in the early 1970s. Husna, whom we encountered briefly in Chapter 4, was born in Sylhet in 1948 in the newly formed province of East Bengal in Pakistan. Her mother died when she was only six years old, and Husna grew up in an extended family compound with her father, uncles, and cousins. While she was still at school, her father and uncles arranged her marriage to a distant relative (the brother-in-law/*debor* of her cousin/*khalato bon*) who worked in the Foreign Service of the Pakistan government; in April 1966, they were married. Almost immediately, Husna moved away with her new husband, first to his family home in Sylhet, then to a posting to Lahore in West Pakistan, and next, in December of the same year, to Saudi Arabia. They lived there until 1970 and had three children before returning to West Pakistan shortly before the outbreak of the Liberation War in 1971.

Husna remembered the war as a very difficult time for Bengalis in West Pakistan:

> . . . our belongings were looted. The time was very hard, we were passing every moment with great anxiety with our three children. We had to whisper even when we were inside the house. If I had to go out, I had to wear a burkha just to hide myself so that they (the Pakistanis) wouldn't know if I was Bengali or Pakistani.

After five months the family flew back to Saudi Arabia, where for nine months they were held in the Pakistani Embassy under house arrest. After the war ended in 1972, Husna's family, along with another sixteen Bengali families working at the Embassy, were put on a ship to Bangladesh, arriving in Chittagong in April. From there, they travelled first to Dhaka and then to Sylhet, where 'everyone . . . was amazed to see us. Nobody recognized who we were'. Her children found the new country ('home') strange and unsettling.

At the end of 1972, the family was on the move again. Husna's husband was transferred to the new Bangladesh High Commission in London, where she and the children later joined him. After a year living in Surrey, the family moved to Tower Hamlets, East London, where she still lives.

132 *'Always/already migrants'*

Asked about her recollections of her arrival in Britain, Husna remembers being one of comparatively few Bengali Muslim women. She recalled:

> At that time, there were not many Bengali families living in the UK. Most of the people who were here were single. We could not get Bangladeshi food items. There were no Bangladeshi food shops at that time. We could not get *desi* fish. . . . There were only a few Bengalis living in the area. Gradually [our numbers] grew. . . .

The area was riven with racial tensions, with the National Front attacking the new arrivals:

> We had to face skinheads. They created lots of problems for us. They used to call us 'Paki'. From 1975–1977, they used to beat us wherever they could get us. The situation changed when our children, our boys were grown up. They started to resist, and after that the skinheads started to move. We forced them to leave the area.

But Husna adapted to her new circumstances, taking up work as a sewing machinist for local Turkish and Jewish tailors:[1]

> It was difficult to run a family with the earnings of only one member of the family. . . . I had to learn how to work and then found a job. . . . I worked for twelve years. I did not work outside, I worked at home. I worked for Turkish and Jewish people. They would bring the clothes and I would do the work. In the morning they would bring them, and the day after they would come to pick them up.

Her husband left the foreign service of Bangladesh and was employed as a supervisor in a local glass factory until he retired.

After her husband died in 1995, Husna stayed on in East London with her married children and grandchildren. In the course of her much-travelled life, she has lived longer in Tower Hamlets than in any other place. But she often visited Bangladesh, where the family had a house, and was in regular touch with relatives in Canada, the United States, and Europe. She was actively involved with local Bangladeshi community-based and political organizations such as the Nirmul Committee, the Bangladesh Mohila Awami League, and Jagonari, a women's organization. Her home in Tower Hamlets is a hub for local Bengali activists. Looking back on her life, she reflected:

> We all participated in the demonstrations in different places. We also encouraged people to go to schools, to learn English to have the tools for survival. . . . Everything has changed now. The place has turned into Banglatown, where [before] it was difficult for us to go out at night time. We were very afraid at that time. But we did not sit idle, we fought against them a lot. Going through

all the troubles and fight has made this area 'Banglatown'. Happiness comes after great sorrow.

Bibi Hawa's story could hardly have been more different. She has lived in the Rajshahi district in Bangladesh, on the border of West Bengal and northwestern Bangladesh, since partition. One of only five children who survived early childhood, Hawa was named after Eve when her mother's prayer for a daughter was answered:

> She gave birth to six boys, but only two survived. After that, she couldn't get any more children. For five whole years she prayed and prayed, asking Allah to give her a daughter, and that if her wish was fulfilled she'd name her Hawa after the first woman Allah created. And I was born.

Now in her seventies, Hawa was twelve years old when independence and partition divided Bengal and her family moved from Indian Chapai (in Malda) to East Bengal. Unlike Husna, who had a precise recall of dates, Hawa was unsure of the date of her marriage, which was arranged by her paternal uncle. But she remembered the wedding itself vividly: 'For my wedding two cows and two goats were killed; we also had *pithas* [rice cakes], *pulao* [savoury rice], and *roshogulas* [sweetmeats] and invited about fifty people'. Like Husna, she remembers leaving her father's home straight after her marriage: 'A cart pulled by buffalos was brought in . . . and we rode [by cart] all the way to Kandopur in the Birol district where my in-laws lived'.

Bibi Hawa had two children – a son and a daughter. They lived in Birol for six years before the family sold their land and bought a larger plot some miles away:

> Land there was very expensive, so we sold off our land and bought, with the price we got for it, double the land here. He had 25 *bighas* there and each *bigha* sold for 1,200 *takas*; we got our *bighas* here for 600 *takas* each. So we bought 50 *bighas* here.

Theirs was one of the many Chapai families (see Chapter 2) who did well after partition, but their modestly prosperous world was ripped apart in 1971. During the Liberation War, Hawa's husband, father-in-law, and brothers-in-law were all killed:

> It was a Wednesday morning. People came in and *gheraoed*[2] him and said they would call a meeting. They tied him and his brothers and father and put a handkerchief on their mouths and then shot them one by one. They killed my father-in-law, my husband, and three of his brothers. Then they stole our cows and our cart. . . .
>
> They said they were *mukti joddhas* [freedom fighters], Bengalis, the group of them – whoever they were, they were *Saitan* [evil]. The locals helped them. We were from India. The locals must have thought that if our menfolk

got killed, they would usurp our land. The Indian army saved the rest of us. Those *mukta bahinis*[3] killed 139 people round here . . . [they] thought we'd return to India and they'd take over our lands and hearths.

Hawa witnessed the men of her family being dragged out of the house: she later found their corpses on the outskirts of the village, memories which continued to haunt her. She survived, somehow bringing up her children. When we met her, she lived with her married son, Ghazi, a landholding cultivator in his forties, whom we met in Chapter 3.

Gendering the Bengal diaspora

Their very different histories and experiences notwithstanding, the stories of Husna Ara Begum and Bibi Hawa reveal much about the shaping of diaspora and community that has often been overlooked or erased. As Chapter 1 underlines, many intra-regional migrants in South Asia itself were women moving in the context of marriage. Early postwar migration to Britain, as Chapter 4 shows, was dominated by men, but from the mid-1970s, the arrival of women and children heralded the formation of permanent 'communities' that were to transform the landscape of multicultural Britain.[4] Migrants from South Asia moving for marriage remain a significant proportion of contemporary non-EU migration:[5] they are a key target of legislation and the focus of much anxiety about the effects and imagined failures of migration and multiculturalism.

Yet migrant wives have been silent and invisible in these debates. Pushed to the margins of history in Britain and South Asia alike, they are seen as the objects rather than subjects of social change, the collective and opaque backdrop to the agency of male migrants. This is also true of 'left-behind wives'[6] who brought up their children in the villages back home. In Britain, race and class have compounded their marginalization. Constructed, as they were, as 'third world woman', they were doubly 'othered' through inscriptions of patriarchal control and cultural pathology. As Mohanty has argued, this 'othering' produces the image of an 'average third world woman' who:

> leads an essentially truncated life based on her feminine gender (read: sexually constrained) and being 'third world' (read: ignorant, poor, uneducated, tradition-bound, religious, domesticated, family-oriented, victimized etc.).[7]

At the same time, and integral to this construction, migrant wives – notably those living in the West – appear as the collective embodiment of 'culture' and 'community', the personification of cultural difference. Viewed as being located within and contained by the boundaries of 'community' and outside broader historical and social processes, they are seen as both the source of the replication of this difference and as its victims.[8] This construct is most apparent in debates about international migration, where, for over forty years, 'family migration' (where women are most usually positioned) has been at the centre of political concerns and increasingly draconian controls on immigration. In Britain, family migration from South Asia has been defined by moral panics about arranged, forced, or 'sham' marriages and placed at the heart of the perceived failures of multiculturalism.[9]

South Asian *Muslim* wives have been the particular focus of concerns about the 'self-segregation' of immigrants and their 'parallel lives'. While their entry into Britain in significant numbers in the 1970s and 1980s transformed previously all-male Bengali communities beyond recognition, these changes were not always viewed as positive by the host society. Rather, these migrant brides were believed to have arrived in Britain carrying 'culture' with them in their tatty suitcases,[10] retaining inappropriate 'traditional' cultural and religious practices which created barriers to integration, 'imported poverty',[11] and inculcated values in their children that placed them at odds with 'British values'. It is perhaps hardly surprising, then, that legislation to control marriage migration has disproportionately targeted women[12] through 'virginity testing', 'primary purpose' legislation, laws raising the legal age for marriage for foreign spouses, language testing, and, most recently, income requirements.[13]

Scholars have consistently questioned this positioning of women as the incarnation of the nation, the symbol of culture and its borders, and the carriers of cultural values.[14] The view that South Asian women in particular are more deeply 'acculturated' than men draws, however, upon a long history. In the early 19th century, the British viewed Indian wives as the victims of barbaric religious and cultural practices such as *sati* and justified (then as now) imperial expansion as 'saving' Indian women from their menfolk. At the turn of the 19th century, elite nationalist men in India, for their part, saw (Hindu) wives as the epitome of a national, civilizational, or communal culture, variously imagined, and regarded the homes they managed as sacred spaces of cultural authenticity.[15] In much the same period, British plantation owners across the empire urged the colonial government to arrange the migration of 'decent' Indian women to join indentured male 'coolies' as a 'civilizing' influence, their role being to 'tame' the unruly male workforce and turn it into a respectable, law-abiding, traditional, god-fearing community. This mirrored the reaction of authorities in the 'sugar colonies', where concerns about 'social instability' and high rates of crime were believed to endorse the planters' view of the problem and its solution.[16] Similarly, the arrival of the white 'memsahibs' in South Asia after the Rebellion of 1857 was seen as a critical turning point, changing the fluid, even cosmopolitan, world of the Company era, with its interracial sexual liaisons, hybrid cultures, and mixed-race offspring, into the racially segregated colonial societies of the late 19th and early 20th centuries.[17] The prescriptive views of border guardians in the post-imperial world thus draw on a long history of overlapping imperial and racial attitudes, nationalist ideas, and pervasive stereotypes about gender.

Central to all of these policies – imperial, national, and post-imperial – is the idea of 'culture' as a body of practices performed and reproduced by women, and particularly by wives and mothers, generation after generation, homogenous and unchanging. Men, by contrast, are viewed as more tenuously linked to their 'culture' and more easily decoupled from it when they travel abroad. It is revealing, for example, that it was almost exclusively men who were labelled as 'economic migrants', responding rationally to market forces, while women migrants were inextricably linked to marriage and family, even if travelling as single, working migrants – as in Visram's richly textured portrait of Indian *ayahs* (nannies) in imperial Britain. Women have been consistently positioned as 'cultural' migrants; indeed, this was the very term by which colonial census officers categorized women who migrated to live with their 'economic' migrant husbands.[18] Women appear solely as 'dependents', as secondary, even second-hand, migrants, who travel in the wake of male migrant pioneers, usually in the guises of bride, wife, and mother of dependent children, and the harbingers of (often unwanted) permanent settlement.

Such representations draw upon (and reinscribe) ideas of racially gendered marginality, victimhood, and powerlessness in ways that deny the role of women migrants as active agents in their own lives and as participants in the formation and transformation of cultures, communities, and nations at both ends of the migration process. These gendered discourses about international marriage migration have had the effects of masking and simplifying the more numerous and quite different experiences of women, like Bibi Hawa, whose lives are marked by smaller (though in no sense more mundane) circuits of migration.[19] It also ignores the agency of women who travel internationally, such as Husna Ara Begum, whose experiences and contributions spill beyond the definitional limits ascribed to them as 'brides/wives'.

This chapter draws on the life stories of Bengali Muslim women like Husna and Hawa, both in Britain and in South Asia, to challenge these crude but remarkably pervasive constructs. It explores the journeys of numerous women migrants which are linked to, but not limited by, their experience of marriage. It draws attention to the agency of brides and migrant wives and their capacity to generate cultural change. We show that not only do these women re-create and transform the more intimate spaces of 'home', they also act in communities and engage with the state, sometimes evading and at other times resisting its various forms of power.

Our focus is thus on the agency of women at all these levels. But we do not assume that their actions are unconstrained by broader structures, whether social, political, or economic. We acknowledge that marriage is a key structuring force in female migration but show how this changed over time – and through the process of migration itself – with women playing a part in driving these changes. We recognize the central role of marriage, historically and today, as a *rite de passage* in the lives of most South Asian women – both symbolically and geographically. Yet we also examine the ways in which the category of 'bride' was experienced and contested by brides themselves.

The category of 'bride', we suggest, should be reconfigured to recognize women's role as agents of transformation. Like Charsley and Shaw, we argue that marriage migration sheds light on 'transnationalism from below' and that it is 'an important mechanism for the production and transformation of transnational networks'.[20] But we go further and contend that marriage itself, in virilocal societies, should be understood as a particular and significant form of mass migration worthy of analysis in its own right.[21] We suggest that marriage practices and affinal relationships have been transformed not only by the scale, distance, and pace of contemporary migration but by the attitudes and aspirations of women.

This chapter begins with a historical introduction to marriage in Bengal between 1940 and 1980. We then go on to explore, through the stories of some of the women we met, how processes of change (sometimes already under way 'at home') were intensified and accelerated by migration. The chapter examines the complex tensions between wider structures – whether transnational, national, or 'communal' – and the agency of our respondents. We contend that it is only by understanding these tensions and their intersection with the further dimension of temporality – of changes over time – that a more nuanced account of gendered migration can emerge.

'**Meyebela**' *or girlhood: A preparation for migration*

The women in our study were all born in South Asia in a region that included the districts of eastern Uttar Pradesh (formerly the United Provinces), the Indian states of Bihar and West Bengal, and East Bengal (later East Pakistan and Bangladesh). Most were born between 1940 and 1980 and grew up predominantly (though not exclusively) in Muslim households and experienced 'girlhood' between 1950 and 1990.

In this period 'girlhood', we suggest, was a transitional life stage bracketed by childhood and by marriage. It was a period of apprenticeship for marriage that transformed the girl, by the end of which she achieved full personhood as a married woman. In virilocal Bengal, the end of girlhood almost inevitably heralded migration to the husband's natal home – just as Hawa and Husna travelled immediately after their marriages, so too did millions of women in the region. Girlhood thus prepared girls not only for marriage but for migration.

To untangle the complex relationships between marriage, migration, and culture, the expectations and experience of girlhood during this period need to be teased out. The sources that historians of migration use throw little light on this history. Census officers would mention the number of these marriage migrations, but say little else about the women, let alone children. Where individual female migrants did feature, these were invariably women whom the census officers regarded as 'deviant' and who rejected their ascribed family role: women who had run away, been abandoned, expelled, or widowed, or had turned to sex work or other forms of labour to survive. District gazetteers were no more informative. Standard chapters about 'the people' of a district said little about wives and children. While there might be the occasional observation about how village elders dealt with young women who broke the rules of caste and marriage and who were thus also, in some senses, 'deviant', they remained silent about the millions of women who, at least overtly, did not transgress their roles and status. Young girls were even less visible to the colonial ethnographer.

The picture that follows, then, is constructed necessarily from patchy source materials: anthropological treatises, little-known village studies by missionaries, and even reports on the spread of infectious diseases. Admittedly it is partial, but nonetheless it provides a starting point, or moment of comparison, for the stories of our migrant brides and begins to enable us to map processes of social and cultural change over space and time.

The first point is that the norms for the socialization of girls and expectations of their behaviour across the region were widely shared. Irawati Karve's classic study of kinship in India in 1968 posited 'a north-Indian region' across which rules of marriage were 'essentially similar', arguing that its 'first rule' was that while 'the man lives with his patri-kin among whom he is born and reared . . . the woman . . . spends her life, except for her few childhood years, with her affinal family with whom she is not acquainted up to the moment of her marriage'.[22] Marriage for girls involved *living among strangers*.

Although anthropologists have subsequently questioned some of the details of Karve's model,[23] the broad picture of a 'North Indian' set of norms of marriage holds true for the region in which our study took place. The normative expectation for girls was that they would marry and leave the parental home for the house of their in-laws at (or before) puberty. This was the case for Muslim and Hindu girls alike. Rules of consanguinity differed between the communities: caste Hindus were expected to avoid marriage to anyone removed by less than seven degrees from their father and five degrees from their mother.[24] Muslim families were expected to observe Quranic proscriptions on incest and exogamy.[25]

Village studies conducted during the period suggest that older girls spent years being prepared for marriage. In the late 1960s, they suggest, young girls enjoyed 'childhood' and were allowed to run around the village playing games as much as male children until about the age of seven or eight. But in Bengal, they may well have been rocked to sleep as infants to a popular lullaby evoking their impending dislocation: *'Dol, dol, duluni, ranga mathaye chiruni, bor ashbe ekhuni, niye jabe takhuni'* ('Rock, rock, little bride, with your forehead adorned, your groom is about to arrive, and he will take you away'). Then, at about the age of eight, they entered 'girlhood', a state described evocatively by Taslima Nasrin in her eponymous autobiography, *Meyebela*:

> In this house [in the village where her family fled in 1971], the girls my age were wrapped in saris. . . . At dawn they let out the ducks and hens. They lit the stove, ground spices, used the *dheki* to remove the husks from the rice, and poured the rice onto a wicker basket to shake it clean.
> 'Want to play hopscotch?' I asked. *They smiled but did not move.*[26]

Arens and Van Beurden also witnessed this transition from *chhelebela* – the Bengali word for childhood, which, interestingly and tellingly, translates literally as 'boyhood' – to *meyebela* (girlhood), a term coined by Nasrin herself.[27] In the village of Jhagrapur in Bangladesh, in 1974–1975:

> We saw several girls going through these changes during the year we were in Jhagrapur. Girls who in the beginning had been running around freely, often

naked breasted and wearing only a skirt, had become little ladies by the end of the year, restricting their exuberancy [while] waiting to be married off.[28]

By the age of eight, girls began to perform domestic chores, and their mobility was increasingly restricted as they learned what it was to be a proper woman and future wife.[29] In the Bangladeshi village of Char Gopalpur, for instance, 'young girls spent most of their childhood learning work roles, skills, and tasks that constitute the women's share of the division of labour. The process is largely one of learning by doing'.[30] Girls were given some schooling, but this largely consisted of learning how to read the Quran and write. Any further education was 'regarded as redundant, if not harmful for a happy married life'.[31] After menarche, their movement outside the home was restricted even further, and most adolescent girls stopped going to school altogether.[32]

After the onset of puberty, they were subject to 'strict sexual segregation, close supervision and physical seclusion from the world outside'.[33] Young men, by contrast, were expected to stay in the villages in which they were born and to uphold the norms and status of their paternal families. In their childhood and adolescence, they roamed the village and pastures, playing games; and as adolescents and young adults, they visited the local market town to go the cinema, to go shopping, to visit relatives or to attend political meetings.[34] In the Bengal region, young men typically married much later in life than girls, usually in their twenties (see Table 5.1).

The restriction on the movement of young women outside the home was, as Miranda notes, because 'girls' sexual coming of age [was regarded as] potentially explosive, adolescent girls being highly vulnerable to their own and others' volatile sexual impulses'.[35] The bride was expected to arrive at her husband's house as a virgin: the critical moment of marriage being *kanya-daan*, or 'the gift of the virgin', by one family to another.[36] Hence the bride's chastity had to be carefully guarded and her sexuality policed until the handover.

With marriage came the bride's departure from her parents' home. The marriage rites for the bride and her family were marked by the sadness of her imminent departure and exile – and the traditional tears shed by the bride and the women from her paternal home[37] – signalled the loss and rupture involved in her transformation into a new adult person with a different role in an altogether strange and unfamiliar household. As with Hindus, it was expected that Muslim girls would, upon marriage, travel to another village to live with their husbands

Table 5.1 Mean age at marriage, by sex and economic class, Char Gopalpur, 1976.

Mean age at marriage	Large landowners	Small landowners	Landless
Male	21.9	23.2	23.0
Female	13.9	13.5	13.1

Source: Mead T. Cain, 'The Household Life Cycle and Economic Mobility in Rural Bangladesh', *Population and Development Review*, 4, 3, September 1978, p. 435.

and in-laws.[38] The status of '*ghor jamai*' (a son-in-law who lives with his wife's parents) was highly unusual, and regarded, in most cases, as deeply shameful:[39] A detailed study conducted in the Matlab area of Bangladesh showed that only between 1 and 5 per cent of all male migrants migrated in the context of marriage (see Table 5.3). Cross-cousin marriage, widely prevalent in southern India,[40] and marriage within the *biradari* or *kunba* (clan), as practised in parts of Pakistan,[41] was comparatively rare. In Char Gopalpur in Mymensingh, Cain noted that between 1976 and 1978, 71 per cent of all married women were born outside the village. Families in the village observed 'a preference for lineage and village exogamy [that] attenuates a woman's ties with her family of birth and reduces the possibility that her family will intervene on her behalf after her marriage'.[42]

This pattern of marriage migration demanded that young brides swiftly acculturate in their new settings. As Fruzetti's study shows, on arrival in their *shashur-bari* (in-laws' home), brides were clearly expected to *relearn* their duties and responsibilities as wives, mothers, daughters-in-law, and household workers. They had to adopt the ways of their husbands' lineages' and *learn* their particular *niyom koron* (codes of conduct). The new bride had to learn the *stri achars* (the rites performed by married women: *stri*) of that household, which were often different from such rites in her father's home; and from which, as an unmarried girl (*kumari*), she would in any event have been excluded.[43] She would be instructed in her household duties by her *shashuri* (mother-in-law) from the very day of her arrival: 'In the course of the first day, the *shashuri* will specify what she wants the bride to do in the *shongshar* (household)'s daily work and how she expects her to behave towards the people of the house'. The mother-in-law would decide, for instance, whether the new bride should cover her head in the presence of the elder males of the house and how to greet her husband every time he entered or left the house.[44]

'Acculturation' for the girl-bride thus began anew in her husband's household and village. This requirement to expect change, to learn to labour, and to adopt the ways of the husband's household was reinforced by the fact that marriages, for women, were expected to be hypergamous. In Bangladesh, the pattern of female neighbourhood migration showed a marked preference for girls from certain districts to marry men from particular neighbouring districts where 'high status' grooms were available.[45]

But this is not to suggest that marriage practices did not change over time, nor that there were no significant variations over class and region. For one thing, over time, lines between Muslim and Hindu practices seem to have blurred. Maulana Thanawi, the Deoband-trained Islamic theologian, wrote his religious manual, the *Bahishti Zewar* ('Heavenly ornaments'), in the 1930s precisely to urge North Indian Muslim wives to give up the practices of marriage borrowed from Hindus and other nonbelievers.[46] But his exhortations appear not to have been heeded. In the early 1970s, Miranda noted among the Muslims of Bangladesh 'a certain extent of mimesis', with upwardly mobile Muslims adopting many Brahmanical taboos in relation to marriage practices.[47] When Fruzetti conducted her own fieldwork in Bengal in the late 1970s, she concluded that practices were widely shared by Muslims and Hindus. The very fact that Thanawi's *Bahishti Zewar* is still given as a bridal gift to millions of South Asian Muslim women and that his Tablighi movement is so strong in Bangladesh (see Chapter 3) suggests that anxieties about Muslim women's superstitious (Hindu) ways still resonate powerfully in the region. However, in one respect the difference was pronounced: 'Muslim first marriages [were] dissolved almost twice as frequently as non-Muslim (that is, essentially Hindu) first marriages. Moreover, while three in five of all Muslim widows and divorcees remarried, only one in five Hindu women did so.[48] This suggests that many Muslim women embarked on new journeys and forged new relationships later in life if they remarried, and this gave them some room for manoeuvre in their personal lives. Bibi Hawa's decision to remain a single widow might then be read not as an act ordained and scripted by 'culture' but as an expression of choice.

Another change – gradual but nonetheless noteworthy – was in the age of marriage. In 1947–1950, the average age at first marriage for girls in Bangladesh was 11.7 years.[49] This rose gently over the next three decades. Between 1971 and 1975, it rose more rapidly (not least due to the dislocations of the 1971 Liberation War and the famine of 1974–1975). By 1975, the average age for girls at marriage had reached 14.8 years (see Table 5.2). According to the Bangladesh Fertility Survey, about one in five of all marriages between 1971 and 1975 involved girls aged twelve or younger, so the sharper rise of the mean age suggests that many marriages involved girls or women who were significantly older than the average.[50]

The age of marriage also varied across regions, in general rising 'as one proceeds from the west to the east of Bangladesh' – and in Sylhet it was as many as ten points[51] higher than in western districts. Miranda also notes differences in the age of marriage between towns and cities – the Census of 1974 showed that urban girls married much later, with a mean age of 17.6 years.[52]

Another important change was in the distances travelled by brides upon marriage. As Hannah Bradby has argued, and as we underline, 'womanhood implies travel'.[53] But over time, the distances travelled by married women grew longer. In Bangladesh itself, the extent of interdistrict female migration increased, with

Table 5.2 Mean age at first marriage by year of marriage, for females.

Year of marriage	*Age at first marriage*
1947–1950	11.7
1951–1955	12.0
1956–1960	12.1
1961–1965	12.9
1966–1970	13.8
1971–1975	14.8

Source: Miranda, *Demography*, p.85.

Table 5.3 Immigrants and emigrants by sex and major categories of reasons for migration, Matlab, 1978.

Reasons given	Immigrants Males		Immigrants Females		Emigrants Males		Emigrants Females	
	Number	%	Number	%	Number	%	Number	%
Dependent movement	809	36%	1,240	45%	1,009	30%	1,738	49%
Independent movement	1,418	64%	1,505	55%	2,402	70%	1,828	51%
– due to marriage and marriage disruptions	17	1%	892	33%	14	e	1,149	32%
– due to work and better living conditions	792	36%	493	18%	2,139	63%	630	18%
– return migration	532	24%	80	3%	153	4%	27	1%
–other reasons	77	3%	39	1%	96	3%	22	e
All reasons	2,227	100%	2,744	100%	3,411	100%	3,566	100%

e = less than 5%

Source: *ICCDR Demographic Surveillance System*, Vol. VII, p. 36, cited in Miranda, *Demography*, p. 211.

a sharp trend upwards from the 1970s onwards. The Bangladesh Census of 1974 showed that in several districts, Sylhet included, women made up between a third and two-thirds of all interdistrict migrants.[54] The assumption that most of these female migrants were women moving between their parents' villages and their husbands' villages is borne out by the more fine-grained results of the surveys carried by an unlikely source: the International Centre for Diarrhoeal Disease Research (ICCDR) in the Matlab area of Comilla. Between 1968 and 1978, the ICCDR collected data continuously in a 'trial area' covering 228 villages with a population of approximately 270,000 people. The survey classified immigrants and emigrants in the 'trial area' according to the reasons they had given for their movement. These are set out in Table 5.3. Notably, women who had migrated as 'dependents' on account of marriage or due to disruptions in marriage made up the great majority of all female migrants.

As this survey shows, female migration *outstripped* that of males in the Matlab area. To be sure, most of these women travelled as 'dependents' and in the context of marriage, but their journeys were no less significant for that. Furthermore, the data from Matlab encourage us to rethink marriage migration to take into account the significance of 'marriage disruptions'. These studies – admittedly small but nonetheless exceptionally detailed – suggest a redrawing of conventional images of what a 'typical' migrant looks like and a need to recognize the huge presence of women in the migration process at different life stages.

The laws of property and inheritance both constrained and informed women's choices. While Muslim family law entitled women to a half-share of that which their brothers inherited from their fathers, every study suggests that in practice, even in the 1970s and 1980s, most Muslim women renounced their share of their paternal inheritance so as not to lose the goodwill and support of their brothers.[55] After their husbands' deaths, women were entitled by religious law to an eighth-share of their deceased husband's property, but they were not always able to claim it. Cain's studies of Char Gopalpur in Mymensingh district show how widows all too often were reduced to vagrancy and begging in order to survive.[56] Yet the fact that 'marriage disruption' was so significant a factor in movement, about one of five of all marriages dissolved, and, among Muslims, six out of ten widows and divorcees remarried[57] suggests the importance of change and flux in the lives of brides and married women.

As our respondents' stories show, the lives of Bengali brides in the post-partition era were at once prescribed and uncharted. They were shaped by broader cultural continuities around expected gendered roles – but women did not always play the roles expected of them. Social change – as reflected in the increased age of marriage and the greater distances women travelled, the uncertain boundaries between cultural and religious norms and practices, and the ways in which norms of one religious community tended to leak into the other – allowed space for more varied personal aspirations, experiences, and expectations of the groom, his family, and, of course, the bride herself. As the stories that follow will demonstrate, the idea(l)s of 'culture' and normative 'tradition', which so often define and constrain how women migrants are understood, needs to be both recognized and treated with caution since they are only one part of a complex and changing picture.

Unsettled lives, unsettled times: Borders, states, marriage, and migration

Migration also entails encounters with other structural forces which place migrants within larger historical and social landscapes. The women in our cohort lived in profoundly unsettled times. Their journeys were sometimes prompted by, and at other times had to negotiate through, the nation-making and state-building taking place all around them. The new borders of South Asia affected all migrants but had particular implications for women.

The briefest overview shows the pace and scale of border-making in this period. In 1947, the Radcliffe line divided Bengal.[58] To begin with, the new borders were porous, but authorities on both sides sought (with different degrees of urgency) to control them. In 1952, passports and visas for travel between the two countries were introduced.[59] In 1955, India enacted citizenship laws which created a hierarchy of rights, ruling out citizenship for persons who had at any point migrated to Pakistan or been domiciled there. Pakistan had legislated along the same lines four years earlier in 1951. In 1965, India and Pakistan fought a brief war, and in 1968 both nations promulgated 'enemy' property ordinances which gave the state draconian powers to seize property owned by an 'enemy'. India defined 'an enemy' as any Muslim who had migrated from India to Pakistan in the wake of partition, and Pakistan, for its part, deemed any Hindu or Sikh who had migrated to India as the same. The enemy acts applied to all their territories, bringing East Pakistan, West Bengal, Assam, and Tripura within their remit. Long after the wars of 1965 and 1971 had ended, the acts in both countries continued to be strengthened by amendment, and the laws remain in force to this day. These laws made it more difficult than ever before for people to move. They also made it hazardous for people to maintain contact with relatives on the other side since fraternizing with 'the enemy' across the border could render their property liable to seizure.[60]

In 1972, after its breakaway from Pakistan and a war that produced 10 million refugees, Bangladesh enacted its own Vested Property Ordinance mirroring the provisions of the evacuee and enemy property acts of its neighbours, with calamitous implications for its large Hindu population and also for its Urdu-speaking (so-called 'Bihari') minorities.[61] For its part, the Indian government sought in 1972 to repatriate every single refugee from East Pakistan in one of the most wide-ranging acts of *refoulement* in the past century.[62] Since the 1980s, India has expended huge sums to build a high security border fence to keep out Bangladeshi immigrants who, some believe, threaten to 'swamp' the country.

Yet, despite this, it remains possible to cross the Radcliffe line, particularly (though not only) for women. As Sur notes, both states' construction of women as 'infantile victims or docile citizens' has constrained but also enabled women's movements across the border zone, permitting degrees of 'illegal but licit' movement, particularly for marriage.[63] In Bangladesh, from the 1980s onwards, the government placed a range of legislative measures onto the statute book to prevent the migration of women as independent labour migrants, but marriage migration was exempted from these restrictions.[64]

Meanwhile, Britain has steadily strengthened its own borders in the postwar period. Even as the British Nationality Act of 1948 allowed free entry to the UK to 'Citizens of the UK and Colonies' (CUKC) and 'Citizens of Independent Commonwealth Countries' (CICC),[65] informal controls put a ceiling on their numbers.[66] In 1962, the Commonwealth Immigrants Act restricted the entry of, particularly, 'unskilled' Commonwealth citizens for settlement and employment. Prospective immigrants had to obtain an employment voucher from the Ministry of Labour before being allowed into Britain – creating the 'voucher system' of which so many of our interviewees in Britain spoke.

South Asian migration was increasingly seen as unwelcome, and legislation was targeted at this group. In June 1964, a 'standstill' was placed on new 'non-priority' applications for labour vouchers from India and Pakistan.[67] The 1968 Commonwealth Immigrants Act restricted the entry into Britain of Asians from East Africa who had UK citizenship to 1,500 heads of families and their dependents.[68] Whereas the 1962 Act preserved the absolute right of entry for the wife and children under sixteen of any Commonwealth citizen, new legislation undermined this right, although such children could be admitted on a discretionary basis.[69] In 1971, a new Immigration Act decreed that only 'patrials' were to have the right of abode in the UK.[70] Nonpatrials, meanwhile, now required leave to enter the UK – something that impacted heavily on wives and children 'back home', curtailed the circular movement of male migrants, and led to the wave of family migration from Bangladesh to Britain (see Chapter 4). In 1977, the government found itself under pressure from a media campaign against illegal immigration, 'racketeering', and 'brides for purchase' and introduced provisions against 'marriages of convenience' – a precursor to the 'primary purpose' legislation that was to be instituted and repealed several times thereafter and which has seen the successive and specific targeting of South Asian marriage migration in recent years, as discussed earlier in the chapter.

This spate of legislation – which, as we can see, was profoundly gendered – has had a considerable impact on international migrants. This is true not only for long-distance migrant wives but also for brides who stayed closer to home, but around whom, as with Bibi Hawa, the world shifted. What comes across most powerfully from the married women we spoke to in India, Bangladesh, and Britain, however, is how their lives – which involved multiple migrations of various kinds – required resilience, adaptation, and adjustment to the dramatic changes that occurred in the world around them. For some, their experience was of loneliness, disappointment, heartbreak, and even destitution; for others, change created space for them to chart their own destiny, pursue new connections, and shape their lives and the lives of those around them.

Roshanara Begum's story reveals some of these themes. She speaks of multiple migrations across the borders and repeated separations in which the upheavals in the subcontinent played a large part. Roshanara was born in 1958 in Calcutta, the eldest daughter of three children. Her mother, Waheeda, was an Urdu-speaking Muslim from Calcutta's Zachariah Street area who, at the time of her own marriage, crossed the Bengali/'Bihari' ethnic divide – her husband, Abed, was a

Bengali-speaking man with shipping connections and business interests in Chittagong and Dhaka. Unusually, Roshanara spent the early years of her childhood in Calcutta with her maternal family – her mother Waheeda, as we shall see, was a strong-willed woman who was reluctant to leave Calcutta. Abed, Roshanara's father (it seems, although she does not spell this out) was a '*ghor jamai*', though often absent on business.

In 1964, however, during the riots, Waheeda fled with Roshanara and her other children to Dhaka. They returned to Calcutta during a lull in the violence but then left the city 'for good' when trouble broke out again. But Waheeda 'hated Dhaka', where people 'were all the same kind, all Bengalis'. She missed Calcutta's cosmopolitan culture and simply 'did not want to live there [in Dhaka]'. During the 1971 War, Waheeda was able, through her Urdu-speaking connections, to secretly get tickets for the family to go to Karachi, under the ' "Bihari" quota'.[71] This time, it was Abed who refused to join his wife: he 'was furious' and announced that he would not accompany his wife to 'a foreign land'. Fearing for his eldest daughter's safety, Abed quickly married Roshanara off to a friend's son in Dhaka. He promised to join his wife and their other two children in Karachi once peace broke out, but he never did.

One striking feature of this story is that it was Waheeda who took all the big decisions (with one exception), deciding whether and when to leave first Calcutta and then Dhaka and arranging their migration to Karachi, which must have required great ingenuity since the ' "Bihari" quota' was very small indeed[72] and tickets to Pakistan desperately hard to come by. But there is also a hint that she rather welcomed this separation from her husband – as Roshanara recalled, 'my parents had never got along too well and he never went to Karachi'. They were never reunited, both dying soon after the war ended.

The dispersal across borders continued into the next generation. Roshanara remained in Dhaka, but she remained close to a maternal aunt who had stayed on in Calcutta, and she and her husband often crossed the border to visit her. Roshanara's younger sister, who had accompanied their mother to Karachi, married a Pakistani and settled there. She longed to visit Roshanara in Bangladesh but could not afford the fare.

Roshanara travelled a great deal. Her businessman husband had 'the travelling bug', she said. He travelled to India 'over a hundred times', and Roshanara often accompanied him. Indeed, when we met her, she and her husband were on a train with their 20-year-old granddaughter, to 'show her India'.

'So what are you? "Biharis"? Bengalis?' we asked her.

Roshanara replied: 'Does it matter anymore? One day we're here, another day we're there. We have roots and branches all over this land, stretching from Bangladesh to Pakistan. We're here one day, we become something else another day. *A bit like a woman, who through her life belongs to different families*'.

Roshanara's analogy, comparing shifting national belonging with the life transitions of women, is striking. Her own life was shaped first by migration decisions taken by her Indian mother Waheeda – herself a party to a 'mixed marriage'. Her mother's tenuous and shifting status as an Urdu-speaking Muslim can be traced both in her reluctance to leave Calcutta and her ability to obtain tickets to Pakistan during the Liberation War and also in Abed's fear for his family's safety during that dangerous period of transition.

Marriage for Roshanara was thus not simply a question of belonging to a new family. It coincided with the break-up of her natal family on account of her father's commitment to a newly independent Bangladesh. Roshanara too was 'Bangladeshi', but her life was punctuated with departures and partings and with connections to Pakistan but also to India, which facilitated numerous journeys and affective links. The marriages of both Roshanara and Waheeda thus involved multiple migrations and transitions which reshaped and subverted traditional expectations and conventions. Their stories show that South Asian women actively bargain with 'traditional' patriarchal structures through cross- or intraborder marriage migration.[73] Sometimes – like Waheeda – they even took advantage of borders to distance themselves from unhappy relationships.

The war and the subsequent civil, economic, and political unrest changed attitudes in 'sending' families in Bangladesh as well as among 'receiving' families in Britain, as did the changing legislative contexts in which migrations took place. This impacted upon the process and rituals of marriage in Bangladesh and across national borders, sometimes creating new 'rituals' that blended with the old. Laila Rahman, who arrived in Britain in 1971 to join her husband at age sixteen, recalled:

> Our marriage took place over the telephone. My guardians – mother, uncles – were present on one side of the phone, and he was here on the other side of the phone. . . . After going back home we organized a Muslim ceremony of marriage. Because our marriage was on the phone, we needed to do that.

Increasingly restrictive immigration policies in Britain, combined with the precarious conditions of post-independence Bangladesh, also encouraged journeys for 'family reunification' which might otherwise have been delayed or resisted. Morium Choudhury's story illustrates some of these trends.

A widow in her late sixties, Morium arrived in Britain in 1989 towards the end of the reunification process. Born in a village in Sylhet, Morium's marriage to a man already settled in London was arranged by her father, a doctor, and her grandfather, a schoolteacher, when she was fourteen years old. Morium spent most of her married life with her six children in her husband's family home in Biswanath *thana* in Bangladesh. She saw her husband (a community worker in London) only now and again, and seemed quite content with this arrangement. She told us:

> He did not bring me. He was not interested to bring us. He thought it was better if we stay in Bangladesh, particularly our children . . . if they come here, they might be influenced by the environment here. . . . He would always say that good people do not come to London.

Her husband was eventually persuaded by the elders to bring his family to London, though Morium herself was reluctant to leave her extended family behind:

> All the *murabbi* [elders] told him to take us. They said it will be good for us. By this time the children were grown up, so he probably thought now it's good to bring them here.

Morium did not really want to move:

> It was his wish . . . I did not tell him to bring us to London . . . because I had everyone – parents, relatives – all in Bangladesh.

When she arrived in London, she was desperately lonely, so her husband would take her and the children sightseeing, but he was reluctant to allow his children to mix with other local Bengalis:

> He would take the children to the park, but my children would not play with other Bengali children. We did not find them good . . . some might have come from the village. They had bad habits. . . . Although my children grew up in a village, they did not mix with the bad boys.

Morium's story illustrates the shifting attitudes towards family migration shaped by changing circumstances in both Bangladesh and Britain. It also provides a revealing commentary on how decisions to migrate were negotiated in changing familial, cultural, and legal contexts. As Gardner has noted, wives left behind in Bangladesh played a crucial facilitatory role in transnational migration by managing the family home in Bangladesh and maintaining links between places, which transformed the 'traditional' role of wife and daughter-in-law[74] and allowed these women greater power and latitude in the domestic setting. For example, Morium told us that she had returned to her parental home for the birth of each of her six children – whereas 'tradition' only encouraged this for the birth of the first child.

Morium's story also reveals the ways in which ideas of family, home, and belonging are themselves transfigured in the process of transnational movement. When Morium and her six children arrived in London, despite her reluctance and initial loneliness, she formed connections in her new home and forged links with new relatives and friends, so much so that when her husband died suddenly of a heart attack in 1998, Morium chose not to return to Bangladesh because of the strong ties she had created in the UK. The family chose to bury her husband in Britain, close to his children who had settled there:

> We decided to bury him here, because his children are living here. My eldest son can go and pray for him. During Ramadan, every day they went to his grave to pray for him.[75]

Her links with Bangladesh had also weakened through the death of close family members – her parents and parents-in-law had all passed away after her emigration. Her closest ties 'back home' were with her younger sister in Chittagong, and Morium had recently arranged the marriage between her eldest son and her niece. Nowadays, she told us, she did not like to return to Bangladesh, even for short visits: 'The last four years I have not gone. My children and grandchildren are living here. I do not like to go to Bangladesh leaving them behind'.

As these stories illustrate, while marriage migration can traverse national borders and disrupt traditional certainties, nation states, with their particular histories and regimes of power, have been central in shaping – and fracturing – processes of movement and settlement. The movement of brides thus calls to be placed in the context of national borders and practices, not just in the regulation of who can enter and stay within a country's borders, but in the broader sense of who 'belongs' and who does not. The role of the nation state was central to the experience of many of the women we interviewed, shaping the places in which they lived and worked and the quality of their lives. In Britain, state intervention and, in particular, increasingly restrictive immigration legislation also worked to reshape family networks as well as the intimate spheres of women's lives. As already noted, the irony was that – at least in part – changes in immigration legislation that curtailed the free circulation of early Bengali migrants between Britain and Bangladesh underpinned the decision of so many to relocate their wives and children permanently to the UK. The same legislation also worked to fracture transnational family links, dividing families and restricting easy movement.

The often devastating impact of these transitions can be seen in the story of Fazilatunnesa, a 67-year-old woman who arrived in Britain in 2001 to join her husband. She married her husband, a distant cousin from the same village, before the Liberation War. Her husband had lived in Britain since the 1960s, when he entered on a 'voucher visa' and, like many women of her generation, Fazilatunnesa stayed behind in Sylhet to raise their family. Her husband would visit every few years, and in between he would write letters and 'send money sometimes, and there was some income from land. I had to run the family with financial constraints'. As with Morium, Fazilatunnesa's husband was reluctant to bring his family to Britain but was persuaded to do so by his family in Bangladesh. 'He said this country is bad. Then everyone convinced him to bring us here. . . . Now everything has changed. It's almost like Bangladesh'.

Fazilatunnesa was herself reluctant to move: 'At first I did not want to come. I did not agree to come', in part because immigration legislation meant that only one of her three children, her youngest daughter, had been able to migrate with her: 'I have left my son and daughter behind'. Fazilatunnesa's first child was a boy, who died, and she later adopted a boy from her village:

> His father and mother died. [His] mother died a couple of days after his birth and his father died after a couple of years. When they took the [mother's]

dead body to the graveyard, the boy's uncle brought the boy to me, and since then I am his mother.

The boy had lived with Fazilatunnesa from when he was 21 days old and did not know he was adopted. She had wanted to bring him to Britain, but permission was denied because she could not prove the relationship:

> People from the embassy went to our village and found that he is not my son. . . . They asked me to submit papers that I have adopted him. I hope they will give him a visa soon, as we have submitted all the required papers. . . . I cry every day for my son.

Perhaps because of these links, and in contrast to Morium, Fazilatunnesa felt strong ties back home. 'I have left the soil of my country. How can I not cry? Slowly I am adapting to this country'.

Fazilatunnesa planned to bring her older daughter to the UK on a visit visa and to find her a UK-based husband to enable her to stay, while her younger (UK-based) daughter had recently married an illegal immigrant. These seemingly intimate choices were, first and foremost, predicated on the demands of a migration regime external to both her family and the broader Bengali community. At the same time, however, these regimes opened space for her British daughter within the confines of the marriage pact. As Fazilatunnesa told us, the most important fact in their choice of a groom for their daughter is that he should enable her to remain close to her natal family and avoid potential conflict with her in-laws: 'Most of all, he is single. He does not have family here . . . as he is alone in this country, we are his family . . . my daughter will have a smooth life'.[76]

Similar trends could be seen in the subcontinent. In a small village in Midnapur, in southwestern West Bengal, lived a family of 'Patua' artists. As with many Patuas, they have both Muslim and Hindu names. Kamala, a single mother, headed an all-woman household in which she supported her own mother and her two daughters, Fatema and Shyama-Suri. They survived by selling their scroll-paintings at craft fairs around India.

One day, two young men came to the village asking for Kamala's house. She learned that they were both Muslim Bangladeshis, with grandparents who had been Indian migrants from Dinajpur. One was called Imtiaz. He was, he admitted to us, an illegal migrant from Bangladesh who had taken the Hindu name 'Ganesh' to conceal his identity. Kamala, who had met him on her travels, invited Imtiaz to stay in their house and treated him as a son. But there was one condition: Imtiaz 'had to choose one of her daughters as a wife'.

Imtiaz agreed and married Shyama-Suri. He wanted to take her back to Bangladesh but was afraid of crossing the border to go home, having once been caught: 'My *dalal* (middleman) was clumsy . . . our whole group of illegal migrants were caught by the BSF (Border Security Force) and locked up and beaten, electrocuted, and starved'.

Imtiaz was uncomfortable in his role as '*ghor jamai*', and wanted to take his wife back to Bangladesh. But he felt trapped. 'What if we're caught again? I could manage those prison-camps, but my wife and baby never will. . . . I will find a way as I don't want to live with my in-laws – what is there for me to do here – I will take them both to Bangladesh'.

These stories illustrate the ongoing role of the nation state in shaping the process of migration and settlement and the ways in which national discourses and nationalist practices impact on gender roles in the lives of women migrants, their families, and communities all across the complex diaspora. The nation state thus works to transform cultural practices around marriage and family formation while simultaneously positioning these cultural practices as being outside of, and in contradistinction to, the modern nation. As Fazilatunnesa's final comment captured, however, these processes also work to reshape internal 'community' expectations around marriage and family formation and have complex outcomes for migrant brides and grooms as well as for their wider communities, both old and new.

Transforming 'community'

Migration thus entails change in the expectations and practices surrounding marriage, both in the country of origin and of arrival. This includes dramatic and sometimes unpredictable consequences for migrant brides, their families, and the broader settled communities. Although marriage remains a significant life stage for both men and women among Bengali Muslims in Britain, reflecting continuity with practices 'back home', there are also clear changes over space and time. In the UK, rates of marriage are high, at 74 per cent, with two in three women marrying between the ages of 20 and 24 years – considerably later than on the subcontinent.[77] Rates of out-marriage are very small, but growing, and figures suggest that practices of consanguineous marriage are declining.[78] Recent figures also suggest that subcontinental marriage is declining due, in part, to shifting attitudes among the 'second generation' exacerbated by legislation that raised the legal age for marriage for 'foreign' spouses to 21[79] and increased the financial requirements for spousal sponsorship.[80]

South Asian marriage migration in Britain is often linked to 'the problem' of integration and social cohesion, which is itself inseparable from essentialized ideas of ethnic 'community' in which gendered practices are believed to be a defining marker. These views belie the multifaceted and changing nature of gendered relations within South Asian/Muslim 'communities'.[81] Studies of transnational marriage practices have shown that rather than reflecting anachronistic and static ideas of culture, marriage acts as a crucible for change precipitated by and through migration, whether as a way of creating status,[82] providing care,[83] negotiating risk, and creating or challenging family obligations and social networks.[84] Although comparatively little is known about Bangladeshi marriage migration to Britain, Gardner's study has emphasized the transformative role that Bangladeshi migrant wives have played in negotiating new family formations and shaping the wider 'community'.[85]

152   'Always/already migrants'

The meaning of 'community' is thus shaped and reshaped over time through marriage migration. As Fazilatunnesa's story in the previous section suggests, in more recent years, brides with British citizenship have more power over their migrant husbands than they had in Bangladesh.[86] Laila Rahman, who worked for a community organization for Asian women in the North of England, described the changing gendered patterns of contemporary marriage within the British Bangladeshi community:

> They go home to find an educated girl from a good family background. So they bring girls from home. But they try to find a groom for their daughter here. They say that boys from home are not smart, girls do not like them.

While most girls wanted to marry British Bengalis, Laila echoed Fazilatunnesa's belief that there were some advantages for those who found husbands from Bangladesh, because it gave them power over their husbands:[87]

> The girls who bring boys from Bangladesh, these boys are from good families; they are educated, polite, gentle. They are not rural boys originally. . . . Sometimes they [the grooms] speak about their problems . . . they have to give all their income to their wives, they are working in restaurants and are not getting proper jobs. It is a kind of torture. . . . But the number is few.

The picture was very different for brides from Bangladesh marrying British Bengali men, according to Laila, but again there were advantages:

> The girls tolerate it. In many cases they are half educated. They are happy with their lives, they are getting good meals, good clothes and good environment. It is far better than their situation in Bangladesh.

This is not to imply, even for a moment, that there are no dark tones in the picture. For the migrant bride in Britain, the huge distance from her natal family rendered her more susceptible to abuse. As Laila pointed out:

> The main problem is domestic violence. . . . This is more common among the wives who are coming from Bangladesh. They bring the girls, they don't know English. It is not only the husbands, mothers-in-law are also involved in this . . . they keep the girl at home to do housework. . . . They beat her very hard.

What emerged from these accounts were shifting contemporary patterns of gender relations and gendered power within this 'community' created through migration.[88] Mehjabin, a divorcee and poet in her early thirties, moved to Britain as a child in 1989 to join her father in East London. Her father had migrated in the early 1960s and worked as a breadmaker in Northampton and then, when he moved to

London, in a sweet factory. Later, her relatives in Bangladesh tried to arrange her marriage to a cousin (*boro khala*) to enable him to migrate. She recalled:

> It was my family which arranged the marriage . . . when I was 14 years old they proposed it, but we fought for nine years about whether I would marry him or not. My father said 'No, there will be no marriage between relatives'. One of my uncles . . . told my father: 'If you give marriage in Bangladesh, one of our families will be benefited. Their son will come to this country. . . .' My father did not agree easily, but after so much pressure from the family, my father said, 'Ok, do whatever you want to do'. By this time my grandmother also got involved, and the marriage was arranged.

When her husband arrived, the newlyweds moved to Green Street in London to set up home: 'After marriage, girls have to go to their in-laws house, or they have to move with their husband. My husband cannot stay with my family as a *ghor jamai*'. After eight years and the birth of four children, the marriage broke down.

Mehjabin herself was interestingly sanguine both about the marriage and its eventual collapse:

> As I did not have any choice . . . I had to marry someone, so I thought it would be better to marry someone known rather than a stranger. . . . I did not think our mentality would be so different, like sky and earth. Anyway, that is my fate.

Mehjabin's story illustrates the complex intersection between external constraints, 'tradition', cultural change, and individual choice that challenge simple ideas of ethnic or religious 'community' in a context of migration.

Historically, the boundaries of 'community' in Britain were also not so clear-cut. Korimunessa Begum, who came to join her husband in 1975, told us that her father-in-law had an English wife as well as a wife in Bangladesh:

> My father-in-law married an English woman, and the brother of my father-in-law married an English woman, and two of my own uncles-in-law married English women. Those who came to this country by ship, almost everyone did this. . . . They were single here, they would have to cook for themselves, it was a difficult life.

The father-in-law's Bengali wife later came to Britain, and he maintained both families, having had three children with his English wife. Korimunessa recalled that the English wife helped bring the Bengali wife over to Britain and that she and her children would attend family events:

> When we were in Hull, she would come with her two sons and one daughter. They used to come to our house, say if there was a party, Eid, they would

come to celebrate. Their father would bring them and told me to treat them well when they were here . . . they would eat if I served them food.

Today, as Rimi, a teacher in her thirties who migrated to Newham in 1992 to join her father, told us, the boundaries of marriage for Bengalis in the UK are even more porous and changeable. When she arrived, she said, her single status was a cause for comment:

> Everybody objected to it. They talked a lot about me: 'You've sent [for] the girl alone. At least you could get her married first and then you could send for her'. . . . I could see girls younger than me, around 17, 18 years old, were already married. I was 20 years old, I was ashamed for this.

In Bangladesh at that time, Rimi insisted, many young women were marrying when they were older to allow them to complete their studies – but not in East London. Rimi married in 1994 and in 2008, fourteen years later, when we interviewed her, she commented on the changing attitudes towards women's status, education, and religion among Bengalis in Britain:

> Now girls are studying, they are not interested in marriage. Even we see some girls . . . over age, they are not married. Before, they got married early. There was a reason too – they [parents] were afraid that their girls might marry some other people from another culture. . . . Nowadays Indian, Pakistani, Turkish are acceptable as long as they are Muslims, because parents are more liberal.

Transgression and negotiation were also important factors in marriages in Bengal. Stories from the Bengal borderlands reveal the porous nature of boundaries and of boundary-crossing through marriage, even among people and groups more usually considered to be highly constrained by tradition and status. Reena's life story is a revealing example.

Reena was born in the late 1960s into an 'Adivasi' or tribal family living in the Dinajpur borderland area, who had converted to Christianity at some point. An attractive young woman, she had married a man of a similar background based in Dinajpur town and had moved there to live with him. But the marriage was unhappy since Reena had no children and was assumed by her in-laws to be barren. She told us, 'They used to be constantly discriminating against me because I couldn't have children and kept saying nasty things'. So Reena returned to her parents' home as often as she could.

These visits seem to have caused a bit of a stir, not only because they were more frequent than the norm but because 'I was very beautiful, and because I lived in Dinajpur [town]. I wore better clothes than those worn here [in the village]'. Here, Reena's migrant status and experience, marked through her mobility, demeanour, and clothes, gave her an air of exoticism and sophistication that marked her out in her natal village. A young man who lived in the neighbourhood 'noticed' her (*chokh legeche*). He was also the child of rural migrants, but, in his case, of a household of Chapaiya Muslims. Reena told us:

> He started following me, and, after some time, he would get angry if I spoke to other men. I asked him, 'Why me? I can't have children'. He'd say, 'I don't want anything but you'.... He was completely crazy for me. One woman had offered him a bike; another, I heard, had offered him a jeep [as dowry]; but he refused them all, he wanted only me.

Eventually, they married. Her new husband, Shahid, asked Reena to convert to Islam and named her 'Shahida' after himself. She told him: 'In your religion you are allowed to marry more than once, what if you tire of me? You'll want another wife to have children'. He denied he would ever do this: 'He said he would never remarry, even if we never have children'.

But the love story did not have a happy ending. Reena is now 'full of sadness'. As for her husband's promises:

> All lies. All utter lies.... After our marriage, we had a daughter, but she died in infancy. Then a boy was born years later. We had two boys, one is nine, another is four. But a year and a half ago, he remarried. Our marriage was false, hollow.... His excuse was that he was a 'full' man when he married me, but that I was not a 'full' woman, and as I had remarried, he should be allowed to remarry too. She now lives next door.

Reena showed compassion for her co-wife, a young girl of about seventeen who had just become a mother. The family lived outside the village near the bazaar, perhaps because she and her husband were not allowed to live in the village itself. This geographical marginalization reflects her social marginality and her liminal position as an Adivasi Christian divorcee married to a Muslim Chapai 'Indian' immigrant. Reena's own affiliation with Christianity seemed weak: indeed, she only mentioned it in passing when talking about her first husband. She spoke in the same way of Islam as something to do with her second husband. Nor did she seemed to identify strongly with either 'Adivasi' or 'Chapaiya' labels and made no mention whatsoever of her 'Bengali' identity. Instead, she seemed to see herself first and foremost as a woman who had been let down badly by both the men she married. Nevertheless, as with Laila Rahman, Mehjabin, and Rimi, Reena's story points to the ways in which social and cultural expectations, statuses, and boundaries are simultaneously salient and negotiable in the lives of migrant women.

Conclusion

If there is one thing that stands out most sharply from these richly textured life histories, it is the unsettled quality, not only of the period in which these women lived but of the impact of that pervasive flux on the women themselves, their families, 'communities', and nations – old and new – and on their sense of self.

Avtar Brah has written powerfully of diaspora as a process of dislocation and relocation which is experienced as 'a homing desire',[89] in which journeying and staying put, loss and hope, ends and beginnings, collide to create new spaces, new homes, and new forms of belonging. The women whose lives we have sketched here, others who were part of our study, and the countless more whose stories remain untold traced pathways within and across borders and were entangled in big and little histories which they themselves unwittingly but indelibly shaped – often with pain, loss, and sacrifice, but also with hope and new beginnings. Taken together, these histories test the limits of the concept of a settled 'culture' or, indeed, a settled 'homeland' and, above all, challenge the assumed role of women and wives in sustaining and reproducing their continuities.

Exploring marriage migration 'from below' demonstrates that the movement of brides is integrally concerned with processes of social and cultural change and transformation within and across borders, places, and times. Focusing on the largely hidden histories of migrant Bengali women, such an approach has challenged the easily racialized and culturalist accounts of ethnic, religious, class, and gender identities and placed them centre stage as social, cultural, and political agents who helped shape their own histories.

At the same time, however, we argue against simplistic and romanticized accounts of women's agency, insisting on the often-unresolved tensions between continuity and change, structure and agency, and community and the individual. Migration worked both to open up and close down cultural norms, sometimes reinscribing defensive and authoritarian gendered roles, at others offering space for individual and collective transformation. The focus on brides allows us to recognize marriage as both a personal and intimate 'moment' of transformation and to place this within the larger historical, social, and political landscape. Bringing the stories of migrant brides from India, Bangladesh, and Britain together works to challenge easy and reductive notions of 'here and there', 'home and abroad', 'then and now', recognizing the contingent and shifting nature of social and cultural norms, traditions, and rituals at both 'ends' of the migrant journey.

A comparative perspective allows us to explore the connections and disjunctions between intranational, cross-national, and international migration as part of a holistic but fractured system in which the very different lives of Bibi Hawa, Roshanara, Husna Ara Begum, Reena, and Morium can speak to each other, to shared origins, historical intersections, and cultural understandings, without flattening the complex textures of history, politics, and power 'at play'[90] in their lives. Our aim in this chapter has been to explore the richness and texture of this sphere of encounter and exchange while acknowledging its constraints and inequalities; to assert presence and complexity in the face of erasure, simplification, and stereotyping; and to offer an embodied, lived, and changing vision of the migration process.

Notes

1 Kabeer, *Power to Choose*.
2 'Encircled' or surrounded (from Hindi).
3 Irregular freedom brigades fighting the Pakistan Army.

4 Ballard, *Desh Pardesh*; Gardner and Shakur, 'I'm Bengali', in Ballard (ed.) *Desh Pardesh*. The number of Bangladeshis in Britain rose from 22,000 in 1971 to 163,000 by 1991 – the majority of these being women and children. See Alexander, Firoz and Rashid, *Bengal Diaspora*.
5 Non-EU family migration to the UK increased from an average of 35,000 per year in the 1990s to 51,000 in 2009 (see S. Blinder, *Non-European Migration to the UK: Family and Dependents*, Oxford: Migration Observatory, 2011: www.migrationobservatory.ox.ac.uk). Most came from the Indian subcontinent, comprising 41 per cent of the 33,270 family migrants admitted in 2008 (during the period of our fieldwork) (see K. Charsley, N. van Hear, M. Benson and B. Storer-Church, *Marriage-related Migration to the UK*, London: HMSO, 2011). The vast majority – 97 per cent – entered as spouses. Women made up 68 per cent of those admitted as spouses or fiancé(e)s. See Home Office, *Family Migration: Evidence and Analysis*, London: HMSO, 2011. In 2010, 61 per cent of applicants were from Bangladesh (ibid.). It is important to note that applicants from South Asia are overrepresented in refusal rates. See E. Kofman, S. Lukes, V. Meetoo and P. Aaron, *Family Migration to United Kingdom: Trends, Statistics and Policy*, Vienna: International Centre for Migration Policy Development, 2008.
6 See, for example, Sonalde Desai and Manjistha Banerji, 'Negotiated Identities: Male Migration and Left-Behind Wives in India', *Journal of Population Research*, 25, 3, 2008, pp. 337–55; see also Malini Sur, 'Bamboo Baskets and Barricades: Gendered Landscapes at the India-Bangladesh Border', in Barak Kalir and Malini Sur (eds) *Transnational Flows and Permissive Polities: Ethnographies of Human Mobility in Asia*, Amsterdam: Amsterdam University Press, 2012.
7 Chandra Mohanty, 'Under Western Eyes: Feminist Scholarship and Colonial Discourses', in Williams and Chrisman, *Colonial Discourse*, p. 199.
8 This chapter is partly based on an article previously published in the *Journal of Ethnic and Migration Studies*: Claire Alexander, 'Marriage, Migration, Multiculturalism: Gendering "the Bengal diaspora"', *Journal of Ethnic and Migration Studies*, 39, 3, 2013, pp. 333–51; see also Katharine Charsley and Alison Shaw, 'South Asian Marriages in Comparative Perspective', *Global Networks* 6, 4, 2006, pp. 331–44.
9 Kofman et al., *Family Migration*; Alexander, 'Marriage, Migration'.
10 Joya Chatterji and David Washbrook, 'Introduction – Concepts and Questions', in Chatterji and Washbrook (eds) *Routledge Handbook*.
11 Claire Alexander, 'Culturing Poverty? Ethnicity, Religion, Gender and Social Disadvantage Amongst South Asian Communities in the UK', in Sylvia Chant (ed.) *International Handbook of Gender and Poverty*, Cheltenham: Edward Elgar, 2010.
12 Sara Ahmed, *Strange Encounters: Embodied Others in Postcoloniality*, London: Routledge, 2000.
13 Pratibha Parmar, 'Gender, Race and Class: Asian Women in Resistance', in Centre for Contemporary Cultural Studies, *The Empire Strikes Back*, London: Routledge, 1982; Perveez Mody, 'Marriages of Convenience and Capitulation: South Asian Marriage, Family and Intimacy in the Diaspora', in Chatterji and Washbrook (eds), *Routledge Handbook*; Alexander, 'Marriage, Migration'.
14 Floya Anthias and Nira Yuval Davis, *Racialised Boundaries*, London: Routledge, 1992; F. Anthias, 'Nation and Post-Nation: Nationalism, Transnationalism and Intersections of Belonging', in Collins and Solomos (eds) *Handbook of Race*; Philippa Levine, 'Sexuality and Empire', in Catherine Hall and Sonya Rose (eds) *At Home With the Empire: Metropolitan Culture and the Imperial World*, Cambridge: Cambridge University Press, 2006.
15 Tanika Sarkar, *Hindu Wife, Hindu Nation: Community, Religion, and Cultural Nationalism*, Bloomington: Indiana University Press, 2001; Partha Chatterjee, *The Nation and its Fragments: Colonial and Postcolonial Histories*, Princeton: Princeton University Press, 1993.
16 Samita Sen, 'Wrecking Homes, Making Families. Women's Recruitment and Indentured Labour Migration from India', in Chatterji and Washbrook (eds) *Routledge Handbook*, pp. 96–7.

158 *'Always/already migrants'*

17 Ghosh, *Sex*, p, 44; Erica Wald, *Vice in the Barracks: Medicine the Military and the Making of Colonial India, 1780–1868*, Basingstoke: Palgrave Macmillan, 2014, p. 24; Kenneth Ballhatchet, *Race, Sex and Class Under the Raj: Imperial Attitudes and Policies and their Critics, 1793–1905*, London: Weidenfeld and Nicholson, 1980, p. 144.
18 For example, see *Census of India, 1921, Bengal, Part 1*, p, 130; Chattopadhyaya, *Internal Migration*.
19 Sur, 'Bamboo Baskets'.
20 Charsley and Shaw, 'South Asian Marriages', pp. 331–44; p. 332.
21 Like the 'economic' migration of labour, marriage migration too involves a distinct form of recruitment and control in which the wife's labour, reproductive capacities, and person are transferred from one household to another. Also see Indrani Chatterjee (ed.) *Unfamiliar Relations. Family and History in South Asia*, Delhi: Permanent Black, 2004; and Indrani Chatterjee, *Gender, Slavery and Law in Colonial India*, Delhi: Oxford University Press, 1999.
22 Karve, 'Kinship Map', p. 60; Karve, *Kinship Organisation*.
23 See, for instance, Louis Dumont, 'North India in Relation to South India', in Uberoi (ed.) *Family*.
24 Karve, 'Kinship Map', p. 54.
25 Hastings Donnan, *Marriage Among Muslims. Preference and Choice in Northern Pakistan*, Leiden: Brill, 1988, p. 115.
26 Taslima Nasrin, *Meyebela: My Bengali Girlhood. A Memoir of Growing up Female in a Muslim World*, Vermont: Steerforth Press, 1998, p. 10. Emphasis added.
27 We are grateful to Samita Sen for this insight.
28 Jenneke Arens and Jos van Beurden, *Jhagrapur: Poor Peasants and Women in a Village in Bangladesh*, Calcutta: Orient Longman, 1977, p. 62.
29 See Rohner and Chaki-Sircar, *Women and Children*.
30 Mead Cain, Syeda Rokeya Khanam and Shamsun Nahar, 'Class, Patriarchy and Women's Work in Bangladesh', *Population and Development Review*, 5, 3 (September) 1979, p. 423.
31 Armindo Miranda, *The Demography of Bangladesh* (No. 144), Bergen: Chr. Michelsen Institute Development Research and Action Programme, 1982, pp. 76–7.
32 Rohner and Chaki-Sircar, *Women and Children*, p. 76.
33 Miranda, *Demography*, p. 79.
34 Rohner and Chaki-Sircar, *Women and Children*, pp. 97–8.
35 Miranda, *Demography*, p. 79.
36 Fruzetti, *Gift of a Virgin*.
37 Ibid., p. 78.
38 A study of the caste Hindu Bengali village of Palashpur in western Bengal in 1981, for example, suggested that 'the wives of Palashpur [came] from 87 different villages and towns, most within a thirty-five mile radius', and that the daughters of the village had also all been married off to men from 87 different places outside its limits. Rohner and Chaki-Sircar, *Women and Children*, p. 45.
39 Nasrin, *Meyebela*, p. 20.
40 Dumont, 'North India', p, 91.
41 Donnan, *Marriage*, p. 311.
42 Cain et al., 'Class', p. 406.
43 Fruzetti, *Gift of a Virgin*, p. 65.
44 Ibid., p. 94.
45 Miranda, *Demography*, p. 202.
46 Metcalf, *Perfecting Women*.
47 Miranda, *Demography*, p. 108.
48 Ibid., p. 108.
49 Miranda, *Demography*, p. 75, footnote.
50 Ibid., p. 85.

51 That is, if 100 was the mean age of marriage, in Sylhet it was 110, while in Kushtia in the west it was 93.
52 Miranda, *Demography*, pp. 92–6.
53 Cited in Charsley et al., *Marriage-related Migration*, p. 7.
54 *Bangladesh Census Report, National Volume*, Dacca: Bureau of Statistics, 1974.
55 Arens and Van Beurden, *Jhagrapur*, p. 53.
56 Cain et al., 'Class', p. 409. Also see Mead T. Cain, 'The Household Life Cycle and Economic Mobility in Rural Bangladesh, *Population and Development Review*, 4, 3 September 1978, pp. 421–38.
57 Miranda, *Demography*, p. 108.
58 Chatterji, 'Fashioning'.
59 Haimanti Roy, *Partitioned Lives. Migrants, Refugees, Citizens in India and Pakistan, 1947–65*, New Delhi: Oxford University Press, 2013; Samaddar (ed.) *Reflections*.
60 Chatterji, 'South Asian Histories', pp. 1049–71.
61 Abul Barkat et al., *Political Economy of the Vested Property Act in Rural Bangladesh*, Dhaka: Pathak Shamabesh, 1994; M. I. Farooqui, *Law of Abandoned Property*, Dhaka: Sultana Suraiya Akter, 2000; Ghosh, *Partition*.
62 Datta, *Refugees*.
63 Sur, 'Bamboo Baskets', pp. 127, 147.
64 Kabeer, *Power to Choose*; V. Redclift, 'Changes in Family Reunion Migration from Bangladesh to the UK 1985–2004: Policy, Gender and Social Ties', MSc thesis, London School of Economics and Political Science, 2006.
65 Randall Hansen, *Citizenship and Immigration in Postwar Britain*, Oxford: Oxford University Press, 2000, p. 46.
66 Joya Chatterji, 'From Subjecthood to Citizenship in South Asia: Migration, Nationality and the Post-Imperial Global Order', in Alfred McCoy, Josep M. Fradera and Stephen Jacobson (eds) *Endless Empire. Spain's Retreat, Europe's Eclipse, America's Decline*, London: University of Wisconsin Press, 2012.
67 Cabinet Memorandum, 'Commonwealth Immigration: Consultation with other Governments', Memorandum by the Secretary of State for the Home Department and the Secretary of State for Commonwealth Relations, 3 November 1964, C. (64). 11.
68 Infamously, this involved breaking a pledge made to the East African Asians in 1963 that they would have unrestricted entry into the UK for as long as they retained their CUKC status.
69 Solomos, *Race*; Hansen, *Citizenship*; Zig Layton-Henry, *The Politics of Immigration: Race and Race Relations in Postwar Britain*, Oxford: Wiley-Blackwell, 1992.
70 A 'patrial' was defined as a CUKC who had that citizenship by birth, adoption, naturalization, or registration in the UK; or such a citizen who had a parent or grandparent with that citizenship; or who was a citizen of the UK and Colonies and had been ordinarily resident in the UK for five years or more. A Commonwealth citizen whose parent was born in the UK and held UK citizenship was also a patrial, as was a Commonwealth citizen who was the wife or widow of a patrial.
71 In 1974, the government of Pakistan agreed to 'repatriate' to Pakistan c. 113,000 people, including government employees and divided families. Ilias, *Biharis*, p. 143.
72 Ilias, *Biharis*; Anthony Mascarenhas, *Bangladesh: A Legacy of Blood*, London: Hodder and Stoughton, 1986.
73 Deniz Kandiyoti, 'Bargaining with Patriarchy', *Gender and Society*, 2, 3, 1988, pp. 274–90
74 Katy Gardner, 'The Transnational Work of Kinship and Caring: British-Bengali Marriages in Historical Perspective', *Global Networks*, 6, 4, 2006, pp. 373–87. See also Desai and Banerji, 'Negotiated Identities'.
75 See Chapter 3 for a discussion of the role of graveyards in South Asia.
76 See Katharine Charsley, 'Unhappy Husbands: Masculinity and Migration in Transnational Pakistani Marriages', *Journal of the Royal Anthropological Institute*, 11, 2005, pp. 85–105.

160   *'Always/already migrants'*

77 Yunas Samad and John Eade, *Community Perceptions of Forced Marriage*, London: Foreign and Commonwealth Office, 2002.
78 Santi Rozario and Sophie Gilliat-Ray, 'Genetics, Religion and Identity: A Study of British Bangladeshis 2004–2007', Working Paper No. 93, Cardiff University School of Social Sciences, 2007. See: www.cardiff.ac.uk/socsi/resources/wrkgpaper-93.pdf
79 This practice was initiated in 2008 to prevent 'forced marriage' but was declared illegal by the Supreme Court in 2011, which also reduced the legal age for marriage to 18. This is still two years higher than the legal age for marriage in the UK itself. The amendment came into force on 28 November 2011. See www.workpermit.com/news/2011-11-08/uk/uk-reinstates-minimum-age-of-18-for-foreign-spouses.html
80 Since July 2012, a minimum earnings requirement to bring a non-EU spouse into the UK was introduced. The threshold is £18,600 for a spouse, rising to £22,400 for a family with a child, and a sum of £2,400 for each additional child. The Home Office report *Family Migration* notes that although 96 per cent of Bangladeshi sponsors were employed at time of application for their spouses, their median monthly earnings were £875 – a figure that falls well below new requirements. Home Office, *Family Migration*; Matt Cavanagh, 'Immigration: A Policy Distorted by Targets', *Guardian*, 17 November 2011.
81 Charsley 'Unhappy Husbands'; Gardner, 'Transnational Work'.
82 Kanwal Mand, 'Place, Gender and Power in Transnational Sikh Marriages', *Global Networks*, 2, 3, 2002, pp. 233–48.
83 Kanwal Mand, *Social Capital and Transnational South Asian Families: Rituals, Care and Provision*, London: Families and Social Capital ESRC Research Group, South Bank University, 2006; Katharine Charsley, 'Risk, Trust, Gender and Transnational Cousin Marriage Among British Pakistanis', *Ethnic and Racial Studies*, 30, 6, 2007, pp. 1117–31.
84 Charsley 'Unhappy Husbands'; K. Charsley, 'Risk and Ritual: The Protection of British Pakistani Women in Transnational Marriage', *Journal of Ethnic and Migration Studies*, 32, 7, 2006, pp. 1169–87; Charsley and Shaw, 'South Asian Marriages'.
85 Gardner, 'Transnational Work'.
86 Ibid. See also Charsley, 'Unhappy Husbands'.
87 See Charsley, 'Unhappy Husbands.
88 Kandiyoti, 'Bargaining with Patriarchy'; Charsley 'Unhappy Husbands'; Gardner, 'Transnational Work'.
89 Avtar Brah, *Cartographies of Diaspora*, London: Routledge, 1996, p. 180.
90 Stuart Hall, 'Cultural Identity and Diaspora', in, J. Rutherford (ed.) *Identity: Community, Culture, Difference*, London: Lawrence and Wishart, 1990.

6 Building a *tazia*, becoming a *paik*

'Bihari' identity amid a hostile Bengali universe

During the first ten days of the Islamic month of Muharram, young boys run through the streets of Dhaka wearing brightly coloured salwar kameezes, embroidered skullcaps, and scarves of red or parrot green. Called '*paiks*' or '*paikis*' (footmen or foot-soldiers), they carry vivid standards (*alam*) atop bamboo poles. All have coloured ropes strung around their chests and shoulders. Attached to these are little bells which tinkle as they dart in and out of the narrow lanes of their camps and past mosques and *imambaras*[1] (see Figure 6.1).

As they run, the boys cry, 'Ya Husain', 'Ya Hassan', invoking the names of the Prophet's grandsons, Imam Husain and his brother, Hassan. Shias around the world mourn the martyrs who died in the battle of Karbala,[2] and commemorating Muharram is usually thought of as expressing a particularly Shia religious identity. In consequence, the *paiks* are often taken by onlookers – Bengali-speaking Hindus and Muslims alike – for Shias. But they are, in fact, Sunni Muslims drawn from those known as 'Biharis' in present-day Bangladesh.

In Dhaka, Muharram is observed by Shias, many of whom are prominent businessmen and merchants, but also by 'Biharis' – Sunni migrants who were once prominent in the administration, railways, and mills and who today work chiefly as mechanics, barbers, tailors, and *zardozi* (gold thread embroidery) embroiderers. On Ashura – the tenth day of Muharram – both groups process through the streets bearing *tazias* (replicas of the bier and tomb of Imam Husain). But in all other respects, the Shia and Sunni versions of Muharram create a strikingly different mood. Shia Muharram is sombre, marked by deep, almost cathartic, mourning. On the morning of Ashura, Shia tributes to the Imam and his fellow martyrs are hushed: processionists sing solemn dirges as they walk behind their own *tazias* through the city. Their destination is a symbolic burial ground called 'Karbala', sanctified with holy earth brought from the original site of the Imam's martyrdom in Iraq.[3] They walk barefoot, their heads exposed to the blistering sun. For Shias of Dhaka, just as for many Shias around the world, from Isfahan to New York, remembering Husain's death is a symbolic act of redemption, commemorated during Muharram by penance. As a Shia woman in Dhaka told us: 'We Shias do not eat fish, get married or wear colourful clothes during those days as we believe that these, representing joy, would be inappropriate in the month of mourning'.

162 *Building a* tazia, *becoming a* paik

Figure 6.1 Smiling *paiks* in Town Hall camp.
Courtesy: Annu Jalais, Bengal Diaspora Project

By contrast, Muharram events organized by 'Bihari' are boisterous, even carnivalesque. Few 'Biharis' wear black, unlike Shias, who invariably do so. None of them performs *matam*, the ritual of self-flagellation by which Shias re-enact Husain's suffering. 'Bihari' Sunni *tazia* processions are rowdy affairs, often joyous, sometimes fraught with tension between the marchers and the crowds through whom they move. In this respect, they resemble the Hosay and Tajda processions of *poorbea* labour migrants in the Caribbean[4] and of working-class Muslims of late-colonial Bombay or Tamil Nadu.[5]

Sunni Muharram has rarely been a subject of enquiry among scholars of South Asia.[6] Outside academia, it is commonly regarded as a form of deviance from Shia practice. In Bangladesh itself, there was widespread public ignorance of its observance: in Dhaka, the Bengali Muslims we spoke to had no idea that the procession was not of Shias, but of 'Bihari' Sunnis.[7] In Calcutta, elite Muslims also tended to ignore it. When we asked about the rituals, they were condescending, saying, 'Why would you be interested in uneducated peoples' practices?' Even 'Biharis' of higher status often dismissed these processions as 'un-Islamic practices, [which] should be banned'. David Pinault writes of encountering similar prejudice when he studied Sunni Muharram rituals in India, in Darjeeling and Hyderabad.[8]

This chapter looks at 'Bihari' Sunni Muharram in Dhaka in its own right and on its own terms. We see it as a prism through which to achieve a better understanding of complex, often incoherent and incomplete, processes of community formation among migrant groups. We suggest that while migrants draw upon elements of their history as a symbolic resource, what is played out on the streets of Dhaka is in no sense a replica of the Muharram of 'old Bihar' or, indeed, of Sunni belief in 'the "Bihari" homeland'. Nor is it a hybrid or creolized adaptation of a 'traditional' form in a new cultural context.

Dhaka's ' "Bihari" Muharram' is not in any literal sense an 'expression of community'. It is action that helps to create a sense of community but also resonates across many other registers of politics. It is the outcome of cooperation but also signals competition between people thrown together willy-nilly in crowded camp neighbourhoods after 1971. It reflects 'Bihari' negotiation with other groups in the city, whether with Urdu-speaking Shia Muslims, with other Sunnis who describe themselves as 'native' Bengalis or, indeed, with other 'Biharis', who are Sunnis like themselves yet condemn their practices from a variety of stances.

This account of ' "Bihari" Muharram' reveals how a group of people, immobilized today in camps, remembers its mobile and turbulent past. Bihari *paiki*-running and *tazia* processions also give an insight into how a reviled 'low-class', migrant 'ethnic' minority represents itself in the 'Bangladeshi' public sphere. By occupying – in public and distinctive ways – space from which they are normally shut out, 'Bihari' participants show themselves to be an undeniable, even subversive, presence in the city on these sacred days of the Islamic calendar.

Migrants immobilized

The so-called 'Biharis' of Dhaka's camps are best understood as part of one of the largest and most enduring labour diasporas in South Asian history. The Awadhi- and Bhojpuri-speaking parts of North India from where they came straddles the region described by the British as 'the North Western Provinces and Oudh' (or Awadh), roughly coterminous with present-day eastern Uttar Pradesh and western Bihar in India. For at least four centuries, the men of this *poorbea* region of armed peasantries worked away from home for years at a time in the mercenary armies of competing powers of early modern India.[9] In British times, as Chapter 1 shows, this mobile work force was integrated into the vast labour market of eastern India, with the railways playing a critical role.

In the early decades of the 18th century, this swathe of territory, and Bengal to its east, came under the influence and rule of Shia dynasties. The Shia nawabs of Awadh and Bengal not only recruited soldiers from the area, they also embarked on enormous building projects in new capital cities that sucked labour away from their agrarian hinterlands. None was more extravagant and ambitious than Lucknow, the court city of the kingdom of Awadh. Indeed, Lucknow's dramatic cityscape is the product of mass migration: in the 1780s, severe drought drove desperate people off the land in the thousands to seek work in the city, and to absorb this influx, Nawab Asafu'd-daula (1775–1797) launched a construction programme 'on an almost pharaonic scale'.[10] Notable among his projects was the Great Imambara complex, completed in 1791, whose immense unsupported ceiling and lavish decorations were believed to have cost a million rupees.[11] Over the next few decades, the nawab's courtiers emulated his bold building programme in their own neighbourhoods, commissioning the construction of numerous *imambaras* in what came to be known as the Realm of the Shia (*Dar ash-Shia*).

As migrant labourers and artisans worked on these building sites, Shia cultural and religious forms percolated into the city's more humble *mohallas* (neighbourhoods), and its proletarian populations are thought to have adopted some Imami practices.[12] However, the particular aspects they took up were influenced by the sharp divisions in Nawabi Lucknow between private Muharram rituals – such as the *majalis* (gatherings for mourning), attended almost exclusively by the city's elite families – and those held in public, such as the grand public processions of *tazias* on Ashura, which were open to all. Shut out from the *marsiya* recitations at which Shia theologians held elite audiences in thrall with their poetic accounts of the tragedy of Karbala and drew out the finer points of Muharram's moral and religious significance, the city's labourers and artisans no doubt derived their own meanings from the *tazias* and their internment at the end of the processions at local sites designated as 'Karbala'. We can only conjecture what these might have been – but the message of Husain's heroic sacrifice for Islam in a doomed battle in which his army was vastly outnumbered seems not to have been lost on them. Cole suggests that both Hindu and Muslim common folk, including Sunnis, took to mourning during Muharram: even women fasted, loosened their hair, and broke their bangles.[13]

But in popular practice, Karbala often escaped the framework of mourning, becoming invested instead with miraculous powers. One such symbol was the (to begin with) modest shrine to the standard of Hazrat Abbas, Imam Husain's half-brother, who died at Karbala in his heroic effort to bring water to parched children.[14] Lucknow's urban poor (who knew drought only too well) began to flock to the shrine, bringing offerings and seeking the intercession of the saint to cure their ills. Similarly, practices linked to the 'Karbala paradigm'[15] were adopted (and adapted) by the inhabitants (both Hindu and Muslim) of the outlying rural areas around Lucknow under the patronage of landed magnates close to the Shia court.

The British may have conquered North India in the 19th century, but they did not – indeed, could not – destroy its culture of mobility. If anything, as Chapter 1 shows, the Raj accelerated it. But as Lucknow began to decline, Bhojpuri- and Awadhi-speaking labour sought out new destinations,[16] and, increasingly, they were joined by migrants from regions that lay between Lucknow and Calcutta, where rural people spoke in various Magadhi and Maithili dialects (see Table 6.1). At the turn of the century, the *poorbea* region suffered, with devastating regularity, from famine, plague or fever in 1897, 1903, 1905, 1909, and again in 1910.[17] These disasters drove more and more men off the land in search of work, and Calcutta and its industrial hinterland absorbed them. Chattopadhyaya writes:

> All kind of employment [was] welcomed by the migrants from Bihar (from U.P. as well) [in Bengal]. . . . The Brahmin migrants, for instance, were found serving as peons, policemen, shop-keepers, cooks. The *tantis*

(weavers) from Bihar (mostly from Monghyr) were . . . almost invariably employed as day-labourers, earth workers, and *palki* (sedan chair)-bearers. The great majority of the 'Bihari' Rajputs sought employment as constables, door-keepers, jail-warders, peons and railway porters. The 'Goalas' (or milkmen) who moved into Bengal earned their living as labourers, domestic servants, and shop-keepers. The Kahars, Kurmis, and Dosadhs usually worked as labourers or mill-hands, a section of the first two classes were also employed as indoor [domestic] servants, while some of the Dosadhs were often employed as *syces* (grooms).[18]

But the migrants also travelled further afield. Men from the United Provinces and Bihar were prominent among the workforce that built and manned the railways,[19] and this work took some of them into eastern Bengal – in what is today Bangladesh – and into Assam. Already by 1903, Grierson estimated, 11,000 Bhojpuri speakers were to be found in Dacca district, 24,800 in Mymensingh, 18,000 in Rangpur, 41,000 in Murshidabad, and 9,400 in Bogra.[20] In the late 19th century, when there was a demand for Indian labour from plantation owners across the empire, it was the Awadhi- and Bhojpuri- speaking countryside that was the source of indentured labourers in the largest numbers, whether to British possessions in Fiji, Mauritius, British Guinea, Trinidad, and Jamaica, or even in the Dutch colony of Surinam.[21]

By the early 20th century, as Table 6.1 shows, there were already almost a million Bhojpuri speakers and another half-million Maithili speakers in Bengal. By the mid-20th century, Calcutta's 'Biharis', as they had come to be known, had lived in that sprawling metropolis for many decades.[22] They provided much of the workforce for the jute mills but also did casual menial work as palanquin-bearers, night watchmen (*darwans*), masons, and construction workers.[23] As Grierson remarked in 1903, 'the Bhojpuri-speaking country . . . furnishe[s] a mine of recruitment to the Hindustani army. . . . Thousands of them have emigrated to British Colonies and have returned rich men; every year still larger numbers wander over Northern Bengal and seek employment. . . . Every Bengali *zamindar* keeps a posse of these men, euphemistically termed *darwans*, to keep his tenants in order. Calcutta, where they are employed . . . is full of them'.[24]

This narrative is, of course, well known to scholars of labour. Its outlines are rehearsed here to remind readers of the long and rich history of mobility – both

Table 6.1 Migrants from eastern United Provinces and Bihar in Bengal, 1903.

	Maithili	*Magadhi*	*Bhojpuri*
Number of speakers in Assam	66,575	33,365	165,670
Numbers of speakers in Bengal	196,782	231,485	775,145
Total	263,357	265,850	940,815

Source: Grierson, *Linguistic Survey of India*, Vol. V, Part II, p. 5.

global and local – of this remarkably cosmopolitan group of working people. It also underlines that they had long ago become an *urban* proletariat in upper India, Bengal, and Assam. The term 'Bihari' captures some aspects of this history but elides (or derides) others. It points, very roughly, to the regional origins of this labour diaspora. But, as deployed by Calcutta's genteel classes, the term had already acquired pejorative connotations by the mid-20th century: 'Biharis' were regarded as rustics, crude and uncultured labourers, 'outsiders' from rural upper India, despite the fact that many had lived in Bengal for decades, had protected the private property of the well-to-do, built its cities, roads and railways, and constructed much of the fabric of modernity of which Bengal's middle classes were so proud. By 2007, when we began our field research, most 'Bihari' families could trace back their urban presence in Bengal, whether in Calcutta, Dacca, Rangpur or Syedpur, for over a century. It is important to recognize, then, that forms of 'Bihari' piety in Dhaka today are not as much a reflection of the 'age-old' traditions of rural Bihar as they are 'a response to the modern urban life of a 20th-century proletariat'[25] and to its location as a 'national minority' in a hostile nation state.

Nor is the term 'Sunni', as applied to these communities, as straightforward as it may first seem. Since the late 19th century, reform-minded Sunni intellectuals and clerics had inveighed against the influence in the region of *pir* cults.[26] *Pirs* were the descendants of holy men or warrior-saints[27] revered across Bengal[28] and Bihar who were thought to have brought Islam to this part of the subcontinent. In 1907, O'Malley remarked that the 'lower and uneducated classes of Muhammedans' in the Patna area (where many of Dhaka's 'Biharis' traced their origins) were noted for their 'adoration of departed Pirs', whose tombs or *dargahs* were 'places of pilgrimage to which many persons resorted for the cure of disease or the exorcism of evil spirits' and whose *urs* (death anniversary) gatherings were vastly popular.[29] From Bihar to eastern Bengal, their shrines, dotted across town and country alike, were invested with miraculous powers; and devout pilgrims from far and wide (Hindus included) sought their intercession against infertility, disease, and other disasters.

But in the late 19th and early 20th centuries, Sunni Muslim reformers denounced these popular practices with increasing shrillness.[30] Even as Shia and Sunni clerics drew sharper sectarian lines between their respective religious traditions,[31] a growing number of learned voices condemned the 'illiterate' among their own, whose practices deviated from those sanctioned by the Quran and Hadith. The proselytizing reformers of the Ahl-i-Hadith had their Patna 'headquarters'[32] in Bihar, but not all local Muslims were persuaded by their preaching: indeed, in the very same area which the British believed was the heart of a grand 'Wahabi conspiracy', the fair commemorating the wedding of *pir* Ghazi Mian, one of the first 'martyrs of Islam' to die on Indian soil, was one of the greatest gatherings of the year.[33] Even as the reformist Tablighi Jama'at spread into Bengal (see Chapter 3), *pir* shrines flourished and spread vigorously in the late 19th and early 20th centuries. 'Replica shrines' (*mazars*) built by migrants who settled in new places also attracted visitors in their thousands. Bibi ka Roja, the shrine to the soul of

Fatima (the daughter of the Prophet, regarded as an exemplar of womanly perfection by many Muslims), attracted pious travellers from all over the world. Despite (and arguably, because of) the efforts of a growing number of reformers, modern 'Sunni Islam' was hardly discrete and bounded: it constituted a bewildering variety of claims, counter-claims, and rival traditions in which, to use Nile Green's phrase, religious consumers made choices in an increasingly 'plural and competitive religious economy'.[34] What it meant (and means) to be a 'Sunni' was (and is) different for different people in the same region. Individuals – particularly urban migrants – chose, then mixed and matched their preferred forms of piety in a bewildering variety of ways.

By the early 20th century, in both Bihar and Bengal, Muharram had become a largely urban phenomenon. Admittedly, some aspects of Muharram had been absorbed into popular religious practice in rural areas close to Lucknow,[35] but further to the east and west of that city, it did not figure among the festivals and fairs the British went to such pains to chronicle.[36] In the mill areas of Hooghly – abutting Calcutta – known for housing large numbers of *poorbea* immigrants, Muharram was observed 'with unusual pomp and circumstance', which is hardly surprising, since Lucknow's Nawab Wajid Ali Shah had moved to Hooghly after the fall of Awadh, setting up camp in Metiabruz. In 1912, O'Malley reported that 'Sunnis [there] observe[d] the Muharram as a period of silent mourning, offer[ed] up prayers and distribute[d] alms to the helpless',[37] a very different observance to that seen in the 'Bihar' camps of Dhaka. Sources also refer to *tazia* processions in Murshidabad town, another urban centre of Shia influence, in the early 1940s.[38] Sunnis and Shias alike continue to perform Muharram in Hooghly today, and these practices will also be discussed later in this chapter for purposes of comparison.

In the early 20th century, Muharram was increasingly an occasion for conflict between Shias and Sunnis across North India, and also between Hindus and Muslims. As Justin Jones points out, the growing competition for religious authority between a host of claimants led to heightened efforts by reformers not only to police the practice of the 'lower orders' but also to mark out more sharply the boundaries between Sunni and Shia communities.[39] Distinctions between Hindus and Muslims were also being demarcated more clearly on the ground, not only in Bengal[40] but also in the *qasbas* (or market towns) of Bihar and the United Provinces.[41] In 1939, the worst Shia–Sunni riots ever recorded broke out over Muharram in the United Provinces. When Muharram overlapped with Holi, the Hindu festival of colours, clashes became ever more frequent in Bengal. In 1941, severe violence broke out in Dhaka over rumours (later proved false) that Hindu women celebrating Holi had been molested by Muslim men.[42] By the middle of the 20th century, Muharram rituals had become highly contested and fraught with sectarian and communal tension. It is unsafe to assume that the Sunni 'Biharis' who continue to observe Muharram today are blithely unaware of its more charged meanings or its association with political conflict.

In late 1946, communal carnage broke out in Bihar. On 22 and 23 November, Hindu mobs fell upon Muslims in what many at the time saw as a reprisal for attacks on Hindus in neighbouring Bengal. Lord Wavell (then viceroy of India) described the violence 'on the scale of murders and degree of brutality, far beyond anything that . . . has yet happened in India under British rule'. Worst affected were the districts of Patna, Gaya, Monghyr (Munger), Bhagalpur, and Saran.[43] (Some, but not all, of these were part of the Bhojpuri belt: all were places which for decades had sent migrants to Bengal.)

This time the context was not Muharram, but instead Hindu–Muslim violence in neighbouring Bengal caused by the Pakistan issue. After August 1946, when the Muslim League had declared 'Direct Action Day' to press their demands, Bengal had witnessed gruesome violence, first in Calcutta and then in Noakhali. In Bihar, between five and ten thousand people are thought to have lost their lives. Wavell estimated that about 120,000 people had fled from the affected districts[44] and that there were 'hundreds and thousands of refugees' who dared not go back to their villages and consequently lost all their property.[45] About half of them ended up in camps in Bengal, where its Muslim League government offered them relief and rehabilitation.[46]

Given the deep-rooted links between the affected districts in Bihar and urban Bengal, it is not surprising that so many 'Bihari' refugees fleeing the rioting made their way to the towns and cities of Bengal. But they were clearly not expected: relief efforts were chaotic, to say the least.[47] Their arrival led to an ugly arm-wrestle between Bengal's chief minister, Huseyn Suhrawardy, and the leader of the Hindu Mahasabha, Syama Prasad Mookerji, who accused Suhrawady of seeking to overrun western Bengal with Muslims from Bihar. In July 1947, Mohmmad Younus of the Bihar Muslim League confused matters further by appealing to these displaced riot victims 'either to seek state protection if they felt unsafe, or to migrate to Pakistan if they were dissatisfied'.[48] The government of Sind (soon to be part of West Pakistan) invited the Bihar refugees to Sind, offering to rehouse and rehabilitate them. Jinnah himself had contributed Rs 42,000 towards the rail fares of 'Bihari' refugees.[49]

But before the fate of the Bihar refugees could be settled, India was partitioned. Eastern Bengal and the Sylhet district of Assam became 'East Bengal', the eastern wing of the new state of Pakistan. This unleashed a fresh stream of migration between eastern India and eastern Pakistan. By May 1950, after a second wave of rioting in both East Bengal and the jute mill areas of Calcutta, the numbers of refugees in East Bengal reached close to a million.[50]

We do not know for certain who precisely these refugees were. Some, without doubt, were people already displaced by the Bihar riots, fearful of returning home and persuaded to migrate to Pakistan by the blandishments of Bihar's Muslim League leaders and Jinnah's own opaque pronouncements. But they accounted for only a part of the million-strong refugee population in East Bengal. On 19 July 1947, the *Morning News* noted that almost all of Bihar's Muslim Indian Civil Service officers, the less grand but more numerous Muslim employees in military and accounts departments, and its Muslim telegraphists and railway employees had opted for Pakistan. According to the newspaper, while 'a very large number of middle-class Muslims were migrating to Sind [in West Pakistan] . . . *workers and labourers [went] to East Pakistan*'.[51] In November 1947, a British High Commission source confirmed that railway employees who had opted to serve in Pakistan were making their way to Parbatipur and other stations in the Rajshahi division in East Bengal 'in their thousands'.[52] Another wave of migration after the 1950 riots included many Bhojpuri jute mill workers, who abandoned the mill areas in Hooghly and Howrah in West Bengal and crossed over to Dhaka.[53] This picture is supported by the 1951 Census of East Bengal and by our own interviews in Dhaka's Town Hall, Mirpur, or Geneva camps and in the railway township of Syedpur (see Chapter 2). If the 'Bihari' diaspora in East Bengal already had a predominantly working-class character before partition, this was accentuated by the influx of refugees after 1947, giving the urban proletariats of the new Pakistani province a distinctive, North Indian profile.

Yet if this 'Bihari' population in Pakistani East Bengal was neither exclusively 'Bihari', it must be emphasized, nor was it uniformly 'Urdu-speaking'. Of course, there were Urdu speakers among them, particularly among the clerks, professional groups, and men of letters who, as Chapter 2 shows, migrated to Dhaka and other urban centres after partition. But given the association of Urdu with the Lucknow court and the professional services groups of the United Provinces, and its distinctive development as a literary language separate from bazaar Hindustani, it was hardly a demotic tongue. It was not the lingua franca of railway drivers, fitters, or mill hands. Their vernaculars were more likely to be Bhojpuri – a cluster of dialects peculiar to this region of the Bhojpur-Shahabad area of Bihar – Maithili or Magadhi Hindi, leavened by street Bengali and bazaar Hindustani. As for the thousands of 'Bihari' soldiers who served the army in East Pakistan in the days of Ayub Khan, a great many of them spoke Punjabi, Pashto, Balochi, or Saraiki, not Urdu, as their first language, although they no doubt understood the language of Pakistani officialdom and military command.[54]

The *Muktijuddho* (Liberation War) of 1971 was fought to free the Bengali nation from Pakistani oppression. It is well known that Bengali national identity was closely identified with language: 'Bengalis' were people whose mother tongue was Bangla.[55] In that war, this motley population of migrants – palpably outsiders who spoke little Bangla, predominantly employed by the Pakistani state (whether directly in the railways, army, schools, or municipal offices) or in state-supported enterprises such as the jute mills – were identified as non-Bengalis and became the target of ethnic nationalist militias. Believed to be collaborators (*razakars*) of the Pakistani army, they were hunted down and killed in large numbers.[56] Of those who survived, a few managed to escape the country, but most flocked to makeshift camps and shelters, mainly in Dhaka, Syedpur, Chittagong, Rangpur, and Bogra. Some attempted to flee to Pakistan, but its prime minister, Zulfikar Ali Bhutto, agreed to accept very few of these people. The rest remained in overcrowded camps where they live to this day.[57] Deprived, until recently, of the citizenship of Bangladesh and denied refugee status by the UNHCR, for decades the camp dwellers have lived in a limbo of statelessness.[58] Their mobility has been highly restricted: camp dwellers are required to present identity papers if they wish to commute or travel as well as certificates confirming that the bearer is of good character and has not been involved in antisocial or antinational activities (see Figure 6.2).

This picture is beginning to change. As Chapter 3 shows, many younger 'Biharis' speak fluent Bangla and have moved out of the camps, some even marrying into 'native' Bengali families, usually from poorer backgrounds. But the crucial point is that each of these camp 'communities' formed after 1971 was in no sense an organic whole developed over time by the usual workings of chain migration, village recruitment, and kinship networks. Rather, they comprised stayers-on from many different sectors of the economy flung together at a stroke by harsh and sudden circumstance. Some were related by blood – like Salima, for instance, whose story was mentioned in Chapter 2, who was widowed in 1971 and fled from Syedpur to Dhaka to join her sister. But many were not and had no connection with each other at all before the horrors of 1971 threw them together. Not all spoke the same language. Most were from working-class families – but frequently from quite different occupational groups who came from different places. In Town Hall camp, Khadija's Allahabad-born father was a lascar and her husband, a mechanic in railways; Hanifa's Darbhanga-born father was an agriculturist, Farida's father was a mill-hand from Belgachia in Calcutta. A very small number had been modestly prosperous before the war: Shabnam's Azamgarh-born father had owned a

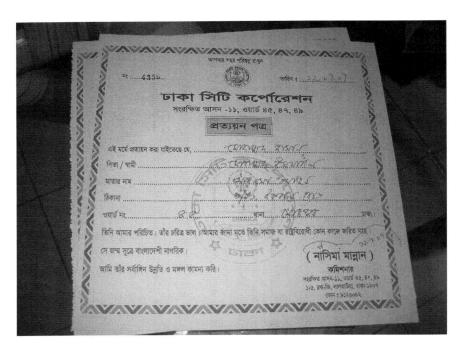

Figure 6.2 Character certificate issued by the Dhaka City Corporation.
Courtesy: Annu Jalais, Bengal Diaspora Project.

tailoring business in 'Old Dhaka' before 1971. But most had been poor and are now poorer still, eking out a living in an informal economy as piece workers in the garment trade or mechanics – and, in some cases, as the servants or clients of small-time drug dealers.[59]

What unites the inhabitants of the camp today, then, are neither kinship or village ties, nor their 'Bihari' roots or their 'Urdu' language. It is their poverty, their migration history, and their particular marginal location within the Bangladeshi nation state that marks them out as a group. Most are survivors of mass killings or the children of survivors. Muharram rituals occasionally bind them to one another and to the city they inhabit in ways that are powerfully influenced by this history of dislocation and how they remember it.

Making space, marking history

Turning from the past to the present, let us follow the *paiks* on their journey. As they jog along in boisterous packs, the boys laugh as they push and tease each other. Yet their levity notwithstanding, how, when, and where they run says much about how camp 'Biharis' construct their history, perform 'community', and engage with others in the city.

'Bihari' *paiki* boys are, so to speak, 'consecrated' for three days to Imam Husain – they act as his 'postmen', 'soldiers' or 'horses' (depending on whom you ask). They run through streets that lead to the *mazars* of saints, to *imambaras* in their own locality and then in adjoining areas. Older boys are more adventurous and venture further afield. For three nights they do not return home, often sleeping in the grounds of 'Bihari' Sunni mosques.

The *paiks* also visit Shia *dargahs* and *imambaras*. Often a Shia mosque becomes the point of assembly and starting point of their trip, especially for the youngest *paiks*. Since Shia mosques in every locality tend to be aligned with rival neighbourhood factions, there are usually several such points of assembly. There is not a single 'Bihari' *paiki* group, then, but many; each sets off on its way after a brief *fatia*[60] and blessing by the elders of their locality. The boys' mothers are much in evidence at these ceremonies, making special *paiki*-appropriate dishes, dressing up their young wards, and organizing prayers for the young girls and women of their neighbourhood who wish them on their way.

Weeks before the *paiks* begin to run, there is a build-up of excitement and activity in 'Bihari' localities. At night, the little enclosures around *imambaras* become the hub for Muharram preparations. Banners and standards *(alams)* flutter atop long bamboo poles, brightening up *imambara* compounds, often left in a desultory and untended state for the rest of the year. With all the bustle and excitement, wafting aromas of cooking, and the hammering as men prepare *tazias*, these places become, for just a few weeks a year, focal points of 'Bihari' sociability.

Most flags have two symbols placed at the highest point of the pole: either the crescent or star and the hand. As a result, observers often conclude that they parade the continued allegiance of the 'Biharis' to Pakistan. But, as Asad explained, 'the crescent and star you see on flags symbolize Islam and not Pakistan. . . . We've always hoisted these flags during Muharram, even before the creation of Pakistan'. The five fingers of the hand symbolize the 'five pure souls' – the Prophet Mohammad; his daughter, Fatima; his son-in-law, Ali; and his grandsons, Hassan and Imam Husain. When asked what the hand stood for, interestingly, many 'Biharis' offered a more ecumenical interpretation – they replied that the hand was a symbol of the fact that the many strands of Islam are one, parts of a single whole.

The public festivities associated with Muharram, such as *paiki*-running, lathi-play, fire-eating, and dancing, are all-male events, displaying physical prowess. The very word *'paik'*, or infantry man, has martial resonances; the term was adopted for this reason by Bengali *zamindars* for their informal armies of rent collectors. (Whether the boys are aware of this is a different matter.) Yet their *paiki* runs are undoubtedly important identity-forging occasions; they engender a strong sense of the collective – even brotherhood – among cohorts of boys and men of the same age. We often heard our informants speak of other young men who ran with them as their *'paiki-bhai'* (*paiki*-brothers).

Three days before Ashura, *paiks* start their running. For these three days, they 'live the life of horses'. Like horses, the boys sleep in open spaces, sometimes in the compounds of mosques, and eat neither rice nor fish. Horses have a special resonance in the Karbala narrative since it was Husain's steed, Zuljeneh – colloquially 'Duldul' – who brought the tragic news of the Iman's martyrdom to his supporters. But, interestingly, not a single informant actually described the *paiks* as symbols of 'Duldul'.

The boys run from *imambara* to *imambara*, from slum to slum, from camp to camp, from neighbourhood to neighbourhood. Sometimes they drop in on relatives, deliver news and letters, and take short breaks to participate in the festivities of the locality in which they find themselves. As families and occupational groups often have been scattered across many camps, the *paiks* serve as messengers ('postmen'), carrying their news from one to the other.

Paiki running is revealing about the ways in which 'Biharis' express both internal differences and shared customs. Boys of the same age linked to the same *imambara* (usually therefore also neighbours) stick together in distinct *paiki* groups, and in so doing express their allegiance with particular *mohallas* and particular cohorts. But all the groups – broadly speaking – nonetheless do the same things and follow similar routes (see Figure 6.3).

These routes are fascinating and significant. They encompass two types of 'centre', marked out on Figure 6.3. The first are sites of special religious significance to the migrants – what one might describe, after Green, as the local 'architecture of enchantment'.[61] The second are areas that have a particular significance to 'Bihari' migration history: Dhaka's migrant zones, whether camps or middle-class neighbourhoods, both Shia and Sunni. For instance, they run past 'Panch Tolla camp', which is not a camp at all but a fairly affluent neighbourhood where Urdu-speaking officers lived in the past and where many still live, having been spared in 1971 (or so rumour has it) because they were well connected to the Bengali-speaking middle classes.

In other parts of Bangladesh where 'Biharis' are concentrated, such as Syedpur, Chittagong, and Narayanganj, *paiki* routes followed similar tracks. In Calcutta,

Building a tazia, *becoming a* paik 173

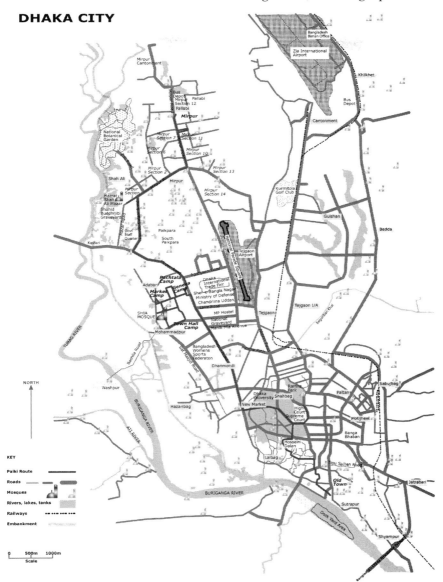

Figure 6.3 Route taken by *paiks* through Dhaka.

too, *paiks* ran through areas that had high concentrations of 'Biharis' or were of special religious significance to them. Some older boys in Pilkhana ran to *dargahs* and *mazars* of various saints so far away that they had to return by train.

When a particular road was abandoned as a *paiki* route, it was usually for a good reason. For instance, the boys stopped running through Kobi Nazrul Islam

Sarani, which passes through Dhaka University, because it was deemed too dangerous: in the 'old days', apparently, students from Dhaka University routinely subjected the young *paiks* to beatings when they passed via that route. This is revealing about how the 'Biharis' negotiate urban space, often retreating from or skirting round danger zones rather than standing their ground and fighting back. Since colonial times, the rule for allowing public processions through thoroughfares had been based on claims of precedence – if a procession had been allowed in the past, its right to continue to use that route was almost always recognized and upheld by the authorities.[62] But as minorities without citizenship rights in Dhaka, 'Biharis' clearly often felt the best course for them was not to insist on 'customary' rights or precedence to urban space.[63] Some parents have stopped sending their boys out altogether, fearing for their safety. The fact that others continue to do so might therefore be interpreted as a sign, if not of defiance, then at least of a certain quiet doggedness.

Significantly, *paiks* deliberately used routes that took them to Shia *dargahs* and *imambaras*. When they visited these Shia sacred spaces, *paiks* stood and prayed together. The caretaker of these Shia mosques usually led their prayers. Even at the Hosseini Dalan, the most significant Shia *imambara* in Bangladesh, *paiks* were allowed access to the *sanctum sanctorum*. However, the young boys entered it using a special stairway reserved for Sunnis. As they entered, a shrine attendant blessed the boys and touched theirs banners to the crest of Hazrat Abbas's banner. (None of the boys could explain why it was Abbas of the Karbala paradigm to whom they were so linked – but it might well be a symbolic reference, in Shia eyes, of proletarian reverence for the shrine of Hazrat Abbas, common in Lucknow's heyday.) This also reveals how 'Bihari' Sunnis of Dhaka manage their relationship with the city's Shias: *paiks* go to great trouble to include Shia holy places in their ritual; Shias, for their part, accept them into these places and bless them – but they ensure that they enter by a specially demarcated, separate entrance. For their part, 'Bihari' *paiks* accepted these terms of engagement without comment as the appropriate order of things.

Better-off Shias, and even educated and wealthy 'Biharis', often raised issues of class, status, and education when they spoke of 'popular Muharram'. In contrast, 'Bihari' practitioners of these popular rituals rarely did so, at least not explicitly. But this is not to say that they did not express views about what Muharram meant for them. Many were so articulate on this subject that one might even speak of an emerging 'Bihari' popular theology.

Young 'Biharis' stressed that, for them, Muharram was about honouring Imam Husain. But significantly, it was also about venerating, simultaneously, *all* the saints who had brought Islam to the subcontinent. Asad, an extremely articulate young man from Geneva camp who ran as a *paik* as a child, explained, 'Husain was the first martyred prophet of Islam, one who was betrayed by his family, but also one who inspired his followers to take the message of Islam to the four corners of the world'. Asad told us that many members of his community venerate *mazars*, who are associated with all the holy men who brought Islam to South Asia. They identified particularly with the Sufi Chishti lineage of Ajmer. Many

'Biharis' believed that the 'Khaja'[64] of Ajmer, Moinuddin Chishti, had himself observed the rituals of Muharram. It was only right, they argued, that they continue this tradition in the Khaja's honour. Asad also said: 'More "Biharis" want to visit Ajmer than Mecca, because Ajmer is the Mecca of the poor and it lies in the country of our forefathers'.

The history of migration and sacrifice is also a central theme. As an elderly 'Bihari' man explained, 'Bihari' migrants feel,

> a bit like Husain, you know; we're sacrificial victims, and it's over our bodies that the politics of the two states of Bengal have been played. Is this why we identify so closely with Husain the martyr? We're a good, honest, hard-working people. We built this city just like we taught the Bangladeshis all about good food, good clothes, and electricity. Don't you find the best kababs of Bangladesh in Mohammadpur [the largest refugee colony of 'Biharis' in Dhaka]? Who do you think work as their tailors? Who does the work as their electricians, their car mechanics, their railway operators? We've been the ones working away for the Bengalis, and yet, what have they given us in return? Only abuse, whether it be on this side of the border or on the other.

Here we see a fierce pride in the history of labour, skill, craft, and hard work combined with the weary knowledge that none of this buys the 'Biharis' real respect in a 'foreign' land. This pride in a shared history of labour combined with awareness of how contemptuous people on the 'outside' were of that history was evident among many respondents.

When we asked why Muharram was such an important event for Sunni 'Biharis' (but not for Sunni Bengalis), 'Biharis' invariably went back to their perceptions of the advent of Islam in South Asia. Muharram was a way for them to maintain their link with the geographies and histories of early Islam and of Islam's spread in the subcontinent as well as with their own migration history. Lomba Jomidar, the elderly (and as his name suggests, tall) caretaker of one of the *imambaras* of the slum of Pilkhana (in Indian West Bengal), explained:

> Bihar was Islamized through the *pirs* and was therefore the land of many *dargahs* and *imambaras*, and wherever 'Biharis' went, they took a bit of their saint with them, carrying his memory safely across the land and seas they crossed. This is why you see us practise Muharram – wherever we go, we take our saints along and build *tazias* to commemorate the first saints of Islam each year.

For Lomba Jomidar, the migration of 'Biharis' was like the 'migration' of the Islamic saints. 'Biharis' revered the mausoleums of saints who had actually lived and died in the Dhaka area, but they also venerated 'replica shrines', symbolizing links (both historical and spiritual) to specific places (and shrines) left behind, whether in Bihar, Uttar Pradesh, or Calcutta. Like their saints before them, 'Biharis' see themselves as pious migrants taking their faith wherever they go.

In this oft-narrated history of a 'common migration', India, Awadh, Lucknow, Ajmer, and Bihar kept resurfacing as places to which they continued to feel a deep religious connection.

The largest and most famous *imambaras* were built not by them but by Shia notables from Lucknow. Yet Dhaka's 'Biharis' would often point to the most important of these with great pride, particularly the ornate and imposing Husaini Dalan and the Bibi ka Roja – believed to be the oldest Shia shrines in Bangladesh. They spoke of these places as 'theirs' as much as they belonged to the Shia. They seemed to regard the saints, the Shia, and themselves as bound together in a complex web of genealogies taking them back to India, Arabia, and Persia, where common histories of migration were played out through the specific rituals of Muharram.

Some Shias also stressed the importance of the mausoleums of the saints in the sanctification of the soil of Bengal. Rokeya Bibi, a Shia woman in her mid-thirties, explained:

> The story goes that after Husain's death, people began to mistreat Khatun-e-Jannat – the 'lady of paradise' – another name for Fatima,[65] the daughter of our Prophet. So before dying she announced that when she died her soul would not stay in Saudi Arabia but go to Hindustan, where women were better treated. It is believed that this is what happened – her soul floated down the Buriganga all the way to Farashganj,[66] where we have kept her memory by respecting her grave.

In such accounts (often repeated by 'Bihari' Sunnis as well), the advent of a holy figure in old 'Hindustan' was linked to a particular grave; the branch or *silsila* was not a formal religious order but rather comprised people who had come together to honour the memory of the saint. Whether they were Shia or Sunni was less of an issue.

But if, just like the 'migrants', the saints were 'foreigners', linking them to communities of followers who were spread throughout the world, they were also made 'local' through their association with particular spaces of veneration that had become their resting places. The caretaker of Bibi ka Roja's *dargah*, Mohammad Sajjh Husain, proudly proclaimed that his lineage was from Egypt and that his family and friends 'lived everywhere: Pilkhana, Calcutta, Iran', but he insisted he was 'Bengali'. He said that the *dargah* was visited by the ambassadors of Egypt, Iran, Iraq, and Pakistan: as the resting place of the illustrious Fatima, in his eyes, it is not reducible to denominational differences or national boundaries. What was important for him was that they were all her followers, 'connected' by virtue of their reverence for *all* messengers of Islam.

Paiki running thus evokes the recent history of a marginal group located in a particular city and nation while simultaneously calling to mind wider spiritual connections across time and space. It links the camp poor with others on the 'outside' – whether the Shia of Old Dhaka, the Urdu-speaking middle classes living outside the camps, or devotees of the Imam worldwide. It thus celebrates, simultaneously, the advent and spread of Islam, the sacrifice of Imam Husain and the pioneer saints, and the Muslim brotherhood of the labouring 'Bihari' poor.

Taziadari: Cooperation, competition, and negotiation

The *tazia* procession is the high point of the Bihari Muharram. As Hakim, a boy from Town Hall Camp, explained:

> The *tazia* procession is one of the most important events in a 'Bihari's' life. The whole community comes and participates, walking along with the *tazias* for a bit or watching from rooftops. We make comparisons between *tazias* and debate which ones are the most beautiful. It is a way for us Biharis to come together.

Tazias are built during the ten days leading up to Ashura. Made of bamboo, cane or even steel, they were often quite large, with three or more storeys. Some were strikingly beautiful; most were richly decorated with coloured paper, glass, and lace. Different *tazias* commemorated the death of Husain and Hassan and all the seventy-two martyrs of Karbala, even the baby Ali Asghar, son of Imam Husain, who was killed by an arrow while in his father's embrace. On Ashura, all these *tazias* were paraded through predominantly 'Bihari' areas of the city in slow procession.

Achieving this spectacular finale was obviously a complex affair, involving cooperation at different levels between many people as well as much delicate negotiation – among other things – about the order in which the *tazias* are paraded. Careful observation of *taziadari* revealed much about internal divisions and competition within camp neighbourhoods. It also threw fascinating light on how 'Biharis' negotiated with each other and with other residents of Dhaka to bring out a successful procession on Ashura and, in so doing, achieve – however partially and momentarily – a sense of community.

The organizers of the procession were often those who tended particular *imambaras* who represented neighbourhoods (*mohalla*) of about two hundred people. To fulfil the many tasks required by a successful procession, 'Biharis' formed small leadership groups directed by '*khalifas*' (or caliphs), usually the chief caretakers of a local *imambara*. Each *khalifa* gathered around him a '*Khalifa* group' of between ten and forty men. These invariably included a senior artisan with specialist skills in *tazia*-building whose job it was to build the frame of the *tazia* or repair an old frame. Others, usually junior craftsmen and apprentices, decorated it. Younger, less skilled members of the group were sent out to collect donations or subscriptions (*chanda*) from the inhabitants of the specific *mohalla*.

Like all processions that use public roads, the organizers first had to obtain permission from the government and then arrange for police protection since the event has often sparked violent confrontation with other groups. Apart from dealing with the authorities, the *khalifa*'s role was to bring special earth from a graveyard (of which more below) and distribute 'consecrated' food (*shirni*) and sugared drinks (*sherbet* or *sabil*) to all those who visited *imambaras* or watched the procession. The younger men accompanied the procession, some as *tazia*-bearers, others beating drums or playing with *lathis* (staves) and fire.

There are four *imambaras* in Town Hall Camp (the larger Geneva Camp has fourteen). When we did our fieldwork in 2008, the *khalifa* of the main *imambara* of Town Hall Camp was Chan Mia, and we observed his role closely. His key assistants included Muhammad Iqbal Munna, the 'second *khalifa*' and chief artisan of the *tazia*, who otherwise earned his living as a car mechanic. Chan Mia was also assisted by Aslam, the son of the camp shopkeeper, Wakil, a barber in his thirties, Sohid the butcher, and Showfik the fishmonger. These men were modestly prosperous by camp standards, and their involvement in the *khalifa* group both reflected and entrenched their standing in the neighbourhood.

The 'second *khalifa*', Iqbal Munna, described himself as a professional *tazia*-maker. A migrant from Metiabruz in Hooghly whose ancestors were from the Lucknow area, he said:

> We have been making *tazias* for generations. My grandfather came to Calcutta as a tailor master. My other job is as electrician. I have never married and feel that making *tazias* is a kind of calling. The way I understand making *tazias* is that in our tradition, one day the angel Gibreel brought some mud to Prophet Mohammad; the Prophet knew that the mud was from Karbala and that Hassan and Husain would become martyrs and that this mud which was slowly taking the shape of a *tazia* would become red; this is also why at the end we place the mud in water, to 'cool' it. Our 'caste' believes that we should make these imaginary tombs to commemorate Husain's sacrifice to protect Islam. The Shias here take out one procession, but we Sunnis take out thousands.

For the event to succeed, *khalifas* together decided upon the precise position of each *tazia* within the grand parade. But harmony was not always possible to achieve. In 2008, one *tazia* builder, Jhula Nannu, refused to conform to the agreed order. He had built his *tazia* in the form of a palanquin, a 'Jhula Tazia' or 'Bibi ka dola' (the palanquin of Bibi, a reference to Fatima). According to one of our survey assistants, 'He always does his own thing and never wants to come in line with us'. Despite days of negotiation between the different *khalifa* groups, when the *tazias* were actually brought out for the final grand procession on Ashura, a heated argument broke out over who would go first and what time they would set off.

The main events started on the sixth day, after the prayers of Magrib and the sighting of the moon. The *khalifas* of Town Hall and Geneva camps, each accompanied by their assistants, took flags to the nearest graveyard as darkness fell. After a brief *fatia*, each gathered up a little earth from the graveyard and wrapped it up in a flag. This earth, we were told, represented the earth from the tombs of Hassan and Husain. Nobody can see it without going blind, so great is its power. On returning to their respective *imambaras*, each *khalifa* placed the earth, wrapped in cloth, at its centre and recited a *fatia* over it. Later, each discreetly inserted this clod of earth inside his *tazia*.

For 'Biharis', *tazias* were the acme of Muharram – their craftsmanship a mark of their devotion to the Imam. (This is in marked contrast with the Shia processions, where the *matam* – the self-flagellation ritual – is the main event.) On the afternoon of the tenth day of Muharram, the *tazias* came out in the final grand procession amid much pomp and ceremony. Thousands of people watched or accompanied the procession, while young men vigorously banged drums, played with swords, and 'ate' fire.

The whole procession wound slowly through the streets, always keeping within the working-class neighbourhoods or camp areas inhabited by 'Biharis'. The confinement of the parade to 'Bihari' areas sent out an interesting message – it announced the presence of 'Biharis' in the city and celebrated it while avoiding conflict by intentionally bypassing Bengali-speaking localities. It thus marked out, and staked a claim, to a very local geography while invoking idioms that resonate throughout the Islamicate world, thereby linking the camps to that world.[67]

At the end of the tenth day, when the festivities came to an end, the *tazias* were taken to a nearby body of water to 'cool'. According to our informants, the clods of earth inside the *tazias* were extremely 'hot' (because Husain and Hassan were very daring, *teji*), and their tombs had to be 'cooled' so that they could rest in peace. In the past, we were told, whole *tazias* were immersed in the rivers or lakes of Bengal. In Dhaka, until about twenty years ago, they were submerged in Dhanmondi lake, or the man-made lake in front of Sansad Bhavan, Bangladesh's imposing parliament building. But two decades ago, the Dhaka City Corporation and the Dhanmondi lake authorities refused permission for these immersion ceremonies. Now, *khalifas* secretly pull out the small clod of earth in each *tazia* and dip it into a large pond or lake. Here again we see their willingness to avoid confrontation with the authorities or with other inhabitants of the city.

This concept of 'cooling' *tazias*, or at least of parts of them, is shared by Shias, who also 'cooled' the flowers that decorated their standards. In West Bengal, processionists immersed whole *tazias* in the river Hooghly or in ponds or lakes adjacent to *imambaras*. (This practice is distinctive to the eastern region – further west, whether in Lucknow, Delhi or Mahmudabad, *tazias* are still interred in the ground.[68]) But despite this strong thread of common practice, relations between Shia and Sunni migrants were shot through with inflections of difference and of hierarchy. In Hooghly, the Shia caretaker of the Metiabruz *imambara* explained the relationship between the two processions:

> Ours is a different kind of procession – it is one of mourning where we sing soulful songs and where some of the younger ones beat themselves with chains. The Sunnis who come with their *tazias* and join our procession are of a totally different kind; they believe that the making of a *tazia* is a form of piety and that their craftsmanship and ability to make such beautiful works of art are due to divine blessing. Ours is a procession of mourning; theirs one of fervent veneration.

Relations between the two communities were often tense. Every year, some Sunni *paiks* (usually much younger than the Shia processionists) run shouting through the Shia procession, disturbing Shia mourning, and fights frequently break out. In 2008, although things remained calm between the Shia and Sunni processionists, students at Dhaka University once again blocked one of the roads the 'Biharis' had received official permission to use. The matter almost came to blows.

Most 'Bihari' camp dwellers (including women and children) stood by the side of the road and watched the Shia procession as it went by, but several actively joined in. Asked why, a few 'Biharis' said that they regard Shias as part of their wider community of migrants from North India. Others were less high-minded, saying merely that Shia mourners beating themselves until they bled was a thrilling spectacle. 'A sight not to be missed', one young 'Bihari' boy said excitedly.

When we asked whether Shias joined in their own Sunni procession in the afternoon, they replied in the negative. Shias, they maintained, were 'a caste above' them. This simple statement reveals that despite occasional ecumenism and ambiguity, Muharram's complex rituals are sites not only for the performance of 'community' and 'identity' but for the expression of cleavages, both subtle and stark. At times, the differences were horizontal, revealing tensions between different sects or 'ethnic' groups. At other moments, they were vertical, revealing distinctions of class, status, and education within the Sunni 'Bihari' community. Yet another kind of distinction – albeit sometimes overlapping with the former – was between the 'educated' and the 'unenlightened'. Perhaps the most controversial was the schism between reform-minded Sunni 'radicals' and the 'unreformed' mass of others, who – in the eyes of the reformers – participated in the 'sin' of superstition. And then there were the 'secular' critics who were simply uninterested in the whole affair and tried to ignore it. They were neither embarrassed nor enthused by Muharram: they were simply bored by the whole business. They had no particular love for *imambaras*, even those in their own neighbourhood. One or two actually saw them as something of a nuisance. One man in Town Hall Camp wanted the *imambara* his deceased father had built to be shut down. He lived just above it, on the first floor, and after his father died he did not want this practice to continue as it was 'disturbing his peace'. He liked to 'smoke a fag, chat with his friends and listen to music' – and these pastimes were difficult with the *imambara* right below him. Shakil, the owner of the Honda shop just opposite, did not want the *imambara* there either because it affected his business. This led to a heated argument between Shakil and those who were determined to keep the *imambara* where it was, and the police had to be called in. In the end, Shakil agreed that the *imambara* could stay, but with a marked lack of enthusiasm.

Muharram as a site of difference

In his fascinating account of Sunni Muharram in Darjeeling in West Bengal, David Pinault writes that Muhammad Maqbool, the person who introduced him to it, was 'both proud and ashamed' of the participation of his *anjuman* or association. 'Proud', he explained, because it gave the town's Muslims a way of asserting their presence publicly, but also 'ashamed' because 'so many of our Muharram practices are against Islam'.[69] When Pinault asked him for an example of such a practice, Maqbool spoke of *tazias* and how 'making a *tazia* is like drawing a picture'[70] and therefore against the tenets of Islam.

As in Darjeeling, so in Dhaka, where Sunni Muharram rituals reflect the ambiguity of migrant identities and also tensions within and between migrant 'communities'. Most marked was the fault line between Shias and Sunnis. Since the late 19th century, as Justin Jones reminds us, these differences have grown deeper. But interestingly, in Bengal, the tensions were more subtle and complex than the outright hostility Shias faced in many parts of contemporary Pakistan.

Shias we interviewed in Calcutta and Dhaka expressed mixed feelings about the way in which 'their' procession had been 'hijacked' by the Sunni 'Biharis'. Even those who described an 'understanding' between the two communities, spoke in terms of 'tolerating' the 'Bihari' Sunni Muharram. Since 'toleration' implies living with or even accepting something viewed as wrong or discomforting, we probed further.

Shias in Dhaka were, on the whole, uncharitable about 'Bihari' Muharram. They spoke angrily about the alleged 'inability or refusal' of 'Biharis' to 'integrate'. This insistence that 'Biharis' should assimilate into 'the mainstream' of 'national' culture suggested that some Dhaka Shias have adopted majoritarian conceptions of Bangladeshi nationalism (see Chapter 8). Other Shias feared that as they too were non-Bengali immigrants from the same *poorbea* region who had migrated to Bengal along with the nawabs, they might be tarred with the same brush as the 'Bihari' *razakars* in the Bengali nationalist perception. They were therefore keen to maintain their distance from the 'Biharis'.

Relations between Shia and Sunni processionists were not particularly cordial. Several Dhaka Shias explained why the two groups had separate processions in the city (whereas they held only one in many parts of Calcutta). Their reasons could be condensed into one single phrase: 'their lack of respect for our customs'. Ali, a bank employee in his mid-forties, claimed to summarize what many Shias thought:

> They aren't respectful of Shias' practices of Muharram. See, they wear all sorts of colourful clothes and do not undertake penance the way we Shias do (such as wearing only black in mourning during the forty days of Muharram, not eating fish, etc.), and they run around like monkeys disturbing our mourning and sorrowful processions.

Flare-ups were common because sometimes young *paiks* ran shouting through the Shia procession of mourning, and fights between the two sides were not unusual.[71] After a 'Bihari' boy was killed during one such fight, the government closed off certain roads to *paiks*.

We asked why the 'Biharis' continued to join the Shia procession despite this rather condescending and half-hearted welcome. We were told that the 'Biharis' see the Shias as part of their own wider community of 'migrants from India', even though they accept that Shias came long before them, accompanying the nawab of Awadh to Bengal in the 19th century.[72]

Cleavages between two groups were as much about status, rank, and class as they were about religious practice. Most Shias we met were relatively wealthy and believed themselves to have descended from 'nawabi' or aristocratic lineages. In the main, 'Biharis' who practised Muharram were not and had no such illusions about their ancestry. Even upwardly mobile 'Biharis' (those who were born in camps but had moved to other parts of the city) made no such claims. The feelings of self-respect and dignity of camp 'Biharis' rested on their self-perception as skilled, industrious craftsmen and hard-working people. They seemed aware of the fact that their Muharram was regarded by Shia elites as a crude carnival of the crowd, something that was 'beneath' the higher status groups and middle classes of the city.

Tension between *poorbea* Sunnis and Shias was less marked in Calcutta. Bohra Ali Mirza, a genial descendant of the last nawab of Awadh, was chief custodian of the grand *imambara* at Metiabruz. He explained why Shias in Calcutta accepted what also seemed to them a rather insensitive tribute to Husain's martyrdom. 'You know', he said,

> they're at heart good people, the younger ones who become *paiks* are . . . well . . . 'young'. As for the older ones, well . . . the older ones are . . . let's say 'sincere'; for them, the very act of 'making' a *tazia* is piety, it is showing Allah that we rejoice in the craftsmanship He has gifted some of us with, showing Him that we honour His saint Imam Husain by building something beautiful for him as he was the first man to die for Islam. Tell me, how can we not allow these people to express their devoutness for our very own saint?

This explanation – at once poignant and patronizing – revealed how much the great days of Awadh and Lucknow lived on in Shia memory and, from their perspective, continued to bind the *poorbea* Sunni proletariat to them in a close relationship, albeit one that was unequal and deferential.

Despite the Shias' ambivalence towards them, however, 'Biharis' continue to observe Muharram at Shia *imambaras*, whether at Hossaini Dalan in Dhaka or the Metiabruz *imambara* in Calcutta. The routes they took in both cities have a high concentration of Shias living around them. It seemed as though, by determinedly marching in these areas, the 'Biharis' publicly insisted on a shared heritage of a single 'North Indian migrant community' – rich and poor, Shia and Sunni alike.

This sometimes made younger, middle-class 'Biharis', particularly those who lived outside the camps, uncomfortable. As one said:

> It reminds me too much of the taunts and attacks of my Bengali neighbours. They would attack us when we went to play in the park, calling us 'dirty "Biharis"' and '*Biharir bachcha*' [son of a 'Bihari'] as if being 'Bihari' in itself was wrong, like being a thief or something.

Another again spoke about how, a couple of decades previously, a fight had broken out between *paiks* running along Kobi Nazrul Islam Sarani and Dacca

University students. Deriding and hurling insults at the young 'Bihari' *paiks*, the students had refused to allow them to pass, claiming they would defile the memory of *Oporejeyo Bangla*[73] by their very presence on the street. Many young educated 'Biharis' also said they felt embarrassed by the 'spectacle' 'Biharis' made of themselves during Muharram. They said that their Bengali neighbours often ridiculed them for this unsophisticated custom of 'their community'.

Another young man from Town Hall Camp was particularly eloquent about his unease with the local Muharram. A bit like David Pinault's informant in Darjeeling, he said that 'as an educated person', he felt he should not practise Muharram in the Bihari way, as it was 'backward'. He felt mortified that his community represented itself publicly in this way. He was, he told us, actively trying to get them to stop by explaining that the Bihari Muharram was not a very old festival. He had read somewhere that 'Biharis' had only started to celebrate Muharram on account of the Hindus. 'During their various festivals, especially Kali puja . . . the Hindus would bring out their arms and parade with them through the streets so the 'Bihari' Muslims, who felt threatened every time that happened, decided to do the same on Muharram', echoing (deliberately or otherwise) Hodson's critique of 'Bihari' Muharram as a set of syncretic customs shared by the 'uneducated persons at the bottom of the social scale'.[74] In his eyes, the festival's dubious historical pedigree meant that 'there was no reason to continue with this custom', and he was trying hard (without much apparent success, it must be said) to persuade less-educated 'Biharis' to give it up.

The similarity between certain 'Bihari' Muharram practices and those of Hindus (such as the 'cooling' of the *tazias* and the immersion of the images of Hindu deities) has also attracted the opprobrium of reform-minded Sunnis, who denounced it as a borrowing from local Hindu customs.[75] But interestingly, ardent supporters of the *tazia* procession took the opposite view: they insisted that the practice allowed them to *distinguish* themselves from Hindus. As Hassan, a young 'Bihari' boy from Town Hall. told us:

> There was, once upon a time, a saintly baba who lived in a Hindu-dominated area. The king of the place was a Hindu, and every time the Muslims wanted to do something they wouldn't be allowed to. The baba decided he should do something so impressive that the king, and the rest of the Hindu population, would start looking well upon Muslims. So he built a *tazia* and started playing drums to attract attention.
>
> The king heard the commotion and ordered the drum-beaters to stop. The man replied, 'You're not doing right'. The king then said, 'What's inside your *tazia*?' The man replied, 'If you want to look inside, please be my guest'. The king peered inside and was completely floored by what he saw: in the tiny room he saw Hassan and Husain talking to each other. The baba then said, 'There's still time for you to repent'. The king then converted to Islam and all his people with him. To commemorate this event, and in honour of the baba, we build *tazias*.

Everything about this story captured the mood of the 'Bihari' Muharram – the sense of being outnumbered by an overbearing majority; the desire to impress and persuade, rather than to fight; the emphasis on the courage of the minority in the face of overwhelming dominance. Also evident was the deep pride in the skills of a working-class community which included many artisans, even if they were no longer able to earn a living by their craft.

But, of course, these were precisely the themes that attracted the censure of radical Sunni reformers. There was the 'saintly baba' – a reference to *pir* cults. There was the creation of human images of Husain and Hassan 'talking to each other'. But most serious in their eyes, perhaps, was the notion of the charismatic power of the *tazia* and its miraculous ability to cure ills and triumph over all obstacles – pure 'superstition', in their eyes. Increasingly, 'Bihari' Muharram incurred their wrath, whether of the 'Wahabi', the Tablighi, the Jamaat-i-Islami, or Ahl-i-Hadith persuasions. While they had differences among themselves, they protested in unison that 'Biharis' behaved like apostates and that their practice of Muharram was 'un-Islamic'. Many of them were, interestingly, from 'Bihari' backgrounds themselves. As one of them said to us: 'By joining these processions, they give a bad name to Islam'.

Both in Dhaka and in Calcutta, several 'Biharis' complained that even though the Wahabis had always been against the practice of Muharram, they had now started attacking the shrines of saints and *tazias* on the grounds that both were 'un-Islamic'. As Lomba Jomidar explained, 'We Muslims are divided into two main groups: Sunnis and Wahabis':

> Our main fight is with the Wahabi or the Taliban. This fight goes back to Karbala – the fight between the spiritual and political forces of Islam. Those who think only the Prophet is worthy of their veneration are Wahabis. The rest of us believe that not just the Prophet but also his family and his followers should be venerated. He couldn't have done everything alone; Islam was brought to South Asia by those who loved and followed him, and all we do is honour their memory.

Another elderly Shia from Dhaka's old town added, 'We enlightened Shias forgive the *paiks*, but the ones to really get provoked are the Wahabis. But then, they get provoked by anything'.

Mohammed Iqbal Munna, the *tazia*-maker from Metiabruz, captured the sense of defiance that many 'Biharis' feel at this attack on their religious rituals. 'We have been making *tazias* for generations', he said. Today, he explained, he continues to make *tazias* deliberately to 'defy the Wahabis'.

Conclusion: Memory, history, and community

Lomba Jomidar, caretaker of the Pilkhana Imambara, claimed that his *imambara* was once called Dargahtala and was built in the year 1800. Similar to the stories Richard Eaton describes, redolent of the charisma of the *pirs* of Bengal, Jomidar told us that, once upon a time, *pir* Mir Amanatullah Ali had received the land from a generous king. The king had promised to give the *pir* all the land that his favourite elephant walked on in a single day. When the British asked him about his title to the 52 *bighas* of land on which the *dargah* and its adjoining tank stood, the *pir* miraculously produced the required papers. This story was in itself revealing: a 'Shia' monument was built on a site with Sunni Sufi mystical provenance.

For Jomidar, the 'interesting part' of the *imambara*'s history was that people from all communities came and settled 'here in Pilkhana'. 'Biharis' came to work in the jute and cotton mills of Howrah and on the railways, and they brought with them their tradition of building *tazias* and praying for intercession from the saint. When these pleas for help were granted, one of their sons would be chosen to be a *paik* or a 'foot soldier' to honour the memory of 'the first saint and martyr of Islam', Imam Husain. Place and travel, settlement and memory, faith and enchantment were intertwined in the remembered history of an *imambara*.

Dhaka's 'Bihari' Muharram's rituals, too, spoke to these themes. But in addition, the 'Biharis' commemorated loss and sacrifice (both at Karbala in the past and in recent history) and celebrated craft, labour, and love. They mapped out, geographically, a place to which they now felt they belonged while asking (albeit deferentially) for a place in Bangladesh's present.

In contemporary Bangladesh, however, many found such a celebration of a 'different' – indeed, reviled – minority ritual deeply challenging, and 'Bihari' *paiks* and processionists who continue with their performance do so in an atmosphere where violence always threatens. So there is an element of resistance, even a staking of claims, in 'performing' 'Bihari' identity in public, in 'coming out' of the camps and 'reclaiming' the streets of the nation's capital. Muharram rituals thus cannot be understood as ageless 'tradition' replayed again and again in the same ways, regardless of place or context, but as constantly changing performances grounded in particular places and their shifting local contexts.

Muhrram rituals also played out an account of the 'migration story' of the 'Biharis' which was in no sense simplistic or linear. The bid was always to be recognized simultaneously as a 'migrant' as well as a 'local'. In chaste Bengali, Lomba Jomidar insisted that he was 'from Pilkhana', even though we had established in our conversation that he was from Bihar. In Metiabruz, an elderly 'Bihari' man sang Bengali folk songs to his heart's content, '*o majhi, ar koro na deri*' ('oh boatman, do not delay') and '*cholo nobir barite*' ('let's go to the Prophet's house'). He said his family was 'originally' from Lucknow and that this was why he had a love for music and beauty. He maintained that it was *because he was a 'Bihari' from Lucknow* that he so loved Bengal's language and culture.

Speaking of their Muharram and its contemporary, cross-cutting, political resonances, all our 'Bihari' respondents showed an acute awareness of how they are viewed by 'the locals' and by their many critics. Whether on the streets of Dhaka or in the narrow bylanes of Hooghly, those who observed, indeed celebrated, Muharram seldom did so unreflexively. They were aware of the debates and saw themselves as participants in them. Some of them, like the *tazia*-maker

186 *Building a* tazia, *becoming a* paik

Iqbal Munna, literally described *tazia*-making as a gesture of defiance – a riposte even – to those who denounce the custom.

We can only conjecture whether Husain's martyrdom was so important in the camps because it allowed their inhabitants to commemorate their own war dead. Damned as traitors to a nation which, like Kwon's Vietnam, has 'promoted the worship of the war dead to a civic religion',[76] the 'Biharis' who lie dead can never be publicly owned nor be brought home and buried by their loved ones. Perhaps the veneration of Husain brings the camp dwellers briefly together because it offers them a moment to remember their dead and grieve for them. But not a single informant told us this.

What, then, does Muharram tell us about how 'Biharis' create and perform 'community'? As we observed in Chapter 3, the 'Bihari' camps of Dhaka are no longer exclusive spaces. 'Biharis' lived alongside others (dozens of Bengali *rickshawalas* from Dinajpur now lived in the 'Bihari' camps, for instance). Their children played together. A significant number of 'Biharis' also 'had family' with Bengalis (*rickshawalas*, porters, fishmongers, shopkeepers). Several have established *pir-bhai* relations with Bengalis when they visited the same shrine or travelled together as migrant workers to Gujarat or the Gulf, and in rare cases (as of two people in Geneva Camp), they had even been on the hajj together. These Bengalis spoke street Urdu with ease, and most 'Biharis' were totally bilingual. Many 'Biharis' were solicited by their rural Bengali in-laws to facilitate land-buying in the suburbs as they were seen to have better relations with the 'town Bengalis' than 'village Bengalis' had themselves.

'Bihari' areas were not exclusive, nor were they 'controlled spaces'. When 'outsiders' enter, their inhabitants go out of their way to help as guides. Usman *chacha* was curious, but not overbearingly so, about who was coming and going as they passed his shop, but he was always happy to chat over a cup of tea with those who came and went. There seemed to be no sign whatsoever of 'community' policing, there were no obvious 'community leaders', and authority seemed rather diffuse. Power in the camps was shared by many. There was the imam, of course, but not everyone went to the camp mosque. The camp 'leader' was Musharaf, but his nickname was 'Baldy', a sign that the respect he commanded was not universal. He shared influence with the schoolteacher, the bright student who was training as a computer engineer, and with the *khalifa* groups. Each had their own understanding of Muharram, of their community, and of how to go 'forward' in life. These understandings rarely matched, and authority did not flow seamlessly from one font.

It was only during Muharram that most – but not all – 'Biharis' in these neighbourhoods come together. As Lomba Jomidar stressed, 'Eid is shared by all Muslims, but people go to their own mosque, so the space is not necessarily shared; but the road, like the *imambara*, is an open space, one where any "Bihari" can feel at home'. For the camp dwellers, Muharram was a festival of the road at which all 'Biharis' were welcome and in which all could participate (albeit in roles defined by age, gender, religious authority or artisanship). It is only when Muharram came round that there was any palpable sense of 'communitas', in

Victor Turner's sense of that term, among the 'Biharis' of these neighbourhoods. Even bitter rivals temporarily ceased their hostilities, or at least worked round them, and joined in, whether actively in the *paiki*-running or *taziadari* or just by cheering on the parade as bystanders. Even the 'secular' critic could sometimes be coaxed to participate in a stick game or to help complete a *tazia*.

Perhaps, then, just as 'class', 'community' is not a 'thing', an objective and identifiable social fact with a permanent, quantifiable existence. Bihari Muharram suggests, rather, that it is evanescent, changing, 'something that happens'[77] at particular moments in response to particular historical conjunctures and processes. Perhaps Muharram is one such moment that enables 'Biharis' to play out their account of their history and, in so doing, fleetingly 'become' a community.

Notes

1 *Imambara*, the Urdu term for 'house of the Imam', describes structures in which eulogies for Imam Husain are recited, biers are housed, and other Muharram rituals observed.
2 See, for instance, Vernon James Schubel, 'Karbala as Sacred Space among North Indian Shia: "Every Day is Ashura, Everywhere is Karbala"', in Barbara Daly Metcalf (ed.) *Making Muslim Space in North America and Europe*, Berkeley: University of California Press, 1996, pp. 186–203; David Pinault, *Horse of Karbala. Muslim Devotional Life in India*, New York: Palgrave, 2001; J.R.I. Cole, *Roots of North Indian Shi'ism in Iran and Iraq. Religion and State in Awadh, 1722–1859*, Berkeley: University of California Press, 1988; Justin Jones, *Shia Islam in Colonial India. Religion, Community and Sectarianism*, Cambridge: Cambridge University Press, 2002; Kamran Scot Aghaie (ed.) *The Women of Karbala. Ritual Performance and Symbolic Discourses in Modern Shi'a Islam*, Austin: University of Texas Press, 2005; Syed Akbar Hyder, *Reliving Karbala. Martyrdom in South Asian Memory*, Oxford: Oxford University Press, 2006; Kamran Scot Aghaie, *The Martyrs of Karbala. Shi'i Symbols and Rituals in Modern Iran*, Seattle and London: University of Washington Press, 2004.
3 These 'creative strategies to metaphorically bring Karbala to local sites' were, according to Korom and Chelkowski, 'devised as a way of bridging geographical distance, in order to attenuate the problem of alienation from the original site'. Frank Korom and Peter Chelkowski, 'Community Process and the Performance of Muharram Observances in Trinidad', The Drama Review, 38 (2), Summer 1994, p. 152. Also, for the significance of pilgrimage to Karbala for Shias, see Mahmoud M. Ayoub, *Redemptive Suffering in Islam: A Study of the Devotional Aspects of Ashura in Twelver Shi'ism*, The Hague: Mouton Publishers, 1978, pp. 180–96.
4 Frank Korom, *Hosay Trinidad, Muharram Performance in an Indo-Caribbean Diaspora*, Philadelphia: University of Pennsylvania Press, 2003; Mohapatra, ' "Following Custom?" '.
5 Nile Green, *Bombay Islam. The Religious Economy of the West Indian Ocean, 1840–1915*, Cambridge: Cambridge University Press, 2011, p. 53–69; Torsten Tschacher, *Islam in Tamilnadu: Varia*, Halle: Institut für Indologie und Südasienwissenschaften der Martin-Luther-Universität Halle-Wittenberg, 2001.
6 Pinault, *Horse of Karbala*; Green, *Bombay Islam*; Jones, *Shia Islam*; Korom, *Hosay Trinidad*; Schubel, 'Karbala'; Cole, *Roots*.
7 Even as recently as 15 November 2012, the BengalNewz, a portal which purports to be the 'Official twitter account for Bengal Newz Dot Com – The first and most reliable daily news portal dedicated to entire Bengali speaking region, since 01–06–2007' describes a photo that shows 'Bihari' Sunni Muslims as 'Shiite Muslim breathes out fire during

188 *Building a* tazia, *becoming a* paik

   #Muharram procession, #Bangladesh': https://twitter.com/search?q=bengalnewz%20muharram%20bangladesh&src=typd
8 When he asked about Shia Muharram practices in Hyderabad, the man he was speaking to responded exasperatedly that, 'Yes, such groups existed, but they were not worth the time and attention of an educated person like myself'. 'Why not?' asked the author. 'Because', he said with evident irritation, 'these groups were uneducated. They were dirty. They knew nothing about Islam and so would be bad people from whom to learn about the religion. End of discussion'. Pinault, *Horse of Karbala*, p. 3.
9 Dirk Kolff, *Naukar, Rajput and Sepoy: The Ethnohistory of the Military Labour Market in Hindustan, 1450–1850*, Cambridge: Cambridge University Press, 1990. Also see, by the same author, 'The Market for Mobile Labour in Early Modern North India', in Chatterji and Washbrook (eds), *South Asian Diaspora*, pp. 26–7; and Chapter 1 of this book.
10 Cole, *Roots*, p. 94.
11 Ibid., p. 95
12 Ibid., p. 69–117; Jones, *Shia Islam*, pp. 75–113.
13 Cole, *Roots*, p. 110.
14 Ibid., p. 99.
15 The term 'Karbala paradigm' draws on Michael Fischer, *Iran: From Religious Dispute to Revolution*, Cambridge, MA: Harvard University Press, 1980.
16 C.A. Bayly, *Rulers, Townsmen and Bazaars, North Indian Society in the Age of British Expansion, 1770–1870*, Cambridge: Cambridge University Press, 1983.
17 L.S.S. O'Malley, *Bihar and Orissa District Gazetteers, Saran*, 1930, Reprinted New Delhi: Logos Press, 2007, p. 36.
18 Chattopadhyaya, *Internal Migration*, pp. 275, 279.
19 Kerr, *Building the Railways*, p. 110 ff.
20 Ibid., p. 45.
21 See, for instance, Brij Lal, 'Girmitiyas: The Origins of the Fiji Indians', *Canberra Journal of Pacific History Monograph*, 1983; and Mohapatra, '"Following Custom?"'. Also see Chapter 1.
22 Chattopadhyaya, *Internal Migration*, pp. 252–85.
23 Ibid.
24 Kenneth McPherson, *The Muslim Microcosm. Calcutta, 1918–1935*, Wiesbaden: Streiner, 1974.
25 G.A. Grierson, *Linguistic Survey of India*, Vol. V, Part II, Calcutta, 1903, p. 5.
26 Green, *Bombay Islam*, p. 2.
27 See, for instance, Rafiuddin Ahmed, *The Bengal Muslims 1871–1906. A Quest for Identity*, Delhi: Oxford University Press, 1988; Jones, *Shia Islam*; Francis Robinson, 'Islamic Reform and Modernities in South Asia', *Modern Asian Studies*, 42, Double Special Issue, 'Islam in South Asia', 2008, pp. 259–281.
28 Eaton, *Rise of Islam*.
29 Ahmed, *Bengal Muslims*; Asim Roy, *The Islamic Syncretistic Tradition in Bengal*, Princeton: Princeton University Press, 1983.
30 L.S.S. O'Malley, *Bengal District Gazetteers, Patna*, Calcutta: Bengal Secretariat Book Depot, 1907, Reprinted New Delhi: Logos Press, 2005, pp. 68–9.
31 Ahmed, *Bengal Muslims*.
32 Jones, *Shia Islam*, pp. 1–74.
33 O'Malley, *Bihar District Gazetteers, Patna*, 1924, pp. 68–71.
34 Ibid., pp. 66–67.
35 Green, *Bombay Islam*, p. 15.
36 Cole, *Roots*, p. 103.
37 In his account of Saran, O'Malley devotes far more space to cow-protection movements and to a mysterious wave of 'tree daubing' than to Muharram. See L.S.S. O'Malley,

Bengal District Gazetteers, Saran, Calcutta: Bengal Secretariat Book Depot, 1908, pp. 39–41. In Monghyr, a region of high emigration, and so profoundly affected by famine that O'Malley listed for a full three pages the roots, creepers, and leaves eaten by starving people, there appears to have been no Muharram commemoration at all. See L. S. S. O'Malley, *Bengal District Gazetteers, Monghyr*, Calcutta: Bengal Secretariat Book Depot, 1909, p. 68.
38 L. S. S. O'Malley, *Bengal District Gazetteers, Hooghly*, Calcutta: Bengal Secretariat Book Depot, 1912, p. 108.
39 Chatterji, *Bengal Divided*, p. 146.
40 Jones, *Shia Islam*.
41 Chatterji, *Bengal Divided*, p. 146.
42 Sandria B. Frietag, *Collective Action and Community. Public Arenas and the Emergence of Communalism in North India*, Berkeley, Los Angeles and London: University of California Press, 1989.
43 Chatterji, *Bengal Divided*, p. 141, n. 168.
44 Lord Wavell to Sir Pethick-Lawrence, 22 November 1946, in Nicholas Mansergh and Penderel Moon (eds) *Constitutional Relations Between Britain and India. The Transfer of Power*, 12 volumes, London: HMSO, 1981–83, Vol. 9, p. 140.
45 Ghosh, *Partition*, p. 3.
46 Lord Wavell to Sir Pethick-Lawrence, 22 November 1946, in Mansergh and Moon, *Constitutional Relations*, Vol. 9, p. 140.
47 Ghosh, *Partition*, pp. 3–8.
48 Wavell's diary.
49 Ghosh, *Partition*, p. 6.
50 Ibid., p. 8.
51 British Library (hereafter BL), L/P&J/ 5/326, East Bengal Weekly Reports from the UK High Commissioner, reports for the months of February, March, April, and May 1950.
52 *Morning News*, 19 July 1947, cited in Ghosh, *Partition*, pp. 12–13. Emphasis added.
53 BL, L/P&J5/231, special reports for the fortnights ending 26 October and 27 November 1947.
54 Ilias, *Biharis*.
55 Ibid., p. 120.
56 For an insightful overview, see Willem van Schendel, *A History of Bangladesh*, Cambridge: Cambridge University Press, 2009, pp. 159–90.
57 Mascarenhas, *Bangladesh*.
58 For details, see Hashmi, '"Bihari" Muslims'; Ghosh, *Partition*, pp. 28–32.
59 Redclift, *Statelessness*.
60 Ilias, *Biharis*. Also see Saif's story in Chapter 3.
61 Prayer ceremony, so-called because it involves the recitation of Al-Fatiha, the opening verses of the Quran.
62 Green, *Bombay Islam*, p. 52.
63 Katherine H. Prior, 'The British Administration of Hinduism in North India, 1780–1900', PhD thesis, University of Cambridge, 1990.
64 In West Bengal, likewise, in the postindependence era, Muslim minorities gave up many 'customary' rights of public worship in the face of danger. See Chatterji, *Spoils*, pp. 178–81.
65 'Khaja' is the local Bhojpuri pronunciation of 'Khwaja', a revered saint, or founder, in this case, of a Sufi religious order.
66 On the special place of Fatima, or Fatemeh, in the Karbala narrative and in Muharram rituals around the world, see Aghaie, *Women of Karbala*, Introduction, pp. 1–21.
67 An area in Old Dhaka where the French are believed to have traded.
68 Marshall Hodgson, *The Venture of Islam*, (Vols. 1, 2 and 3), Chicago: Chicago University Press, 1961.

Building a tazia, becoming a paik

69 A. K. Mahmudabad, 'Muharram in Awadh', in Muzaffar Ali (ed.), *A Leaf Turns Yellow: The Sufis of Awadh*, New Delhi: Bloomsbury, 2013.
70 Pinault, *Horse of Karbala*, p. 94.
71 Ibid.
72 Peter Gottschalk, 'The Problem of Defining Islam in Arampur', *International Institute for the Study of Islam in the Modern World Newsletter*, August 2001, p. 23.
73 Of course, this is not strictly accurate: Bengal's nawabs were not all Shias. The nawab of Dhaka was not a 'Bihari', nor a Shia. But because he enjoyed Persian literature, was the de facto patron of the Husaini Dalan, and patronized Muharram in the city, the general view among 'Biharis' was that 'Nawabi culture' and 'Shia culture' were one and the same.
74 *Oporejeyo Bangla* is an iconic statue that stands in front of the university and symbolizes the resistance against Pakistani oppression by Bengali, considered to be the nation's martyrs.
75 *Bengal, Bihar, Orissa and Sikkim, 1911*, in Thomas Callan Hodson, *Analysis of the 1931 Census of India*, New Delhi: Government of India Press, 1937, p. 251.
76 This is not a new observation. European travellers, such as Garcin de Tassy and Emma Roberts, remarked that 'Muharram, like the festival for the Goddess of Death, Durga, lasts ten days. On the tenth day of Durga *puja* Hindus cast a figurine of the goddess into the river, paralleling the Shi'i custom of often casting the Imam's cenotaph into the river on the tenth day of Muharram. The Muslims made the same offering to the Imam that Hindus proffered their sacred figures'. M. Garcin de Tassy, *Mémoire sur des particularités de la religion musulmane dans l'inde*, Paris: L'Imprimerie Royale, 1831, pp. 11–12, 30, 38–41, in Cole, *Roots*, pp. 116–17.
77 Heonik Kwon, *After the Massacre. Commemoration and Consolation in Ha My and My Lai*, Berkeley, Los Angeles, and London: University of California Press, 2006, p. 2.
78 E. P. Thompson, *The Making of the English Working Class*, London: Victor Gollanz, 1963, pp. 10–11.

7 Rituals of diaspora

The Shahid Minar and the struggle for diasporic space

Just before midnight on a freezing cold 20 February 2008, Altab Ali Park on the Whitechapel Road in Aldgate, East London, began to fill with people gathering to mark 'Ekushe', a ceremony to commemorate the Bangladeshi Language Martyrs. Over 200 people – mostly British Bangladeshis, men and women of all ages and social stratas – gathered, from restaurant owners and their employees to professionals and Bangladeshi international students studying in London. Individuals mingled with cultural and political organizations, some chanting slogans from their political parties based in Bangladesh, others evoking the 1971 Liberation War – *'Ekattorer dalalera hushiyar shabdhan'* ['Collaborators of '71, be careful!'], still others appealing to a more global collectivity – *'Duniar mojdur ek hou, lorai koro'* ['Workers of the world unite and fight']. A tea vendor circled through the crowd selling tea from a flask, another selling *jhal muri*;[1] in one corner of the small park, a group of young men and women – probably students – sat with a guitar singing Bengali pop songs. Towards midnight, the crowds formed a ragged line to the Shahid Minar, the monument to the Language Martyrs that stands towards the back of the park, now lit up by spotlights. Many were holding flowers and wreaths or a single rose, some singing *'Amer bhaier rokte rangano Ekushe February, Aami ki bhulite pari'* ['I cannot forget the 21st February, that has been coloured with the blood of my brothers'].[2]

The programme, as in previous years, was organized by Shahid Minar UK, part of the Nirmul Committee in East London. At 12:01 a.m. on *Ekushe* February[3] itself, the Bangladeshi High Commissioner led the tributes, placing a garland at the base of the Shahid Minar. He was followed by the Mayor of Tower Hamlets, the leader of Tower Hamlets Council, and representatives of both British and Bangladeshi political parties, cultural and professional organizations, Bengali TV stations, and other social and regional organizations. When they reached the monument, a few removed their shoes as a sign of respect, standing barefoot for the few moments when they placed their flowers before they were moved on. The flow of people past the monument was organized by employees from Tower Hamlets Council, with the Metropolitan Police standing nearby and occasionally moving people along. The ceremony lasted around an hour.[4]

Later that day and over the following weekend, local organizations held discussion and cultural events to mark *Ekushe* in East London. The largest, on *Ekushe* itself, was staged by the London Bangla Press Club at the nearby Brady Centre in Whitechapel and was attended by local politicians, community leaders, and media personalities. The weekend events included a concert of sitar fusion music in neighbouring Bethnal Green and an art competition for children.

Like the Muharram celebrations in Dhaka, discussed in Chapter 6, *Ekushe* marks part of the annual cycle of Bengali diaspora life in Bangladesh and among Bengali Muslim diaspora communities across the world. In East London and elsewhere in the UK, the Shahid Minar monument, along with the yearly *Ekushe* ritual surrounding it, has become a primary site for a version of nationalist/cultural identity work and politics. While on the one hand the ceremony is a private, almost intimate, memorialization of loss, struggle, and sacrifice, it also functions as a public and outward-facing performance of Bengali identity, an evocation of the ties to the homeland and to other Bengali communities in diaspora, as well as a claiming of space in the place of arrival: what we might think of as the 'rituals of diaspora'. The memorial and the surrounding rituals inscribe the Bengali presence in terms of time and space through an appeal to places and points of origin both historical and 'mythical' (see Chapter 8), and through the enactment of the fragmented, sometimes fractious, formations and transformations of contemporary 'community' identities. They thus constitute a performance of 'long distance nationalism'[5] which conjures at once a diasporic 'non-territorial form of essentialized belonging'[6] and a transported and relocated ideal of nation and community that traverses and transcends time and distance between Bangladesh and Britain. *Ekushe* enacts multiple temporalities and spatialities including a contested national (hi)story, the transplanted local histories of British Bengali communities, and their place within a new national imaginary. As with Muharram, *Ekushe* speaks to the formation of Bangladeshi nationhood, here through the lens of the dominant nation-story[7] – from the perspective of its winners rather than its losers – though one that has not remained uncontested in contemporary Bangladesh. But it also speaks to the creation of travelling nationhoods which take root within, and as part of, other national stories. The Shahid Minar memorial in East London emerged at the same multicultural moment as, and as part of, the bigger Banglatown project,[8] and is thus integral to the story of diasporic community-building discussed in Chapter 4. At the same time, divisions within British Bengali communities and their links to ongoing political and religious struggles in Bangladesh are played out within these rituals and memorial sites in the UK[9] – testifying both to the unfinished nature of Bangladeshi nationhood and its continued resonance for its diasporic children. The rituals of diaspora thus interweave local struggles with the national-British and transnational-Bangladeshi dimensions, which constitute a multilayered web of meanings, contexts, and contestations that shape Bengali diaspora identities in Britain. Like Muharram, then, these rituals constitute contemporary sites of struggle and contestation, inclusion and exclusion, narration and silence, which tell a more complex story about the struggle for recognition and belonging and open up demotic and discordant local, national (British and Bangladeshi), and diasporic stories.

This chapter seeks to unpack some of the workings of the rituals of diaspora through an exploration of the Shahid Minar and *Ekushe* in Tower Hamlets, East London.[10] Where earlier chapters have focused on the social formations of Bengali diaspora identities, the emphasis here, as with Chapter 6, is on the cultural and performative dimensions of diaspora.[11] Rituals of memorialization (*Ekushe*) are considered to constitute forms of cultural identity work which exemplify some key transitions and tensions in Bengali diaspora identities. Here, through the Shahid Minar and the associated ritual of *Ekushe* and building on the analysis of Muharram in the previous chapter, we explore the ways in which collective memory and identity are evoked, layering the multiple meanings of transnational, national, and local belonging and the ways in which these histories are contested in the contemporary moment of religious and generational transformation.

Conjuring home: The 'roots' and 'routes' of the Shahid Minar

The Shahid Minar in Tower Hamlets, East London, stands in Altab Ali Park across the Whitechapel Road at the southern end of Brick Lane. The monument can be found towards the back of the small park, formerly the churchyard of the medieval St Mary Matfelon's White Chapel, which gives the area its name. The entrance to the park is marked by a wrought iron arch commissioned by the council in 1989 and designed by Welsh artist and blacksmith David Peterson. Combining Bengali and European design traditions, the arch is made up of a tubular structure woven through with bands of red-coated metal, and was commissioned as a memorial to Altab Ali and the struggle against racism.[12] The path through the park is studded with brass letters imprinting a quote from a poem by Nobel Prize-winning Bengali poet Rabindranath Tagore: 'The shade of my tree is offered to those who come and go fleetingly'. On *Ekushe*, the site is surrounded by flowers and people, but more usually it is strewn with rubbish and scarred with the occasional, and occasionally racist, graffiti that defaces the monument and archway.[13] The monument is a replica of the larger original memorial in Dhaka and of its first diasporic reincarnation, which is situated in Oldham in the northwest of England. The abstract design – a white metallic structure consisting of a central, three-pronged pillar standing before a red circle with two smaller pillars at either side – symbolizes a mother with her fallen sons backed by the crimson rising sun, resonant of the Bangladeshi national flag.

The original Shahid Minar stands outside the Dhaka Medical College and was built to commemorate the students and political activists who, on 21 February 1952, were shot by the Pakistani police force during a demonstration against the imposition of Urdu as the official language of East Pakistan. 'Shahid Minar' translates, in fact, as 'Tower of the Martyrs' or 'Martyrs' memorial'. The roots of this event can be traced back to an earlier attempt at nation-building in the aftermath of partition, in what Van Schendel has termed 'the Pakistan experiment',[14] and the attempt by West Pakistan to impose Urdu as the language of the newly emerging Pakistani nation. Language quickly became a primary terrain for struggle against West Pakistani domination and exploitation. The imposition of Urdu was seen as part of a mission to 'Islamicize' East Bengal and reinforced the perception of social and religious inferiority.[15] The language movement was created and led by university students, and the first Language Action Committee was formed as early as December 1947. In February 1952, students at Dhaka University staged a mass demonstration against plans to make Urdu the state language and replace written Bengali with Arabic script. Thousands of students and school pupils confronted armed police outside the gates of the university campus. The police attacked the protesters with batons, launched tear gas when the students retaliated, and then fired into the crowd, killing five people, including a 9-year-old boy, and injuring many others. Over the next few days, there were further demonstrations, arrests, and killings. The language movement continued until 1956, when Bengali was accepted as a state language, but the resistance and the sacrifice of the language 'martyrs' are popularly understood as the starting point of the nationalist struggle, which culminated in the 1971 Liberation War (*Shangram*) and Bangladeshi independence.

The first memorial to the language martyrs was erected on the site within days of the first killings and itself became a site of resistance and confrontation, destroyed by the authorities and re-created by supporters several times before the establishment of a permanent memorial in 1962. The original monument in Dhaka remains a key focal point for nationalist secular identity politics, and like the *tazias* discussed in Chapter 6, martyrs' memorials are found, or made, in every town in the region. Where *Ekushe* was once a 'popular act of defiance' against the West Pakistani regime,[16] it is now a national holiday in Bangladesh and is marked by Bengali songs, plays, and poetry and the wearing of a combination of white, grey or black clothing, sometimes imprinted with Bengali script. Van Schendel quotes Rounaq Jahan that the '1952 language movement created myths, symbols and slogans that consolidated the vernacular elite'[17] which were foundational to the formation of an idealized secular Bangladeshi national identity and remain relevant today.

Nevertheless, the memorial and the commemoration have been, and remain, contested sites.[18] Van Schendel notes that the Shahid Minar, a key site of nationalist aspirations, was razed to the ground in the run-up to the outbreak of the Liberation War in March 1971.[19] The memorial, the language martyrs, and, indeed, the liberation struggle itself have remained sources of contention and contestation – perhaps most notably in the precarious citizenships of the 'Biharis',[20] discussed in Chapters 3 and 6; in the ongoing and unresolved controversies over the prosecution of those individuals who collaborated with the West Pakistani regime; and, most recently, in the Shahbag intersection demonstrations around the prosecution and sentencing of the Jamaat-i-Islami leader, Abdul Quader Mollah.[21] The significance of the Liberation War and the status of the Shahid Minar and *Ekushe* have thus waxed and waned according to who is in government.[22]

The Shahid Minar and the commemoration of *Ekushe* have become primary sites for a version of nationalist/cultural identity work and politics within the Bangladeshi community in East London, as well as in Bangladesh itself, and reflect both the continuities and tensions of memory work 'at home' (as well as more diasporic disjunctures, which will be explored later). The monument and the rituals surrounding it commemorate the mythical birth of the nation – language, blood, sacrifice – and enact a lived performance of links to Bangladesh, its history, the remembrance of the national struggle, and a set of intertwined values around secularism, language, culture, and nationalism. It is the claiming of a national and cultural identity that privileges notions of shared origins, of belonging, and of 'roots' which find their apotheosis in the liberation struggle.

Mahmoud Rauf, a local accountant and community leader who has lived and worked in East London since 1968 and was one of the founders of the Shahid Minar memorial committee in Tower Hamlets, explained:

> This is purely a cultural identity. It is the symbol of the language movement of Bengali people to keep their Bengali language, . . . [which] was the big turning point of Bengali sentiment, Bengali culture, and Bengali nationalism . . . that is our movement of self-determination and a symbol of our independence.

Mostaq Ahmed similarly commented, 'I think Shahid Minar is a symbol, it is an emotion. It is not only a sculpture, so many things are involved with it'. Sayeeda Shikha, who runs Nari Chetona,[23] a diaspora organization concerned with women's rights in Bangladesh and Britain, told us that she always attended *Ekushe*, but that:

> I celebrate it every day . . . it's my identity, it's *our* identity. If I don't mark it, I don't know my roots . . . if you are coming to the Shahid Minar, you are showing that you value our independence, you value our 21st February.

Shikha is also a member of the Nirmul Committee, the organization that is responsible for the annual *Ekushe* ceremony in Tower Hamlets. The Nirmul Committee was originally established in 1992 in Bangladesh by a group of 'pro-liberation' activists and has, as Van Schendel notes, 'become an important rallying point for secular and anti-Fundamentalist forces'.[24] The committee is concerned with the prosecution of war criminals in Bangladesh and elsewhere (including the UK) and has been central in shaping public perceptions of the war. These activities led to a number of high-profile prosecutions, demonstrations, and counterdemonstrations throughout 2013 which were played out in both Shahbag intersection, Dhaka, and Altab Ali Park, East London, in February that year.[25] Along with other political and cultural organizations which participate in *Ekushe*, the UK Nirmul Committee embody a version of 'long distance nationalism', which re-creates ties between the homeland and the diaspora that are at once historically rooted and immersed in contemporary concerns in Bangladesh itself.[26] Ansar Ahmed Ullah, a leading member of the Nirmul Committee in Britain, explained:

> It's a political campaign that was set up in Bangladesh in 1992 with the primary aim of combating the rise of fundamentalism, religious extremism, and also to demand the trial of war criminals from Bangladesh's war. We have branches here . . . and there are other branches in Europe . . . America, Australia. We have branches across the globe to support the campaign going on in Bangladesh.

Golam Mustafa, coordinator of Udichi Shilpi Gosthi, a cultural organization based in East London which was also centrally involved in establishing the Shahid Minar, told us that the memorialization provided living links to Bangladesh and its history and culture. Udichi has been running in Bangladesh since 1968 and has been established in East London for over 20 years. Golam Mustafa spoke of the links between then and now, here and there, performed in *Ekushe* commemorations, in particular linked to Bengali language and culture:

> From Martyrs' Day, from that language movement, we say was the actual starting of our independence. And that is marked in February 21st to remember those people who died for our mother tongue. So we built this monument, and this is a symbol of our cultural struggle.

For Golam Mustafa, the purpose of Udichi UK is twofold: first, to 'keep up with our culture, with our heritage, with our tradition, with the people within the country' (both migrants and their British-Bengali descendants); and, second, 'to represent Bengali people in this country . . . to bring our rich heritage to the mainstream communities in this country . . . and contribute to the multicultural society'. Mustafa spoke of the Shahid Minar and *Ekushe*, along with the annual Boishakhi Mela celebrations, as central to this more outward-facing engagement with wider British society.

War stories: Remembering *Shangram* in diaspora

Beyond these institutional contours, however, lies a more personal set of stories of war, struggle, loss, and remembrance. Sylhet was one of the largest areas held by the freedom fighters by November 1971 and had been a site of fierce fighting that extended over many weeks.[27] For many of our interviewees, the Liberation War and its aftermath were living memories – not least, perhaps, because in many cases the war and the political and economic turmoil which succeeded it had led to their migration to Britain, particularly for wives and children. For some, their memories of the Liberation War were still stark and emotive. Abul Hashem is a former journalist in his early forties who was granted political asylum in Britain in 1994 and later married and had three children. When we interviewed him, he was divorced and living in Newham, working part time in a local restaurant. Abul described his family's involvement and losses:

> When I was four or five years old, my father and second eldest brother were killed by the Pakistani military during the Liberation War in 1971. During the war, the Pakistani military, with the help of the *razakars*, killed my father and brother as they supported the war. . . . My eldest brother was a freedom fighter. He was in India. After they killed my father, we left our house secretly with the help of my grandmother. We went to India to take shelter, and after the Liberation War, probably in 1972, we came back to our house.

In 1971, around 13 per cent of Bangladesh's population were Hindu (about 10 million people),[28] and these communities were a particular target for the Pakistani military, with many hundreds of thousands killed or displaced through the violence.[29] Ashim Sen, a Bangladeshi Hindu who came to Britain in 1992 through marriage and now owns a restaurant in Bradford, was a young child when the war broke out. He recalled:

> What about my story? I have only one story to tell – the great story, the Liberation War. . . . I was around eight years old. I can remember the story of *Shangram*. People used to say 'the Punjabis are coming'. We would go and take shelter behind the bushes so many times. Whenever anyone would say 'they are coming', we would start running, although the Punjabis were ten miles away from there. Probably we heard the sound of a bomb blast. We would think they were coming to kill us all, so we had to do something. We would hide in the jungle, we hid our utensils and valuables in a hole covered by mud, we gave our domestic animals to reliable people for if we came back. . . . Our boat was on a nearby river bank. We went to camp because we could not live there.

He remembered the arrival of relatives from nearby villages escaping the violence, and the kindness of his Muslim neighbours in sheltering the family:

> We did not go to India in the end. Our relatives from other villages came to our house. Their villages were destroyed by the [Pakistani] military; their houses were burned to ashes; they [the soldiers] did bad things [rape]. Then we thought we should not leave our village. . . . In our area there were many people who were pro-liberation and carried those values. They said 'Why do you want to leave? You might get caught in the middle'. So we decided not to go.

In Bradford, he told us, the small community of Sylheti Hindus (about twenty to twenty-five families) had strong relationships with their Muslim countrymen:

> In Sylhet, Hindus and Muslims were living together; in Bangladesh, we were living together. We are so similar in our minds that religion was not a problem

in our relationships. That is why among the hundreds of my friends, 99 per cent are Muslim friends.

Korimunessa Begum came to Britain as a bride aged 15 in 1975 in the aftermath of the violence and settled in first in Yorkshire. She was born in India in 1958 in a tea garden where her father worked. The family moved to East Pakistan when she was very young and settled in Sylhet. One of her brothers joined the Pakistan army but left when the conflict broke out. She told us:

> During the Liberation War I was only 13, but I can remember everything. My mother used to cook *dal* in a huge pot for the Freedom Fighters, who were hiding in our house. Some Hindu families also took shelter in our house. . . . My niece's husband [*khalato bon*] was a leader of the Freedom Fighters.

She recalled that, 'We would not eat fish. It was available, but as the Pakistani army would kill people and throw them into the water, we would not eat fish from hatred'. She carried this anger with her to Britain: 'Only one community I hate, which I will not name – those who opposed us in the Liberation War, I do not like them'. Nevertheless, in her small community in Shaw (near Oldham), she bought her groceries in a Pakistani-owned shop: 'I go there, but it's not only them. It is mixed. There are more Bengalis than them. They have learned how to eat fish. They even sell dry fish, but they do not eat it'.

As Korimunessa suggests, the ramifications of the Liberation War were felt across the diaspora. The involvement of Bengalis in Britain in the struggle was key in shaping the events 'back home', particularly in raising funds for the Liberation Fighters, so it was perhaps especially fitting that Sheikh Mujibur Rahman was declared president of the newly formed Bangladesh during a visit to East London.[30] Nurunnobi Miah, who has lived and worked in Bradford since 1963, vividly recalls watching the events of the Liberation War unfold from the UK while his family were still in Bangladesh:

> The Liberation War started. For nine months, from 25th (March) to 16th December, we were worried. . . . There was no news from home; we did not know the situation in our village, no letters, nothing. There was a boy who was a student, he was my nephew . . . sometimes he would give us news. He would go to our village and tell us the situation, 'Don't worry, everybody is OK'.

In the days before satellite TV, the British media was crucial in giving the community information about the events in East Pakistan:

> British media gave good coverage of our Liberation War. They highlighted all the logical reasons for liberation, all the justified causes. Through their coverage, we saw on TV the Pakistani army torture the people of Bangladesh. They set fire to the houses of Bengalis. At that time, coming home from work, we sat to watch the TV to see what we can learn from BBC or Indian news.

Nurunnobi Miah recalled the role of diaspora Bengalis in raising money to support the struggle and raising its profile within Britain:

> We, the *probashira* (the overseas community) tried to help in support of the Liberation War . . . 95 per cent of the community were concerned about Bangladesh. After two, three months, we called a meeting on Bangladesh and formed committees with the purpose of helping the country. We contributed financially to the Liberation War. . . . We protested against the Pakistanis. We went to Hyde Park in London with a procession. . . . We went to different embassies and demonstrated. These nine months we were very worried and concerned. . . . The Pakistan Army tortured people, killed many people. In my village also, they killed many people. Many of our relatives were killed. . . . Anyway, the Liberation War ended. I left my Pakistani passport and took a British passport.

After Independence, Nurunnobi Miah and his brother travelled to the newly formed Bangladesh:

> We went to Bangladesh on 10th April [1972]. . . . I went for the first time after coming [to Britain] in '63. We saw the broken Bangladesh. There were signs of suffering everywhere. . . . After arriving, I heard all the stories from our relatives and village people. These types of stories are rare in the history. But in our village also there were some people who would support Pakistan. They acted against the freedom fighters. They helped the Pakistan Army to catch the freedom fighters. This way, they killed many Bengalis. If the collaborators did not help, the Army would not have got them.

Shanu Miah, who came to London as a teenager in 1967 to join his father and seaman grandfather, told us that he raised money while at school in East London to support the struggle in Bangladesh:

> During the Liberation War, we were organizing fundraising programmes. That was a great time. I feel proud of that time. . . . All the Bengalis were united during the Liberation War. At that time, I was a schoolboy, but I worked hard for Bangladesh.

This activity took place wherever Bengalis were living. Tasarul Ali, whom we met in Chapter 4, lived and worked in the textile mills in Oldham at the time. He similarly recalled:

> We would go to people to make them understand the situation. 'If our country does not exist, where will you call home? We are not able to go home. We need money to buy weapons and other things'. I alone collected £1,500, . . . and my four or five friends also collected money and handed it over.

As discussed in Chapter 4, the events also impacted on community formation and tensions within the UK itself. Nurunnobi Miah noted that the majority of Bengalis supported the struggle for Independence: 'There were a few people in favour of Pakistan, but they were very few – 2, 3 per cent. They would talk about religion – "Pakistanis and we are the same Muslims" – and [they thought] India and their collaborators were trying to break Pakistan'. Samuz Miah was in his late seventies when we met him and had been living in the northern mill town of Burnley since his arrival in the UK in 1964. He was in Dhaka preparing to bring his family to Britain when the war broke out, and he returned to Britain to organize support for the struggle. He recalled that tensions between neighbouring Bengali and Pakistani communities in the northern mill towns were high during this period. In Burnley:

> We had a Pakistani Association. . . . In our area, we built a mosque with the Pakistanis. I saw the Bengalis walk out of the mosque, they wouldn't pray over there. . . . Immediately after Liberation, it was a little bit hot. Particularly those who lost their relatives in the War had hatred against them.

In the aftermath of independence, the Bengali community in Burnley demanded separate mosques and community centres:

> If we wanted to get our flag flying over the mosque, we needed another mosque. We went to the council. They said, 'But you are all Muslims, why do you need another mosque?' . . . We said 'It is true, we are all Muslims, but we have two languages. That is why we've fought with them. . . . We are two different nations'. Then the council gave us permission to build another mosque. Then Shahzalal Mosque was built. Our flag started flying over it.

He noted, however, that these tensions were soon largely forgotten in a local and national context of migration and wider racial hostility:

> My logic is that we've been with the Pakistanis before, so we can live together with them. The British do not see any difference between us – they call us all 'Pakis'. Here in Burnley the relationship is good. We're on good terms with them.

If some of the fracture and fissures within and between South Asian migrant communities in the UK caused by the conflict were ameliorated over time, as Samuz Miah suggests, the significance of the Liberation War and Bangladeshi independence has also been seen as declining for the second and third generations of Bengalis born and bred in Britain. Nurunnobi Miah commented:

> Now it is a new generation. Almost 37 years are gone. The batch of Bengalis who saw the Liberation War . . . are mostly dying. Their children who have

not seen this do not think of it. Most of them do not know the history, do not read the history, and do not want to know about it.

As Kamal Hossain, who was central in establishing the Shahid Minar in Oldham, noted, however, these generational shifts and disengagements made the commemorative links to the war even more significant in shaping the identity of the next generation of Bengalis in the diaspora. He commented:

> Here we observe *Ekushe* for specific reasons. One is patriotism, and the other is to let the next generation, who are born and brought up here . . . to know about the occasion. We should let them know our history, make them understand the history and what happened to our country. . . . Then our children will feel a relationship with them – our country, our culture, our history.

As Kamal suggests, the purpose of *Ekushe* is then as much about the 'here and now' as about the 'there and then'. This is not to argue, however, for a utilitarian reading of commemoration as spatially and temporally presentist, but to recognize the ways in which these rituals of the past shape, facilitate, and enact cultural and political links between contemporary Bangladesh and its diaspora. The 'roots' of diaspora thus generate political and cultural 'routes' that travel both ways – in time and in place – between Bangladesh and Britain, the past and the present.

At the same time, too, the story of the struggle for Bangladeshi independence carries multiple strands, opening the space for negotiation and ambivalence. The narratives of sacrifice and triumph erase more contestatory and controversial presences and ghosts, including the stories of women raped during the conflict, the discarded children born from the violence, the beating and bayoneting of the *razakars*, and the exclusion of both Hindu- and Urdu-speaking minorities from this national narrative in the ensuing decades.[31] The 'story' of the Shahid Minar and of *Ekushe* thus encapsulates multiple temporalities and spatialities which the convenient bracketing of the national struggle from 1952–1971 belies, and reflects the longer histories and struggles over Bengali identity and its contested contemporary borders and citizenry. As the work of the Nirmul Committee, Nari Chetona, and Udichi suggest, these histories also have an unresolved impact on the present, and beyond Bangladesh's borders as well as within them.[32]

The 'roots' of the Shahid Minar and *Ekushe* are thus ambiguous and contested, while its 'routes' suggest alternative formations and transformations of meaning. Memorialization thus shifts from 'an imagery of dwelling' to one of 'journeying'[33] – in diaspora, both literal and metaphorical. On the one hand, the history of the language movement and the struggle for Bangladeshi independence can be viewed as having broader, global significance. The date of *Ekushe* – 21 February – has, for example, been recognized as by the United Nations as International Mother Language Day. On the other hand, the Shahid Minar and the meaning of *Ekushe* in Britain takes shape within a post-imperial national context and, indeed, within the local specificities – of Oldham, Greater Manchester, and the London

202 *Rituals of diaspora*

borough of Tower Hamlets – where it engages with different narratives, different histories, and different struggles. It is to these that we now turn.

Locating memory: The Shahid Minar in Oldham and London

The Shahid Minar monument and associated *Ekushe* rituals thus function on multiple levels, as a story of diaspora consciousness, as a symbol of multicultural Britain, and as a more local narrative of the Bengali presence in specific sites. Indeed, *Ekushe* is marked by Bengali communities across the UK and across the diaspora in temporary places, such as community centres, and with disposable monuments. It is only comparatively recently that these commemorations have assumed a more public and permanent form. While the Shahid Minar in East London is perhaps the best known, it is worth remembering that it is not the only – nor even the first – such permanent monument in Britain. This honour belongs to the British Bengalis' second city, Oldham.

Shahid Minar: Oldham

The first permanent Shahid Minar outside of Bangladesh was established in Oldham in 1997 and arose out of the history of local community associations and activism discussed in Chapter 4. Kamal Hossain, who had been a member of the Bangladeshi Youth Association, led the campaign for a permanent memorial, which was placed in the Westwood ward of Oldham, locally known as *Bangla Para*. He told us, 'Every year we would construct a Shahid Minar and then break it down'. He recalled, 'First we celebrated our Independence Day on 26th March in '91. We made the memorial with clothes'. His British-born Bengali friends, he said, did not know about the memorial: 'There was no picture of it. I drew the picture and showed them what the Shahid Minar and National Mausoleum looked like'. The following February, they observed *Ekushe* for the first time. The monument was built with wood and was mobile – an idea the community borrowed from Tower Hamlets – but in 1990 the community applied to the Single Regeneration Budget to establish a permanent monument, at the cost of £22,000.[34] Kamal recalled, with pride, 'It was finished at the end of '96, and in '97 we opened it and presented flowers. Before it, there was no other Shahid Minar in any foreign country outside of Bangladesh'. Abdul Jabbar, who arrived in Oldham in 1962, said that among the early arrivals, 'Shahid Day would be observed, but there was no Shahid Minar'. He described the changes to *Ekushe* after the establishment of the permanent Shahid Minar:

> [Before] we would organize meetings, discussion and distribute leaflets. The leaders in other cities would be invited and they would participate in the discussion. It would be observed in the way a Shahid Day is generally held. After [the establishment of the permanent] Shahid Minar, the tradition is changed. Now when 21 February comes, flowers are offered at the Minar at one minute past 12 midnight. Many organizations come to offer flowers. The Youth Association comes, political parties, for example, the Awami League,

BNP [Bangladesh National Party]. All come with flowers to offer.... Special prayers are arranged for the Shahid ... the day has great significance.

While the local position was significant in an area dominated by Bengali settlers and adjacent to the Bangladesh Welfare Association Community Centre, Kamal described the wider significance of the memorial and *Ekushe* rituals for Bengalis from across the North and Midlands in providing a link with 'back home':

> People come from Manchester, Hyde, Burnley, Bradford, and even Birmingham to place flowers at the Shahid Minar from 12 midnight.... When people come, the road in front of the Shahid Minar is blocked.... It's a huge gathering. The Shahid Minar is covered with flowers.... I feel good when I see people from all corners. A different feeling comes to my mind. *It feels like we are placing flowers at the Dhaka Shahid Minar* [our emphasis].

Mohammed Aziz similarly spoke of the significance of the Shahid Minar and the later Shapla Chhattar (established in 2000) in representing Bengali identity to the broader British population and to the next generation. For him, the story arises out of the process of migration and community-building described in Chapter 4. Funded by the same Single Regeneration Budget that built the local community centre, it is a story of arrival, of distinctiveness, of contribution, and of continuity:

> It is our unique contribution to uphold the image of Bengalis to the eyes of foreigners. Thinking about our generation and the generations to come, we tried to do something for the spirit of the Liberation War.... It was inaugurated by officials from the Bangladesh High Commission. Then we thought of Shapla [water lily]; it is our national flower. But the next generation might not know anything about it. So we wanted to show our love for it.

Shahid Minar: Tower Hamlets

As described above, the Shahid Minar in London stands in Altab Ali Park, across the Whitechapel Road from the southern entrance to Brick Lane and Banglatown in Tower Hamlets, at the heart of Britain's Bangladeshi community. Neighbouring the East London docks, the historical lifeline of the British empire[35] and the arrival point of immigrants for centuries, this part of East London has long stood as a symbolic hub of British imperialism, of a melting pot that predates London's status as a 'global city',[36] and of an often virulent 'Little Englander' nationalism that both expelled and subsumed successive waves of foreigners and outsiders. As Rivington Place director Mark Sealy, who in 2008 curated the *Bangladesh 1971* exhibition, commented, this past makes East London a powerful, symbolic backdrop for any discussion of empire, nationhood, and diaspora identity:

> The East End has a very specific diasporic history. You know, the labour from the Huguenots through the Jews through to whoever, layers and layers of migrants have settled in the East End ... it's a rich mine of history.

204 *Rituals of diaspora*

In telling the story of the Bangladeshi nation in East London, the location thus makes tangible and evocative links to another national story – that of Britain itself, its imperial past, and its own national-historical memories and erasures, Sealy continued:

> It's a partition story . . . all these things are part of our story. I mean, this is very much part of the postcolonial story – you cannot separate these two spaces, you can't unhinge that history . . . we are implicitly tied to this place, these people are implicitly tied to us.

The neighbouring presence of a large and iconic Bangladeshi community in and around Brick Lane makes the siting of the Shahid Minar particularly resonant, making visible and linking the historical and contemporary presence in ways that challenge the dominant narratives of Britishness and the ambiguous position of Bangladeshi Muslims within this.[37] As discussed in Chapter 4, Tower Hamlets stands, too, as a symbolic site within the British Bangladeshi community itself – if in different ways – representing what many people we spoke to described as a 'safe haven' for Bangladeshis and 'the heartland' of the community in diaspora. The visible Bangladeshi presence locally, particularly since the regeneration of the area in the 1990s, which saw the emergence of Banglatown, the founding of the Mela, and the establishment of the Shahid Minar, has been viewed both as underscoring this identity internally to an imagined diasporic community in Britain and as a way of claiming space within a broader British national story.[38] The Shahid Minar, for example, is one of the landmarks in a new Bengali heritage trail through the area sponsored by the Heritage Lottery Fund[39] and a history walk organized with Tower Hamlets Council called 'Exploring Banglatown and the Bengali East End' (Culture Walk 3), which the site proclaims 'offer[s] a fascinating insight into the British Bengali community's significant contribution to contemporary UK culture'.[40]

On the one hand, then, the establishment of the monument tells a story of engagement with wider British society and the bid for recognition within this national and multicultural landscape. On the other, it speaks of the creation of a shared 'diaspora consciousness' and a focal point of identification for the Bengali community within and across Britain. Rajonuddin Jalal, who was chair of the Regeneration Committee that developed the Shahid Minar in East London, commented that the Shahid Minar was important in generating a sense of Bengali identity in the UK:

> Whatever happens, any Bengali that comes to this country, or a Bengali who might move to Manchester . . . and wants to have a connection with the Bengali community, will come to Brick Lane and come to this Altab Ali Park. So that is why it is significant to have it [the Shahid Minar] there. . . .

Mahmoud Rauf similarly told me:

> Bengali people, about 70,000 live in this borough. And it [the Shahid Minar] is the symbol of our cultural identity. So where is the better place? . . . Every

year, 21st February, we have over three, four, five thousand people turn up on that cold British night.... From all over London, people come. Even people from outside London come with their cars to pay their respects.

The permanent monument in Tower Hamlets was constructed in 1999 as part of a larger process of regeneration of the area centred on the creation of Banglatown.[41] As in Oldham – and indeed, in Bangladesh itself – community activist and local historian, Ansar Ahmed Ullah, told me:

> Before that, Bengalis were observing Martyrs' Day by creating a temporary Shahid Minar with wooden plans and stuff and using community centres. They've been doing it for years, since 1952, so it's nothing new. So ... the council thought we ought to have a permanent monument.

Mahmoud Rauf noted that the demand for a Shahid Minar monument began much earlier than the Banglatown project: 'There was a lot of pressure for a long, long time. We started this movement to have a Shahid Minar since 1974, actually'. It was only made possible, along with the development of Banglatown, however, as the Bangladeshi community became more powerful in terms of the local economy and local political arena:[42]

> Our muscle was not that strong at that time. We were not that organized, we were not in the council to put forward our proposal.... So in '94, the Bengali people openly helped Labour come to power.... We had fourteen councillors at that time in the council.... We started our demands again: 'We want our Banglatown'... and here you are.

Rajonuddin Jalal noted that the Bengali vote held the balance of power between the Labour and Liberal parties vying for control of the council and was significant in establishing the Shahid Minar and renaming Altab Ali Park:

> It was talked about for quite a while ... so this Stepney neighbourhood was run by Labour, and we pressed them for the park to be renamed.... The electorate was 70 per cent Bengali, so [they] couldn't say anything.... I think most of the white people in the Labour Party did not support it, but I think in time they realized there are some things not worth arguing about. And then the Shahid Minar came later on as part of the Banglatown project.

On one level, then, the building of the Shahid Minar is inseparable from the integration of Bangladeshis within local and national political structures.[43] The permanent Shahid Minar arose from a partnership between the state (in this case, the local council) and the community (or its representatives) which recognized the blurred and overlapping boundaries between these two constituencies. Ansar Ahmed Ullah explained:

> Fifty groups came together, and they contributed £500 each, which went to a central pot, and the council facilitated the permission on the land,

acquirement, permissions, and all that. So, [it was] the community's money, but with support from the council.

Mahmoud Rauf estimated that the input from the council was £100,000, but reflected,

> The council *should* pay, because the council are serving 70,000 [Bengali] people. They're paying their tax, their rates, their council tax. The council *should* look after their needs as well and this is one of their needs

It is possible then to see the establishment of a permanent monument as a 'coming of age' of the Bengali community – a recognition of the permanence of their presence, their increased confidence, and their visibility and contribution to the area politically, economically, socially, and culturally. However, as one might expect, this cultural claiming of space is neither as seamless nor as complete as the above narrative suggests, and the Shahid Minar in East London speaks too to a more local history, local struggles, and, indeed, local martyrs.

Local histories: Siting the Shahid Minar

As discussed earlier, the London Shahid Minar is located in Altab Ali Park, formerly known as St Mary's Churchyard.[44] The park was renamed in 1998 in memory of Bangladeshi garment worker Altab Ali, who was murdered in a racist attack in the park one evening in 1978 on his way home from work.[45] Shiraj Haque, who was a founding member of the Bangladeshi Youth Forum at the time, recalled:

> Altab Ali was not directly a member, but he used to come to one of our youth clubs we ran in Hanbury Street. He used to work near there. He was a quiet boy. He was going home to Wapping and was crossing through the park, and he was attacked in the park. And he tried to run for safety to where the community would have been – he was running back to Whitechapel, and he couldn't run anymore, and he fell onto the street. And the first person to find him was a friend of mine. He phoned me, I was in a cafe – that's where we used to sit . . . he phoned me on a public phone and said, 'Somebody got killed'.

Not unlike the Language Martyrs in Bangladesh, Altab Ali's murder is seen as the start of a UK-centred struggle against racism which marked a turning point for the local Bangladeshi community. Shiraj Haque continued:

> That same night I called everyone. . . . We went around inviting everybody, making them aware of what happened. The meeting took place in the mosque because the mosque secretary was the employer of that boy. . . . I wasn't very popular with some people because they simply didn't think that it was

something they should explore at all. [They thought] if they are beating us, if they are attacking us, we should ignore it.

Later, however, the mood changed:

> They woke up a bit, you know. It was a bit of a wake-up call, that we shouldn't take that easily, that we should fight back. And it took me two years, from '78 to '80, to really make everyone understand that, as you start to bring your family here, we must look forward for our community to be here and settling round here.

Helal Abbas, a member of the Bangladeshi youth movements at this time and later the first Bangladeshi leader of Tower Hamlets Council, told us:

> Altab Ali was a watershed point for us; people felt very bitter, very angry at the injustice, young and old. I remember – I was very active in those days – we walked up and down Brick Lane, we went down to every shop and every factory and said to people: 'We're going to come out, we're not going to put up with this'.

In the days after the murder, the Bengali community organized a protest march. Shiraj Haque explained:

> So a lot of things happened. We mobilized a big demonstration demanding justice for Altab Ali that took place on the 10th [May]. In six days, we managed to mobilize a very big crowd. . . . It was a rainy day, people started marching, with a symbol of the coffin of Altab Ali, to Hyde Park.

Jalal, who also took part in the youth movements, similarly described the demonstration:

> For the first time, Bengalis marched from Whitechapel to Parliament House on the way round Hyde Park corner and back to Whitechapel. It took about eight hours. About 10,000 people. That was the first time Bengalis came out.

The renaming of the park in Altab Ali's memory was viewed as important in marking these struggles and this sacrifice and inscribing the presence of the Bangladeshi community as a legitimate and integral part of the British landscape. Mahmoud Rauf, who was a founder of the Shahid Minar and campaigned for the renaming of the park, told us:

> Altab Ali was killed on that corner . . . in 1978. So that became a sentimental thing for a lot of us, the activists of the time. . . . So when we came to choose a place [for the Shahid Minar], we thought that this is a better place. Why not

here? Altab Ali was killed there, and this is a corner of the park which is not very much used, people just pass through.

Ansar Ahmed Ullah, who was a community worker at the time of the murder, commented:

> Altab Ali Park... had importance to the community because of the murder of Altab Ali there and the park being a rallying point for lots of demos, meetings and protests, so it was always seen as a symbol of protest and of celebration.

Jalal similarly stated:

> Altab Ali Park is like our mini Hyde Park locally – local Bengalis use it to have their meetings, even to have rallies about politics in Bangladesh... That's why that monument is there and that's why I think it's the right place.

As Jalal implies, the (hi)stories of Altab Ali Park and the Shahid Minar are closely interwoven for British Bangladeshis. Indeed, many of those who shaped the youth movements in East London traced back their political activism to the liberation struggles in Bangladesh, in which they were involved.[46] Jalal commented, 'I think Bengalis were more politicized. That may be something to do with the new Bengali nation, so they had more political experience', while Shiraj Haque similarly argued, 'Because of the liberation struggle, people were more motivated, more freedom seekers in their minds. They had to be. This is how Bengalis became the leaders of the antiracist movements in the UK'. Ansar Ahmed Ullah drew clear connections between the local antiracist struggle during the 1970s and the liberation struggle and saw both as central to understanding the contemporary significance of the Shahid Minar to the local community:

> A lot of people who fought the antiracist struggle were all inspired by Bangladesh's independence movement, so it's all kind of connected. Many of the activists of the '70s and '80s felt inspired by the Bengali independence movement, which was also inspired by the language movement, so they were all connected.

Contesting memory: A tale of two mosques

It would be misleading, however, to see this alternative (hi)story as itself uncontested – indeed, within the British Bengali community, as in Bangladesh itself, the monument itself has been, and remains, a source of disagreement and conflict. In Tower Hamlets, this can be read particularly as a struggle between more secularized nationalist activists within the community, such as those associated with the Nirmul Committee, and more Islamist inspired groups,[47] which can be broadly mapped onto an ideological struggle between the two most important local mosques[48] – Brick Lane Mosque and East London Mosque, which stand about equidistant from Altab Ali Park and the Shahid Minar.

Brick Lane Mosque, or the Jamme Masjid, stands about halfway up Brick Lane and itself constitutes an important feature of the Tower Hamlets heritage trail. The building housing the Mosque was purchased by local Bangladeshis in 1976, but its history can be traced from the 18th century. In the following three centuries it has served as a Huguenot chapel, a Methodist chapel, and then a synagogue, reflecting the area's complex history of migration. The chair of Brick Lane Mosque, Sajjad Miah, spoke with pride of the ways in which the building spoke to this broader history, reflecting the waves of migration and settlement that characterize the East End: 'This building has a unique history itself, and that interests lots of people, not only from the Muslim community but from other communities'. Dominated by the syncretic *Barelvi* tradition, the mosque's history is closely linked to Bangladeshi community organizations such as the Bangladesh Welfare Association, which is next door, and it has close political ties to the UK Awami League, reflecting a continued commitment to more secular and nationalist ideologies of Bangladesh.[49] Sajjid Miah told us that the building, then a synagogue, was purchased by local community elders:

> They contributed £1,000 each, which was a large sum of money at that time. But they were business people and so on, about twelve of them contributed, who became director and trustees of the Mosque, and there is about another £30,000 or so [raised locally]. We paid about £40,000 on the building.

According to Sajjid Miah, the mosque attracts over 3,000 people for Friday prayers and is largely funded locally through personal donations, with some support from local businesses and from the council for education projects, such as a supplementary school and mother tongue classes. The identity of the mosque is closely tied to the surrounding community both in terms of place and ethnic identity, with a congregation drawn from local Bangladeshi men, often first-generation migrants. Sajjid Miah agreed, 'It is a community-based mosque . . . it's basically Bangladeshi people who mostly come here'. However, as with the Shahid Minar, he also noted the significance of the mosque for the wider British Bengali community:

> Some people come from different parts of London and different parts of the country. And people know of Brick Lane Mosque, [because] you know, it's historical. People from Birmingham, Liverpool and Oldham, everybody knows Brick Lane Mosque.

At the time of our fieldwork, the Mosque was undergoing extensive renovations, with multimillion-pound plans to modernize the building and facilities and erect a steel minaret outside on Brick Lane itself in a bid to give the building a stronger Islamic appearance, which was proving controversial locally. The money for the extension (an estimated £4 million) was to be raised from the local community and businesses, from English Heritage (to restore the fabric of the original building and the roof), and some (about £175,000, according to Sajjid Miah)

210 *Rituals of diaspora*

from Bangladesh ex-President Ershad and Prime Minister Sheikh Hasina. These transnational links underscored the identity of the mosque as Bangladeshi and its strong ties to the homeland: 'They [Ershad and Hasina] prefer to come here rather than other purpose-built mosques because it is totally run by the Bangladeshi Muslims themselves'.

East London Mosque stands on the Whitechapel Road about 100 yards away from the entrance to Brick Lane and Altab Ali Park. The mosque claims to be the oldest Muslim organization in the area, tracing its roots back to a charity established in 1910 and to the purchase of properties on the neighbouring Commercial Road in the 1930s to create local mosques to serve the diverse groups of lascars from the nearby docks. Shaynul Khan, director of the London Muslim Centre, explained:

> The need for a mosque obviously came about because an area like Tower Hamlets attracted a lot of sailors from the Middle East, Asian subcontinent, Bangladesh, people from Yemen and so forth. . . . Initially, people were hiring local community halls . . . it was like a 'floating mosque', and every now and then when they could find a space they would use it for prayer facilities. . . . In the 1930s, the mosque acquired a couple of properties on Commercial Road and used that as its base.

The land for the current impressive and expanding modern building was purchased in 1975, with around half of the £2 million costs raised from local community donations and the other £1 million by a donation from the King of Saudi Arabia. The mosque itself opened in 1985 and has since expanded to a £10.5 million complex that includes the neighbouring London Muslim Centre, shops and offices, and a recent social housing project. At the time of our fieldwork, the mosque announced future plans for an additional prayer hall and expanded facilities for women.[50] Over half of the £8 million expansion, we were told, came from community donations:

> It would be your average poor East Londoner who would have donated their jewellery or some of their savings; there would be children who would have done sponsored walks, or local gangs doing car washes – these were the little things that the community did, and people came forward very generously.

According to Shaynul Khan, East London Mosque has an estimated 22,000 people passing through its doors every week to access the thirty weekly religious services as well as a range of education and training programmes, the crèche, social welfare programmes, economic regeneration, and interfaith work. He told us, 'This mosque has always been very, very progressive in its thinking', and includes both Muslims and local non-Muslims in its remit:

> The majority of the time it's the Muslim community, [but] we do also have members of the non-Muslim communities come here, although the numbers

are less and they come in for specific projects. . . . So the community that comes here is actually very, very broad . . . and our motto is 'There's something for everyone here'.

Dilowar Hussain Khan, executive director of East London Mosque, defined its constituency in the inclusive, globalizing terms of 'the Muslim community': 'They come from all communities – Somali, North African, Bangladeshi, Moroccan, and all these places . . . it's people from all over London . . . we have one of the youngest congregations as well'.[51] He contrasted East London Mosque with more traditional organizations – like Brick Lane Mosque, perhaps – arguing:

> Most of the other mosques are run by first-generation Muslims, and they have a very narrow understanding of what mosques should be, and basically it's a replica of their village mosque in Bangladesh; all they do is prayers and Quran reading for the children, that's all.

There are ideological divisions too, with East London Mosque most strongly associated with Islamist organizations such as *Jamaat-e-Islami*,[52] themselves strongly linked to both Pakistan and Saudi Arabia.[53] Shaynul Khan commented of the Brick Lane Mosque:

> Particular viewpoints that are outside of the mainstream Islamic viewpoint are not accepted here. . . . There's a particular Sufi tradition that we don't accommodate here, which is accommodated over around the Brick Lane sort of area. So you'll have that little bit of tension going on, but that's just a viewpoint difference, it doesn't necessarily mean that the essence of what is Islam . . . is something that's missing.

In the interviews we conducted, representatives of both mosques were understandably reluctant to speak of divisions and conflict between them, although other interviewees were more vocal, particularly around concerns over the perceived dominance of the East London Mosque in the area. Ansar Ahmed Ullah, a member of the Nirmul Committee, claimed that there were a number of former Pakistani collaborators who fled Bangladesh after 1972 among its founding membership:

> A number of war criminals, Bengali ones who worked with the Pakistanis, fled Bangladesh after '72 when Bangladesh became independent because obviously they were wanted. Some of them went to Pakistan, some of them went to Middle Eastern countries, and some of them found their way to England . . . East London Mosque is their kind of stronghold.

He continued:

> They are Fundamentalists. They are very much opposed to anything Bengali . . . they believe that they are Muslims first and foremost and nationality,

ethnicity, or division should not come into it – you know, they are all part of the same community, the same global *ummah*... So they don't believe in Bengali nationalism, and if they could, they would delete Bengal's history and heritage.... Melas, Shahid Minar, even our clothing, you know, saris and everything. It's all no-no for them.

The Shahid Minar and the *Ekushe* memorialization have been a source of – sometimes violent – contention, with some interviewees alleging that the East London Mosque would send its younger members to disrupt the memorialization. One interviewee, who runs a cultural organization in East London and described himself as 'more from the Islamic camp', but who did not wish to be named, explained:

It's ideological – the Islamists don't like it. The story is very complicated, but the Islamists don't like it for two reasons: one is that the Islamists don't like any symbols that come close to idolatry. So the Shahid Minar they see as a little bit of idolatry. But also, the Shahid Minar, how it has developed in Bangladesh, it has become a secularist, anti-Islamic kind of challenge.

The tension, he explained, is between those who see themselves as Bengalis, those who position themselves as Bangladeshis, and those more marginal groups who pursue a more global Islamist agenda.[54] Again, the intertwining of local and transnational political agendas and struggles through the monument and the memorialization can be clearly identified, linking Britain and Bangladesh through this local site. In addition, ideas of religion, culture, politics, and community are played out in negotiating the meanings and claims of the memorial.[55] Sajjad Miah, who is chair of the Brick Lane Mosque and a founding member of the Nirmul Committee and was involved in the building of the Shahid Minar, told me that the mosque's imams opposed the monument but not the act of memorialization. He commented further, and with resigned good humour, on the tensions between the nationalist and religious perspectives within the local community, and often within individuals themselves:

I was involved with the building of the Shahid Minar . . . but religiously, it is two different things. I have a role as a community leader and then I have a role in the mosque management committee. . . . The mosque cannot oppose anything, the people who are religious scholars, they oppose, they make their views clear that this is not good and we shouldn't go there. But people still go there, and we as community leaders feel it is our obligation as well and we go there . . . [there is] no tension, no conflict.

In contrast, Dilowar Hussain Khan of East London Mosque insisted that the memorialization was incompatible with Islamic belief and practice and argued that the monument and the ceremony surrounding it were Western fabrications, imported from British culture:

You see, we as Muslims have a particular way of revering those who died. We are supposed to make prayers for them, and this kind of thing which are just copying the West, if you like – having a memorial and on the night you give flowers and all these things – it has no basis in our religion. We should pray for the ones who died in the language movement. But making a monument, no.

Shaynul Khan similarly continued:

> Our own fathers and grandfathers fought in that, so obviously our hearts have an affinity with those who died, but it's the process in which you recognize them. For me, it's a personal thing. I would want to pray for my uncle that died in the war in my personal way – I don't have to show a wreath, for example, like is done on Poppy Day. . . .

Dilowar Hussain Khan concluded firmly:

> That's the problem – people just make up these kinds of commemoration these days. . . . The secular community is very much involved in this. . . . You will not find any imams laying wreaths on 21st February in Altab Ali Park and praying. Nobody will go.

What can on one level be read simply as a religious or ideological division within the Bengali diaspora in East London (and elsewhere[56]) can also be understood as a struggle over the meanings of home and histories in a place of diaspora, which points to generational divisions and transformations. Implicit in these struggles over the meanings and memories of the Shahid Minar, past and present, is a struggle over the future of the British Bangladeshi community – and in particular over the shifting sense of identity for the next, British-born, generation and the place of Bengali history within this. As discussed above, one primary motivation for the staging of the *Ekushe* ceremonies in Britain has been to transmit this sense of history, identity, and belonging across the generations and between the homeland and the diaspora. Yet, as Ansar Ahmed Ullah noted, the struggle is to make this history meaningful to young people in a new multicultural context like London and against the tide of a globalized Muslim identity which subsumes or erases difference. He argued:

> I think most young people aren't really bothered. . . , to be honest. They're just being young . . . they are going to youth clubs, they are into fashion, into music, like any other young person. . . . But there is a small number of people . . . who have become religious or found religion to be their identity. . . , and we [secular nationalists] are like a drop in the ocean, and there needs to be more of us to give our young a sense of Bengali identity.

As Dilowar Hussain Khan intimated earlier in the chapter, East London Mosque's globalized Islam is one which appeals more to the younger, aspirant British Bengali population more than the nationalistic, Bangladeshi-rooted Brick

Lane Mosque, something that even its opponents acknowledged. Rajonuddin Jalal told me that:

> I think it's culture, it's heritage. . . . And those of us who belong to the 'Bengali-ism' part of the community would still like to promote 'Bengali-ism' as opposed to Fundamentalism. I'm Bengali first, Muslim second. I'm Bengali *and* a Muslim, but I'm not going to sacrifice being a Bengali for being a Muslim.
> But I think that kind of view would not be held by 95 per cent of the young people you come across. I think we have been defeated, ideologically . . . they have won the battle.

At the same time, however, and perhaps the more so because of this perceived ideological 'defeat', the struggle for history – and for Bengali history and identity – was viewed as an essential and integral part of the struggle for belonging in contemporary Britain. As Helal Abbas commented:

> I think history is important. Some people think that life is easy. I don't believe that you have to go through the same things that I did, but I do think it's important that people know how they ended up where they are.

Contested memories: Framing rituals of diaspora

The Shahid Minar and the *Ekushe* commemorations can, then, be seen to exemplify one aspect of the 'private life' of the Bengal diaspora in Britain, pointing to the ongoing roots and routes of diaspora memory and identity, the layering and intersection of transnational, national, and local histories, and the contours of contemporary struggles over diaspora identities marked through the shifting formations of religious and generational identities. One of the key shifts in conceptualizations of diaspora in the past three decades has been from descriptive, top-down, empiricist accounts towards a focus on the ways in which diaspora is experienced and sustained in the lives and imaginations of diasporic communities. Indeed, we might argue that diaspora is itself maintained and lived largely in the minds of its members, produced and sustained through the performance, transmission, and circulation of stories, events, rituals, and objects – what Philip Crang describes as 'the stuff of diaspora'[57] – through and across time and space. Collective memory and identity, as well as the stories and rituals of memorialization, are central to the formation and conceptualization of diasporic communities – commemoration and narration lie, indeed, at the heart of classic notions of diaspora (see Chapter 8).[58] As Stuart Hall has argued, diasporic cultural identity 'is always constructed through memory, fantasy, narrative and myth',[59] which 'is a matter of "becoming" as well as of being [and] belongs to the future as much as to the past'.[60] Practices of commemoration, as with diaspora itself, mobilize ideas of an imagined shared past as a way of staking claims in the present and as a basis for future belonging, inscribed and performed in a contested present.[61] The narration of collective memory and identity serves as a way of constituting identity through 'the everyday stories we tell ourselves individually and collectively',[62] and as a bid for inclusion within other (hi)stories – global, national or local.

Such practices are by no means straightforward or uncontested, however. Rather, they stand as exemplars of what Paul Gilroy has termed 'diasporic consciousness', which 'highlights the *tensions* between common bonds created by shared origins and other ties arising from the process of dispersal and the obligation to remember a life prior to flight' and 'drawing attention to the *dynamics* of commemoration'.[63] The rituals of diaspora memory run the risk not only of the reification and sedimentation of 'culture' and cultural practices that reinscribe marginalized positions as the exotic 'other'[64] but also of homogenization that ignores or erases diverse positionalities and struggles. We need, then, to position diaspora rituals and commemorations as products of collective organizations and histories which are structured socially and which concretize collective and cultural meanings but which are also open to change, resistance, division, and transformation and which take shape as part of broader social, political, and cultural fields.[65]

These tensions and contestations can be clearly observed in the Shahid Minar monument and the annual *Ekushe* commemoration. As a monument to the Bengali Language Martyrs and the liberation struggle, the Shahid Minar serves as a staging post in the (hi)story of Bangladesh and its diaspora, working to 'book end' the narration of the Bangladeshi nation itself. At the same time, it testifies to the unfinished stories of Bangladesh and its peoples, at home and in diaspora, to continued and new struggles, new nationhoods, and contested belongings. The Shahid Minar and *Ekushe* furnish telling insights into the multilayered and contested dimensions of community and memorialization – transnational, national, and local – and raise important questions about the role of memorialization and the place of diaspora in at once summoning and unravelling the notions of shared histories, memories, communities, and places. The place of the Shahid Minar, and the commemorative practices of *Ekushe*, thus constitute a site through which collective diasporic memory can be explored not solely in relation to imagined pasts and origins but in delineating contested borders and travelling 'homes'.

Notes

1 A Bengali street food made from puffed rice and lentils.
2 The song was, fittingly, written by Abdul Gaffar Choudhury, a resident of Tower Hamlets. See: http://static.visitlondon.com/assets/maps/guides/bengali_history_walk.pdf
3 *Ekushe* means literally '21st', but is used to denote Martyr's Memorial Day on 21 February every year.
4 This account is from field notes supplied by Shahzad Firoz.
5 Benedict Anderson, *Long Distance Nationalism: World Capitalism and the Rise of Identity Politics*, Amsterdam: CASA, 1998.
6 Brubaker, 'The "Diaspora" Diaspora', p. 12.

216 *Rituals of diaspora*

7 Homi Bhabha (ed.) (1990) *Nation and Narration*, London: Routledge, 1990.
8 John Eade and David Garbin, 'Competing Visions of Identity and Space', *Contemporary South Asia*, 15, 2, 2006, pp. 181-93; ; Begum, 'Commodifying Multicultures'.
9 Redclift, *Statelessness*; Victoria Redclift, 'Rethinking "the Muslim Community": Intra-minority Identity and Transnational Political Space', in C. Alexander, V. Redclift and A. Hussain (eds) *The New Muslims*, London: Runnymede Trust, 2013. See: www.runnymedetrust.org/uploads/publications/Runnymede_the_New_Muslims_Perspective.pdf
10 This chapter is based on an earlier article published in *Ethnic and Racial Studies*. See Claire Alexander, 'Contested Memories: The Shahid Minar and the Struggle for Diasporic Space', *Ethnic and Racial Studies*, 36, 4, 2013, pp. 590–610.
11 Virinder Kalra, Raminder Kaur and John Hutnyk, *Diaspora and Hybridity*, London: Sage, 2005.
12 Ullah and Eversley, *Bengalis*.
13 Michael Keith, *After the Cosmopolitan? Multicultural Cities and the Future of Racism*, London: Routledge, 2005.
14 Van Schendel, *A History*, p. 107.
15 Chapter 6 also explored this religious/status boundary drawing in the performance of Muharram. Ibid., p. 111. See also Chatterji 'Bengali Muslim'.
16 Van Schendel, *A History*, p. 121.
17 Ibid., p. 152.
18 At the time of writing, in February 2015, *Ekushe* commemorations have been thrown into the international spotlight with the public murder of the secular US-Bangladeshi writer, Avijit Roy, by apparent Islamist attackers as he left a book fair in Dhaka that was part of the *Ekushe* festival. Saad Hammadi and Mark Tran, 'Anger in Dhaka at Secular Blogger's Killing', *Guardian*, 28 February 2015.
19 Van Schendel, *A History*, p. 162.
20 Redclift, *Statelessness*.
21 Tahmina Anam, 'Shahbad Protesters versus the Butcher of Mirpur', *Guardian*, 13 February 2013. The historic resonance of Shahbag intersection, where Dhaka University is located, with the language movement, the Liberation War, and the Shahid Minar, is significant. Redclift, 'Rethinking'.
22 Van Schendel, *A History*, pp. 215–18.
23 Nari Chetona translates as 'Women's Power Awake' (Sayeeda Shikha, interview).
24 The Nirmul Committee is also known as the 'Committee for the Uprooting of Traitors and Collaborators of 1971'. Van Schendel, *A History*, p. 217.
25 Redclift, 'Rethinking'.
26 Sarah Glynn, 'The Spirit of '71: How the Bangladeshi War of Independence has Haunted Tower Hamlets', *Socialist History Journal*, 29, 2006, pp. 56–75. David Garbin, 'A Diasporic Sense of Place: Dynamics of Spatialization and Transnational Political Fields Among Bangladeshi Muslims in Britain' in M.P. Smith and J. Eade (eds) *Transnational Ties: Cities, Identities and Migrations*, London: CUCR (9) Transaction Publishers, 2008.
27 Van Schendel, *A History*, pp. 163, 167.
28 Ibid., p. 261.
29 An article in *Time* magazine claimed: 'The Hindus, who account for three-fourths of the refugees and the majority of the dead, have borne the brunt of the Muslim military hatred'. 'World: Pakistan: The Ravaging of Golden Bengal', *Time*, 2 August 1971, http://content.time.com/time/magazine/article/0,9171,878408,00.html
30 Glynn, 'The Spirit'.
31 A photographic exhibition, *Bangladesh 1971*, held at Rivington Place, East London, from 4 April to 31 May 2008, captures some of these hidden histories and voices (see www.autograph-abp.co.uk and Alexander, 'Contested Memories' for a longer discussion). Redclift, *Statelessness*.

Rituals of diaspora 217

32 Glynn, 'The Spirit'; Garbin, 'Diasporic Sense'.
33 Barbara Misztal, 'The Sacralization of Memory', *European Journal of Social Theory*, 7, 1, 2004, pp. 67–84.
34 Tasarul Ali, interview.
35 Wemyss, *Invisible Empire*.
36 Jacobs, *Edge of Empire*.
37 Alexander, 'Making Bengali Brick Lane', pp. 201–20; Wemyss, *Invisible Empire*.
38 Alexander, 'Making Bengali Brick Lane'; Keith, *After the Cosmopolitan*.
39 www.ideastore.co.uk/assets/documents/local%20History%20Archives%20Online/walks/Bengali_History_Walk.pdf
40 http://static.visitlondon.com/assets/maps/guides/bengali_history_walk.pdf
41 Alexander, 'Making Bengali Brick Lane'; Begum, 'Commodifying Multicultures'; Jacobs, *Edge of Empire*; Keith, *After the Cosmopolitan*.
42 See Eade, *Politics of Community*; and Glynn, 'The Spirit', for a discussion of Bangladeshi involvement in local Labour Party politics in East London.
43 Eade, *Politics of Community*; and Glynn, 'The Spirit'.
44 The church was destroyed during the Blitz in 1940, and its absence testifies to another war and other local struggles and sacrifices.
45 Leech, *Brick Lane*.
46 John Eade, Isabelle Fremeaux and David Garbin, 'Political Construction of Diasporic Communities in the City' in Pamela Gilbert (ed.) *Imagined Londons*, Albany: State University of new York, 2002; Glynn, 'The Spirit'; Garbin, 'Diasporic Sense'.
47 One interviewee described this as a division between Bangladeshi nationalists and Bengali nationalists, who can be broadly politically aligned to the Bangladesh National Party and Awami League respectively. Bengali nationalists, he noted, could be characterized as 'slightly anti-Islamic', while Bangladeshi nationalists included both secular and Islamist orientations.
48 Tower Hamlets had over 40 mosques at the time the research took place, most coordinated by a local Council of Mosques (Sajjad Miah, interview).
49 Eade and Garbin, 'Competing Visions'.
50 Shaynul Khan, interview; *ELM News: The Official Bulletin of the East London Mosque*, September/October 2008.
51 East London Mosque has established links with Islamist groups such as the *Jamaat-e-Islami* through its youth organizations such as Young Muslim Organisation and Islamic Forum Europe. See Eade and Garbin, *Bangladeshi Diaspora*.
52 Eade and Garbin, *Bangladeshi Diaspora*; Eade and Garbin, 'Competing Visions'.
53 Bhatt, *Liberation*.
54 See Van Schendel, *A History*, Chapter 19, for an insightful discussion of these issues in Bangladesh.
55 As with Muharram in Chapter 6, it is possible to trace issues around class and status in these discourses, inflected through an additional Sylheti/Dhaka regional divide and different migration histories, but this is beyond the scope of the current discussion.
56 Cf. Eade and Garbin, 'Competing Visions'.
57 Philip Crang, 'Diasporas and Material Culture' in K. Knott and S. McLoughlin (eds) *Diasporas: Concepts, Identities, Intersections*, London: Zed Books, 2010, p. 139.
58 William Safran's foundational formulation, for example, stresses the maintenance of a '*memory*, vision *or myth* about their original homeland' as a defining feature of diasporic communities. See William Safran, 'Diasporas in Modern Societies: Myths of Homeland and Return', *Diaspora*, 1, 1, 1991, pp. 83–99; pp. 83–84 (our emphasis).
59 Hall, 'Cultural Identity', p. 226.
60 Ibid., p. 225.
61 Maurice Halbwachs, *On Collective Memory*, trans. Lewis Coser, Chicago: University of Chicago Press, 1992.
62 Brah, *Cartographies*, p. 183.

63 Paul Gilroy, 'Diaspora and the Detours of Identity' in K. Woodward (ed.) *Identity and Difference*, London: Sage, 1997, p. 328, our emphasis.
64 J.R. Gillis, *Commemorations: The Politics of National Identity*, Princeton: Princeton University Press, 1994; Kalra et al., *Diasporas*.
65 Gillis, *Commemorations*; Sean McLoughlin, William Gould, Ananya Kabir and Emma Tomalin (eds) *Writing the City in British Asian Diasporas*, London: Routledge, 2014.

8 Narrating diaspora

Community histories and the politics of assimilation

In 1993, the Sylheti Social History Group in London published a little book called *The Roots and Tales of Bangladeshi Settlers*. Ten years later, in 2003, *Biharis. The Indian Emigres in Bangladesh: An Objective Analysis*, was brought out by the Shamsul Huq Foundation, a non-governmental organization (NGO) based in Syedpur, the old railway township in Bangladesh. *Roots and Tales* is an account of the Sylheti diaspora in the United Kingdom. Written in the first person by Yousuf Choudhury, who migrated to Britain in the 1950s as a young bachelor, it purports to be the view of the migrant-insider, and its style is personal and confessional. *Biharis* tells the history of the so-called 'Biharis' of Bangladesh, a community twice displaced by violence. Its author – the journalist, social worker, and poet Ahmed Ilias – is himself a 'Bihari' who migrated from Calcutta in 1953 to what was then East Pakistan. As the subtitle of the book suggests, he strives to write as 'objectively' as a professional historian might, supporting his narrative with references to primary and secondary sources.

On the face of it, the two texts have very little in common. One – *Roots and Tales* – is a classic story of economic migration. It chronicles the sojourning and eventual settlement of 'Bangladeshi' people in the United Kingdom. Choudhury traces their history back to the heyday of the Raj, when young men from Sylhet worked as lascars in the British merchant marine, some jumping ship in London in search of better working conditions. Others followed their lead and, through typical chain migration, significant clusters of Sylheti migrants gradually developed within working-class neighbourhoods of London's East End, Manchester, and Birmingham. In due course, these men were joined by family – elderly parents, wives and children, and other relatives – and became a typically self-sustaining diasporic community. Choudhury's is an optimistic story of (upward) mobility: of people deploying their connections and their wits to survive, who, through hard work and sacrifice, prospered and built a better life for themselves and their children.

Ilias's *Biharis*, by contrast, is a stark account of forced migration. It tells the grim tale of how in 1946, months before India's partition, Urdu-speaking Muslims fled from the deadly communal violence in Bihar. They sought and found shelter first in Bengal (then run by a Muslim-dominated government). After partition, they fled to Pakistan's eastern wing, only to once again become, in 1971 during the Liberation

War, the victims of genocidal violence. Today, perhaps 300,000 'Biharis' remain in Bangladesh, most of them still living in the squalid and desperately overcrowded camps where they took refuge during the war and its aftermath. This is the story Ahmed Ilias attempts to tell in *Biharis*, 'objectivity' being his declared aim. But inevitably it is a much darker work than *Roots and Tales*. Reflecting, as it does, on the defeat of a once-proud community, it is an excellent example of the 'histories of the vanquished' that Wolfgang Schivelbusch describes.[1]

Yet a closer look at these two very different works reveals interesting parallels between them. Both are written in English, the third language of Choudhury and Ilias alike. Both authors might be described as 'organic intellectuals', members of the group or community whose experience they sought to articulate. Choudhury, however, comes from a working-class background, while Ilias is a product of a North Indian, Urdu-speaking service elite. Both began their research and writing at roughly the same time, Choudhury in 1981 and Ilias in 1978. Both works were published by community groups. On careful scrutiny, the two books prove to have similar themes, similar internal structures, and similar patterns of emphasis.

This chapter argues that both texts produce 'origin myths' as well as 'migration myths' and have many tropes in common. Teasing out the features shared by the two books will explore the inwardness of how, when, and why migrant groups come to write their own histories. It suggests that both these histories were written with a view to enabling the 'assimilation' of the community for which they claim to speak, to seek rights and recognition for that 'community' in its place of settlement. By looking at these texts through a comparative historical prism, the complex processes by which migrant communities try to 'assimilate' into 'host' cultures are seen in a different light.

'Assimilation' itself is a controversial concept. Since the early 1970s, it has been subjected to sustained scholarly critique. It is no longer seen as a one-sided process by which alien communities are incorporated into an apparently homogeneous host culture, gradually (but inevitably) shedding their own ways while adopting those of their hosts. As Rogers Brubaker has argued, this perspective was 'analytically and normatively Anglo-conformist. It posited, endorsed, and expected assimilation towards an unproblematically conceived white Protestant "core culture." '[2] In challenging it, the 'differentialist' critique has informed (and was in turn inspired) by the politics and practices of multiculturalism, supported by a growing body of scholarship that showed that ethnic diversity among 'new migrants' in the West persists and survives, so much so that the new orthodoxy proposed that the melting pot 'never happened'.[3] Instead, scholars underlined the centrality for migrant groups of transnational networks.[4] It is now widely accepted that migrants remain embedded simultaneously in a variety of locations and 'networks',[5] deploying them to 'circulate'[6] between locations, rather than permanently settle in one. Many scholars now see migrants as cosmopolitans who constantly and creatively renegotiate 'hybridity'[7] rather than as conformists who either maintain their 'traditional' culture or adapt to the lifestyles of Western hosts. Indeed, studies regard the practice of 'hybridity' as challenging the logic of modernity and the nation state.[8]

These are valuable insights. Yet they gloss over the harsh realities of the contemporary world, where nation states monopolize 'the legitimate means of movement',[9] control borders ever more stringently, and erect ever higher barriers against entry and naturalization, making it increasingly difficult for migrants to 'circulate', let alone to enter and stay on as full citizens. This is true not only in the West (which implicitly or explicitly has been the focus of these new theories of diaspora) but, as we have seen in the preceding chapters, also of nations in the Global South.[10] For many compelling reasons – dominated by constraints upon their options – many migrants today, in the West and elsewhere, seek to settle permanently in the locations where they presently dwell. Like Yousuf Choudhury's 'Bangladeshi settlers' and Ahmed Ilias's '"Bihari" emigres' (and indeed like the 'Biharis' of Dhaka and the Bangladeshis of Tower Hamlets and Oldham), they aspire to live with dignity and in security in their new locations. By examining how two migrants seek to negotiate their assimilation in two very different national contexts, the chapter reveals the constraints within which such projects work and their implications for 'hybrid' subjectivities.

Whereas the previous chapters explored how migrant groups perform diasporic history in different locations, this chapter examines how history is remembered and narrated by organic intellectuals. But, first, an important caveat: one of the authors of the works discussed here is still alive and well, and both have living children and families. *Roots and Tales* and *Biharis* are two works of great significance, not only for the communities they describe but also for scholars of migration. Both contain much vital information: they are rightly seen as key sources. As Chapter 3 shows, the publication of *Biharis* was also a crucial political intervention in Bangladesh. By suggesting that these works construct migration 'myths', which deserve close analysis, there is no intention to impugn their value. Rather, the chapter demonstrates that these books have far more to tell us than meets the eye.

Mythical pasts and sacred origins

Both books begin with an account of the origins of the author's 'community'. But both represent these origins using tropes that betray their intent to invest them with a special moral quality and purpose. Choudhury's *Roots and Tales* is the more obviously 'fabulous'. According to the author, the origins of the 'Bangladeshis' can be traced back to the central lowlands of Sylhet at the beginning of the 13th century. In ancient times, he tells us, this low-lying territory to the south of the kingdom of Kamrup in Assam lay partially submerged under the waters of the Bay of Bengal. But a swan-shaped gulf rose out of the sea and nestled among 'low hills covered with lush monsoonal forest, in an area rich in natural beauty . . . full of exotic fruit trees, splendid flowering plants and birds such as parrots, mynahs and seagulls'. This came to be the site of a market town and port – known for its rare beauty as 'Sri Khetro' or 'Beautiful Field' – as well as a commercial centre 'for traders from many nations. . . . Seafaring Arab merchants used to call at that port regularly for silk, spices and other oriental products'.[11]

Given the work's rather prosaic style (as the foreword by the Oxford theologian Clinton Bennett puts it, Choudhury 'makes no claim to literary finesse in his third language, although he is an accomplished writer in Bengali'[12]), this passage of almost lyrical quality stands out.[13] 'Home' is a landscape of extraordinary loveliness, a veritable Garden of Eden. Significantly, Choudhury chooses to stress Sylhet's original and ancient connection with the sea. Present-day Sylhet is far from the water's shoreline, and yet the ocean plays a crucial part in his story. The ancient Sylhet of *Roots and Tales* is a hub of trade and exchange: Choudhury's Sylheti ancestors in the long-distant past were already itinerant seafaring cosmopolitans.

In 1209 and 1300, according to Choudhury, two earthquakes changed the landscape around 'Sri Khetro', lifting the gulf out of the deep and severing its connection with the sea.[14] At that time, the land around the town was still partly submerged and largely uninhabited. But in 1313 it was conquered by Gour Gobindo, 'a cruel Hindu king who had no mercy for anyone'.[15] At this early juncture in its history, so we are told, there were only thirteen Muslim families in the area, descendants of seafaring merchants and Islamic missionaries, who lived together in a village by the River Surma, the waterway which connected the hills of Assam to the Bengal delta. In 1340, the wife of one of these Muslim pioneers, Borhanuddin, gave birth to a baby boy, and to celebrate, the proud father slaughtered a cow. On hearing of this offence to Hindu sensitivities, Raja Gour Gobindo ordered that the baby be beheaded and the arms of the mother be cut off. After the death of mother and child, Borhanuddin sought the protection of neighbouring Muslim rulers in Bengal and then travelled to Delhi to raise an army to challenge and defeat the 'cruel king'.

It was in Delhi, Choudhury tells us, in the presence of the great Sufi mystic Nizamuddin Auliya, that a fateful meeting took place between brave Borhanuddin and the 'leading Muslim saint', Shah Jalal, who had travelled to Delhi from Yemen with 313 followers. On hearing Borhanuddin's story, Shah Jalal 'decided to volunteer himself along with his followers'[16] to fight Gour Gobindo. Together with an army of 360 saints, Shah Jalal marched eastwards into Bengal and defeated Gour Gobindo in a battle replete with miracles in which the saints deployed supernatural powers and witchcraft to bewitch and destroy the enemy.[17]

And then Sylhet revealed its sacred destiny. Before he set out on his mission in Al-Hind, Shah Jalal had been given a clod of Arabian earth by his spiritual mentors, who instructed him to settle wherever he found similar soil. Miraculously, the marshy soil of Sri Khetro exactly matched this sacred lump of earth from dry and distant Arabia. So Shah Jalal settled permanently in 'Shil-hotto', and the 360 saints 'spread all over Sylhet' to propagate Islam. They also set to work reclaiming the land, building simple structures as their mosques, fishing in the waters, and farming the land:

> Most of the saints got married, and many of them had a farm and a family. They worked all day long, growing crops or vegetables, looking after their cattle and catching fish. When the work was done they swam in the open

clean water, then they sat and had some food. At the end of the day, they could go to their own straw built mosque and pray to their heart's content. Many of the saints were married to the new converts, had families, ran farms by themselves . . . but the saintliness of the working saints was never washed away or wasted. Their faith was always with them and passed on to their descendants.[18]

The story of conversion deploys the sexual metaphors of fertility and insemination so prominent in descriptions of Islam's spread in Bengal.[19] But while in other parts of Bengal the exotic 'soil' (or host society) produced a version of Islam distorted by caste hierarchy and contaminated by other Hindu manners and customs, Sylhet's wondrous soil – in Choudhury's account – nourished the true faith. The homeland emerges from *Roots and Tales* as a green paradise adorned by the graves of saints, a land of plenty sustaining a casteless society of hard-working, peace-loving, and god-fearing peasants,[20] a truly Islamic brotherhood, governed by the robust but simple values of their forefathers.

Some of these themes recall other, better-known foundation myths,[21] and the story as a whole powerfully echoes Eaton's account of the role of '*ghazi-pirs*' or soldier-saints in establishing Islam and settled agriculture on the Bengal frontier.[22] But the point here is a rather different one. Choudhury's story is not only a myth of origins, it is also a parable about settlement. He constructs 'the Bangladeshi settlers' as living descendants of saints from all over the Muslim world who long ago settled in Sylhet, bringing their faith with them and establishing Islam in the delta. By tracing the community's roots back to these pioneering settler-saints, his parable validates the peripatetic struggles of present-day migrants and sets them up as vectors for the expansion of the Islamic frontier in the Western world. Implicitly, it gives their story of migration *and settlement* legitimacy derived from this origin myth, but also a deeper moral and religious meaning.[23]

But there is also another process at work in this account of origins: the construction of a notion of a single 'Bangladeshi community'. That process begins, of course, with Choudhury's choice of title, which alludes to 'the Bangladeshi settlers'. In his preface or introduction, the author admits that his story is 'mostly about the settlers from Sylhet as . . . they are 95% of Bangladeshi settlers. The remaining 5% came from other places. I have tried my best to cover these people too'.[24] Yet Choudhury makes hardly any reference to these 'other people', and, when he does, his remarks are disparaging and dismissive. But by describing his subjects as 'Bangladeshis' rather than as Sylhetis and then by assigning a single foundation myth set in ancient Sylhet to all of them, he has launched the enterprise of incorporating (and indeed assimilating) different groups with disparate histories into a single national 'community' with shared origins and with a destiny in common.

Ahmed Ilias's account of the origins of the 'Biharis' is not as colourful as Choudhury's tales of Syhet. Nonetheless, they share some significant features. *Biharis* begins with description of 'The Home and Culture', which, in ten pages, sets out 'the glorious history of Bihar'. Even though in the second paragraph of his preface Ilias states (accurately) that 'Biharis did not come from the Indian state of Bihar alone',[25] a few pages later, he contradicts himself and states that 'the Biharis are proud of their ancient history', which he locates in the Indian state of Bihar. This is reminiscent of Choudhury's strategy, where he first admits that all Bangladeshi settlers in Britain are not, in fact, from Sylhet, but then proceeds to give the whole community a single foundation myth located in ancient Sylhet.

Ilias constructs 'the home' of the 'Biharis' not only as a place lost forever but as representative of a vanished golden age of Indian achievement. The thrust and tone of his argument are captured in the following paragraph:

> Historically, Bihar is a land of faiths and religions, myths and mysticism, parables and legends. Islam began to spread in this part of India from around the twelfth century. Both its Hindus and Muslims were always seen at the forefront of every movement launched for the glory and greatness, liberty and independence of India.[26]

At 'home', the 'Muslim minority lived scattered in villages and towns with all their [pride] and [prejudice], with the low standards of skills and education and the high esteem of old orthodox society. They were happy with their own way of life, culture, customs and traditions'.[27]

In the same way that Choudhury's Sylhet is idealized, Ilias' 'Bihar' is also a rich and bountiful land. Ilias confidently asserts that 'as a geographical unit, Bihar is the richest State in India',[28] when, in fact, it is one of the poorest. It is also, just as Choudhury's Sylhet, a land sanctified by faith. Ilias describes Bihar as a sacred site where Islam first took root in the subcontinent:

> Long before the arrival of Muslim rulers, many Sufis and saints came to Bihar to preach Islam among the cast-ridden [sic] Hindu community.... Hazrat Shahbuddin reached Bihar before the attacks on Punjab by ... Mahmud Ghaznazi (999–1027). Imam Mohammed Taj Fakir, another Muslim saint [,] came from the Middle East in 1104. His grandson Makhdum Sharfuddin Yahia Muniri belonged to the oldest and most widely dispersed Sufi orders in Bihar, the Suhrawardy and Chisti. A branch of the Suhrawardy order later emerged [and] was known as Firdausia under Yahia Muniri.[29]

Both accounts thus trace the origins of the migrant community back to a single place; both describe that place as a land of peace and plenty; both locate the ancient 'homeland' as a sacred site that witnessed the birth of Islam in the Indian subcontinent; and both claim cosmopolitan and saintly ancestors who played a key role in expanding the frontiers of the Islamic world.

But there are also important differences between Ilias' account and Choudhury's, and their significance will become apparent when the authors' political intentions are considered. Ilias situates his 'Bihar' within a robust tradition of syncretism and constructs it as a place where, besides Islam, Hindu, Muslim, Buddhist, and Jain cultures and polities also thrived. The understanding of culture in *Biharis* is more syncretic than that in *Roots and Tales*, claiming as part of the community's 'glorious history' the achievements of religions other than Islam. Ilias takes pains, for example, to inform his readers that 'the two founders of Buddhism and Jainism inspired the world from this land. Ram's wife Sita, the most significant character in Hindu mythology [,] was born in this land of faiths and religions'.[30]

Ilias also insists repeatedly on a powerful 'Bihari' tradition of 'anti-imperialism'. He claims that 'Bihar gave birth to many valiant sons, who fought for the liberation of India from the yoke of British Empire'. From the earliest times, Ilias tells us, Bihar's rulers have repelled invaders. Chandragupta Maurya 'put an end to Greek rule in India'.[31] Mir Quasem 'shifted his capital from Murshedabad [sic] to Munghyr to defend his rule against the forces of the East India Company'.[32] To a far greater extent than Choudhury, Ilias claims for his community a history of political sacrifice in the national struggle against British rule. Choudhury's text, by contrast, is muted in its criticism of the Raj, for example, quickly glossing over an uprising in Sylhet against the British in 1782.[33] Its heroes are not rebels who fought the British, but trade unionists like Aftab Ali who organized and defended Sylheti seamen, and community leaders like Ayub Ali 'Master' who helped illiterate lascar migrants cut through the red tape in Britain. Ilias' emphasis on Bihar's traditions of high culture has no counterpart in Choudhury. Unlike Choudhury's idealized but rustic Sylhet, Ilias's Bihar was

> an ancient seat of learning which attracted people from far and wide, ever since Kumaragupta founded the Nalinda [sic] university near the capital Patna . . . where more than a thousand teachers and scholars used to teach about ten thousand students drawn from middle and Far East countries.[34]

Home to the Khuda Baksh library, 'the richest library of manuscripts on Islam in the world',[35] Bihar was the seedbed for poets such as Kazi Nazrul Islam and Ramdhari Singh Dinkar. 'Bihar also produced many eminent writers, poets and critics in Urdu literature'.[36] The author's pride in this tradition shows how different his class perspective is from Choudhury's. Ilias views history from the vantage point of a cultured literati which has suffered catastrophic decline, while Choudhury's angle of vision is that of a working-class community making its way up in the world. These different perspectives helped to shape strategies for assimilation which, as will be seen below, were subtly but significantly different.

Migration myths: Tales of loss and exile

Having established their singular origins in an idealized 'homeland', the next task for both authors is to explain why their subjects left their homeland behind. Both struggle to produce a seamless narrative of migration. In both works, this distinctive (if strained) narrative is repeated throughout the text at regular intervals, so that it assumes a normative power – appearing to elevate and encapsulate a 'truth' about the community that is more compelling than mere fact.

226 *Narrating diaspora*

In Choudhury's *Roots and Tales*, the central theme of this migration narrative is that *all 'Bangladeshi settlers' in Britain are seafarers or their descendants*:

> Most Bangladeshi settles are the descendent flesh and blood of those who were lost in the seas and survived to tell their tale, so it is our duty to keep our history alive and remind everyone of who we are and why we are here.[37]

This assertion is repeated three times on the very first page of the Introduction. It is then rehearsed *no less than fifty times* in the book.

So how did Sylhetis – whose homeland was so far away from the sea – come to be seafarers? According to Choudhury, the explanation is that the River Surma, the only waterway connecting Assam to Bengal and the sea, passes through Sylhet. In consequence, Sylhet had a long tradition – beginning with the early settler saints – of mercantile boats carrying goods from Assam to Bengal and beyond. Although Sylhet's farmers were prosperous, its 'spare young men' (younger brothers and cadet sons) traditionally worked as boatmen. When the region came under British rule, things changed, particularly after the British introduced steamer stations linking Calcutta to upper Assam. Aware that 'the new water way arrangement [had] hit the boatmen' hard, Choudhury argues, 'the [British] steamer companies perhaps realised the need to compensate the boatmen by recruiting them mainly as engine room crew. . . . This is the story of the Sylheti boatmen and how they became the steamer's crew'.[38] Here again we see that Choudhury prefers to take a benign view of British rule in Sylhet, even though these Sylheti lascars, he has to admit, began to be 'illtreated and illfed'.[39] They were exploited by British navigation companies, who paid them a sixth of what British crews received, but even more by the Indian '*sarongs*' and '*bariwalas*' (or jobbers) who took a large part of their wages in return for finding them jobs and housing them at ports. 'Out of frustration, they decided to desert their ships and go wherever they would find a chance', whether Rangoon, Singapore, or London.[40] But it was only during the First World War, when 'over one thousand Bangladeshis' were brought to Britain 'to replace British seamen', that a few began to settle in London.[41] And it was during the Second World War that 'the Bangladeshi population began to increase in the U.K'. When the Second World War ended in 1945, and with India's independence and partition in 1947, more and more Sylheti seamen found themselves unemployed and sought work in Britain to support their families. The present Bangladeshi community in Britain, Choudhury insists again and again, are all descendants of these first seafaring settlers, of persons who fought and died in the two world wars.

This account, while superficially plausible, does not bear historical scrutiny. As Chapter 2 shows, a few Sylheti lascars did indeed jump ship in London, and some of them did eventually settle in Britain. In turn, they assisted others to follow suit.[42] But to claim that all of today's 'Bangladeshi settlers' are their descendants stretches the point. If this assertion were correct, the migrations from Sylhet to Britain would have peaked in the 1940s and 1950s, since after independence and partition in 1947, very few Sylheti lascars (by Choudhury's own account,

Narrating diaspora

supported by scholars[43]) found work on British ships. Instead, the numbers of Bengali migrants in Britain remained tiny in this period: by the early 1950s, there were perhaps no more than 300 Sylhetis in London. By 1962, their numbers in the whole of Britain had grown to only about 5,000.[44] It was only after this date that the numbers of Sylhetis began to grow rapidly, in the context of new British rules about immigration[45] and the dangers and uncertainties of life in Bangladesh during and after the 1971 war. By 1986, when the British government published its first White Paper on Bangladeshis in Britain, it estimated that there were about 200,000 Bangladeshis were in the country.[46] By 2001, as the Census of that year suggests, that number had grown by another 100,000 in just 15 years.

Contrary to Choudhury's account, then, the vast majority of Bangladeshis now settled in Britain were never lascars on British ships and were born long after the Second World War. Most Bangladeshis who migrated to Britain did so in the two decades *after Bangladesh achieved independence from Pakistan in 1971*. The claim to lineal descent from lascars is overstretched, at the very least.

So why does Choudhury repeat his claim over fifty times in the course of his book? For one thing, of course, it gives the 'community' a single shared history and glosses over the deep political divisions that have long beset it.[47] It provides it with a simple genealogy which connects today's British Bangladeshis – through the lascar seamen who served on British ships during the world wars, and through them back to the Sylheti boatmen who were recruited to work on steamships on the River Surma in Sylhet – right back to the original band of 360 saints who accompanied Shah Jalal on his mission to spread Islam on the frontiers of Bengal. This genealogy serves both to unify 'the community' as fictive kin and gives it an intelligible history imbued with a continuing moral purpose. But, no less significantly, as we shall see below, it provides the foundations on which the 'settlers' built their claim to rights as citizens in Britain.

In Ilias's history, the communal riots in Bihar in late 1946 are depicted as 'the root cause' of the emigration of the 'Biharis' from Bihar. Throughout the book, Ilias returns again and again to these horrific events, which (in his account) claimed 50,000 lives[48] and forced many thousands more to flee from their homes. When Pakistan was established in 1947, he tells us, many of these terrified people sought shelter in its eastern wing. Later on, their numbers swelled as anti-Muslim violence in India in 1950 and again in 1964 drove more and more people out. Ilias' purpose is to imprint on the reader's mind the 'fact' that the people he writes about were victims of catastrophic events, refugees who, through no fault of their own, were evicted from the land of their birth and had to seek shelter elsewhere: 'The Muslim minority in Bihar were ... happy with their way of life, when India fell for communalism and Bihar became the target'.[49] The very language he uses to describe these events emphasizes the passive victimhood of the 'Biharis': they were 'sorted out' and 'shunted off''[50] and 'forced to leave their country of origin'.[51] Ilias' recurrent theme is that the 'Biharis' 'are descendants of those optees and emigrants who came to East Bengal after the great divide in India in 1947'.[52]

Yet there are contradictions, and a noticeable instability, in this construction of events. As Ilias himself admits (and as discussed in Chapters 1 and 6), from the late 19th century onwards, the British had employed large numbers of 'Biharis' on the railways when these were extended into eastern Bengal and also many others in 'the police, judiciary and other civil departments'.[53] So when the calamitous events of 1946–1947 took place, there were already many 'Biharis' long settled in parts of what now became East Pakistan.[54] After partition, some were joined by their families, but they were not refugees from violence. By Ilias' own account (which the censuses and other studies support), many of the Urdu-speaking service elites who migrated to East Pakistan after 1947 did so in fits and starts over more than two decades between 1947 and 1970, attracted by the better opportunities for employment in East Pakistan.

As we read on, then, it becomes clear why Ilias describes his 'community' as 'Bihari', even though he himself admits its members do not all come from Bihar, and despite the fact, as he would be the first to acknowledge, that 'Bihari' has become a derogatory term in present-day Bangladesh. Yet by calling them 'Bihari', he fixes in the reader's mind an association between this migrant group and the carnage in Bihar in 1946. The Bihar riots have long been held up as 'the moment when Pakistan was born', when the sheer brutality of the attacks demonstrated that reconciliation or rapprochement between India's Hindus and Muslims was impossible. They hold as large a place in the collective memory of partition in the east as do the Calcutta killings of 1946. Used in particular contexts, the very word 'Bihar' conjures up all the horrors of 'the deadly ethnic riot'.[55] By calling his community 'Biharis', perhaps Ilias seeks to recall these outrages in order to evoke the sympathy of fellow Muslims and 'hosts' in Bangladesh, sympathy which his community patently deserves despite their later 'mistakes' (more of which later in this chapter). The word 'Bihari' in Ilias' book thus carries a powerful moral charge.

But at another level, the 'myth' of their enforced exile from Bihar also works to provide a single, straightforward common 'history' for the 'Bihari' community in Bangladesh today. Present-day 'Biharis' are represented as linear descendants of those who fled the carnage, who in turn are descended from the saintly pioneers who brought Islam to 'caste-ridden' India, and all are legatees of the great revolutionaries who resisted imperial incursions. They are standard bearers of a sacred mission with a long history and heirs to a great culture. This 'history' seeks to unify the 'community' and sanitize and simplify its complex and multistranded chronicles by providing a single and intelligible 'root cause' for its presence in Bangladesh. In this sense, it has much in common with the foundation myths of so many migrant groups, which typically see their migration as the consequence of a single catastrophic event, even though historians might agree that they migrated gradually over a long period, sometimes over centuries.[56]

Both these accounts, then, simplify complex histories of migration. Choudhury ignores the fact that most Sylhetis migrated to Britain during and after the upheavals of the Liberation War in Bangladesh, and he greatly exaggerates the role of lascars – typically enterprising economic migrants – in that history. For his part, Ilias plays down the long process of 'economic' migration from Bihar and upper India to eastern Bengal, proposing instead that all 'Biharis' were 'forced migrants', victims of communal violence. These constructions enable both writers to provide simple answers to the question 'Why are we here?' But, as we shall see, they deliberately privilege one particular answer over others because it suits their purposes 'here' and 'now'. These histories are thus not only about the past, they are about the present, about contemporary challenges and how to respond to them. They also offer prescriptions for the future.

Myths for assimilation: Intertwining community and 'host' histories

In what way do these histories advance the cause of assimilation if, as has been shown, one of their purposes is vigorously to claim the unity, the integrity, and the separate identity of 'the community'? We will suggest that people must first be 'assimilated' into a community with a single story or construct about itself before it can begin to negotiate its acceptance as a part of a host nation. Maintaining 'ethnicity' does not prevent assimilation, as some critics have argued. Instead it is often a necessary prolegomenon to it.

The first technique in this 'work of assimilation' is the insertion of 'community history' into the 'national history' of the 'host' country. Of course, no nation has a single national narrative, no matter how much nationalists might claim it does. But at certain times and in certain places there may be a measure of consensus about which historical events crucially shaped a nation's identity, and migrant intellectuals seem to be quick to spot these areas of 'national' agreement. In Britain in the late 1970s and 1980s, when Yousuf Choudhury wrote his book (and indeed even today, as the recent votes for Churchill as 'the greatest Briton' suggest), the world wars, and particularly the Second World War, seemed to be such defining events.[57]

The very first page of Choudhury's *Roots and Tales* makes plain his intention to insert 'the Bangladeshi settlers' into this narrative of British patriotic sacrifice. It calls to be quoted in full:

> Many people have misconceptions about the Bangladeshi settlers because they either have wrong information or lack of the same. Many do not know that the Bangladeshis were asked to come and fight for Britain in the two world wars. We fought both wars for them. We were in the warships and troop carriers when they were facing enemies. We were in British cargo-ships to bring in the vital supplies. Bangladeshis worked on the deck, went down to the bottom of the ships, and ran the engines for them. We were part of the British war power.
>
> The ships were attacked and sunk on the high seas. Many of our men were killed, not all of their dead bodies floated to the surface of the water. The dead bodies were eaten by sharks or simply decomposed.
>
> Many dead bodies went down with their ships leaving no trace, no grave or headstone is there to be seen, so our dead Bangladeshi seamen have been forgotten for all time.

230 *Narrating diaspora*

> Most Bangladeshi settlers are the descendent flesh and blood of those who were lost in the seas or survived to tell their tale, so it is our duty to keep our history alive and remind everyone of who we are and why we are here.[58]

This is a remarkable passage for many reasons. On the one hand, it makes explicit the author's intention to inform 'many people' about his community's sacrifices on their behalf, and it is clear that his intended audience is the 'host' society, 'the British'. But what is particularly interesting is how he maintains the boundary between 'us' and 'them' ('we fought both the wars for them', etc.), even as he weaves the history of 'the settlers' into the tapestry of British national history.

Once it is recognized that Choudhury's history is also a polemical tract, staking claims in the present and for the future, many peculiarities of its language and structure become intelligible. It explains the author's decision to write the book in English rather than Bangla. It explains why the author insists repeatedly that *all* 'Bangladeshis' are descended from lascar seamen; why his brief account of his community's origins stresses its primeval connection with the sea; why his Sylhet is literally born out of the ocean and why his 'community' (just as its British hosts) is presented as a seafaring people. It explains why so much of the book is about the period of British rule over Sylhet, and why its account of colonial rule is so uncritical, downplaying the fierce conflicts between Sylhetis and 'Britishers' and positing instead a largely cordial interdependence between rulers and ruled. It explains why it stresses the kindness and paternalism of the British owners of steamer ships in employing the Bengali boatmen their ships had put out of business, and the decency of the British people towards them when they first arrived on British shores.[59] And of course it explains why the crucial and recurrent theme – which stresses Bangladeshi sacrifice for Britain during the wars – is the leitmotif of the work. This is the basis on which Choudhury rests his case for the community's *right* to settle in Britain. It is a right they have *earned* by their sacrifices on behalf of Britain.

But it also explains why Choudhury strives so hard to compress and simplify that history of 'the settlers' into a single narrative. That narrative has to be controlled tightly if Choudhury is to be able to sustain this claim. If the variety of histories and experiences of Bangladeshi migrants were acknowledged, this would weaken his claim to rights for the community in Britain today. The 'community' has first to be constructed as 'Bangladeshi' in order for it to be accepted as British. Those migrants whose stories palpably strain the unified account of the community and its origins – for instance, the snobbish 'Dhaka gentlemen' who turn up their noses at their more humble countrymen from Sylhet[60] and the 'Arabic-educated' pro-Pakistanis (persons of the same group Ilias describes as 'Biharis') who become the imams at their new mosques[61] – are 'reconciled' with the larger Sylheti population, soon 'gain their forgiveness',[62] and are apparently 'assimilated' into the community before disappearing from the account as suddenly as they entered it. It is only after this work of constructing, inventing, and assimilating migrant Bangladeshis of very different sorts into one community has been achieved by the myths of origin and migration that Choudhury begins to describe his 'community' as 'British Bangladeshi'. Significantly, the term is first used only on page 196 of a 230-page work. Thereafter, the book refers repeatedly to 'British Bangladeshis', their culture but also their secular problems – particularly their underperformance in education – and their politics in Britain.

Another interesting point is that the author simultaneously aligns his community with a 'general' British past and also with *particular* sections of 'British' society. His discussions of the lifestyles of the early postwar migrants – their liaisons and marriages with working-class white women, their sharing of food and lodgings with migrant workers from other parts of the world, their long shifts in the factories, their renting of premises and leasing of shops from East End Jews – identifies 'Bangladeshis' with a kind of enterprising, working-class cosmopolitanism that, Choudhury suggests, characterized the 'Britain' in which they lived and worked. Palpably it is this convivial[63] 'Britain' into which he seeks the incorporation of his community. In this sense, Choudhury bears out Brubaker's suggestion that assimilation must be understood as a process by which a community repositions itself with regard to many different cultural referents, rather than to a single, monolithic, 'core' culture.[64]

Towards the end of the book, moreover, Choudhury begins to describe 'Bengalis' as 'part of the immigrant population'.[65] They are represented as part of 'Black' movements,[66] an integral element in the fight against racism in the 1980s: 'Bangladeshis had done a lot of fighting and were still fighting for their existence and rights'.[67] Increasingly, he discusses their politics: their long-distance nationalism[68] vis-à-vis Bangladesh (through their support of the Liberation movement), but also their political activism in the local councils in Britain to improve living conditions in the inner cities. He mentions certain liberal Britons as friends of the community: the social worker and historian Caroline Adams, Ken Livingstone, and even Prince Charles, proudly reproducing a photograph of the Prince's visit to Aldgate. So one can see that Choudhury is positioning his 'community' within a certain construct of 'Britain' and of 'Britishness', one that is by turns hard-working and enterprising, cosmopolitan, egalitarian, tolerant, and inclusive. In some senses, one might argue, he is constructing the multicultural 'Britain' into which the community of 'Bangladeshi settlers' seeks to be assimilated quite as much as he is constructing the community itself.

Ilias adopts similar strategies in *Biharis*. He, too, strives to insert his community into the national history of Bangladesh. But his is a rather more difficult enterprise and one that is fraught with many pitfalls. Above all, it requires him to admit repeatedly to his community's past mistakes and seek forgiveness for them.

The first move Ilias makes is a bold one, considering that some of the deepest differences between 'Biharis' and their hosts revolve around the question of language: 'Biharis' are widely believed by Bangladeshi nationalists to have stood aloof from the language movement. In his first chapter, Ilias simply asserts that the Bengali language and ' "Bihari" Urdu' have a common origin, that both descend from a single great linguistic tradition: that of 'Magadhi Prakrit'.

> Bengali, Oriya and Assamese have their root in Bihar. Bengali is a typical descendent of the great language that, under the name of Magadhi Prakrit, was the vernacular of eastern North India for many centuries. This was the

232 *Narrating diaspora*

official language of the great Emperor Asoka and the Buddha and Mahavira, the apostle of Jainism. . . .

'Bihari' Urdu [is] unlike the [literary] Urdu evolved in Delhi and UP, [it] was overwhelmingly plain and simple. . . . Even today, most 'Bihari' Muslims speak Magadhi, Maithili and Bhujpuri rather than Urdu.[69]

In this passage, Ilias seeks to construct a common linguistic heritage for 'eastern north India' and places Bihar squarely at its centre. Ilias thus disentangles and distances 'Bihari' from the courtly and aristocratic world of North India, claiming that it is part of a syncretic family of 'plain and simple' spoken languages. By making this claim, he seeks to defuse the tension engendered by the language question, and also to rid Urdu, as spoken in Bangladesh, of its elitist and North Indian associations. He rhetorically shifts the Bihar 'homeland' eastwards – in the direction of its Bengali neighbourhood and away from Upper India and Pakistan. He also pushes 'Bihari' Urdu speakers down the social ladder, associating them not with the elite or *ashraf* North Indian tradition of Persianized Urdu but with the more lowly *atrap* or *ajlaf* everyday bazaar dialects of the eastern region.

In his next set of strategic moves, Ilias faces up squarely to the greatest obstacle to 'Bihari' assimilation into Bangladeshi society – the charge that the community fought against the 'nation' in the war of 1971, joining hands with the Pakistani army in its brutal and merciless suppression of the people's uprising. Ilias attempts to explain this in a variety of ways – and autocritique is central to them. The 'Bihari' refugees from India, he admits, made grave mistakes. But they did this largely because they were misled, misguided, and, ultimately, betrayed by their leaders who took them into 'the wilderness'.[70] Despite the fact that the 'local Bengali community was . . . very sympathetic towards [them]',[71] they kept themselves aloof from the locals, living apart in 'reservations'.[72] By adopting the title and status of *mohajirs* – the Islamic term that the Pakistani state used for refugees – they isolated themselves from other groups in society, adopting a 'psyche' which led them to mistakenly regard the struggles of the local people as being against their interests. Instead of demanding that they should be treated equally as citizens of Pakistan,[73] they claimed a special status as *mohajirs* who had made particular sacrifices for the state and who therefore deserved special privileges. Unlike the *mohajirs* of Karachi and Hyderabad in West Pakistan, who were harsh critics of the Pakistani regime, the 'Bihari' *mohajirs* in Bengal remained apathetic[74] and were won over by special allotments of housing and other facilities. Under General Ayub Khan's martial law regime, 'Bihari' Basic Democrats 'were submissive to the political programmes of Ayub Khan. They performed their duty not as representatives of their community but as agents of the ruling clique'.[75] Their failure to adapt and assimilate, Ilias admits, was a huge error. Their separatist 'psyche' prevented them from throwing their weight behind the rightful political struggles of Bengalis against successive Pakistani regimes, hence the dreadful reprisals against the 'Bihari' community after the war ended.

These are profoundly moving passages. Like many 'interested' historians of vanquished peoples, Ilias labours under the burden of having to explain why events turned out as they did, and this leads him to reflect with great seriousness on the past. In common with others in this predicament, he laments the short-sightedness of his people but also blames their former leaders, now deposed.[76] Again and again, he shows how the 'Biharis' were let down by their leaders. Ilias' 'Biharis' were misled first by the creator of Pakistan,[77] and then by the Muslim League leadership and their 'religion-based politics'.[78] After partition, they were misled by the Pakistani state, which encouraged them to cling to their refugee status and their Urdu language.[79] In the late 1950s, they were betrayed by corrupt 'Bihari' representatives who were too busy making money to give proper leadership to the community; and in the 1960s, they were exploited by Governor Monem Khan 'who had very close contact with notorious [criminals]', and who used them 'to create a wedge between locals and non-locals'.[80] In the late 1960s, when the campaign for the autonomy of East Pakistan gained ground, West Pakistani-based Urdu newspapers misled them with false propaganda against the Bengali leader, Mujibur Rahman.[81] In the months before the outbreak of the war, they were betrayed again by the media, which falsely alleged that the Mohajer Convention had called for the partition of East Bengal,[82] and after the war began, they were led astray by a false prophet – Warasat Khan, the leader of the Mohajer Party – who dragged orphaned 'Bihari' boys into the war on the side of Pakistan.[83] In the aftermath of the war, when 'Biharis' were hunted down and killed in their thousands by the so-called Bengali 'Sixteenth Divisions', they were betrayed by the Red Cross, which encouraged and organized 'bewildered people' to register themselves for 'repatriation to Pakistan'.[84] Terrified victims of grisly reprisals, as they huddled in their makeshift camps after the war, they were exploited by the Indian soldiers who, instead of protecting them, took all their money on the false promise of getting them out of Bangladesh.[85]

This theme of betrayal is repeated so often, and at such regular intervals in the book, that it demands reflection on its deeper discursive intent. Arguably, it takes forward two crucially important strategic purposes. On the one hand, it clearly seeks to drive a distinction between the innocence of the general 'Bihari' community and the culpability of their 'false' leaders. By this device, Ilias suggests that it is right for the 'soft-hearted' Bangladeshi nation to forgive these poor misguided people, in their own way as much victims of the old Pakistani order as the Bengalis.

But on the other hand, a less explicit, but nonetheless potent, message is directed at the 'Biharis' themselves. Ilias warns his fellow 'Biharis' to beware the siren calls of the false prophets of today. In particular, he appeals to them not to be misled by the likes of Nasim Khan, the retired railway guard who organized 'Bihari' railway employees to fight for their repatriation [to Pakistan], and his organization, the Stranded Pakistanis General Repatriation Committee (SPGRC). Since the mid-1970s, the SPGRC has waged a long and highly publicized battle to arrange the transfer of all 'Stranded Pakistanis' back to Pakistan, albeit with very little success.[86] Ilias describes the followers of Nasim Khan as 'frustrated and uneducated and half-educated youths'.[87] He clearly believes them to be misguided, and their goals for 'repatriation' to a country they have never seen and which has repeatedly repudiated them to be unrealistic and naive.

Since 1980, Ahmed Ilias himself and the 'Al Falah' NGO he directs have worked for the rehabilitation of 'Urdu-speaking Bangladeshis'[88] living in camps. His very description of them as 'Urdu-speaking Bangladeshis' (as opposed to Khan's 'Stranded Pakistanis') reveals his goal to negotiate their assimilation into the society and polity of Bangladesh. Hence Ilias writes with approval of those individuals among the 'Bihari' community 'who are struggling for a place in the soft heart of the Bengali society', 'the literate and educated, representing the young generation [that] wants to come out from the depressed situation and overcome the agony they have suffered for the last three decades'.[89] The deeper intent of his whole 'history' is to suggest that 'the literate and educated' syncretists reflect the true 'progressive' spirit of the community's history and hence represent the true leadership for the community today. Of course, in making this claim, Ilias glosses over the cracks within the community,[90] particularly, but not exclusively, those that distance Bhojpuri-speaking camp dwellers from the Urdu-speaking literati. His aim is to persuade the community and their hosts alike that 'Biharis' *are* in fact 'Urdu-speaking Bangladeshis'. The fact that this term is first used only towards the end of his book (on page 154 of a 200-page text) suggests that, through this usage, Ilias seeks to transform 'Biharis' into 'Urdu-speaking Bangladeshis' in much the same way that Yousuf Choudhury metamorphoses Sylheti lascars into 'British Bangladeshis'.

Ilias's other objective is to provide this community of 'Urdu-speaking Bangladeshis' with an impressive record of service to the cause of Bangladesh. He painstakingly catalogues every act by which Urdu speakers – whether as individuals or groups – demonstrated their loyalty to Bengal and the national ideals of Bangladesh. He notes with pride that on 21 February 1952, when Bengali students took up the fight for the Bengali language, the 'Urdu-speaking civil servant' Hussain Haider refused to issue orders proscribing the movement and was transferred for his pains. In this way Ilias 'inserts' 'Biharis' into the history of *Ekushe*, symbolically the moment that Bangladeshi nationalism was born.[91] He then goes on to describe the contribution of 'progressive' Urdu 'poets, writers, journalists and students' to 'the Language Movement':

Dr. Yusuf Hasan, Arif Hushyarpuri, Ayaz Asmi, Massod Kalim, Akhtar Payami, Akhtar Hyderabadi, Adeeb Sohail, Khwaja Mohammed Ali, Qamar, Manzur Rahman, Salahuddin Mohammed, Badruddin Ahmed (Engineer), Perwez Ahmed (Barrister), Hasan Sayeed, Abu Sayeed Khan and Zainul Abedin were prominent among the supporters of the language movement. Dr. Yusuf Hasan being a member of the Urdu speaking community played a significant role in the language movement. He issued press statements on behalf of the Urdu *Progressive* Writers Association in favour of the movement. He was also selected as one of the founder members of the '*Rashtro Bhasha Sangram Parishad*' [the National Language Movement Council].

At a later stage, others like Ataur Rahman Jalil, Naushad Noori, Suroor Barabankwi, Habib Ansari, Bamo Akhter Shahood, Umme Ammarah and Anwer Farhad joined the movement. It was Salahuddin Mohammed, who had

Narrating diaspora 235

even said that if Urdu and Bangla were not accepted as two state languages of Pakistan, he then would demand only for Bangla as the state language.

The Language Movement also greatly influenced the *progressive* Urdu poets and writers in both wings of Pakistan. . . . In East Pakistan, Urdu poet Naushad Noori wrote a very powerful poem, '*Mohenjodaro*', in Urdu. . . .

[Ilias then quotes the full text of the poem 'Mohenjodaro', first in Urdu and then in English translation.]

. . . The Urdu-speaking writers expressed their solidarity with the Language Movement. *Anjuman Taraqqi-e-Urdu* (Organisation for the Development of Urdu) in East Pakistan severed its tie with the All Pakistan Anjuman . . . for its support to the government on language policy. . . . The *progressive* Urdu students formed *Anjuman-e-Adab*, a literary organization in Dhaka University[,] to support the contemporary *progressive* Bengali writers for their cultural struggle.[92]

And so on. Later, according to Ilias, when political movements against Ayub Khan gained momentum, 'the *progressive* and pro-democratic Urdu students, youths, journalists, teachers, writers and poets' mobilized themselves in their support.[93] 'The 'Bihari' railway workers in Syedpur Railway Workshops joined the anti-Ayub movements following the directive of the "Bihari" labour leaders Azim Nomani and Mohammed Ibrahim'.[94] On the eve of the fateful general election in 1970, Ilias tells us, 'a *progressive* Urdu-speaking businessman Mahmood Hasan of Chittagong', associated with '*progressive* movements since 1952', brought out a new weekly *Jaridah*, whose first banner headline *Hamari Nijat Tumhari Nijat, Chey Nukat, Chey Nukat*[95] ('Our salvation, your salvation, Six Points, Six Points') explicitly supported the Awami League's Six Point Charter for autonomy for East Pakistan.[96] In 1971, many 'Bihari' labour leaders and journalists 'joined the liberation movement'.[97] He recalls that two officers in the army – the 'Bihari' Saghir Ahmed Siddiqui and the Bengali Nurul Islam – were incarcerated and killed by the Pakistani army. 'Two bloods', he tells us, had *'mingled together to live in union'*,[98] graphically demonstrating the syncretistic character of the freedom struggle and (Ilias suggests implicitly) the true spirit of the Bangladeshi nation.

At every stage in the nation's struggles for liberation, Ilias therefore insists, 'Biharis' had played a role. While some had admittedly been misled, coerced or inveigled into joining the Pakistani army and its depredations on the people of Bangladesh, the community's true leaders – intellectuals and writers – had fought and died for the nation. So too had the hard-working 'Bihari' masses, notably the railway workers of Syedpur. Here again we see Ilias's strategy of incorporating 'Bihari' workers into the 'progressive' history of the educated elites.

Ilias thus skillfully weaves 'Biharis' into the patriotic history of the Bangladeshi nation while significantly aligning his community with *specific* sections of Bangladesh's polity. As highlighted in the passages cited above, Ilias repeatedly uses the adjective 'progressive' to describe his list of 'Urdu-speaking Bangladeshi' heroes. Clearly, he is seeking to enlist the support of similarly 'progressive' segments of local Bengali society to rehabilitate his community as true members

236 *Narrating diaspora*

of the Bangladeshi nation. Here again we see at work the subtle and complex mechanics of assimilation. Just as Choudhury positioned his 'community' within a certain kind of 'Britain', Ilias positions his 'Biharis' as part of a certain kind of Bangladesh – one that is 'progressive' in a specifically South Asian meaning of that term: secular, anti-imperialist, egalitarian, tolerant, and inclusive, one that celebrates the pluralism and syncretism of South Asia's faiths and cultures. There is a subtle suggestion that this 'progressive' vision of Bangladesh has as yet to be to be realized, and Ilias seems to urge 'Urdu-speaking Bangladeshis' to join with like-minded Bengalis in its construction and achievement. Just as Choudhury seeks to fashion multicultural 'Britain', Ilias seeks to join with 'progressive' Bengalis to create a more inclusive – indeed, multicultural – 'Bangladesh'.

The 'myth of return': The context and politics of assimilation

The final set of questions raised by these texts has to do with their timing. Why were they written and published when they were? What was it about the moment of their production that made them appropriate, relevant, or even possible? And if we can uncover these 'conditions of production', might we be able to get a better insight into the conditions under which migrant groups in times past wrote histories or genealogies of their communities?

The first set of answers lie in generational changes within the community. The coming of age of a generation of children who have grown up in the diaspora (in the case of Choudhury) or in camps (in the case of Ilias) is a compelling concern that animates both works. Choudhury refers directly in his introduction to these changes as one of his motives in writing his book:

> Now in 1993, most work-mates, room-mates and close friends of my earlier times have passed away. Their sons and grandsons became the family head, living in this country with their own wives and children. . . . The new generation in our community need to know more about us. What we were, what we are and where we come from. It is their roots, their identity, which are unknown to many of them. That identity is vital, no matter where they live. Without it, they will be lost.[99]

Ilias is less explicit about his intention to write for the young, but he too refers repeatedly to the rise of a new generation of young people who have grown up in camps and who understand little about the history of their situation. Ilias seems keen not only to educate, but also to guide the young towards a brighter future which, he believes, can only come if they embrace an 'Urdu-speaking Bangladeshi' identity.

However, a deeper imperative appears to come from a recognition that the 'myth of return' can no longer be sustained. Choudhury writes poignantly of the gradual fading of the dream of going back 'home':

> After spending ten or fifteen years here, some Bangladeshis often decided to go home to resettle. They sold their properties . . . whatever they owned,

then went to Bangladesh with a lump sum of money . . . quite confident of a happy life.

As the dealing . . . really started, obstacles began to emerge. [The typical British Bangladeshi] realised that, without his conscious knowledge, he himself had picked up a lot of habits from the host country and was used to another pattern of life.

He found himself inexperienced in many day-to-day matters. He needed a guide at every step and gradually began to discover himself as a foreigner in his own home land. Still [he kept hoping] to get over it. . . .

As time passed on, either money or health went down, if not both. Otherwise, if he was unlucky, he might get involved with a court case. . . . The people stayed on until their patience ran out.

Eventually the spirit to resettle in the homeland began to fade away. . . . The first generation of Bangladeshi settlers might have had several tries to settle in the homeland and failed. Some are still alive. . . . [Now] they grow a beard, dress up in white and attend the nearest mosque and spend hours praying. . . . Although the father and son [may live] under the same roof, sharing the same food, with love, affection and care, yet in their minds they are living in different worlds.[100]

With the long, slow and painful death of this dream, Choudhury and many of his contemporaries had to reconcile themselves to the fact that their children were not keen to return, and they themselves have been so changed by their years abroad that they could no longer slip back easily into life at 'home'. Perhaps (as suggested by the references to court cases and conflicts) they also have to recognize that 'home' too has changed forever. A key purpose of writing this history is to try to come to terms with this loss, accepting that 'the Bangladeshi settlers' are really 'here to stay' in Britain.

For Ilias, too, the book signals a recognition that the dream of 'repatriation' to Pakistan is just that – a dream. In a chapter titled 'The Long March' he describes, at some length and in much painful detail, the process of disillusionment by 'the step-motherly attitudes of the Pakistan government'.[101] The Red Cross had raised false hopes among 'Bihari' displacees that they would be 'repatriated' to Pakistan if they signed 'declarations of intention', but immediately after the Delhi Agreement of 1973, the Pakistan government made clear its determination not to accept these stranded people. So too did its citizens: Pakistanis in Sindh raised the slogan *"Bihari' na khappan'* ('Biharis are not wanted'), 'taking advantage of the known views of [Bhutto's ruling] People's Party regarding Biharis'.[102] Despite the efforts of the SPGRC and the Saudi-sponsored organization Rabita, the government of Pakistan stuck to its guns that 'Biharis will have to live in Bangladesh'.[103] Ilias urges his community to face the harsh fact that there is no place for them anywhere else than Bangladesh – they have been abandoned by Pakistan and forgotten by the international community. They have no choice, he suggests, but to come to terms with this fact and seek finally to settle (and assimilate) in Bangladesh.

So both our authors reach the same conclusion at roughly the same time – four decades after partition and two decades after the birth of Bangladesh. The natural cycle of generations – as has been suggested above – helps to explain why this should be the case. But it would be unwise to ignore the changing political context in both 'host' countries, which encouraged the migrant community to take bold steps towards greater integration, if not total assimilation. The postwar decades in Britain saw ever-harsher rhetoric against nonwhite immigration (Enoch Powell's 1968 'rivers of blood' speech was only one example of a wider trend) and deepening racial conflict. Throughout the 1970s and 1980s, Asians in Thatcher's Britain experienced 'a further entrenchment of institutionalized racism, particularly in the form of immigration laws and the British Nationality Act [of 1981]'.[104] As we have discussed in Chapters 4 and 7, these were also decades of escalating racist violence:[105] in a poignant passage Choudhury lists the names of 'victims of racist attacks' killed during this period, including Altab Ali. The same period saw the growth of organized antiracist resistance in black and Asian communities and of harsh policing of this increasingly vocal and 'home-grown' movement.[106] The early 1980s witnessed the outbreak of 'race riots' across the country and the shift towards a policy of multiculturalism. This sought to recognize the histories, cultures, and contributions of Britain's diverse ethnic minorities but also saw the fragmentation of 'black' antiracist activism and shifts towards the celebration of ethnicity and 'difference' – what Sivanandan has described as the growth of 'ethnic enclaves and feuding nationalisms'.[107]

This splintering of solidarities can be most clearly seen in 1988, when the publication of Rushdie's *Satanic Verses* prompted widespread demonstrations among outraged Muslims in Britain's inner cities[108] and placed 'Muslims' in the spotlight for the first time.[109] But of no less importance (Choudhury makes no mention at all of Rushdie's book) was the British government's publication in 1986 of the first policy document on *Bangladeshis in Britain*.[110] This revealed official concern about the continuing 'backwardness' of the Bangladeshi population, showing that their children were underachieving at school, faring far worse than the children of Indian and Pakistani descent. Significantly, Choudhury's book ends with a long discussion of the white paper. He argues that it shocked the community – hitherto complacent about the education of its children – into action, and he shows how British Bengalis began to enter local politics to tackle these problems. (Again, this bears out Brubaker's insight that assimilation for 'secular' purposes continues to be salient for many migrant groups.[111]) Instead of focusing their energies solely on Bangladeshi politics – as they had done in the past – they increasingly began to see good reasons to seek to influence, or even to enter, local councils in Britain. Local politics appears to have become a vital arena for interaction between new spokesmen for the community and particular British people: constituency MPs, of course, but also local councillors, school head teachers, social workers, and representatives of church groups. These interactions can be seen to have created a new space – perhaps what Brah calls a 'diaspora space'[112] – in which assimilation could begin to be negotiated by certain Bangladeshis and certain Britons. It is highly significant that Caroline Adams' path-breaking study of the community, *Across Thirteen Rivers and Seven Seas*, came out of her interaction with Bangladeshis as a social worker in the East End.[113] Her book 'explains' the Bengali presence in

Britain in precisely the same terms as Choudhury's does, recalling the sacrifice of Bengali lascars in the world wars. It is also noteworthy that Choudhury's book was published by the Sylheti Social History Group in London – a small group of British liberals and left-leaning Bangladeshi community leaders such as Tassaduq Ahmed, who is also the author of the foreword to Adams' book. The fact that the preface to *Roots and Tales* was written, in a neat symmetry, by a leading Christian theologian underlines the enabling role played by such individuals, and by civil society and religious groups, in the processes of Bengali assimilation.

But the most interesting feature of Choudhury's last chapter is its suggestion that assimilation (at least with the secular purpose of raising educational standards of the community, and improving its access to healthcare and housing) is a *national duty* for all 'British Bangladeshis'. They must encourage educational achievement, he suggests, because their failure in this regard lets the nation (Bangladesh) down. The fact that both Indian and Pakistani children had outstripped Bengalis at school is stressed again and again. It is as if Choudhury is seeking to play upon Bangladeshi anxieties about their overweening neighbours in South Asia to provoke them into taking steps to 'improve' themselves in Britain. Thus we see the playing out of an apparent paradox – 'long-distance' Bangladeshi nationalism being deployed to drive forward Bengali assimilation into *British* politics and *British* culture.

Ilias's *Biharis* must also be placed within the political context in which it was published. In 2003, months before *Biharis* came out, Bangladesh's Supreme Court ruled in the case of *Abid Khan and others* that the Urdu-speaking 'Bihari' petitioners were citizens of Bangladesh by birth and could not be deprived of their voting rights. As Chapter 3 has shown, this followed other rulings in favour of 'Bihari' petitioners upholding their rights as citizens. In their turn, these rulings came in a context where Bengali civil society groups began to challenge discrimination against 'Biharis' as well as against Hindu minority groups and Muslim women. Sections of the academic community (notably the Refugee and Migratory Movements Research Unit, RRMRU) and the media took up the 'Bihari' cause.[114] Soon after Ilias's book came out, Tanvir Mokkamel's documentary *Swapnabhumi* ('The Promised Land') portrayed the 'Bihari' community in a deeply sympathetic light.[115] That film, made in the Bengali language, 'explained' the predicament of the 'Biharis' to local Bengalis in much the same way that Caroline Adams had explained the Sylhetis' history to white British readers. The fact that Ilias mentions some of these rulings and trends in his book[116] suggests that he was aware that his goal of 'Bihari' assimilation enjoyed the support of many 'progressive' Bangladeshis.

Like Choudhury, Ilias identifies the pressing need for his community to attend to its secular needs in Bangladesh. He urges it to consider the future of 'the young generation' here and now, a generation that 'want[s] to come out of the depressed situation and overcome the agony'[117] instead of continuing to hanker after 'repatriation' to Pakistan in an indefinite future. His particularly concern is that without better provision for their education in Urdu and Bengali, the community would fail to improve its circumstances. But he also warns of the danger that the great Urdu literary tradition to which they are the heirs might die forever. A plea for cultural survival[118] sits comfortably with his case for assimilation: indeed, it is deployed to advance arguments for assimilation. He sees no contradiction between the survival and persistence of the 'ethnic' or 'national' culture and secular incorporation into the national life of Bangladesh.

So both projects work with and through nationalisms, but in complex ways. Both are 'multicultural': they ask for recognition and survival locally, while identifying the community with not one but *two* territorial nations (Britain *and* Bangladesh/Sylhet in the case of Choudhury; Bangladesh *and* Bihar/India for Ilias). But both also construct diasporic, deterritorialized 'transnations'.[119] The 'British-Bangladeshi' people and 'Urdu-speaking Bangladeshi' people are both shown to have been formed, in a fundamental sense, by *repeated* migrations: they are 'migrant-nations' who have successively sacralized the spaces in which they have settled.

But it would not do to gloss over the differences between these two projects. Choudhury's shows greater self-confidence and aspiration. It actively seeks to build coalitions to influence the direction of British national politics by working through and with local government, the church, the 'race relations industry',[120] and other civil society groups. Ilias's goals appear to be rather more tentative: he seeks recognition for 'Urdu speakers' to supplement the very basic political rights they have finally achieved. Their respective projects for assimilation appear to work within the particular political space their authors see as being open to them: they respond creatively to contingent local possibilities and negotiate particular, local, challenges while pursuing similar (but not identical) goals.

Conclusion

In *Roots and Tales*, Choudhury recalls that when he and his friends were young men working in Britain, they used to laugh when people described them as immigrants. They knew that they were in Britain temporarily. They counted the money they earned in terms of Bangladeshi *takas* (rupees). Now, however, 'their sons didn't regard his pounds as *takas* to invest in paddy farmland in Sylhet, as his father did. He preferred the things here – red brick houses, good carpets, modern furniture, fashionable clothes to wear and a nice car to drive. When he got a pound he spent it as a pound in the place where it was earned and where he lived'.[121]

This chapter has attempted to uncover the processes by which *takas* became 'pounds' and sojourners became settlers. It has suggested that the apparently clumsy and anachronistic but in fact revealing title of Choudhury's book – *The Roots and Tales of Bangladeshi Settlers* – provides a clue to the process by which Sylhetis simultaneously became both 'Bangladeshis' and 'settlers'. Assimilation, it has showed, is a 'doubled' process. It has underscored the Sylhetis' strong emotional bonds with the national project in Bangladesh but has shown how they came to view assimilation (or true settlement) in Britain as a *Bangladeshi* patriotic duty. Both community histories by Choudhury and Ilias reveal the complexities and inwardness of the long-distance nationalisms of migrant groups, complexities which previous studies have tended to overlook.

Both histories suggest, moreover, that the concept of 'hybridity' calls to be refined in order to capture such drives for assimilation. For our migrants, constructing and recognizing their own cultural hybridity is a process replete with pain and confusion and is part and parcel of the ending of their dreams of returning 'home'. Their stance towards the nation state – whether of origin or of settlement – is also rather less critical than some authors have suggested. The possibilities of hybridity may be limited by the need for survival, recognition, and citizenship. Most migrants (like Choudhury and Ilias) are caught up in a deeply asymmetrical relationship with the 'host' society, and their tentative steps towards assimilation can only succeed if they are supported by civil society groups in the host country. They have no choice but to couch their claims for rights in terms that the host country (or sections of its political classes) deems to be 'legitimate'. These works reveal the profound impact of nationalism and racism on contemporary formations of diaspora and on diasporic projects of making claims. The 'third space' about which Bhabha has written proves, in their case at least, to be profoundly constrained by these limits.

Notes

1. See Wolfgang Schivelbusch, *The Culture of Defeat. On National Trauma, Mourning and Recovery* (translated by Jefferson Chase), London: Macmillan, 2003.
2. Rogers Brubaker, 'The Return of Assimilation? Changing Perspectives on Assimilation and its Sequels in France, Germany, and the United States', *Ethnic and Racial Studies*, 24, 4, July 2001, p. 540.
3. Nathan Glazer and Daniel Moynihan, *Beyond the Melting Pot: The Negroes, Puerto Ricans, Jews, Italians and Irish of New York City*, Cambridge MA: MIT Press, 1963, cited in Rogers Brubaker, 'Return of Assimilation', p. 532.
4. Peggy Levitt, *The Transnational Villagers*, Berkeley and Los Angeles: University of California Press, 2001; Khachig Tololyan, 'Elites and Institutions in the Armenian Transnation', *International Migration Review*, 37, 3, 2003 (also see Alejandro Portes' concluding remarks in the same special issue); Tony Ballantyne, *Between Colonialism and Diaspora. Sikh Cultural Formations in an Imperial World*, Durham and London: Duke University Press, 2006.
5. *Migration: A Welcome Opportunity*, RSA Migration Commission Report, 2005.
6. Markovits et al. *Mobile People*.
7. Homi Bhabha, 'The Third Space', in Rutherford (ed.) *Identity*; Bhahba, *Location of Culture*; Brah, *Cartographies*; Appadurai, *Modernity at Large*. For a critical discussion of the concept of 'hybridity', see Alexander, 'Diaspora and Hybridity', in Collins and Solomos (eds) *Handbook of Race*.
8. James Clifford, *Routes. Travel and Translation in the Late Twentieth Century*, Cambridge MA: Harvard University Press, 1997.
9. John Torpey, *The Invention of the Passport: Surveillance, Citizenship and the State*, Cambridge; Cambridge University Press, 2000. Also see Mark Salter, *Rights of Passage: The Passport in International Relations*, Boulder: Lynne Rienner Publishers, 2003; and Daniel Turack, The Passport in International Law, Lexington: Lexington Books, 1972.
10. On the control of borders in South Asia, see Zamindar, *Long Partition*; Chatterji, 'South Asian Histories'; Datta, *Refugees*; Chatterji, 'From Subjecthood'; and Roy, *Partitioned Lives*.
11. Choudhury, *Roots*, p. 10.

242 *Narrating diaspora*

12 Ibid., p. viii
13 Deliberately or otherwise, it evokes Bankim Chandra Chatterjee's *Bandemataram*, which describes the 'motherland' as a place of sweet waters, ripe fruit, and cool breezes (*sujalam, suphalam, malayaja sheetalam*).
14 Choudhury, *Roots*, p. 11.
15 Ibid., p. 12.
16 Ibid., p. 14.
17 Although this account shares some features with the 'conventional legend' of the Muslim conquest of Sylhet, it is significantly different. Rizvi (ed.) *Bangladesh District Gazetteers*, pp. 55–56.
18 Choudhury, *Roots*, p. 17.
19 Chatterji, 'Bengali Muslim'.
20 Choudhury, *Roots*, pp. 20, 26.
21 Gour Gobindo's infanticide resembles, of course, the evil acts of King Herod and also of King Kansa of Mathura in Hindu mythology. Kansa, the maternal uncle of Lord Krishna, imprisoned his sister and killed each one of Krishna's siblings at birth.
22 Eaton, *Rise of Islam*.
23 Also see Ho, *Graves of Tarim*.
24 Choudhury, *Roots*, p. xii.
25 Ilias, *Biharis*, p. ix.
26 Ibid., p. 17.
27 Ibid., p. 25.
28 Ibid., p. 16.
29 Ibid., p. 18.
30 Ibid., p. 17.
31 Ibid., p. 17–19.
32 Ibid., p. 18.
33 Choudhury, *Roots*, p. 21.
34 Ilias, *Biharis*, p. 17.
35 Ibid., p. 25.
36 Ibid.
37 Choudhury, *Roots*, p. ix.
38 Ibid., p. 31.
39 Ibid., p. 33.
40 Ibid., p. 43.
41 Ibid., p. 50
42 Joseph Salter, *The Asiatic in England. Sketches of Sixteen Years of Work Among Orientals*, London: General Books, 1873; Joseph Salter, *The East in the West. Work Among the Asiatics and Africans in London*, London: Henry Morris, 1895; see also Visram, *Ayahs*.
43 Balachandran, 'Circulation'.
44 Adams, *Across Seven Seas*, pp. 54, 64.
45 See Chapter 5 for details.
46 UK House of Commons Home Affairs Committee, *Bangladeshis in Britain*, Vols 1 and 2, London: HMSO, 1986.
47 The community was divided by its attitudes towards Pakistan before 1971; since then, supporters of different regimes and parties have frequently clashed.
48 The numbers killed in riots are never easy to verify, but 50,000 is not a secure approximation. The viceroy estimated that between 5,000 and 10,000 people lost their lives. Wavell to Pethick Lawrence, 22 December 1946, in N. Mansergh and E.R. Lumby (eds) *The Transfer of Power*, Vol IX, London: HMSO, 1980, p. 140. Also see the discussion of numbers killed and displaced by the violence in Ghosh, *Partition*, pp. 2–3.
49 Ilias, *Biharis*, p. 26.

Narrating diaspora 243

50 Ibid., pp. x, xi.
51 Ibid., p. xiii.
52 Ibid., p. ix.
53 Ibid., p. ix.
54 See Chattopadhyaya, *Internal Migration*.
55 Daniel Horowitz, *The Deadly Ethnic Riot*, Berkeley: University of California Press, 2001. Horowitz sees the 1946 Bihar killings as an exemplar of this type of violence.
56 See, for instance, the foundation myths of mobile weaving communities in Roy and Haynes, 'Conceiving Mobility'.
57 For scholars' perspectives on the wars and 'Britishness', see C. Waters, ' "Dark Strangers in our Midst": Discourses on Race and Nation in Britain, 1947–63', *Journal of British Studies*, 36, 2, 1997. Also see C. Waters, 'J.B. Priestly' in Susan Pederson and Peter Mandler (eds) *After the Victorians. Private Conscience and Public Duty in Modern Britain*, London: Psychology Press, 1994; S.O. Rose, 'Race, Empire and British Wartime Identity', 1939–45', *Historical Research*, 74, 184, 2002; R. Weight, *Patriots. National Identity in Britain, 1940–2000*, London: Macmillan, 2003.
58 Choudhury, *Roots*, p. ix.
59 Ibid., pp. 90, 118–20.
60 Ibid., p. 196.
61 Ibid., p. 177.
62 Ibid., p. 179.
63 Paul Gilroy, *After Empire: Melancholia or Convivial Culture? Multiculture or Postcolonial Melancholia*, Abingdon: Routledge, 2004.
64 Brubaker, 'Return of Assimilation', pp. 543–44.
65 Choudhury, *Roots*, p. 195.
66 Ibid., p. 192.
67 Ibid., p. 195.
68 Benedict Anderson, *The Spectre of Comparison. Politics Culture and the Nation*, London: Verso Books, 1998; and Nina Glick Schiller and Georges Eugene Fouron, *Georges Woke Up Laughing. Long-distance Nationalism and the Search for Home*, Chapel Hill: Duke University Press, 2001.
69 Ilias, *Biharis*, pp. 19–20
70 Ibid., p. 66.
71 Ibid., p. 60
72 Ibid., pp. 67–68
73 Ibid., p. 61.
74 Ibid., p. 88.
75 Ibid., p. 85.
76 Schivelbusch, *Culture of Defeat*, pp. 3–13.
77 Ilias, *Biharis*, p. xi.
78 Ibid., p. 66.
79 Ibid., p. 68.
80 Ibid., p. 92.
81 Ibid., p. 93.
82 Ibid., p. 95.
83 Ibid., p. 114.
84 Ibid., p. 132.
85 Ibid., p. 133.
86 Ghosh, *Partition*, pp. 57–122.
87 Ilias, *Biharis*, p. 151.
88 Ibid., p. 154.
89 Ibid., pp. 155–6.
90 These are discussed in Chapters 3 and 6.

91 Ilias, *Biharis*, p. 75. Also see Sufia M. Uddin, *Constructing Bangladesh: Religion, Ethnicity, and Language in an Islamic Nation*, Chapel Hill: University of North Carolina Press, 2006; and Chapter 7.
 92 Ilias, *Biharis*, pp. 77–78. (Emphasis added.)
 93 Ibid., p. 94.
 94 Ibid., p. 95.
 95 Emphasis added to 'progressive'.
 96 Ilias, *Biharis*, p. 102.
 97 Ibid., p. 118.
 98 Ibid., p. 119. (Emphasis added.)
 99 Choudhury, *Roots*, pp. ix-x.
100 Ibid., pp. 219–223.
101 Ilias, *Biharis*, p. 150.
102 Ibid, pp. 150–1.
103 Ibid., p. 153.
104 Brah, *Cartographies*, p. 37–8.
105 Ibid., p. 39.
106 A. Sivanandan, *A Different Hunger: Writings on Black Resistance*, London: Pluto Press, 1982; Centre for Contemporary Cultural Studies, *The Empire Strikes Back*; Ramamurthy, *Black Star*.
107 Claire Alexander, 'Beyond Black: Rethinking the Colour/Culture Divide', *Ethnic and Racial Studies*, 25, 4, 2002, pp. 552–71; A. Sivanandan, 'A Radical Black Political Culture' in K. Owusu (ed.) *Black British Culture and Society*, London: Routledge, 2000.
108 Charles Taylor, 'The Rushdie Controversy', *Public Culture*, 2, 1, Fall 1989, pp. 118–22.
109 Alexander, 'Re-Imagining the Muslim Community', pp. 439–50.
110 UK House of Commons Home Affairs Committee, *Bangladeshis in Britain*.
111 Brubaker, 'Return of Assimilation?'
112 Brah, *Cartographies*, p. 208.
113 Kenneth Leach, 'Caroline Adams: Youth Worker Devoted to the Welfare of London's Bangladeshi community', *Guardian* (Obituaries), 23 June 2001.
114 See, for instance, Md Ruhul Quddus, 'Recognising Citizenship Right', *The Independent* (Dhaka), 6 October 2007; A.B.M.S. Zahur, 'Enrolling Stranded Pakistanis', *The Daily Star*, 1 October 2007; 'Quazi Quamruzzaman et al., 'The Camp-dwelling Ilias, Biharis and Bangladesh', *New Age*, 17 September 2007.
115 See Chapter 3 for a fuller discussion of its impact on Ilias, *Biharis*.
116 See Ilias, *Biharis*, 'Legal Aspects', pp. 191–5, and the reference to RRMRU, p. 157.
117 Ilias, *Biharis*, pp. 155–6.
118 See Charles Taylor, 'The Politics of Recognition', in Charles Taylor (ed.) *Multiculturalism. Examining the Politics of Recognition*, Princeton NJ, Princeton University Press, 1994, pp. 25–73.
119 As in Tololyan, 'Elites'.
120 Brah, *Cartographies*, p. 28.
121 Choudhury, *Roots*, p. 223.

Conclusion

If, as this book has suggested, the notion of diaspora 'origins' are myths for the present, endings prove to be no less poignantly mythical. Endings suggest finality, resolution (whether physical, intellectual, or emotional), and settlement – allowing those who have embarked on journeys to reflect on them, on destinations reached, and transformations completed. Yet just as beginnings are often inchoate and various, places of arrival too have constantly to be fought for and 'remade', and endings are at best a moment or place to pause, sometimes with the illusion of permanence, before the journey continues.

Diasporas are inherently fragmented and dispersed, with undetermined borders and uncertain outcomes. As we have tried to show in this sprawling, eclectic work, they have multiple points of entry and pathways that proliferate – not all of them similar to each other or recognizable as part of a single process. Any attempt to produce a singular narrative of 'the Bengal diaspora' buckles in the face of this fragmentation. Indeed, some will challenge our focus on Muslim migrants (questioning whether a Muslim can truly be 'Bengali'), while others will bristle at our inclusion of 'Biharis' within this framework. Perhaps few of our interviewees would see themselves as part of a 'diaspora'. Nevertheless, it was this challenge – of decentring and questioning the very analytical framework we worked with – that (for us) gives the concept of diaspora its distinctive interrogative strengths.

This is not a book of theory, nor has the pursuit of new theoretical insights been its driving force. The challenge of our project was to draw very different experiences, different concepts, and different methods of analysis into a fresh dialogue. Our project sought, first and foremost, to provide historical and ethnographic 'flesh' to the often-abstract 'bones' of diaspora and migration theory and to see how they might resolve or reveal points of tension within these universalizing frameworks. It is perhaps best understood as a set of interventions that raise questions for theory. Drawing on the insights of Stuart Hall, we used theory as a 'toolbox'[1] whose instruments enabled us to prise open historical and ethnographic material, while always recognizing the limitations and specificities of these insights. Rather than following one analytical pathway or theoretical byway, we sought consistently to be led by our material and draw out its implications for the understanding of the subject. If theory has remained implicit in this study, informing but not determining the analysis, that was always our intention.

Nevertheless, there are some lessons to be drawn, and here we pause to consider how they relate to the wider fields of study that most concern us. Given how broad and rich are these interlocking fields, and how narrow the constraints of a proliferating word count, we offer only some briefa observations.

The question of diaspora

While the notion of 'diaspora' lies at the heart of the current study, the definition of this key concept was left deliberately opaque. In part, this was because of the proliferation of meanings of the term across the humanities and social sciences in the past few decades and the explosion of its boundaries to include a plethora of migrant trajectories and formations.[2] In part, we wanted to remain open and alert to different understandings of 'diaspora' in different disciplines and the productive tensions between them. Our main concern throughout, however, was not to delimit and essentialize the object of our study – either as 'Bengali' or as 'a diaspora' – thereby allowing new insights to emerge from our understanding of the ways in which it was historically shaped and empirically experienced.

Diaspora as a concept has long been recognized as inherently ambivalent – as encapsulating both 'roots' and 'routes' – reifying imagined origins and imposing coherence and connectedness on lives lived in dispersal and fragmentation. At the same time, the question of 'origins' has vexed social theorists more than it has troubled historians, and this has led to a bifurcation of the field. Rogers Brubaker's influential article on 'the "diaspora" diaspora'[3] characterizes this as a division between more historical and empiricist accounts of groups defined through categorization and quantification (as 'bona fide actual entities'[4]) and sociological and cultural studies accounts which emphasize stances, heterogeneity, movement, and change.[5] Avtar Brah has argued that 'at the heart of the notion of diaspora is the image of a journey'.[6] However, as Brah recognizes, travelling implies an initial impetus (or origin) which is crucial to the definition of diaspora – 'not every journey can be understood as diaspora'.[7] For Gilroy, diasporas are collective journeys undertaken 'in a process of non-voluntary displacement, usually created by violence or under threat of violence or death'[8] – and the moment of rupture or dislocation is definitive in 'classic' notions of diaspora, as, indeed, is the idea of 'homeland'.[9] Nonetheless, unlike historians, who are more concerned with the roots of violence and the causes of departures, sociologists have largely focused on arrival and settlement, on claims-making in contexts of hostility and marginalization. It is not accidental, then, that the leading *social* theorists of diaspora have emerged from the field of racial and ethnic studies located in, and preoccupied with, the global cities of the West and North.[10]

In theory, at least, all scholars of this subject insist on the necessary interplay between the historical and the contemporary in the production of diaspora identities.[11] In practice, however, their orientations are distinct and, if anything, the disciplines have grown further apart. Partly, this flows from their different focus and method, with historians looking backwards towards origins and causes and social scientists more concerned with the heterogeneous encounters of the 'here

Conclusion 247

and now'. Historians investigate changes (or continuities) over time, sociologists look at disruption and transformation, although both have been criticized for not giving due weight to power and structure. A consequence of this parting of the ways has been, so to speak, the flattening and thinning of our understandings of diaspora. Ironically, diaspora has been richer and more complex in theory than in its scholarly investigation.

But these differences in emphasis or method do not by themselves explain this outcome: it is also connected with the wider politics of knowledge. In Britain, for example, diaspora scholars pay lip service to the significance of history yet remain profoundly suspicious of questions of origins and continuities. This stems from a legacy of postwar ethnographic (and mainly anthropological) research on 'race relations', where claims about cultural continuities and 'traditions' underpinned decades of hostility, in both policy and attitudes, to racial and ethnic minorities – notably South Asians in the UK.[12] Such attitudes informed notions of 'cultural conflict' and 'parallel lives', and the recent backlash against 'multiculturalism' which has stigmatized (South Asian and particularly Muslim) 'diasporas' as a threat to the nation. As James Clifford has noted, one of the dangers of diaspora (as a concept) is the way it positions minorities as '"not here" to stay',[13] even though, as our findings have shown, it can also be used as a way of opening up spaces in which to belong. As Paul Gilroy puts it, 'It ain't where you're from, it's where you're at'.[14] From these perspectives, historical accounts of diaspora have been criticized (often unfairly) for reifying contingent and shifting entities and for ignoring processes of cultural change.[15] For their part, historians have looked askance at 'presentist' and 'snapshot' views of 'communities' and 'cultures'. The disciplines have largely misunderstood and talked past each other.

Our hope, by contrast, was to bring these different approaches to diaspora together within a more unified framework. In the preceding chapters of this work, we have combined and counterposed historical, sociological, and anthropological approaches to examine, empirically, interlocking layers and histories of diaspora experience and to explore how these shape contemporary identities. The Bengal diaspora shares many of the features of 'classic' diasporas of exile, but our research shows that moments of rupture and flight have to be placed within a longer history of regional and global mobility which both precedes and succeeds them. We have explored how these historically inscribed 'routes' – whether within Bengal itself or overseas – both facilitated and constrained movement. At the same time, we have shown that the process of making new homes does not simply involve recreating historical patterns and 'traditions' of 'the homeland'. Agency, and its many textures, has been a key preoccupation of this work. It conjures up various narratives and performances of 'diaspora remembered', which make claims that draw on rich and various, and sometimes unexpected, sources and resources. Yet these claims or 'stances',[16] in their turn, are not autonomous: they are 'rooted' in particular versions of group histories (and how they are remembered) and made authoritative by (and in) transnational and local circuits of power.

A key finding is that to understand 'diaspora', it needs to be reconfigured to incorporate smaller forms of movement. Conventionally, diaspora was most often understood in terms of dramatic ruptures and long-distance movements. Yet our research in the borderlands of Bengal, and in particular the mobility of brides, suggests that 'diaspora' also includes small journeys which are nonetheless characterized by profound rupture and the impossibility of return. The story of the Gazi brothers in Chapters 2 and 3, whose family was ripped apart in the process of nation building and who lost contact with each other despite living only a few miles apart (albeit in different countries) or of the many brides whose lives were irrevocably altered by the domestic, but still defining, dislocations of marriage illustrate that diaspora is not necessarily – or even mainly – a matter of distance. A bride's journey to her husband's home in the context of marriage is as intrinsically diasporic (perhaps even more so) than the long-distance circulation of a seafaring lascar. If diaspora theory takes on board the conclusions of social histories of space[17] so as to recognize that diaspora is a matter of social distance travelled and emotional dislocation (and relocation)[18] rather than simply movement through physical space, it will better be equipped to understand the transformations of today's world.

Our findings also underline how important it is to recognize the configuring role of place. Although they travelled from the same broad region at much the same time, the experiences of our respondents at different sites were not of a piece. These differences are as important as their (often intriguing) similarities. As we have demonstrated, place-making can be found in disparate, hostile, and unexpected spaces but can incorporate within it very different local, national, and transnational connections as well as multi-layered histories.[19] In our work we have given them sustained attention, and this too has implications for the subject.

Diaspora theory has sought to balance these different perspectives: to derive benefit from the productive tensions between history *and* culture, similarity *and* difference, tradition *and* transformation, being *and* becoming, 'roots' *and* 'routes'.[20] However, this subtlety has largely remained at the level of theory rather than practice; history has remained firmly on one side of the fence and sociology on the other, and empirical studies have tended to fix diaspora on one or other of these boundaries. Diaspora studies, some scholars suggest, are now entering a 'consolidation' phase which seeks to combine the critical social and political insights of the 'social constructionist' (or metaphorical) diaspora theorists with the historical insights of the more empirical approaches to diaspora[21] – what we might think of as 'critical diaspora studies'. Such an approach would examine the intersections of historical experiences of diaspora with contemporary politics of engagement in various local, national, and global contexts. Our work is a tentative step in this direction.

Migration and transnationalism

Migration theory, too, has undergone significant transformations in the last three decades or so, with compelling theories of migration emerging from a range of disciplines. As with diaspora theory, disciplinary divides remain significant, with economists and demographers interested in 'push' and 'pull' factors in a global (if increasingly bifurcated) labour market and in 'human capital' (even though the 'human' aspect of 'human capital' remains, in their accounts, strangely disembodied and without historical context). Structural accounts of globalization, particularly ideas of global cities and labour flows,[22] have yielded rich insights but continue to focus on (supposedly recent) long-distance 'economic' migration. As an interdisciplinary approach to migration begins to emerge, the emphasis has shifted from these macrolevel 'world systems' to the microstructures of 'transnational' networks. These two levels, as Massey's influential thesis proposes, interact to produce 'cumulative causation of migration'.[23]

Our concept of 'mobility capital', which explains why and how some people can migrate and others cannot, draws upon network theory. It defines mobility capital as a bundle of capacities, predispositions, and connections, often rooted in the family and group histories of mobility, which shape patterns of migration and settlement. Yet by studying networks *longitudinally*, though a historical lens, we have found that networks are more fragile and more susceptible to atrophy and rupture than network theorists had assumed. This is one example of how a multidisciplinary approach that takes history seriously can push the subject forward.

Yet historical accounts of migration have their own limits and biases, particularly with respect to South Asia. Undoubtedly, historians of South Asia have made an enormous contribution to the subject by challenging the presumed 'newness' of late-20th century mobility (and the supposed rarity of migration in the past) which still dominates the perspectives of the social sciences.[24] Yet for all its sophistication, the historiography is marked by an almost whiggish notion of a movement through distinct 'stages' of migration – from 'sojourning' and 'circulation' in the early modern period[25] to the 'assisted' and 'indentured' movement of the colonial period, giving way to 'forced' migrations that accompanied nation formation, in their turn followed by economic 'labour migration' to the West in the 1950s and 1960s and then succeeded by 'high-skilled' migration in the late 20th century. This book has revealed the shortcomings of such a view of migration. Within a single household, as we show, migrants might well have undergone these various 'stages' of migration once, twice, or several times in the course of their lives. One individual – Shamsul Huq is a case in point – could be a sojourner, an assisted migrant, an economic migrant, a refugee, and a circulator, sometimes all at the same time. In the Bengal diaspora, 'stages' did not tidily follow one another, marching through the 20th century and into contemporary times. These movements are better understood as 'forms' of migration that co-existed, overlapped, and intersected.

Furthermore, our work suggests that even the idea of different 'forms' of migration is at best a heuristic tool. We must be alert to the instabilities and overlaps in these different forms, so the boundary or distinction between 'forced' and 'economic' 'forms' of migration proves to be very blurred indeed. Despite the dogma (which assumes such a distinction a priori), these boundaries were artificial to begin with and made more rigid by the bifurcation between disciplines, with historians more interested in the movement of labourers and traders ('economic' migration), and sociologists and anthropologists in refugee movements ('forced migration'), usually from a crisis- and case-driven perspective.[26] We have discovered, by contrast, that 'economic' migration is both a precursor and enabler of refugee movement, and our work strongly suggests the sheer scale of refugee movements in modern South Asia cannot be understood without first understanding the histories of mobility that preceded them and carved the pathways along which later migrants flowed. In theoretical terms, this suggests that populous regions with long and dense histories of mobility are likely to generate large diasporas and refugee movements when they are disrupted by dramatic political or environmental crises.

Another important finding is that internal and international migration are most usefully understood within the same analytical framework. Whereas migration studies have tended to concern themselves with international migration (and, indeed, on South-North movement) in which the Global South is usually reduced to shadowy places of embarkation and flight, we insist that the Global South is itself, and has always been, a pre-eminent place of 'arrival'. Sources of migration, then, can also be (and usually are) destinations. This conclusion, and the new perspectives it encourages, may help to challenge the single-minded focus on the points of arrival rather than departure which characterizes so much scholarship in this field of endeavour. Furthermore, by setting long-distance movement alongside smaller journeys and migratory circuits within or across states and regions, we hope to have highlighted the shared historical, social, and emotional processes of dislocation and settlement while explaining rather better than before why certain factors facilitate the movement of some and not others – the stark difference between having some 'mobility capital' and being without it.

By examining processes of mobility *alongside* immobility, we have shown that one cannot be understood without the other. Indeed, the book has turned out to be as much about staying on as it is about migration. Migration studies have been preoccupied by circulation and networks – whether of people, money or objects – but they must also look at those who are left behind and those who are 'stuck'. Our work has also investigated the limits of mobility. These are both external – social, legal, and political structures – as well as internal – different types of mobility capital (or their lack) but also less tangible, 'sticky' factors: emotional, religious, and familial obligations that tie people to place, even in deeply hostile circumstances. By trying to find out how people *think* about their ties to places – as expressed in their migration myths and public performances, or in more intimate everyday acts of place-making in Oldham and East London, the Bengal borderlands, and 'Bihari' camps in Bangladesh – we have tried to draw attention to the imaginative dimensions of both movement and immobility.

Since the 1990s, transnational studies have increasingly drawn attention to emerging forms of circular or temporary mobility and to the role of new technologies which have transformed connectivity between migrants and their homelands.[27] Dominated by sociologists and anthropologists, transnational theory explores global organizations and corporations – 'transnationalism from above' – as well as the actions and identities of migrants themselves – 'transnationalism from below'.[28] It also takes seriously cultural, political, and social aspects of migration and challenges the idea of migration as a unidirectional and one-off movement. It shows instead that migrants are embedded simultaneously in different locations and that migration is a complex 'field' of multiple actors, places, and dimensions.[29] Our research has been influenced by this body of scholarship, and this was why we decided to study both origins and destinations, as well as complex affiliations and networks, and the symbolic, cultural and ritual resources which migrants use to create and maintain conceptions of 'home'.

While deepening our understanding of contemporary forms of migration, transnationalism has been criticized for being ahistorical – for privileging the 'new' over older forms of transnational connection and for ignoring the ways in which ideas of identity and culture are historically structured. Cultural identities, as Hall reminds us, 'come from somewhere, have histories' but are also 'subject to the continuous play of history, culture and power'.[30] Cultures and identities change over time, as we have demonstrated, both 'at home' as well as in spaces of migration, but they carry with them the traces of what has gone before.

Our work suggests further caveats to transnational theory. We find that, in stressing crossborder connections, transnational studies have downplayed the vital role of the state and the nation in shaping, constraining, and enabling the actions of migrants.[31] By being preoccupied with the transnational and (trans) local dimensions of migration, they have rather lost sight of the importance of national borders and controls. They have exaggerated fluidity and connection, and ignored the permanent ruptures that are involved in transnational movement. Long-established links between places and people can and do break down, and these breaks and ruptures are too significant to be ignored. The analysis of processes of *dis*connection, and all their complex consequences, will, we feel, profoundly enrich our understanding of the diverse experiences of globalization.

A vital part of this story is the modern nation state itself. Transnational theory – particularly in its more qualitative and ethnographic forms – pays lip service to the state and to wider questions of power, but in fact its celebratory view of transnational identity and agency privileges elite experience over the more constrained lives of ordinary migrants.[32] As our study shows, the nation state looms large. Every single one of our informants spoke about its role in their lives: for some it hovered like distant thunder, presaging the storm, for others it was a dark, looming presence, and for a few, a beacon of hope. But it was never, ever irrelevant. It is time, perhaps, to bring the nation back into transnational theory.

Another weakness in the work on transnationalism is the profoundly optimistic view its theorists take of its possibilities. As we hope to have shown, however, power circulates not just 'outside' transnational networks (above all, in states), but also deep within them. By looking closely at how transnational networks have worked in practice for our respondents, we show not only how they atrophy and rupture, but how important they were in limiting migrants' choices. These networks were not neutral spaces, capable of being easily penetrated by 'outsiders'. The networks we studied were closed arenas in which hierarchy flourished and was perpetuated more frequently than it was challenged and status reconstituted more often than it was subverted. These points are well understood in many classical studies of migration, but they call to be underlined in the current intellectual context in which theorists of diaspora tend to valorize networks and 'diasporic spaces' as sites of radical possibility.

****

This cursory review of the field reveals as much about our own particular disciplinary, methodological, and ethical perspectives as about their limitations. All of us share a strong preference for qualitative, narrative, and 'messy' humanistic accounts that unsettle tidy theories. Each of us is deeply interested in agency and in the myriad ways – sometimes brutal and sometimes subtle – in which power constrains it. Each of us is drawn to the stories of the marginal, the weak, and the invisible migrants who cannot simply 'speak for themselves'. Our attempt here has been to 'place' their stories within the tapestry of a larger history – that of the Bengal diaspora – and to see what this perspective from the margins tells us about our (different) fields of scholarship. There are other pathways we could have taken, of course, and other stories we could have told, and perhaps other conclusions would have been drawn from them. But our approach, we hope, will resonate, in particular with readers who have observed, experienced, or wrestled with the consequences of migration and diaspora.

Notes

1 Claire Alexander, 'Introduction: Stuart Hall and "Race"', *Cultural Studies*, 23, 4, 2009, p. 459.
2 Alexander, 'Diaspora and Hybridity'; Claire Alexander, 'Diaspora, Race and Difference' in Kim Knott and Sean McLoughlin (eds) *Diasporas: Concepts, Intersections, Identities*, London: Zed Press, 2010; Chatterji and Washbrook, 'Introduction'.
3 Brubaker, 'The "Diaspora" Diaspora', pp. 1–19.
4 Gabriel Sheffer, *Diaspora Politics: At Home Abroad*, Cambridge: Cambridge University Press, 2003, p. 245.
5 Alexander, following Hall, characterizes this as a division between 'historical' and 'metaphorical' accounts of diaspora. See Alexander, 'Diaspora, Race'.
6 Brah, *Cartographies*, p. 182.
7 Ibid.
8 Gilroy, 'Diaspora and the Detours', p. 328.
9 Safran, 'Diasporas in Modern Societies', pp. 83–99
10 Alexander 'Diaspora, Race'.
11 Hall, 'Cultural Identity'.
12 Sue Benson, 'Asians have Culture, West Indians have Problems' in Terrence O. Ranger, Yunas Samad and Ossie Stuart (eds) *Culture, Identity and Politics*, Aldershot: Avebury, 1996; Alexander, 'Beyond Black', pp. 552–71.
13 Clifford, *Routes*.
14 Paul Gilroy, *Small Acts: Thoughts on the Politics of Black Cultures*, London: Serpent's Tail, 1993. Of course, there are differences in how different scholars view ideas of culture and cultural change – Gilroy himself favouring the idea of 'the changing same'.
15 Brubaker, 'The "Diaspora" Diaspora'; Chatterji and Washbrook, 'Introduction'.
16 Brubaker, 'The "Diaspora" Diaspora'.
17 Lefebvre, *Production*.
18 Brah, *Cartographies*; Clifford, *Routes*.

19 Peggy Levitt and B. Nadya Jaworsky 'Transnational Migration Studies: Past Developments and Future Trends', *Annual Review of Sociology*, 33, 2007, pp. 129–56; Brah, *Cartographies*.
20 Hall, 'Cultural Identity'.
21 Robin Cohen, *Global Diasporas: An Introduction*, 2nd edition, London: Routledge, 2008.
22 Saskia Sassen, *The Global City: New York, London, Tokyo*, Princeton: Princeton University Press, 1991; S. Sassen, *The Mobility of Capital and Labor: A Study in International Investment and Labor Flow*, Cambridge: Cambridge University Press, 1988.
23 Massey, 'Social Structure', p. 3.
24 Ludden, 'Maps'.
25 Markovits et al., *Mobile People*.
26 See E. Fiddian-Qasmiyeh, G. Loescher, K. Long and N. Sidona, 'Introduction: Refugee and Forced Migration Studies in Transition' in E. Fiddian-Qasmiyeh, G. Loescher, K. Long and N. Sidona, *Oxford Handbook of Refugee and Forced Migration Studies*, Oxford: Oxford University Press, 2014.
27 L. Basch, N. Glick Schiller and C.S. Blanc, *Nations Unbound: Transnational Projects, Post-colonial Predicaments and Deterritorialised Nation-States*, New York: Routledge, 1993.
28 Alejandro Portes, 'Conclusion: Towards a New World: The Origins and Effects of Transnational Activities', *Ethnic and Racial Studies*, 22, 2, 1999, pp. 463–77.
29 P. Levitt and N. Glick Schiller, 'Conceptualising Simultaneity: A Transnational Social Field Perspective', *International Migration Review*, 38, 3, 2004, pp. 1002–39.
30 Hall, 'Cultural Identity', p. 225.
31 Andreea Raluca Torre, 'Migrant Lives: A Comparative Study of Work, Family and Belonging Among Low-wage Romanian Migrant Workers in Rome and London', PhD thesis, London School of Economics and Political Science, 2013.
32 Alejandro Portes, 'Conclusion: Theoretical Convergences and Empirical Evidence in the Study of Immigrant Transnationalism', *International Migration Review*, 37, 2003, pp. 847–92.

Glossary

Note on transliteration: The words used in the book draw on Bengali, Hindustani, Sylheti, Bhojpuri, Urdu, Persian, Sanskrit, and Arabic, and are pronounced in a variety of ways across the region. We have transliterated them phonetically, in ways that correspond to the pronunciation of a range of vernaculars and dialects we encountered. This also dictated our decision not to use diacritical marks.

alam: flag or standard
aman: winter rice
anchal pradhan: headman
anjuman: assembly or association
ashraf: elite
atrap/ajlaf: Muslim of the lower classes
ayah: nanny
azan: the call to prayer
babu: term of respect (Hindu, male); clerk
baper-bari: father's house
bari: home
bariwalas: house-owners who rent out rooms or apartments; also used for jobbers who provided housing to workers
baro khala: cousin
basha: residence
bhatia: (shifting) cultivator of alluvial bars, shoals or islands
bhodrolok/bhadrolok: educated upper and middle class; genteel
bigha: 1/3 acre
biradari: clan
chanda: donation
chhelebela: childhood/boyhood
chilla: 40 days spent travelling and preaching to Muslims
chor/char: alluvial bar, shoal or island
dalal: middleman
dalil: lease
dargah: shrine
darwan: night watchman

debor: brother-in-law
dhandabaj: maker of (shady) deals
diaria: (shifting) cultivator of alluvial bars, shoals or islands
elaka: area/s
fatia: brief prayer (prayer so-called because it involves the recitation of Al-Fatiha, the opening verses of the Quran).
ghat: jetty
ghat-sarang: port foreman
ghazi-pir: soldier-saint
ghor-jamai/ghar-jamai: son-in-law resident in his father-in-law's house (pejorative)
girmit: agreement
gotra: lineage
gramer lok: village folk
gusti: clan
haat: weekly market
jagirthaka: tutor-in-residence
jhal muri: Bengali street food
jotedar: intermediary tenure holder (often prosperous)
kafir: unbeliever
kangani : system of labour recruitment
kantha: cloth
kanya-daan: gift of the virgin
khalato bon: cousin (mother's sister's daughter)
khalifa: caliph
khas mahal: government-owned agrarian land
kumari: virgin
kunba: clan
kurta: short tunic
lakh: hundred thousand
lungi: loincloth often worn by Muslim men in the region
majalis: gathering for mourning
matam: self-flagellation, associated with Shia Muharram rituals
milad: gathering where songs, often of a devotional nature, are sung
mazar: mausoleum or shrine
mohajir: refugees in Pakistan
mohalla: neighbourhood
mukti bahinis: volunteer freedom brigades (during the Bangladesh Liberation War)
muktijoddha: freedom fighter/warrior
murabbi: elder
namaaz: daily prayer (Muslim)
niyom koron/kanon: code of conduct
paik/paiki: footmen or footsoldiers
palki: sedan chair

para: neighbourhood
pardesi: foreigner
pice: unit of currency (The old Indian rupee was divided into 16 annas, each anna was subdivided into 4 Paise or 12 Pice, There were thus 192 pice in a rupee)
pir: (Muslim) saint or holy man
pithas: rice cakes
poorbea: (men) from eastern United Provinces/Uttar Pradesh and Bihar, colloquial
probashira: overseas community
prodhan: village headman
pulao: savoury rice
punkah: fan
qasba: market town
qurbani: animal sacrifice
razakar: collaborator (pejorative),volunteer
refuz: refugee (pejorative)
rickshawala: someone who pulls a rickshaw
roshogulla: sweetmeat
Saitan: evil; Satan
sal: Shorea robusta, a tall hardwood
sardar/sirdar: 'jobber', foreman, leader
sarongs: jobbers
shaheb: term of respect for a male of higher social status
shamiana: marquee
shashur-bari/sasur-bari: the home of a married woman's in-laws, affinal home
shashuri/sasuri: husband's mother
sherbet/sabil: sweetened water
shirni: consecrated food
silsila: branch
sindoor: vermillion powder
sirdari: system of labour recruitment through jobbers
shongshar/sangsar: household
stri: married women
stri achar: rites performed by married women
subah: province (Mughal)
tantis: weavers
taziya/tazia: bier, replicas of the mausoleums of Shia saints and martyrs
thakur ghar: niche or room housing household deities
thana: administrative district
uposhahr: satellite town
zamindar: landlord
zardozi: gold thread embroidery

Appendix 1
Shamsul Huq's family tree

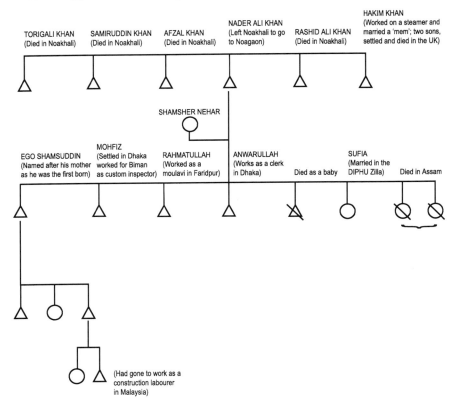

Bibliography

Primary sources

1. Archives

British Library
National Archives of India (NAI)
Nehru Library, Delhi
Supreme Court of Bangladesh, High Court Division (Special Original Jurisdiction)

2. Government and official publications

a) Censuses

Census of India, 1921, Vol. V, Bengal, Part 1, Calcutta: Bengal Secretariat Book Depot, 1923.
Census of India, 1931, Vol. V, Part I, Report, Calcutta: Central Publications Branch, 1933.
Census of India, 1951, Vol. VI, Part 1-A, Report, Delhi: Manager of Publications, 1953.
Census of India, 1961, Vol. XVI, Part I-A, Book (1).
Census of Pakistan, 1951, Vol. 3, East Bengal.
Oldham Council, *2011 Census: Key Statistics for Oldham*, Corporate Research and Intelligence Team, 2012: www.vaoldham.org.uk/sites/vaoldham.org.uk/files/Census%20 2011%20key%20stats%20briefing%2014%20Dec%2012.pdf
2011 Census: Ethnic Group, Local Authorities in the United Kingdom, London: Office for National Statistics, 2012–2014.

b) Reports

Amin, A. *Ethnicity and the Multicultural City*, Report for Department of Transport, Local Government and the Regions, London: DTLG, 2002.
Bangladesh Census Report, National Volume, Dacca: Bureau of Statistics, 1974.
Migration: A Welcome Opportunity, RSA Migration Commission Report, 2005.
Report connected with the Construction of Docks at Calcutta, Part I, *(Selections from the Government of India Public Works Department, No. CCIX, Public Works Department Serial Number 4)*, Calcutta: Superintendent of Government Printing, India, 1885.
Report No. 799 R.C., Railway Construction, Simla: Government of India Public Works Department, 1887.

260 *Bibliography*

Report of the Census of Bengal, 1881, Calcutta: Bengal Secretariat, 1883.

Souttar, W. N. *Annual Report on the Police Administration of the Town of Calcutta and its Suburbs For the Year 1879*, Calcutta: Bengal Secretariat Press, 1880.

A Study of the Report of the Commission of Enquiry (Jabbar Commission) on Expulsion of Pakistani Infiltrants from Tripura and Assam, New Delhi: Government of India, Ministry of Home Affairs, 1964.

c) *Court cases*

Md. Abid Khan and others vs The Govt. of Bangladesh and others, Writ Petition No. 3831 of 2001, Supreme Court of Bangladesh, High Court Division (Special Original Jurisdiction).

Md. Sadaqat Khan (Fakku) and 10 others vs The Chief Election Commissioner, Bangladesh Writ Petition No. 10129 of 2007, Supreme Court of Bangladesh, High Court Division (Special Original Jurisdiction).

d) *Other official sources*

Cabinet Memorandum, 'Commonwealth Immigration: Consultation with other Governments', Memorandum by the Secretary of State for the Home Department and the Secretary of State for Commonwealth Relations, 3 November 1964, C. (64). 11.

Charsley, K., N. van Hear, M. Benson and B. Storer-Church, *Marriage-related Migration to the UK*, London: HMSO, 2011.

Data Management and Analysis Group, *2001 Census Profiles: Bangladeshis in London*, London: GLA, 2004: http://legacy.london.gov.uk/gla/publications/factsandfigures/DMAG-Briefing2004-16-2001CensusProfilesBangladeshisinLondon.pdf

Department for Communities and Local Government, *The Bangladeshi Muslim Community in England: Understanding Muslim Ethnic Communities*, London: DCLG, 2009: www.swadhinata.org.uk/document/Bangladeshi_Muslim.pdf

Eade, J. and D. Garbin, *The Bangladeshi Diaspora: Community Dynamics, Transnational Politics and Islamist Activities*, London: Foreign and Commonwealth Office, 2005.

General Instructions for Pilgrims to the Hedjaz, Calcutta: Superintendent of Government Printing, 1911.

Grierson, G. A. *Linguistic Survey of India*, Vol. V, Part II, Calcutta, 1903.

History of Indian Railways Constructed and in Progress, corrected up to 31 March 1923, Simla: Government of India Press, 1924.

Hodson, Thomas Callan *Analysis of the 1931 Census of India*, New Delhi: Government of India Press, 1937.

Home Office, *Building Cohesive Communities*, London: HMSO, 2001.

— *Community Cohesion* (The Cantle Report), London: HMSO, 2001.

— *Family Migration: Evidence and Analysis*, London: HMSO, 2011.

The Imperial Gazetteer of India. The Indian Empire. Vol. I. Descriptive, Oxford: Clarendon Press, 1907.

The Imperial Gazetteer of India. The Indian Empire. Vol. III. Economic, Oxford: Clarendon Press, 1907.

The Imperial Gazetteer of India. Provincial Series. Eastern Bengal and Assam, Calcutta: Superintendent of Government Printing, 1909.

Mansergh, Nicholas and Penderel Moon (eds) *Constitutional Relations Between Britain and India. The Transfer of Power*, 12 volumes, London: HMSO, 1981–83.
O'Malley, L.S.S. *Bengal District Gazetteers, Hooghly*, Calcutta: Bengal Secretariat Book Depot, 1912.
— *Bengal District Gazetteers, Monghyr*, Calcutta: Bengal Secretariat Book Depot, 1909.
— *Bengal District Gazetteers, Patna*, Calcutta: Bengal Secretariat Book Depot, 1907, Reprinted New Delhi: Logos Press, 2005.
— *Bengal District Gazetteers, Saran*, Calcutta: Bengal Secretariat Book Depot, 1908.
— *Bihar and Orissa District Gazetteers, Saran*, 1930, Reprinted New Delhi: Logos Press, 2007.
Organisation for Economic Co-operation and Development, 'World Migration in Figures', OECD-UNDESA, October 2013: www.oecd.org/els/mig/World-Migration-in-Figures.pdf
Rizvi, S.N.H. (ed.) *Bangladesh District Gazetteers: Sylhet*, Dacca: Bangladesh Government Press. 1975.
Samad, Y. and J. Eade, *Community Perceptions of Forced Marriage*, London: Foreign and Commonwealth Office, 2002.
Statistical Atlas of India (Second Edition, 1895), Calcutta: Superintendent of Government Publishing, 1895.
UK House of Commons Home Affairs Committee, *Bangladeshis in Britain*, Vols 1 and 2, London: HMSO, 1986.

3. Newspapers and magazines

BengalNewz
The Daily Star
ELM News: *The Official Bulletin of the East London Mosque*
The Guardian
The Independent (Dhaka)
New Age
Time

4. Photographic exhibition

Bangladesh 1971, Rivington Place, East London, 4 April to 31 May 2008: www.autograph-abp.co.uk

5. Websites

Oldham Council, www.oldham.gov.uk
Tower Hamlets Council, www.towerhamlets.gov.uk
http://static.visitlondon.com/assets/maps/guides/bengali_history_walk.pdf
https://twitter.com/search?q=bengalnewz%20muharram%20bangladesh&src=typd
www.ideastore.co.uk/assets/documents/local%20History%20Archives%20Online/walks/Bengali_History_Walk.pdf
www.workpermit.com/news/2011-11-08/uk/uk-reinstates-minimum-age-of-18-for-foreign-spouses.html

Secondary sources

A

Abbas, Rameez and Divya Varma. 'Internal Labour Migration in India Raises Integration Challenges for Migrants', *Migration Policy Institute Newsletter* (2013): www.migration policy.org/article/internal-labor-migration-india-raises-integration-challenges-migrants

Abedin, Najmul. *Local Administration and Politics in Modernising Societies, Bangladesh and Pakistan*, Dacca: National Institute of Public Administration, 1973.

Adams, Caroline. *Across Seven Seas and Thirteen Rivers. Life Stories of Sylheti Settlers in Britain*, London: THAP, 1987.

Aghaie, Kamran Scot. *The Martyrs of Karbala. Shi'i Symbols and Rituals in Modern Iran*, Seattle and London: University of Washington Press, 2004.

—— (ed.) *The Women of Karbala. Ritual Performance and Symbolic Discourses in Modern Shi'a Islam*, Austin: University of Texas Press, 2005.

Ahmed, Rafiuddin. *The Bengal Muslims 1871–1906. A Quest for Identity*, Delhi: Oxford University Press, 1988.

Ahmed, Sara. *Strange Encounters: Embodied Others in Postcoloniality*, London: Routledge, 2000.

Ahuja, Ravi. 'Mobility and Containment: The Voyages of Indian Seamen, c. 1900–1960', *International Review of Social History*, 51 (Supplement) 2006.

—— *Pathways of Empire. Circulation, 'Public Works' and Social Space in Colonial Orissa, c. 1780–1924*, Hyderabad: Orient BlackSwan, 2009.

Alba, Richard. 'Bright vs Blurred Boundaries: Second Generation Assimilation and Exclusion in France, Germany and the United States', *Ethnic and Racial Studies*, 28, 1, 2005.

Alexander, Claire. 'Re-Imagining the Muslim Community', *Innovation*, 11, 4, 1998.

—— *The Asian Gang: ethnicity, identity, masculinity*, Oxford: Berg, 2000.

—— 'Beyond Black: Rethinking the Colour/Culture Divide', *Ethnic and Racial Studies*, 25, 4, 2002.

—— 'Re-Imagining the Asian Gang: Ethnicity, Masculinity and Youth after 'The Riots'', *Critical Social Policy*, 24, 4, 2004.

—— 'Imagining the Politics of BrAsian Youth', in Ali, Kalra and Sayyid (eds) *A Postcolonial People*.

—— 'Introduction: Stuart Hall and "Race"', *Cultural Studies*, 23, 4, 2009.

—— 'Culturing Poverty? Ethnicity, Religion, Gender and Social Disadvantage Amongst South Asian Communities in the UK', in Chant (ed.) *International Handbook of Gender and Poverty*.

—— 'Diaspora and Hybridity', in Collins and Solomos (eds) *Sage Handbook of Race and Ethnic Studies*.

—— 'Diaspora, Race and Difference' in Knott and McLoughlin (eds) *Diasporas: Concepts, Intersections, Identities*.

—— 'Making Bengali Brick Lane: Claiming and Contesting Space in East London', *British Journal of Sociology*, 62, 2, 2011.

—— 'Contested Memories: The Shahid Minar and the Struggle for Diasporic Space', *Ethnic and Racial Studies*, 36, 4, 2013.

—— 'Marriage, Migration, Multiculturalism: Gendering "the Bengal diaspora"', *Journal of Ethnic and Migration Studies*, 39, 3, 2013.

Alexander, C., S. Firoz and N. Rashid. *The Bengal Diaspora in Britain: a review of the literature*, 2010: www.banglastories.org

Alexander, Claire and Caroline Knowles (eds). *Making Race Matter: Bodies, Space and Identity,* Basingstoke: Palgrave, 2005.

Alexander, Claire, Victoria Redclift and Ajmal Hussain (eds). *The New Muslims*, London: Runnymede Trust, 2013. See: www.runnymedetrust.org/uploads/publications/Runnymede_the_New_Muslims_Perspective.pdf

Ali, Chaudhuri Muhammad. *Emergence of Pakistan*, New York: Columbia University Press, 1967.

Ali, Nasreen, Virinder Kalra and Salman Sayyid (eds). *A Postcolonial People: South Asians in Britain*, London: Christopher Hurst, 2006.

Allen, Chris. *Fair Justice: The Bradford Disturbances, The Sentencing and The Impact*, London: Forum Against Islamophobia and Racism, 2003.

Amrith, Sunil. *Migration and Diaspora in Modern Asia*, Cambridge: Cambridge University Press, 2011.

— 'South Asian Migration, c. 1800–1950', in Lucassen and Lucassen (eds) *Globalising Migration History.*

Anderson, Benedict. *Long Distance Nationalism: World Capitalism and the Rise of Identity Politics*, Amsterdam: CASA, 1998.

— *The Spectre of Comparison. Politics Culture and the Nation*, London: Verso Books, 1998.

Ansari, Humayan. *The Infidel Within*, London: Hurst and Company, 2004.

Anthias, Floya. 'Nation and Post-Nation: Nationalism, Transnationalism and Intersections of Belonging', in Collins and Solomos (eds) *Handbook of Race and Ethnic Studies.*

Anthias, Floya and Nira Yuval Davis. *Racialised Boundaries*, London: Routledge, 1992.

Anwar, Mohammed. *The Myth of Return: Pakistanis in Britain*, London: Heinemann, 1979.

Appadurai, Arjun. *Modernity at Large: Cultural Dimensions in Globalisation*, Minneapolis: University of Minnesota Press, 1996.

Arens, Jenneke and Jos van Beurden. *Jhagrapur: Poor Peasants and Women in a Village in Bangladesh*, Calcutta: Orient Longman, 1977.

Ayoub, Mahmoud M. *Redemptive Suffering in Islam: A Study of the Devotional Aspects of Ashura in Twelver Shi'ism*, The Hague: Mouton Publishers, 1978.

B

Back, Les. ' "Home from Home": Youth, Belonging and Place', in Alexander and Knowles (eds) Making Race Matter.

Baker, Christopher. 'Economic Reorganisation and the Slump in South and Southeast Asia', *Comparative Studies in Society and History*, 23, 3 (July) 1981.

— *An Indian Rural Economy, 1880–1955*, Oxford: Oxford University Press, 1985.

Balachandran, G. 'Recruitment and Control of Indian Seamen: Calcutta, 1880–1935', *International Journal of Maritime History*, 9, 1, 1997.

— 'Circulation through Seafaring: Indian Seamen, 1890–1945' in Markovits et al. (eds) *Society and Circulation.*

Ballantyne, Tony. *Between Colonialism and Diaspora. Sikh Cultural Formations in an Imperial World*, Durham and London: Duke University Press, 2006.

Ballard, Roger (ed.). *Desh Pardesh, The South Asian Presence in Britain*, London: Hurst, 1994.

Ballhatchet, Kenneth. *Race, Sex and Class Under the Raj: Imperial Attitudes and Policies and their Critics, 1793–1905*, London: Weidenfeld and Nicholson, 1980.

Banton, Michael. *The Coloured Quarter*, London: Jonathan Cape, 1955.

Bari, Abdul. *Isal I Soab Darshan*, P.O., Rajgunj: Noakhali, 1924, p. 5. Datta, *Carving Blocs*.

Barkat, Abul et al. *Political Economy of the Vested Property Act in Rural Bangladesh*, Dhaka: Pathak Shamabesh, 1994.

Basch, L., N. Glick Schiller and C.S. Blanc. *Nations Unbound: Transnational Projects, Post-colonial Predicaments and Deterritorialised Nation-States*, New York: Routledge, 1993.

Basu, Subho. *Does Class Matter? Colonial Capital and Workers' Resistance in Bengal, 1890–1937*, New Delhi: Oxford University Press, 2004.

Bayly, C.A. *Rulers, Townsmen and Bazaars, North Indian Society in the Age of British Expansion, 1770–1870*, Cambridge: Cambridge University Press, 1983.

— *Indian Society and the Making of the British Empire*, Cambridge: Cambridge University Press, 1988.

Bayly, C.A. and T. Harper. *The Forgotten Armies: The Fall of British Asia, 1941–1945*, Cambridge, MA: Harvard University Press, 2006.

Begum, Halima. 'Commodifying Multicultures: Urban Regeneration and the Politics of Space in Spitalfields', PhD thesis, Department of Geography, Queen Mary and Westfield College, University of London, 2004.

Behal, Rana P. 'Power Structure, Discipline and Labour in Assam Tea Plantations under Colonial Rule', *International Review of Social History*, 51 (Supplement) 2006.

— 'Coolie Drivers or Benevolent Paternalists? British Tea Planters in Assam and Indenture Labour System in Assam', *Modern Asian Studies*, 44, 1, 2010.

Behal, Rana P. and Marcel van der Linden (eds). *Coolies, Capital and Colonialism: Studies in Indian Labour History*, Cambridge: Cambridge University Press, 2006.

Benson, Sue. 'Asians have Culture, West Indians have Problems' in Ranger, Samad and Stuart (eds) *Culture, Identity and Politics*.

Bhabha, Homi. 'The Third Space', in Rutherford (ed.) *Identity. Community*.

— *The Location of Culture*, Oxford: Routledge, 1994.

— (ed.) *Nation and Narration*, London: Routledge, 1990.

Bhatt, Chetan. *Liberation and Purity: Race, New Religious Ethics of Postmodernity*, London: UCL Press, 1997.

Bhattacharya, Sanjoy. *Propaganda and Information in Eastern India, 1939–45. A Necessary Weapon of War*, London: Curzon, 2001.

Blinder, S. *Non-European Migration to the UK: Family and Dependents*, Oxford: Migration Observatory, 2011: www.migrationobservatory.ox.ac.uk

Bose, N.K. *Calcutta, 1964: A Social Survey*, New Delhi: Lalvani Publishing House, 1968.

Bourdieu, Pierre. 'The Forms of Capital', in Richardson (ed.) *Handbook of Theory*.

Brah, Avtar. *Cartographies of Diaspora: Contesting Identities*, London: Routledge, 1996.

— 'The Scent of Memory: Strangers, Our Own and Others', *Feminist Review*, 61 (Spring) 1999.

Brah, Avtar, Mary J. Hickman and Máirtín Mac an Ghaill. *Thinking Identities: Ethnicity, Race and Culture*, New York: Palgrave, 1999.

Breman, Jan. *Taming the Coolie Beast. Plantation Society and the Colonial Order in Southeast Asia*, Delhi: Oxford University Press, 1989.

— *Footloose Labour: Working in India's Informal Economy*, Cambridge: Cambridge University Press, 1996.

Brown, Judith. *Global South Asians. Introducing the Modern Diaspora*, Cambridge: Cambridge University Press, 2006.

Brubaker, Rogers. 'The Return of Assimilation? Changing Perspectives on Assimilation and its Sequels in France, Germany, and the United States', *Ethnic and Racial Studies*, 24, 4 (July) 2001.
— 'The "Diaspora" Diaspora', *Ethnic and Racial Studies*, 28, 1, 2005.

C

Cain, Mead T. 'The Household Life Cycle and Economic Mobility in Rural Bangladesh, *Population and Development Review*, 4, 3 (September) 1978.
Cain, Mead, Syeda Rokeya Khanam and Shamsun Nahar. 'Class, Patriarchy and Women's Work in Bangladesh', *Population and Development Review*, 5, 3 (September) 1979.
Carey, S. 'Curry Capital: The Restaurant Sector in London's Brick Lane', Working Paper No. 6, Institute of Community Studies, London, 2004.
Carter, Marina. *Voices from Indenture: Experiences of Indian Migrants in the British Empire*, London: Leicester University Press, 1996.
Carter, Marina and Khal Torabully. *Coolitude. An Anthology of the Indian Labour Diaspora*, London: Anthem Press, 2002.
Castles, Stephen and Mark Miller. *The Age of Migration: International Population Movements in the Modern World*, 4th edition, Basingstoke: Palgrave Macmillan, 2009.
Centre for Contemporary Cultural Studies. *The Empire Strikes Back*, London: Routledge, 1982.
Chakrabarti, Prafulla. *The Marginal Men. Refugees and the Left Political Syndrome in West Bengal*, Calcutta: Lumiere Books, 1990.
Chakrabarty, Dipesh. *Rethinking Working Class History: Bengal 1890 to 1940*, New Jersey: Princeton University Press, 1989.
— 'Remembered Villages: Representation of Hindu-Bengali Memories in the Aftermath of the Partition', *South Asia*, 28, 1995.
Chakrabarty, Saroj. *With Dr. B.C. Roy and other Chief Ministers. A Record Uptil 1962*, Calcutta: S. Chakrabarty, 1974.
Chan, Kam Wing. 'China, Internal Migration' in Ness and Bellwood (eds) *Encyclopedia of Global Migration*.
Chandavarkar, R. *The Origins of Industrial Capitalism in India: Business Strategies and the Working Class in Bombay*, Cambridge: Cambridge University Press, 1994.
— 'The Decline and Fall of the Jobber System in the Bombay Cotton Textile Industry, 1870–1955', *Modern Asian Studies*, 42, 1, 2008.
Chant, Sylvia (ed.). *International Handbook of Gender and Poverty*, Cheltenham: Edward Elgar, 2010.
Charlton-Stevens, Uther. 'Decolonising Anglo-Indians: Strategies for a Mixed-Race Community in Late Colonial India During the First Half of the Twentieth Century', DPhil thesis, University of Oxford, 2012.
Charsley, Katharine. 'Unhappy Husbands: Masculinity and Migration in Transnational Pakistani Marriages', *Journal of the Royal Anthropological Institute*, 11, 2005.
— 'Risk and Ritual: The Protection of British Pakistani Women in Transnational Marriage', *Journal of Ethnic and Migration* Studies, 32, 7, 2006.
— 'Risk, Trust, Gender and Transnational Cousin Marriage Among British Pakistanis', *Ethnic and Racial Studies*, 30, 6, 2007.
Charsley, Katharine and Alison Shaw. 'South Asian Marriages in Comparative Perspective', *Global Networks* 6, 4, 2006.

Chatterjee, Indrani. *Gender, Slavery and Law in Colonial India*, Delhi: Oxford University Press, 1999.
— (ed.) *Unfamiliar Relations. Family and History in South Asia*, Delhi: Permanent Black, 2004.
Chatterjee, Nilanjana. 'Interrogating Victimhood: East Bengali Refugee Narratives of Communal Violence', Department of Anthropology, University of North Carolina at Chapel Hill, n.d: www.swadhinata.org.uk/misc/chatterjeeEastBengal%20Refugee.pdf
Chatterjee, Partha. *The Nation and its Fragments: Colonial and Postcolonial Histories*, Princeton: Princeton University Press, 1993.
Chatterji, Joya. *Bengal Divided. Hindu Communalism and Partition, 1932–1947*, Cambridge: Cambridge University Press, 1994.
— 'The Bengali Muslim: A Contradiction in Terms? An Overview of the Debate on Bengali Muslim Identity', *Comparative Studies of South Asia, Africa, and the Middle East*, 16, 2, 1996.
— 'The Fashioning of a Frontier: The Radcliffe Line and Bengal's Border Landscape, 1947–1952', *Modern Asian Studies*, 33, 1, 1999.
— 'Right or Charity? The Debate over Relief and Rehabilitation in West Bengal, 1947–1950' in Kaul (ed.) *The Partitions of Memory*.
— '"Dispersal" and the Failure of Rehabilitation. Refugee Camp-dwellers and Squatters in West Bengal', *Modern Asian Studies*, 41, 5, 2007.
— *The Spoils of Partition, Bengal and India 1947–1967*, Cambridge: Cambridge University Press, 2007; 2011.
— 'South Asian Histories of Citizenship, 1946–1970', The Historical Journal, 55, 4 (December) 2012.
— 'From Subjecthood to Citizenship in South Asia: Migration, Nationality and the Post-Imperial Global Order', in McCoy, Fradera and Jacobson (eds) *Endless Empire*.
Chatterji, Joya and David Washbrook. 'Introduction – Concepts and Questions', in Chatterji and Washbrook (eds) *Routledge Handbook*.
Chatterji, Joya and David Washbrook (eds). *Routledge Handbook of South Asian Diaspora*, Oxford: Routledge, 2013.
Chattopadhyaya, Haraprasad. *Internal Migration in India: the Case of Bengal*, Calcutta: K.P. Bagchi and Company, 1987.
Chaudhuri, Nirad C. *The Autobiography of an Unknown Indian*, London: The Hogarth Press, 1988.
Choudhury, Yusuf. *The Roots and Tales of Bangladeshi Settlers*, Birmingham: Sylheti Social History Group, 1993.
— *Sons of the Soil*, Birmingham: Sylheti Social History Group, 1995.
Chimni, B.S. (ed.). *International Refugee Law: A Reader*, New Delhi: Sage, 2001.
Clifford, James. *Routes. Travel and Translation in the Late Twentieth Century*, Cambridge, MA: Harvard University Press, 1997.
Cohen, Abner. *Arab Border Villages in Israel*, Manchester: University Press, 1965.
Cohen, Phil. *The Last Island*, London: Centre for New Ethnicities Research, 1998.
Cohen, Robin. *Global Diasporas: An Introduction*, 2nd edition, London: Routledge, 2008.
Cole, J.R.I. *Roots of North Indian Shi'ism in Iran and Iraq. Religion and State in Awadh, 1722–1859*, Berkeley: University of California Press, 1988.
Collins, Patricia Hill and John Solomos (eds). *The Sage Handbook of Race and Ethnic Studies*, London: Sage, 2010.
Crang, Philip. 'Diasporas and Material Culture', in Knott and McLoughlin (eds) *Diasporas*.

D

Daeschel, Marcus. 'Sovereignty, Governmentality and Development in Ayub's Pakistan: The Case of Korangi Township', *Modern Asian Studies*, 44, 1, 2011.

Das, Suranjan. *Communal Riots in Bengal, 1905–1947*, Delhi: Oxford University Press, 1993.

Das Gupta, Ranajit. *Economy, Society and Politics in Bengal: Jalpaiguri 1869–1947*, Delhi: Oxford University Press, 1992.

Datta, Antara. *Refugees and Borders in South Asia: the Great Exodus of 1971*, London: Routledge, 2012.

Datta, Pradip Kumar. *Carving Blocs. Communal Ideology in Early Twentieth-century Bengal*, Delhi: Oxford University Press, 1999.

Davis, Kingsley. *The Population of India and Pakistan*, Princeton, NJ: Princeton University Press, 1951.

Dench, Geoff, Kate Gavron and Michael Young. *The New East End: Kinship, Race and Conflict*, London: Profile Books, 2006.

Desai, Sonalde and Manjistha Banerji. 'Negotiated Identities: Male Migration and Left-Behind Wives in India', *Journal of Population Research*, 25, 3, 2008.

Donnan, Hastings. *Marriage Among Muslims. Preference and Choice in Northern Pakistan*, Leiden: Brill, 1988.

Dumont, Louis. 'North India in Relation to South India', in Uberoi (ed.) *Family, Kinship*.

E

Eade, John. *The Politics of Community, The Bangladeshi Community in East London*, Aldershot: Ashgate, 1989.

— *Placing London: From Imperial Capital to Global City*, Oxford: Berghahn, 2000.

Eade, John, Isabelle Fremeaux and David Garbin. 'The Political Construction of Diasporic Communities in the City', in Gilbert (ed.) *Imagined Londons*.

Eade, John and David Garbin. 'Competing Visions of Identity and Space', *Contemporary South Asia*, 15, 2, 2006.

Eade, J., A. Ullah, J. Iqbal and M. Hey. *Tales of Three Generations of Bengalis in Britain*, London: Swadhinata Trust and CRONEM (Surrey and Roehampton Universities), 2006: www.swadhinata.org.uk/index.php?option=com_content&view=article&id=49&Itemid=53

Eaton, Richard M. *The Rise of Islam and the Bengal Frontier, 1204–1750*, Berkeley: University of California Press, 1993.

F

Farooqui, M.I. *Law of Abandoned Property*, Dhaka: Sultana Suraiya Akter, 2000.

Fiddian-Qasmiyeh, E., G. Loescher, K. Long and N. Sidona. 'Introduction: Refugee and Forced Migration Studies in Transition' in E. Fiddian-Qasmiyeh, G. Loescher, K. Long and N. Sidona, *Oxford Handbook of Refugee and Forced Migration Studies*, Oxford: Oxford University Press, 2014.

Finney, Nissa and Kitty Lymperopoulou. *Local Ethnic Inequalities: Ethnic Differences in Education, Employment, Health and Housing in Districts of England and Wales, 2001–2011*, London: Runnymede Trust, 2014: www.runnymedetrust.org/uploads/Inequalities%20report-final%20v2.pdf

Finney, Nissa and Ludi. Simpson *Sleepwalking to Segregation?: Challenging Myths about Race and Migration*, Bristol: Policy Press, 2009.

Fischer, Michael. *Iran: From Religious Dispute to Revolution*, Cambridge, MA: Harvard University Press, 1980.

Foster, Janet. *Docklands: Cultures in Conflict, Worlds in Collision*, London: UCL Press, 1999.

Frietag, Sandria B. *Collective Action and Community. Public Arenas and the Emergence of Communalism in North India*, Berkeley, Los Angeles and London: University of California Press, 1989.

Fruzetti, Lina. *The Gift of a Virgin: Women, Marriage and Ritual in a Bengali Society*, New Brunswick: Rutgers University Press, 1982.

Furnivall, J. S. *Colonial Policy and Practice: A Comparative Study of Burma and Netherlands India*, Cambridge: Cambridge University Press, 1948.

G

Garbin, David. 'A Diasporic Sense of Place: Dynamics of Spatialization and Transnational Political Fields Among Bangladeshi Muslims in Britain', in Smith and Eade (eds) *Transnational Ties*.

Gardner, Katy. *Global Migrants' Local Lives: Travel and Transformation in Rural Bangladesh*, Oxford: Oxford University Press, 1995.

— 'The Transnational Work of Kinship and Caring: British-Bengali Marriages in Historical Perspective', *Global Networks*, 6, 4, 2006.

Gardner, K. and A. Shakur. 'I'm Bengali, I'm Asian and I'm Living Here: The Changing Identities of British Bengalis', in Ballard (ed.) *Desh Pardesh*.

Gellner, David N. (ed.). *Borderland Lives in Northern South Asia*, Durham, NC: Duke University Press, 2013.

Ghosh, Amitav. *The Hungry Tide*, London: The Borough Press, 2005.

Ghosh, Durba. *Sex and the Family in Colonial India. The Making of Empire*, Cambridge: Cambridge University Press, 2006.

Ghosh, Gautam. '"God is a Refugee": Nationalism, Morality and History in the 1947 Partition of India', *Social Analysis*, 42, 1, 1998.

Ghosh, Papiya. *Partition and the South Asian Diaspora. Extending the Subcontinent*, Delhi: Routledge, 2007.

Gillis, J. R. *Commemorations: The Politics of National Identity*, Princeton: Princeton University Press, 1994.

Gilroy, Paul. *Small Acts: Thoughts on the Politics of Black Cultures*, London: Serpent's Tail, 1993.

— 'Diaspora and the Detours of Identity', in Woodward (ed.) *Identity*.

— *After Empire: Melancholia or Convivial Culture? Multiculture or Postcolonial Melancholia*, Abingdon: Routledge, 2004.

Glazer, Nathan and Daniel Moynihan. *Beyond the Melting Pot: The Negroes, Puerto Ricans, Jews, Italians and Irish of New York City*, Cambridge MA: MIT PRESS, 1963, cited in Brubaker, 'The Return of Assimilation'.

Glinert, Ed. *East End Chronicles: 300 Years of Mystery and Mayhem*, London: Penguin, 2005.

Glynn, Sarah. 'The Spirit of '71: How the Bangladeshi War of Independence has Haunted Tower Hamlets', *Socialist History Journal*, 29, 2006.

Gottschalk, Peter. 'The Problem of Defining Islam in Arampur', *International Institute for the Study of Islam in the Modern World Newsletter*, August 2001.

Green, Nile. *Bombay Islam. The Religious Economy of the West Indian Ocean, 1840–1915*, Cambridge: Cambridge University Press, 2011.
Guha, Amalendu. *Planter Raj to Swaraj*, New Delhi: Indian Council of Historical Research, 1977.
Guhathakurta, Meghna. 'Families, Displacement', *Transeuropéennes*, 19/20, 2001.

H

Hafesji, Khatija. 'Transnationalism, Migration, and Piety in the Growth of the Tablighi Jama'at Between India and Britain from 1926 to 2001', History Tripos dissertation, University of Cambridge, 2011.
Halbwachs, Maurice. *On Collective Memory* (translated by Lewis Coser), Chicago: University of Chicago Press, 1992.
Hall, Catherine and Sonya Rose (eds). *At Home With the Empire: Metropolitan Culture and the Imperial World*, Cambridge: Cambridge University Press, 2006.
Hall, Stuart. 'Cultural Identity and Diaspora', in Rutherford (ed.) *Identity*.
Hall, Suzanne M. 'Super-diverse Street: A "Trans-ethnography" Across Migrant Localities', *Ethnic and Racial Studies*, 38, 1, 2015.
Hansen, Randall. *Citizenship and Immigration in Postwar Britain*, Oxford: Oxford University Press, 2000.
Hashmi, Tajul Islam. 'The "Bihari" Muslims of Bangladesh: Victims of Nationalisms', in Hassan (ed.) *Islam, Communities and the Nation*.
Hassan, Mushirul (ed.). *Islam, Communities and the Nation: Muslim Identities in South Asia and Beyond*, New Delhi: Manohar, 1998.
Hefner, Robert and Muhammad Qasim Zaman. *Schooling Islam: The Culture and Politics of Modern Muslim Education* (Princeton Studies in Muslim Politics), Princeton: Princeton University Press, 2007.
Ho, Engseng. *The Graves of Tarim: Genealogy and Mobility across the Indian Ocean*, Berkeley, University of California Press, 2006.
Horowitz, Daniel. *The Deadly Ethnic Riot*, Berkeley: University of California Press, 2001.
Hunter, W. W. *Statistical Account of Bengal, Vol. 3*, London: Trubner and Co., 1877.
Huntington, Samuel. *The Clash of Civilisations and the Remaking of World Order*, New York: Simon and Schuster, 1996.
Huq, Maimuna. 'Reading the Qur'an in Bangladesh: The Politics of "Belief" Among Islamist Women', *Modern Asian Studies*, 42, 2/3, 2008.
Hyder, Syed Akbar. *Reliving Karbala. Martyrdom in South Asian Memory*, Oxford: Oxford University Press, 2006.

I

Ilias, Ahmed. *Biharis: The Indian Émigrés in Bangladesh. An Objective Analysis*, Syedpur: Bangladesh: Shamsul Huque Foundation, 2003.
Iqbal, Ifthekar. *The Bengal Delta: Ecology, State and Social Change, 1840–1943*, Basingstoke: Palgrave Macmillan, 2010.

J

Jackson, Ashley. 'The Evolution and Use of British Imperial Military Formations', in Jeffreys and Rose (eds) *The Indian Army*.

Jacobs, Jane. *Edge of Empire: Postcolonialism and the City*, London: Routledge, 1996.

Jalais, Annu. *Forest of Tigers: People, Politics and Environment in the Sundarbans*, New Delhi: Routledge, 2009.

— 'Geographies and Identities: Subaltern Partition Stories along Bengal's Southern Frontier', in Gellner (ed.) *Borderland Lives*.

Jeffreys, Alan and Patrick Rose (eds). *The Indian Army, 1939–47, Experience and Development*, Farnham: Ashgate, 1988.

Jivraj, Stephen. 'Geographies of Diversity in Newham', Manchester: Centre on Dynamics of Ethnicity, 2013: www.ethnicity.ac.uk/medialibrary/briefings/localdynamicsofdiversity/geographies-of-diversity-in-newham.pdf

Jones, Justin. *Shia Islam in Colonial India. Religion, Community and Sectarianism*, Cambridge: Cambridge University Press, 2002.

Joppke, Christian. *Immigration and the Nation-State: The United States, Germany and Great Britain*, Oxford: Oxford University Press, 1999.

Joshi, Chitra. *Lost Worlds: Indian Labour and its Forgotten Histories*, London: Anthem Press, 2005.

K

Kabeer, Naila. *The Power to Choose: Bangladeshi Women and Labour Market Decisions in London and Dhaka*, London: Verso, 2000.

Kalir, Barak and Malini Sur (eds). *Transnational Flows and Permissive Polities: Ethnographies of Human Mobility in Asia*, Amsterdam: Amsterdam University Press, 2012.

Kalra, Virinder S. *From Textile Mills to Taxi Ranks: Experiences of Migration, Labour and Social Change*, Aldershot: Ashgate, 2000.

Kalra, Virinder, Raminder Kaur and John Hutnyk. *Diaspora and Hybridity*, London: Sage, 2005.

Kamal, Nahid. 'The Population Trajectories of Bangladesh and West Bengal During the Twentieth Century: A Comparative Study', PhD thesis, London School of Economics and Political Science, 2009.

Kamaluddin, A.F.M. 'Refugee Problems in Bangladesh', in Kosinski and Elahi (eds), *Population Redistribution*.

Kandiyoti, Deniz. 'Bargaining with Patriarchy', *Gender and Society*, 2, 3, 1988.

Karve, Irawati *Kinship Organisation in India*, Delhi: Asia Publishing House, 1968.

— 'The Kinship Map of India', in Uberoi (ed.) *Family, Kinship and Marriage*.

Kaul, Suvir (ed.). *The Partitions of Memory: The Afterlife of the Division of India*, Indiana: Indiana University Press, 2001.

Keith, Michael. *Race, Riots and Policing: Lore and Disorder in a Multiracist Society*, London: UCL Press, 1993.

— *After the Cosmopolitan? Multicultural Cities and the Future of Racism*, London: Routledge, 2005.

Kerr, Ian *Building the Railways of the Raj, 1850–1900*, New York: Oxford University Press, 1995.

— *Railways in Modern India*, Delhi: Oxford University Press, 2001.

Khan, Misbahuddin. *History of the Port of Chittagong*, Dhaka: Dana Publishers, 1990.

Khan, Tamizuddin. *The Test of Time. My Life and Days*, Dhaka: University Press, 1989.

Knott, Kim and Sean McLoughlin (eds). *Diasporas: Concepts, Identities, Intersections*, London: Zed Books, 2010.

Kofman, E., S. Lukes, V. Meetoo and P. Aaron. *Family Migration to United Kingdom: Trends, Statistics and Policy*, Vienna: International Centre for Migration Policy Development, 2008.

Kolff, Dirk. *Naukar, Rajput and Sepoy: The Ethnohistory of the Military Labour Market in Hindustan, 1450–1850*, Cambridge: Cambridge University Press, 1990.

— 'The Market for Mobile Labour in Early Modern North India', in Chatterji and Washbrook (eds), *Routledge Handbook*.

Korom, Frank. *Hosay Trinidad, Muharram Performance in an Indo-Caribbean Diaspora*, Philadelphia: University of Pennsylvania Press, 2003.

Korom, Frank and Peter Chelkowski. 'Community Process and the Performance of Muharram Observances in Trinidad', *The Drama Review*, 38 (2), Summer 1994.

Kosinski, L.A. and K.M. Elahi (eds). *Population Redistribution and Development in South Asia*, Dordecht: Springer, 1985.

Kraler, A. *Civic Stratification, Gender and Family Migration Policies in Europe*, Vienna: International Centre for Migration Policy Development, 2010.

Kuhn, Philip A. *Chinese Among Others: Emigration in Modern Times*, Plymouth: Rowman and Littlefield, 2008.

Kundnani, Arun. 'From Oldham to Bradford: The Violence of the Violated', London: Institute of Race Relations, 2001: www.irr.org.uk/news/from-oldham-to-bradford-the-violence-of-the-violated/

— *The Death of Multiculturalism*, London: Institute of Race Relations, 2002: www.irr.org.uk/news/the-death-of-multiculturalism/

Kwon, Heonik. *After the Massacre. Commemoration and Consolation in Ha My and My Lai*, Berkeley, Los Angeles, and London: University of California Press, 2006.

L

Lal, Brij. 'Girmitiyas: The Origins of the Fiji Indians', *Canberra Journal of Pacific History Monograph*, 1983.

— *Chalo Jahaji: On a Journey of Indenture through Fiji*, Canberra: Australian National University, 2000.

—. 'Indian Indenture: Experiment and Experience', in Chatterji and Washbrook (eds), *Routledge Handbook*.

Layton-Henry, Z. *The Politics of Immigration: Race and Race Relations in Postwar Britain*, Oxford: Wiley-Blackwell, 1992.

Leech, K. *Brick Lane 1978: The Events and Their Significance*, Birmingham: AFFOR, 1980.

Lefrebvre, Henri. *The Production of Space* (translated by Donald Nicholson-Smith), Oxford; Cambridge MA: Basil Blackwell, 2004.

Levine, Philippa. 'Sexuality and Empire', in Hall and Rose (eds) *At Home With the Empire*.

Levitt, Peggy. *The Transnational Villagers*, Berkeley and Los Angeles: University of California Press, 2001.

Levitt, Peggy and Nina G.S 'Conceptualising Simultaneity: A Transnational Social Field Perspective', *International Migration Review*, 38, 3, 2004.

Levitt, Peggy and B. Nadya Jaworsky. 'Transnational Migration Studies: Past Developments and Future Trends', *Annual Review of Sociology*, 33, 2007.

Lucassen, Jan. *Global Labour History: A State of the Art*, Bern: Peter Lang, 2006.

Lucassen, Jan and Leo Lucassen (eds). *Migration, Migration History, History: Old Paradigms and New Perspectives*, Bern: Verlag Peter, 2005.

— (eds) *Globalising Migration History: The Eurasian Experience*, Leiden: Brill Publishers, 2014.
Ludden, David. 'Presidential Address: Maps in the Mind and the Mobility of Asia', *Journal of Asian Studies*, 62, 4, 2003.

M

MacInnes, Tom, Amshree Parekh and Peter Kenway. *London's Poverty Profile, 2011*, London: Trust for London/New Policy Institute www.londonspovertyprofile.org.uk
Mahmudabad, A. K. 'Muharram in Awadh', in Muzaffar Ali (ed.), *A Leaf Turns Yellow: The Sufis of Awadh*, New Delhi: Bloomsbury, 2013.
Malkki, Lisa. *Purity and Exile. Violence, Memory and National Cosmology among Hutu Refugees in Tanzania*, Chicago and London: University of Chicago Press, 1995.
Mand, Kanwal. 'Place, Gender and Power in Transnational Sikh Marriages', *Global Networks*, 2, 3, 2002.
— *Social Capital and Transnational South Asian Families: Rituals, Care and Provision*, London: Families and Social Capital ESRC Research Group, South Bank University, 2006.
Markovits, Claude. *The Global World of Indian Merchants, 1750–1947: Traders of Sind from Bukhara to Panama*, Cambridge: Cambridge University Press, 2000.
Markovits, Claude, Jacques Pouchepadass and Sanjay Subrahmanyam (eds). *Society and Circulation. Mobile People and Itinerant Cultures in South Asia, 1750–1950*, London: Anthem, 2006.
Marshall, Richard and Shibaab Rahman. *Internal Migration in Bangladesh: Character, Drivers and Policy Issues*, Bangladesh: United Nations Development Programme, 2013: www.undp.org/content/dam/bangladesh/docs/Publications/Pub-2013/Internal%20 Migration%20in%20Bangladesh%20UNDP%20Final.pdf
Mascarenhas, Anthony. *Bangladesh: A Legacy of Blood*, London: Hodder and Stoughton, 1986.
Massey, Douglas. 'Social Structure, Household Strategies and the Cumulative Causation of Migration', *Population Index*, 56, 1 (Spring) 1990.
Masud, Maulana Khalid (ed.). *Travellers in Faith: Studies of the Tablighi Jama'at as a Transnational Islamic Movement for Faith Renewal*, Leiden: Brill, 2000.
McCoy, Alfred, Josep M. Fradera and Stephen Jacobson (eds). *Endless Empire. Spain's Retreat, Europe's Eclipse, America's Decline*, London: University of Wisconsin Press, 2012.
McGhee, Derek. *Intolerant Britain? Hate, Citizenship and Difference*, Maidenhead: Open University Press, 2005.
McKeown, Adam. 'Global Migration 1846–1950', *Journal of World History*, 15, 2, 2004.
McLoughlin, Sean, William Gould, Ananya Kabir and Emma Tomalin (eds). *Writing the City in British Asian Diasporas*, London: Routledge, 2014.
McPherson, Kenneth. *The Muslim Microcosm. Calcutta, 1918–1935*, Wiesbaden: Streiner, 1974.
Meer, Y. S. *Documents of Indentured Labour: Natal 1851–1917*, Durban: Institute of Black Research, 1980.
Metcalf, Barbara Daly. *Islamic Revival in British India: Deoband, 1860–1900*, Princeton: Princeton University Press, 1982.
— *Perfecting Women: Maulana Ashraf Ali Thanawi's Bihishti Zevar*, Berkeley: University of California Press, 1990.

— 'Living Hadith in the Tablighi Jama'at', *The Journal of Asian Studies* 52, 3, 1993.
— *Islamic Contestations: Essays on Muslims in India and Pakistan*, Oxford: Oxford University Press, 2006.
— (ed.) *Making Muslim Space in North America and Europe*, Berkeley: University of California Press, 1996.
— (ed.) *Islam in South Asia in Practice*, Princeton: Princeton University Press, 2009.
Miranda, Armindo. *The Demography of Bangladesh* (No. 144), Bergen: Chr. Michelsen Institute Development Research and Action Programme, 1982.
Misztal, Barbara. 'The Sacralization of Memory', *European Journal of Social Theory*, 7, 1, 2004.
Mitra, Asok. *The New India, 1948–1955*, Delhi: Popular Prakashan, 1991.
Moch, Leslie Page. 'Dividing Time: An Analytical Framework for Migration History Periodization', in Lucassen (eds) *Migration History*.
Mody, Perveez. 'Marriages of Convenience and Capitulation: South Asian Marriage, Family and Intimacy in the Diaspora', in Chatterji and Washbrook (eds) *Routledge Handbook*.
Mohanty, Chandra. 'Under Western Eyes: Feminist Scholarship and Colonial Discourses', in Williams and Chrisman, *Colonial Discourse*.
Mohapatra, Prabhu. '"Following Custom"'? Representations of Community among Indian Immigrant Labour in the West Indies', in Behal and Van der Linden (eds) *Coolies, Capital and Colonialism*.
Mukhopadhyay, Aparajita. 'Wheels of Change? Impact of Railways on Colonial North Indian Society', PhD thesis, School of Oriental and African Studies, University of London, 2013.
Munsi, Sunil Kumar. *Geography of Transportation in Eastern India under the British Raj*, Calcutta: K. P. Bagchi, 1980.
Murshid, Tazeen M. 'Nations Imagined and Fragmented: Bengal', in Van Schendel and Zürcher (eds) *Identity Politics*.
Muslim Council of Britain. *British Muslims in Numbers*, London: MCB, 2015: www.mcb.org.uk/wp-content/uploads/2015/02/MCBCensusReport_2015.pdf

N

Nair, Janaki. *Miners and Millhands: Work, Culture and Politics in Princely Mysore*, New Delhi: Sage, 1998.
Nakatani, Tetsuya. 'Away from Home. The Movement and Settlement of Refugees from East Pakistan to West Bengal, India', *Journal of the Japanese Association for South Asian Studies*, 12, 2000.
Nasrin, Taslima. *Meyebela: My Bengali Girlhood. A Memoir of Growing up Female in a Muslim World*, Vermont: Steerforth Press, 1998.
Ness, Immanuel and Peter Bellwood (eds). *The Encyclopedia of Global Migration*, Oxford: Blackwell, 2013.
Nichols, Robert. *A History of Pashtun Migration 1775–2006*, Karachi: Oxford University Press, 2008.
Northrup, David. *Indentured Labour in the Age of Imperialism, 1834–1922*, Cambridge: Cambridge University Press, 1995.

O

O'Hanlon, Rosalind. 'Scribal Migrations in Early Modern India', in Chatterji and Washbrook (eds) *Routledge Handbook*.

274   Bibliography

Omissi, David. *The Sepoy and the Raj*, London: Macmillan, 1994.

Oonk, Gijsbert (ed.). *Exploring Trajectories of Migration and Theory*, Amsterdam: Amsterdam University Press, 2007.

Owusu, K. (ed.). *Black British Culture and Society*, London: Routledge, 2000.

P

Parmar, Pratibha. 'Gender, Race and Class: Asian Women in Resistance', in Centre for Contemporary Cultural Studies, *The Empire Strikes Back*.

Peach, Ceri. 'The Muslim Population of Great Britain', *Ethnic and Racial Studies*, 13, 3, 1990.

Pederson, Susan and Peter Mandler (eds). *After the Victorians. Private Conscience and Public Duty in Modern Britain*, London: Psychology Press, 1994.

Peebles, Patrick. *Plantation Tamils of Ceylon. New Historical Perspectives on Migration*, London and New York: University of Leicester Press, 2001.

Phillimore, R. H. *Historical Records of the Survey of India, Vol. IV*, in Munsi, *Geography of Transportation*.

Pinault, David. *Horse of Karbala. Muslim Devotional Life in India*, New York: Palgrave, 2001.

Plummer, K. *Documents of Life 2*, London: Sage, 2001.

Portes, Alejandro 'Conclusion: Towards a New World: The Origins and Effects of Transnational Activities', *Ethnic and Racial Studies*, 22, 2, 1999.

— 'Conclusion: Theoretical Convergences and Empirical Evidence in the Study of Immigrant Transnationalism', *International Migration Review*, 37, 2003.

Portes, Alejandro, Luis E. Guarnizo and Patricia Landolt. 'The Study of Transnationalism: Pitfalls and Promise of an Emergent Research Field', *Ethnic and Racial Studies*, 22, 2, 1999.

Prior, Katherine H. 'The British Administration of Hinduism in North India, 1780–1900', PhD thesis, University of Cambridge, 1990.

Q

R

Raghavan, Srinath. *1971. A Global History of the Creation of Bangladesh*, Cambridge MA: Harvard, 2013.

Rahman, Mahbubar and Willem van Schendel. '"I Am *Not* a Refugee": Rethinking Partition Migration', *Modern Asian Studies*, 37, 3 (July) 2003.

Ramamurthy, Anandi. *Black Star: Britain's Asian Youth Movements*, London: Pluto Press, 2013.

Ranger, Terrence, Yunas Samad and Ossie Stuart (eds). *Culture, Identity and Politics*, Aldershot: Avebury, 1996.

Ray, Manas. 'Growing Up Refugee: On Memory and Locality', *Hindi: Language, Discourse, Writing*, 1, 3–4, 2001.

Redclift, Victoria. 'Changes in Family Reunion Migration from Bangladesh to the UK 1985–2004: Policy, Gender and Social Ties', MSc thesis, London School of Economics and Political Science, 2006.

— *Statelessness and Citizenship: Camps and the Creation of Political Space*, Abingdon: Routledge, 2013.

— 'Rethinking "the Muslim Community": Intra-minority Identity and Transnational Political Space', in Alexander, Redclift and Hussain (eds) *The New Muslims*.
Richardson, J. (ed.). *Handbook of Theory and Research for the Sociology of Education*, New York: Greenwood, 1986.
Robinson, Francis. *Separatism Among Indian Muslims. The Politics of the United Provinces' Muslims 1860–1923*, Cambridge: Cambridge University Press, 1974.
— 'Islamic Reform and Modernities in South Asia', Modern Asian Studies, Double Special Issue: 'Islam in South Asia', 42, 2008.
Rohner, Ronald P. and Manjusri Chaki-Sircar. *Women and Children in a Bengali Village*, Hanover and London: University Press of New England, 1988.
Rose, S.O. 'Race, Empire and British Wartime Identity', 1939–45', *Historical Research*, 74, 184, 2002.
Roy, Asim. *The Islamic Syncretistic Tradition in Bengal*, Princeton: Princeton University Press, 1983.
Roy, Haimanti. *Partitioned Lives. Migrants, Refugees, Citizens in India and Pakistan, 1947–65*, New Delhi: Oxford University Press, 2013.
Roy, Tirthankar. '"Where is Bengal?" Situating an Indian Region in the Early Modern World Economy', *Past and Present*, 213 (November) 2011.
Roy, Tirthankar and Douglas Haynes. 'Conceiving Mobility: Weavers' Migrations in Precolonial and Colonial India', *Indian Economic and Social History Review*, 36, 1, 1999.
Santa, Rozario and Sophie Gilliat-Ray. 'Genetics, Religion and Identity: A Study of British Bangladeshis 2004–2007', Working Paper No. 93, Cardiff University School of Social Sciences, 2007: *www.cardiff.ac.uk/socsi/resources/wrkgpaper-93.pdf*
Rutherford, Jonathan (ed.). *Identity: Community, Culture, Difference*, London: Lawrence and Wishart, 1990.

S

Safran, William. 'Diasporas in Modern Societies: Myths of Homeland and Return', *Diaspora*, 1, 1, 1991.
Salter, Joseph. *The Asiatic in England. Sketches of Sixteen Years of Work Among Orientals*, London: General Books, 1873.
— *The East in the West. Work Among the Asiatics and Africans in London*, London: Henry Morris, 1895.
Salter, Mark. Rights of Passage: The Passport in International Relations, Boulder: Lynn Reinner, 2003.
Samaddar, Ranabir (ed.). *Reflections on Partition in the East*, New Delhi and Calcutta: Vikas Publishing House and Calcutta Research Group, 1997.
Sarkar, Tanika. *Hindu Wife, Hindu Nation: Community, Religion, and Cultural Nationalism*, Bloomington: Indiana University Press, 2001.
Sassen, Saskia. *The Mobility of Capital and Labor: A Study in International Investment and Labor Flow*, Cambridge: Cambridge University Press, 1988.
— *The Global City: New York, London, Tokyo*, Princeton: Princeton University Press. 1991.
Sayigh, Rosemary. *The Palestinians. From Peasants to Refugees*, London: Zed, 1979.
Sayyid, Salman. *A Fundamental Fear: Eurocentrism and the Emergence of Islamism*, London: Zed Press, 1997.
Schiller, Nina Glick and Georges Eugene Fouron. *Georges Woke Up Laughing. Long-distance Nationalism and the Search for Home*, Chapel Hill: Duke University Press, 2001.

Bibliography

Schivelbusch, Wolfgang. *The Culture of Defeat. On National Trauma, Mourning and Recovery* (translated by Jefferson Chase), London: Macmillan, 2003.

Schmeidl, Suzanne. 'Conflict and Forced Migration: A Quantitative Review', in Zolberg and Benda (eds) *Global Migrants*.

Schubel, Vernon James. 'Karbala as Sacred Space among North Indian Shia: "Every Day is Ashura, Everywhere is Karbala"', in Metcalf (ed.) *Making Muslim Space*.

Seabrook, Jeremy and Imran Ahmed Siddiqui. *People Without History. India's Muslim Ghettos*, London: Pluto Press, 2011.

Seal, Anil. *The Emergence of Indian Nationalism. Competition and Collaboration in the Later Nineteenth Century*, Cambridge: Cambridge University Press, 1971.

Sen, Samita. *Women and Labour in Late Colonial India: The Bengal Jute Industry*, Cambridge: Cambridge University Press, 1999.

— 'Questions of Consent: Women's Recruitment for Assam Tea Gardens', *Studies in History*, 2, 2002.

— '"Without his Consent?" Marriage and Women's Migration in Colonial India', *International Journal of Labour and Working-Class History*, 65 (Spring) 2004.

— 'Wrecking Homes, Making Families. Women's Recruitment and Indentured Labour Migration from India', in Chatterji and Washbrook (eds) *Routledge Handbook*.

Sen, Uditi. 'Refugees and the Politics of Nation-building in India, 1947–1971', PhD thesis, University of Cambridge, 2009.

Sharma, Jayeeta. '"Lazy" Natives, Coolie Labour and the Assam Tea Industry', *Modern Asian Studies*, 46, 6, 2009.

— *Empire's Garden. Assam and the Making of India*, Durham and London: Duke University Press, 2011.

Sheffer, Gabriel. *Diaspora Politics: At Home Abroad*, Cambridge: Cambridge University Press, 2003.

Siddiqui, A.R. *Partition and the Making of the Mohajir Mindset, A Narrative*, Karachi: Oxford University Press, 2008.

Siddiqui, M.K.A. *The Muslims of Calcutta. A Study in Aspects of their Social Organisation*, Calcutta: Anthropological Survey of India, 1974.

— *Muslim Educational Uplift. How to Achieve this Goal?*, Calcutta: Institute of Objective Studies, 2008.

Sikand, Yogender. *The Origins and Development of the Tablighi Jam'aat (1920–2000). A Cross-country Comparative Study*, New Delhi: Orient Longman, 2002.

Simeon, Dilip. *The Politics of Labour Under Late Colonialism: Workers, Unions and the State in Chota Nagpur, 1928–1939*, New Delhi: Mahohar, 1995.

Simpson, L. and V.S. Gavalas. *Population Dynamics within Rochdale and Oldham: Population, Household and Social Change*, Manchester: Centre for Census and Survey Research, Manchester University, 2007.

Sivanandan, A. 'From Resistance to Rebellion: Asian and Afro-Caribbean Struggles in Britain', *Race and Class*, 23, 2/3, 1981/1982.

— *A Different Hunger: Writings on Black Resistance*, London: Pluto Press, 1982.

— 'A Radical Black Political Culture' in Owusu (ed.) *Black British Culture*.

Smith, M.P. and J. Eade (eds). *Transnational Ties: Cities, Identities and Migrations*, London: CUCR (9) Transaction Publishers, 2008.

Solomos, John. *Race and Racism in Britain*, Basingstoke: Palgrave Macmillan, 2003.

Spivak, Gayatri. 'Can the Subaltern Speak', in Williams and Chrisman, *Colonial Discourse*.

— *A Critique of Postcolonial Reason: Toward a History of the Vanishing Present*, Cambridge, MA: Harvard University Press, 1999.

Stark, Oded and J. Edward Taylor. 'Relative Deprivation and International Migration', *Demography*, 26, 1 (February) 1989.
Strachey, John and Richard. *The Finances and Public Works of India from 1869 to 1881*, London: Kegan Paul, 1882.
Sur, Malini. 'Bamboo Baskets and Barricades: Gendered Landscapes at the India-Bangladesh Border', in Kalir and Sur (eds) *Transnational Flows*.
— 'Through Metal Fences: Material Mobility and the Politics of Transnationality at Borders', *Mobilities*, 8, 1, 2013.

T

Tabili, Laura. *'We Ask for British Justice'. Workers and Racial Difference in Late Imperial Britain*, New York: Cornell University Press, 1994.
Tagore, Rabindranath. *The Post Office* (translated from Bengali by Devabrata Mukherjee), New York: Macmillan, 1914.
Tassy, Garcin M. de *Mémoire sur des particularités de la religion musulmane dans l'inde*, Paris: L'Imprimerie Royale, 1831, in Cole, *Roots*.
Taylor, Charles. 'The Rushdie Controversy', *Public Culture*, 2, 1 (Fall) 1989.
— 'The Politics of Recognition', in Taylor (ed.) *Multiculturalism*.
— (ed.) *Multiculturalism. Examining the Politics of Recognition*, Princeton, New Jersey: Princeton University Press, 1994.
Taylor, James. *A Sketch of the Topography and Statistics of Dacca*, Calcutta, 1840, in Roy, '"Where is Bengal?"'.
Temple, Bogusia and Rosalind Edwards. 'Interpreters/Translators and Cross-Language Research: Reflexivity and Border Crossings', *International Journal of Qualitative Methods*, 1, 2, 2002.
Thompson, E.P. *The Making of the English Working Class*, London: Victor Gollanz, 1963.
Tinker, Hugh. *A New System of Slavery. The Export of Indian Labour Overseas 1830–1920*, London: Hansib, (1974) 1993.
Todaro, Michael P. 'A Model of Labour Migration and Urban Development in Less Developed Countries', *American Economic Review*, 59, 1, 1969.
Tololyan, Khachig. 'Elites and Institutions in the Armenian Transnation', *International Migration Review*, 37, 3, 2003.
Torpey, John. *The Invention of the Passport: Surveillance, Citizenship and the State*, Cambridge: Cambridge University Press, 2000.
Torre, Andreea Raluca. 'Migrant Lives: A Comparative Study of Work, Family and Belonging Among Low-wage Romanian Migrant Workers in Rome and London', PhD thesis, London School of Economics and Political Science, 2013.
Tschacher, Torsten. *Islam in Tamilnadu: Varia*, Halle: Institut für Indologie und Südasienwissenschaften der Martin-Luther-Universität Halle-Wittenberg, 2001.
Turack, Daniel. The Passport in International Law, Lexington: Lexington Books, 1972.

U

Uberoi, Patricia (ed.). *Family, Kinship and Marriage in India*, Delhi: Oxford University Press, 1993.
Uddin, Sufia M. *Constructing Bangladesh: Religion, Ethnicity, and Language in an Islamic Nation*, Chapel Hill: University of North Carolina Press, 2006.

Ullah, Ansar Ahmed and John Eversley. *Bengalis in London's East End*, London: Swadhinata Trust, 2010.

V

Van Hear, Nicholas. '"I Went As Far As My Money Would Take Me": Conflict, Forced Migration and Class', COMPAS Working Paper No. 6, University of Oxford, 2001.
Van Schendel, Willem. 'Easy Come, Easy Go: Smugglers on the Ganges', *Journal of Contemporary Asia*, 23, 2, 1993.
— 'Working through Partition. Making a Living in the Bengal Borderlands', *International Review of Social History*, 46, 2001.
— 'Stateless in South Asia: The Making of the India-Bangladesh Enclaves', *The Journal of Asian Studies*, 61, 1 (February) 2002.
— *The Bengal Borderland: Beyond State and Nation in South Asia*, London: Anthem Press, 2005.
— *A History of Bangladesh*, Cambridge: Cambridge University Press, 2009.
Van Schendel, Willem and Erik Jan Zürcher (eds). *Identity Politics in Central Asia and the Muslim World*, London: I. B. Tauris, 2001.
Vertovec, Steven. *The Hindu Diaspora: Comparative Patterns*, London: Routledge, 2000.
Visram, Rozina. *Ayahs, Lascars, and Princes: Indians in Britain 1700–1947*, London: Pluto Press, 1986.

W

Wald, Erica. *Vice in the Barracks: Medicine, the Military and the Making of Colonial India, 1780–1868*, Basingstoke: Palgrave Macmillan, 2014.
Washbrook, David. 'Economic Depression and the Making of Traditional Society in Colonial India, 1820–1855', *Transactions of the Royal Historical Society*, Sixth Series, II, 1993.
Waters, C. 'J. B. Priestly' in Pederson and Mandler (eds). *After the Victorians*.
— '"Dark Strangers in our Midst": Discourses on Race and Nation in Britain, 1947–63', *Journal of British Studies*, 36, 2, 1997.
Weight, R. *Patriots. National Identity in Britain, 1940–2000*, London: MacMillan, 2003.
Wemyss, Georgie. *The Invisible Empire: White Discourse, Tolerance and Belonging*, Aldershot: Ashgate, 2009.
White, C.A. *Waterways in East Bengal and Assam*, Preliminary Report on the Improvement for Navigation of the Most Important Waterways on Eastern Bengal and Assam, 1909, Geography of Transportation.
Williams, P. and L. Chrisman. *Colonial Discourse and Postcolonial Theory*, New York: Columbia University Press, G. 1994.
Willis, Paul and Mats. Trondman, 'Manifesto for Ethnography', *Ethnography*, 1, 1, 2000.
Woodward, Kath (ed.). *Identity and Difference*, London: Sage, 1997.
Wright-Mills, C. *The Sociological Imagination*, Oxford: Oxford University Press, 1959.

Y

Young, Michael and Paul Wilmott. *Family and Kinship in East London*, London: Routledge and Kegan Paul, 1957.

Z

Zachariah, C. *A Historical Study of Internal Migration in the Indian Subcontinent, 1901–1931*, New York: Asia Publishing House, 1964.

Zaman, Muhammad Qasim. *Modern Islamic Thought in a Radical Age: Religious Authority and Internal Criticism*, Cambridge: Cambridge University Press, 2012.

Zaman, Niaz. *A Divided Legacy: The Partition in Selected Novels of India, Pakistan and Bangladesh*, Dhaka: University Press Limited, 1999.

Zamindar, Vazira Fazila-Yacoobali. *The Long Partition and the Making of Modern South Asia: Refugees, Boundaries, Histories*, New York: Columbia University Press, 2007.

Zeitlyn, Benjamin. 'Challenging Language in the Diaspora', *Bangla Journal*, 6, 14, September 2008.

Zolberg, A.R. 'The Formation of New States as a Refugee-generating Process', *Annals of the American Academy of Political and Social Science*, 467, 1, 1983.

— 'Introduction' in Zolberg and Benda (eds) *Global Migrants*.

Zolberg, A.R. and P.M. Benda (eds). *Global Migrants, Global Refugees: Problems and Solutions*, New York and Oxford: Berghahn Books, 2001.

Index

Abbas, Hazrat 164, 174
Abbas, Helal 109, 111, 114, 116, 207, 214
Abedin, Najmul 32
Abid Khan and others 239
Adams, Caroline 231; *Across Thirteen Rivers and Seven Seas* 238–9
Adivasis 82, 85–6, 154, 155
age 46n1; marriage 141, 143, 159n51
agency 14, 136, 156, 247
Ahl-i-Hadith 166, 184
Ahmed, Boshir 107
Ahmed, Jubair 74–5, 102–3, 107, 118
Ahmed, Mostaq 195
Ahmed, Tassaduq 239
Ahuja, Ravi 26, 35, 72
Alexander, Claire 4, 10, 11, 252n5
Al-Falah Bangladesh 97
Ali, Aftab 225
Ali, Altab 111, 112, 114, 123, 129n38, 193, 206, 207–8, 238
Ali, Altaf 107
Ali, Amjad 113
Ali, Ayub 225
Ali, Ishaq 111, 129n38
Ali, Mir Amanatullah 185
Ali, Musa 59
Ali, Rushanara 107–8, 128n27
Ali, Sofed 87
Ali, Tasarul 118, 120, 122, 199
Altab Ali Park 191, 193, 195, 203, 205, 206, 208, 210, 213
Amrith, Sunil 21, 29, 33
Arens, Jenneke 138
Asafu'd-daula, Nawab 163
Asghar, Ali 177
Assam 14n1, 24, 27, 77; agriculture 39; anti-Muslim 19, 82; infrastructure 30; language 32, 45; lascars 43; tea industry 26, 28–9, 40, 44, 72, 73

Assam-Bengal railway 24, 33–4, 39, 56–7, 165
Association of Young Generation of Urdu Speaking Community 97
Awami League 94, 132, 202, 209, 217n47, 235
Aziz, Mohammed 119, 120, 121, 125, 203

Babu, Mohammad Ashraful Haque 97
Baker, Christopher 29, 33, 47nn19–20
Bangladesh 1971 216n31
Bangladesh Fertility Survey 141
Bangladesh National Party (BNP) 94, 124, 125, 203, 217n47
Bangladeshis 95; Britain 6, 7, 10, 71, 157n4, 204–40; Coldhurst 117; London 117, 129n43; Oldham 117, 120, 221; Tower Hamlets 105, 204, 209, 221; origins 221; Urdu-speaking 234, 236; violence 125; *see also* Shahid Minar
Banglatown Consultative Forum 114, 115
Banu, Anisa 57–8
Begum, Abed 145–6, 147
Begum, Husna Ara 128n28, 131–3, 134, 136, 137, 156
Begum, Nafissa 61
Begum, Korimunessa 153, 198
Begum, Roshanara 145–7, 156
Begum, Suraiyya 60, 62
Begum, Waheeda 145, 146
Bengal and North Western railway 24, 34
Bengal Diaspora Project 4–11; Britain 6–8; placing 5–8; research methods 8–11; South Asia 5–6
Bengali Language Martyrs 88, 191, 194, 206, 215
Bengali-Urdu Sahitya Forum 97
Bengal Muslim diaspora, 1947–2007 52–79; ghettoization among 'national

minorities' 67–71; 'imperial' mobility 71–5; migration and displacement in rural borderlands 64–7; migration to Britain 71–5; migration to urban centres in new nation state 56–64; 'national' mobility 56–64
Bennett, Clinton 222
Bethnal Green 112, 128n10, 192
Bhojpuri-speaking people 45, 76n2, 163, 164, 165, 169, 234
Bhutto, Zulfikar Ali 169
Bibi, Rokeya 176
Bibi ka Roja 166–7, 176
Biharis 6, 10, 58, 60, 70, 76n2, 93–8, 161–90, 194, 219–39, 245; killings 52, 63, 243n55; making space, marking history 171–7; migrants immobilized 163–71; *tazias* 177–80
Birbhum 6, 89–93
BNP *see* Bangladesh National Party
Bradby, Hannah 141
Bradford 119, 124, 197–8
Brah, Avtar 104, 156, 238, 246
Brahmaputra River 23, 25, 37, 39
Brahmaputra Valley 41
Brahmins 32, 140, 164
Brick Lane Mosque 112, 208, 209, 211, 212
Britain: migration 71–5, 157n5, 160n80; non-EU spouse migration 160n80
Britain diaspora 102–30; East End 104, 105, 111, 128n19, 203–4, 209, 231, 238; *see also* Oldham; Tower Hamlets
British, in India 14n1, 21, 72, 73, 98
British Nationality Act of 1948 145
British Nationality Act of 1981 238
Brubaker, Rogers 220, 231, 238, 246
Burma: migration controls from India 40
Burnley 107, 118, 124, 200

Calcutta 23, 34, 35, 45, 72, 73, 146–7, 164–6; agreement of 1948 78n48; airstrip 30; canal systems 24; coal industry 26; constabulary 31; 'ghetto' dwellers 10; jute industry 26, 168; killings in August 1946 57, 82, 228; migrants 59, 63; Muslim policemen murdered 78n26; Muslims 6, 12, 69; port 29, 43, 102; railway 24, 26; riots 18; violence 168; weavers 63
Cantle, Ted 124
Carter, Marina 44
Castles, Stephen 2
census, in Pakistan 1951 56

Chamberlain, Walter 124
Chamra Godown Camp 63, 64, 71
Charsley, K. 136
Chatterjee, Bankim Chandra: *Bandemataram* 242n13
Chatterjee, Neelanjana 87, 89
Chelkowski, Peter 187n3
Chota Nagpur 23, 27, 36, 37, 43, 44, 45
Choudhury, Abdul Gaffar 215n2
Choudhury, Morium 147–50, 156
Choudhury, Yousuf: *Roots and Tales* 219–41
Chowdhury, Billal Ali 66, 80
citizenship laws, in India 144
Clifford, James 247
coal industry 26–7, 28, 29, 30, 34, 40
Coldhurst 117, 120
colonial India 12, 21, 22
Commonwealth Immigrants Act 7, 145
community histories and the politics of assimilation 219–44; context and politics of assimilation 236–40; intertwining community and 'host' histories 229–36; migration myths 225–9; mythical pasts and sacred origins 221–5; 'myth of return' 236–40; myths for assimilation 229–36; tales of loss and exile 225–9
Crang, Philip 214

Darjeeling 28, 37, 38; Sunni Muharram 180, 181
Davis, Kingsley 20, 35–6
Delhi 84, 222; agreement of 1950 78n48; agreement of 1973 237
Depression 21, 22, 29, 33, 39, 40, 41
de Tassy, Garcin 190n76
Dhaka 6, 146, 194, 217n55; Bangladeshi 'Bihari' Muslims 93–5; migration 56, 57; Muharram 13, 161–90, 192
Dhaka Medical College 193
Dhaka University 93, 174, 180, 194, 216n21, 235
diaspora: question of 246–8
Dinajpur 6, 19, 37, 58, 59, 62, 65, 85, 150, 154; immigrant '*kafirs*' and '*razakars*' 81–4; West 36, 60

East Bengal 6, 29, 34, 39, 52, 56, 57, 63, 66, 87, 131, 133, 168, 169, 194, 233
East End 104, 105, 111, 128n19, 203–4, 209, 231, 238
East India Company 7

Index 283

East London Mosque 109, 113, 208, 210, 211, 212, 213, 217n51
East Pakistan 1, 2, 5–6, 19, 32, 56, 57, 58, 59, 60, 62, 63, 66, 68, 73, 83, 84, 86, 87, 91, 101n37, 137, 144, 169, 198, 219, 228, 233, 235; civil war 52; language 194
East Pakistan Industrial Development Corporation 63, 78n31
Eaton, Richard 36, 184–5, 223
Ekushe 14, 88, 130n64, 191–3, 194, 195, 196, 201, 202, 203, 212, 213, 214, 215, 215n3, 216n18, 234
'enemy' property ordinances in Pakistan 144
Ershad, Hussain Muhammad 74, 210

Faqir, Jaafar Ali 66, 80, 84
Fatima (Fatemeh) 166, 172, 176, 178, 189n66
Fazilatunnesa 149–50, 151, 152
Firoz, Shahzad 4, 9, 10
First World War 31, 35, 226
Foodgrains Control Order of 1942 33
forced marriage 160n79
Forsyth, Charles 29

Gardner, K. 148, 151
Gazi, Fakhruddin 68, 69
Gazi, Hamidullah 69
Gazi, Jalal 68, 69, 86–8, 248
Gazi, Shahid 68, 86–9, 248
gendering the Bengal diaspora 134–43
Geneva Camp 95, 98, 169, 174, 178, 186
ghettoization among 'national minorities' 67–71
Gilroy, Paul 215, 246, 247, 252n14
Global South 2, 221, 250
Gobindo, Gour 222, 242n21
government: in India 44, 144; in Pakistan 200, 227, 237
Green, Nile 167, 172
Gurkhas 28, 31–2, 38, 45

Hall, Stuart 214, 245, 251, 252n5
Haq, Biswajit 91
Haq, Enamul 91–2, 99
Haq, Surojit 91, 92
Haque, Shiraj 109, 110, 111–2, 206–7, 208
Hawa, Bibi 133–4, 136, 137, 141, 145, 156
Hindu Bengali 42, 91, 92, 158n38, 158n38

Hindus 1, 37, 60–1, 62, 65, 89, 91–3, 95, 101n22, 135, 138, 144, 150, 167–8, 183, 190n76, 197, 222, 223, 224, 228, 239; attire 86; Bengali-speaking 161; Birbhum 89–90; brides 41; government 57; high-caste literate 32; marriage 139–41; migrants 87; Muharram 164; refugees 52, 54, 59, 66–7, 85, 216n29; sacred sites 45; Satkhira 84; Sylheti 197; West Bengal 6
Hooghly 34, 73, 167, 169, 178, 179, 185
Horowitz, Daniel 243n55
Hossain, Kamal 119, 122, 124, 125–6, 201, 202, 203
Huq, Shamsul 18–19, 23, 30, 43, 45, 58, 72, 73, 80, 81, 98, 249
Huq Foundation, Shamsul 219
Huque, Nurul 114
Husain, Imam 13, 161–2, 164, 171, 172, 174, 175, 176–7, 178, 179, 182, 183, 184, 185, 186, 187n1
Husain, Mohammad Sajjh 176
Husaini Dalan 190n73

Ibrahim, Mohammed 235
ICCDR *see* International Centre for Diarrhoeal Disease Research
'imperial' mobility 71–5
Ilias, Ahmed 99, 219, 221, 223–5, 227–8, 230, 241; *'Biharis'—The Indian Émigrés in Bangladesh* 97, 219, 220, 231–7, 239–41
Imperial Gazeteer 20
indenture in India 44
independence in Pakistan 227, 228
Indian army 82, 133
Indian Seamen's Welfare League 106
India-Pakistan War 144
infanticide 242n21
internal migrants in India 35
International Centre for Diarrhoeal Disease Research (ICCDR) 143
Islam 84, 88, 89, 91, 155, 164, 166, 171–2, 174, 175–7, 178, 181, 182, 183, 184, 185, 188n8, 211, 212, 213, 216n18, 217n51, 223, 224–5; anti-217n47; Sunni 83, 167; Sylhet 127n1, 222; *see also* Muharram
Islam, Noor 9–10
Islam, Nurul 235

Jabbar, Abdul 118, 120, 121, 202
Jagonari 132

284 *Index*

Jalais, Annu 4, 9, 10–11
Jalal, Rajonuddin 111, 112, 114, 135, 204, 205, 207, 208, 214
Jalal, Shah 127n1, 222, 227
Jalil, Abdul 64
Jamaat-i-Islami 195, 211, 217n51
Jinnah 168
Jinnahbhai 58, 59
Jomidar, Lomba 175, 184–5, 186
Jubin, Sitara 64
jute industry 25, 26, 28, 29, 30, 34, 39, 40, 48n57, 63, 165, 168, 169, 185

Kakrail Mosque 83
Kalra, Virinder 116–17
Karbala paradigm 188n15
Kerr, Ian 28
Khan, Abid 239
Khan, Ayub 63, 85, 169, 232, 235
Khan, Dilowar Hussain 113, 211, 212, 213–14
Khan, Hamid 73
Khan, Monem 233
Khan, Nasim 233
Khan, Sadaqat (Fakku) 96
Khan, Shaynul 210, 211, 213
Khan, Tamizuddin 32
Khan, Warasat 233
Khastgir, Shyamali 93
Khatun, Fatema 90–1, 92, 95, 150
Khatun, Mehrunissa 71
Korom, Frank 187n3

Labour Force Survey 7
Lalon (Lalon Sain, Lalon Shah, Lalon Fakir) 92, 101n23
language in Pakistan 193–4
lascars: agreements 79n64; Asiatic 43; Bengali 7, 43; Britain 7, 219; Indian 79n63; 'losing' 72; Sylheti 226–7
'legitimate' India 87
Liberation War 12, 81, 85, 102, 109, 111, 120, 121, 131, 133, 141, 147, 149, 169, 191, 194, 195, 196, 197, 198, 199, 200, 203, 216n21, 228
local 'micro-mobility' 33–43
Lohani, Kamal 101n34
London 106, 118, 147, 148, 153, 209, 226; Bangladeshis 4, 6, 105, 117, 129n43; Chinatown 105; East 7, 8, 10, 13, 14, 102, 103, 104, 106, 107, 108, 110, 111, 122, 123, 131, 132, 152, 154, 191–2, 193, 195, 196, 198, 199, 211, 212, 213, 217n44, 250; East End 105, 219; lascars 72; Metropolitan Borough 129n48; *see also* Oldham; Tower Hamlets
London Bangla Press Club 192
London School of Economics and Political Science 4

Maithili-speaking people 164, 165, 169
Maqbook, Muhammad 180–1
marriage: age 141, 143, 159n51; forced 160n79; migration 131–60; out-marriage 151
Marxism 20
Massey, Douglas 54, 249
McKeown, Adam 76
Mehjabin 152–3, 155
Mia, Chan 178
Mia, Muhammad Iqbal 178
Miah, Nurunnobi 198–9, 200–1
Miah, Sajjid 112, 209, 212
Miah, Samuz 200
Miah, Shanu 110, 199
Mian, Ghazi 166
migrants on the 'peripheries' 80–101
migration: Britain 71–5, 157n5; and displacement in rural borderlands 64–7; in India 2, 6, 16n34, 20–1, 44; in India after 1921 35–6; in Pakistan 168, 169; transnationalism and 248–52; to urban centres in new nation state 56–64
migration and marriage 131–60; gendering the Bengal diaspora 134–43; transforming 'community' 151–6
Miller, Mark 2
minorities 89–99; Bangladeshi "Bihari" Muslims in Dhaka 93–5; Birbhum district, western Bengal 89–93; nomenclature, categories, and contestations 95–9
Mirza, Bohra Ali 182
mobility and immobility in Bengal delta and 'eastern zone', pre-histories of 18–51; local 'micro-mobility' 33–43; state expansion and migration, 1857–1945 31–3; upper India, 1857–1945 23–31
Mohila Awami League 132
Mokamel, Tanvir: *Swapnabhumi* 93, 239
Mollah, Abdul Quader 195
Monghyr (Mungher) 57, 165, 168, 188n37
Mookerji, Syama Prasad 168
Muharram 13, 14; 'Bihari' Sunni 161–90, 192, 193, 216n15, 217n55; Hyderabad

188n8; migrants immobilized 163–71; site of difference 180–4; *tazias* 177–80
Munna, Iqbal 178, 184, 186
Muslim identity 3, 213
Muslim Indian Civil Service officers 77n23
Muslim League 168, 233
Muslim policemen: murdered in Calcutta 78n26, 168
Muslims, Sunni *see* Sunni Muslims

Nakatani, Tetsuya 78n36
Nari Chetona 195, 201
narrating diaspora 219–44; context and politics of assimilation 236–40; intertwining community and 'host' histories 229–36; migration myths 225–9; mythical pasts and sacred origins 221–5; 'myth of return' 236–40; myths for assimilation 229–36; tales of loss and exile 225–9
National Front 110, 111, 112, 124, 125, 126, 132
nawabs 163, 164, 181, 182, 190n73
Newham 8, 74, 102, 104, 154, 197
Nirmul Committee 132, 191, 195, 196, 201, 208, 211, 212, 216n24

Oldham 7, 8, 104, 116–25, 127, 130n82, 193, 221, 250; arrivals 118–20; building community 120–3; Pakistan 117; riots 123–6; Shahid Minar 201, 202–3, 205; textile mills 199
O'Malley, L. S. S. 166, 167, 188n37
Oporejeyo Bangla 183, 190n74
out-marriage 151

paiks 161–90; making space, marking history 171–7; migrants immobilized 163–71
Pakistan army 63, 85, 169, 197, 198, 199, 232, 235
Pakistan Welfare Association 110
Palashpur 158n38
'parallel lives' 124, 135, 247
partition in India 1, 18, 19, 52–3, 66, 77n12, 168, 219
patrials 145, 159n70
Pinault, David 162, 180–1, 183
Plummer, Ken 10

Radcliffe line 52, 54, 64, 77n12, 80, 82, 86–9, 144
Rahim, Abdul 61–2

Rahman, Laila 147, 152, 155
Rahman, Mizanur 118
Rahman, Mojibur 80, 99, 108, 198, 233
railways, in India 45, 58
Rangoon: fall 33
Rasul, Abdul 63
Rauf, Mahmoud 108, 114, 115, 195–6, 205, 206, 207
rebellion, in India 26, 31, 135
refugees: in India 78n48; in Pakistan 100n15
'refuz' in Bangladeshi borderlands 81–9; Dinajpur 81–4; Satkhira 84–6; tale of two brothers on opposite sides of Radcliffe line 86–9
repatriation in Pakistan 159n71, 233, 237
riots 242n48
Rivington Place: *Bangladesh 1971* 216n31
Roberts, Emma 190n76
Roy, Avijit 216n18
Roy, Tirthankar 23, 27, 45
Royal Commission of Labour 42
Royal Navy 74
Ruha, Bibi 65–6
rural borderlands, migration and displacement in 64–7
Rushdie, Salman *Satanic Verses* 238

Safran, William 217n58
Saif Ali, Gulam Mohammad 66–7, 80
Salauddin, Mohammad 64
Santals 28–9, 36, 38, 41, 45, 82
Saran 168, 188n37
Satkhira 84–6, 88, 99
Schivelbusch, Wolfgang 220
Second World War 18, 21, 29, 31, 54, 74, 106, 108, 117, 118, 226, 227, 229
Sen, Ashim 197
Sen, Samita 29, 40, 42
Sen, Uditi 58
Shah, Nawab Wajid Ali 167
Shahbag intersection 194–5, 216n21
Shahid Minar 191–218; contested memories 214–15; contesting memory 208–14; East London 14; framing rituals of diaspora 214–15; Oldham 117, 121, 202–3; 'roots' and 'routes' 193–6; tale of two mosques 208–14; Tower Hamlets 203–8; war stories 196–202
Shamsul Huq Foundation 97, 219
Shangram 194, 196–202
Shaw, A. 136

Shias 13, 161–2, 163, 164, 166, 167, 171, 172, 174, 176, 178, 179–80, 181–2, 184, 185, 188n8, 190n73
Siddiqui, M. S. A. 10
Siddiqui, Saghir Ahmed 235
Spitalfields 114, 115, 128n10, 129n43
S.S. Arenda 83
state expansion and migration in India, 1857–1945 31–3
Stepney Green 128n10
Strachey, John 24
Suhrawardy, Huseyn 168, 224
Sunni Muslims 65, 161, 166, 187n7
Sylhet 6, 131, 168, 197–8; diaspora in Britain 219–42; female migrants 143; Islam 127n1; lascars 7, 226–7, 228, 234; marriage age 141, 159n51; migration to Britain 71; Oldham 116; tea industry 26, 73; pre-partition 72; war 196
Sylheti Social History Group 219, 239

Tablighi Jama'at 83–4, 166
taluks 78n37
Tamils 47n19
tazias 177–80
Tower Hamlets: diaspora 104–16; marriage age 141; mosques 217n48; Shahid Minar 203–8
Town Hall Camp 6, 70, 114, 169, 170, 177, 178, 180, 183
trade, in India 43
transnationalism and migration 136, 248–52
Turner, Victor 187

Udichi Shilpi Gosthi 196, 201
Udichi UK 196

Ullah, Ansar Ahmed 106, 112–13, 115, 116, 196, 205–6, 208, 211, 213
Union Board 60, 78n37, 87
upper India 18, 166, 232
upper mobility revolution in India, 1857–1945 23–31
Urdu-speaking people 13, 32, 37, 57, 76n2, 94, 96, 97, 144, 145, 146, 147, 163, 169, 171, 172, 176, 186, 194, 201, 219, 220, 228, 231–2, 233, 234–6, 239, 240
Urdu language in Pakistan 193–4, 235
Urdu Speaking People Youth Rehabilitation Movement 96

van Beurden, Jos 138
van Schendel, Willem 80, 81, 89, 99, 194, 195
Vested Property Ordinance 144

Wavell, Lord 168
West Bengal 1, 5, 6, 16n34, 43, 54, 59, 61, 64, 67–8, 73, 83, 84, 86, 87, 90, 93, 95, 99, 133, 137, 159, 179, 180, 189n64
West India 1, 57, 83, 84, 168, 194, 232, 233
white seamen 72, 79n63
women: gendering the Bengal diaspora 134–43; in India 42–3, 135–6, 140, 145; 'meyebela' or girlhood 137–43; migration 40–2; migration and marriage 131–60; migration preparation 137–43; South Asian Muslim 135–6; transforming 'community' 151–6

Younus, Mohmmad 168

Zolberg, A. R. 4, 54, 77n12